MIGHTY SILENCE Images of destruction

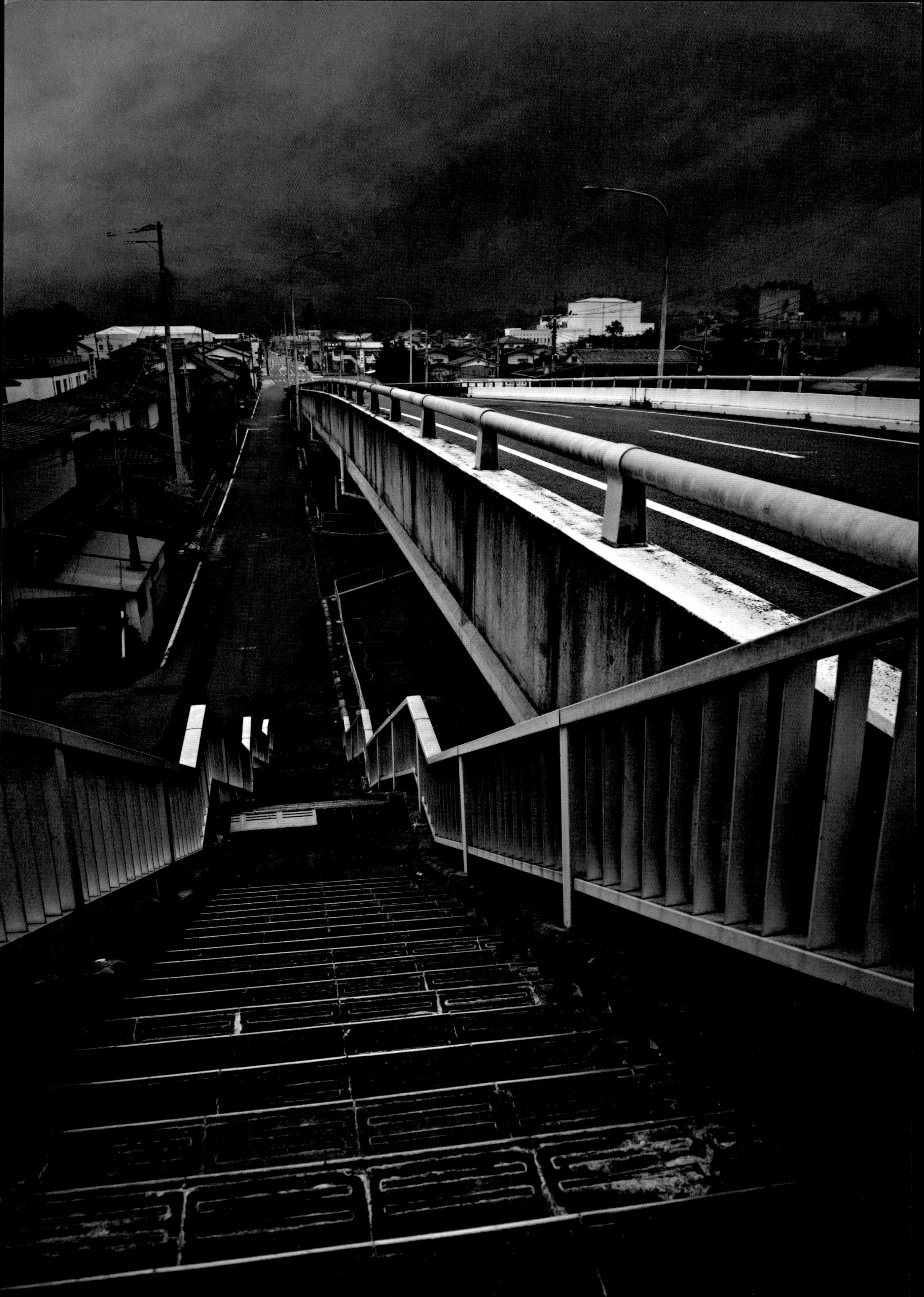

Yasushi Handa

MIGHTY SILENCE

Images of destruction

The Great 2011
Earthquake
and Tsunami of East Japan
and Fukushima

SKIRA

Concept
Graziano Sforza, Urbis Inc.

Special thanks to
Tetsuo Fukaya
Yasumichi Maruyama
Aya Hamao
Travis Close

Design and cover
Marcello Francone

Editorial Coordination
Emma Cavazzini

Editing
Marco Abate

Layout
Paola Oldani

Translations
Ayako Ishida and Joy Onozuka
from original Japanese texts
Sylvia Notini from original Italian text

First published in Italy in 2012 by
Skira editore S.p.A.
Palazzo Casati Stampa
via Torino 61
20123 Milano
Italy

Printed and bound in Italy. First edition

ISBN: 978-88-572-1557-0

Distributed in USA, Canada, Central & South America by Rizzoli International Publications, Inc., 300 Park Avenue South, New York, NY 10010, USA.
Distributed elsewhere in the world by Thames and Hudson Ltd., 181A High Holborn, London WC1V 7QX, United Kingdom.

Printed in Italy

www.skira.net

The book has been published thanks to the contribution of

SHISEIDO

ありがとう。

Arigato.
Thank you.
Grazie.

STAY STRONG! NIPPON

JAPAN DISASTER RELIEF PARTY

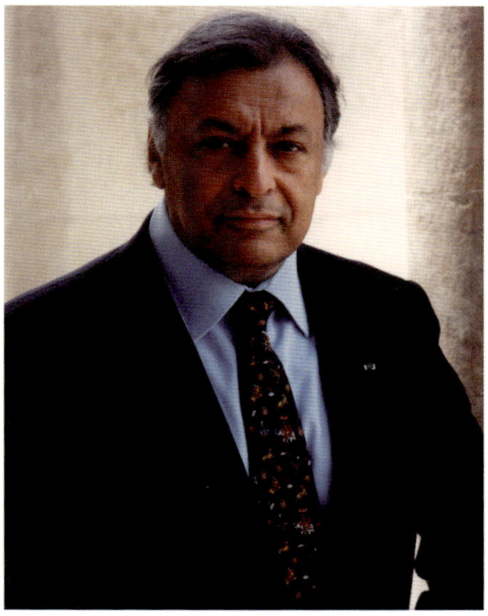

"My wife and I send our blessings and prayers
to all those who are still suffering from the aftermath
of the incredible tragedy. May they once again very soon
regain their peaceful lives as before March 11, 2011."

FONDAZIONE ITALIA GIAPPONE
伊日財団

These images, more dramatically than any description, tell the story of one of the worst catastrophes in the history of human mankind: the frightful earthquake and the subsequent tsumani occurred in Japan on March 11, 2011. I remember perfectly the very instant when it all began. I was on the ground floor of Italy's Cultural Institute in Tokyo: everything was shaking around me and I immediately understood the seriousness of what was happening. Having lived in Japan for five years, I was used to recurrent tremors, but this time the earth movement was more violent, more intense, too lasting. There is nothing doing. Even if you are aware of the natural causes of an earthquake, you perceive something supernatural in this event, as if a hand of a giant in the bowels of the earth was tossing your house and your heart.

The facts and the numbers of the tragedy are well known and I won't recall them. But I do want to recall my two visits to Tohoku and Fukushima. In my memory the faces of old people, cruelly stricken by the calamity, but patient and courageous are deeply impressed. Nowhere else in the world would you experience such stoical dignity, such calm despair after a similar catastrophe.

Italians were particularly moved by these tragic events because they share with the Japanese a dangerous familiarity with earthquakes and disasters. I was a personal witness of the solidarity expressed by the Italian authorities and common people to the Japanese communities victimes of the earthquake and of the tsunami.

The images of this book are a forceful reminder of what happened on March 11, 2011. And an invitation to reflect and understand that we all are in the same boat. A tsunami, even in the remotest part of the world, strikes all of us.

Umberto Donati
Director
Italy Japan Foundation

Contents

20 DAYS

AFTER

20 days post disaster

Yasushi Handa

Twenty days after March 11, 2011, I found myself driving in the direction of Tohoku. The National Road No. 4, Tohoku Expressway, and the other connecting roads to the devastated coastal region, which had been hastily rebuilt according to the government-initiated "Tooth-comb Strategy" after the disaster, were finally opened to the public. The U.S. military and the Japanese Self Defense Forces were in the midst of "Operation Tomodachi (Friends)," a joint effort to find survivors, collect bodies, and transport critical supplies. I had wanted to go earlier; but, there was a severe gasoline shortage, even in Tokyo, so I had to be patient. The moment had to be right otherwise I ran the risk of causing trouble by being there.

Right after the earthquake, which was initially estimated as a massive 8.4 in magnitude—the biggest ever recorded in Japan—things were strewn everywhere, as screens were suddenly filed with images of devastating tsunami that quickly and brutally swept away everything in its path. Gas tanks in Ichihara exploded. The city of Kesennuma went up in flames. A hydrogen explosion rocked the Fukushima Nuclear Power Plant. For 24 hours, almost nonstop, the media broadcasted grisly images of the violent power of nature, which in turn triggered a man-made calamity. The number of dead and missing went up digit by digit, day by day. The size of the earthquake was revised upward to 9.0. The situation at the nuclear power plant grew more worrisome by hour. It was obvious that this was an extraordinary event of death and destruction. Nonetheless, it still seemed abstract. But when I saw a video taken with a cell phone on YouTube, I suddenly felt a burning desire to go there to shoot photos. The YouTube clip was filmed by a man in the midst of the disaster. It showed the tsunami barreling in and sweeping away his home. You could hear his cries and screams of despair. It had such a different impact because it was so personal and real. In the media coverage, reporters often used the word "garbage," which irked me. All these things that had been deemed "garbage" had previously been a part of someone's life. How could they be so insensitive? Even as these thoughts ran through my mind, I felt indecisive about going there. I finally decided that I had a duty to accurately record the devastation with my camera. But how could I best capture this unparalleled catastrophic event? I first thought about using my 8x10 camera. But I needed to be realistic, which meant shooting under the worst possible conditions. Using a darkroom would be out of the question. I ended up deciding on two cameras: PhaseOneP65+ for locations where a tripod worked and NikonD3X for when it did not. At the time, these were the best cameras available to capture the highest quality images. Indeed, they enabled me to capture powerful panoramic images, which had just begun gaining popularity in the digital-camera world. If I captured everything in detail, I felt it would serve as evidence of what had taken place. Such photos might serve a purpose someday. As a professional photographer, that was something I could do.

Twenty days after the earthquake, I drove through clouds of limestone dust, which had been sprinkled to slow the decay, trying to avoid glass and nails along the road that might cause a flat tire. I went there knowing I had a mission; but, in front of the horrible landscape, I couldn't even hold my camera. I stood motionless, unable to do anything. The sludge reeked. An extraordinary number of fish, either swept in by the tsunami or released from the shattered seafood manufacturing companies, lay in varying states of decay along with decomposing bodies. Seabirds and crows picked at the remains, leaving behind piles of their excrement. Gasoline and chemicals leaked from tanks. Grain stores and fermented foods rotted. It was all tangled together, mound upon mound, creating an extraordinary stench. Tears flowed from my eyes. Suddenly, I was in the midst of late-season snowstorms. I was filled with anger, with no one to direct it at. I kept calling out. Eventually, the snow stopped, and I felt the warmth of sunshine. I looked up to find a blue sky gradually expanding. I saw flowers on a Japanese apricot tree. I heard a little cuckoo singing somewhere in the distance. The sky was calm, and it seemed nature was at peace. At last, I came to my senses. Between the end of March and the beginning of May, I made several trips to devastated areas.

My choice in cameras proved correct. When I look at the photos closely, I see a picture, a Buddhist mortuary tablet, and a stuffed doll plastered to a car. What might be described as "garbage" in a media clip, can be seen upon closer observation as the remains of lives torn asunder.

Due to the peculiarity of Japan's geography, the country has a dramatic history of man-made and natural disasters, from wars, crushing earthquakes to tsunami, dating back to ancient times. Consequently, Japanese have experienced a cruel pattern of having to rebuild and restart their lives. Last year reminded me of 737—the year a deadly epidemic broke out, triggering political chaos for the government led by Emperor Shomu. The *Manyoshu* book of Japanese poems, which was compiled in that century, includes these lines from a poem by Otomo no Yakamochi:

If I go to the ocean, I will be a corpse soaking in the water.
If I go to a mountain, I will be a corpse fleeced with grass.

The poet composed it while contemplating the upcoming construction of a colossal statue of Buddha at Todaiji Temple in Nara. It was hoped that such a magnificent statue would reduce political tensions and anxiety, provide repose for the souls of those lost to calamities, as well as prevent future catastrophes. We assume it was customary in those times to compose poetic requiems to mourn the dead. We have genres of poems and paintings dating from this period that vividly depict the disasters, evoking a sense of resignation and the Buddhist notion that all things are in motion and therefore nothing is permanent. They are not overpowering messages of pessimism, but rather affecting and poetic portrayals of what devastation entails. Did our ancestors intentionally embrace such expression as a means to sustain hope against such a seemingly dark destiny? As I stood motionless, beholding the horrific landscape, I knew they must have. I stood there, hands clasped in prayer as I recalled a famous passage from "Spring View" by Chinese poet Du Fu:

In the devastated country, the hills and rivers remain.
It is springtime in the city, and plants and trees grow deep.
Despaired by the times, my tears fall upon flowers.
Grieved by separation, flying birds startle my heart.

Needless to say, nature does not strive to be beautiful nor does it intend to be brutal in its destruction. Awed by the power of nature, we praise its beauty and record what it reveals to us. Such records allow us to relive the awe and beauty of that moment in time; only humans possess such instincts and abilities. Since this tragedy, we have been warned repeatedly about the high probability of an earthquake striking Tokyo. The reality in Tohoku could be our reality tomorrow. We all need to be mentally prepared for such a disaster.

A prayer of hope, from the edge of despair

Toru Takimoto

Director General of the Regional Development Department, Japan Tourism Agency Ministry of Land, Infrastructure, Transport, and Tourism

There are no people in these photos. Nonetheless, they reveal the pitiful scars and the wasteland of debris left behind by the thunderous tsunami that swept through the Tohoku region on the heels of the Great East Japan Earthquake, which struck on March 11, 2011. The images capture the landscape twenty days after the ocean water had retreated. Taken with a 65-million pixel camera, the pictures are almost surreal because they capture details missed by the naked eye. What we've typically seen in the media are people determined to move beyond their misfortune, to deepen their ties with the community, and to overcome the overwhelming adversity. In contrast, this book puts the harsh realities first and forefront. Viewing these photos and contemplating this tragedy, I slip into prayer, hoping for restoration and renewal.

The tsunami engulfed cities and towns that thrive on fishing and agriculture, along the Pacific coastlines of Aomori, Iwate, Miyagi, and Fukushima prefectures. It spared no one and no thing. Over 18,000 people were killed or went missing. Today, there are an estimated 340,000 people living on the edge of survival like refugees. Eighteen months have passed, but only 15 percent of debris has been cleared; the remainder has been piled high in temporary dumps scattered throughout the disaster areas. It's estimated that it will take five years to dispose of it all. And then we have the debris that was carried out into the Pacific Ocean, which is now showing up along the coastlines of the United States and Canada. Local officials are grappling with how to address the issue of their garbage littering the lands of other countries.

Akira Miyawaki, a botanical ecologist, has called for the creation of "green-tide embankments", which would utilize the debris to create a wall to protect people from future tsunamis. With support from former Japanese Prime Minister Morihiro Hosokawa and others, Miyawaki is heading the project, which has been labeled "Green Great Wall Made From Debris". The plan calls for the removal of toxic substances from the debris, which can then be used to construct a wall, with a width spanning between 30 and 100 meters, and with a height of 10 to 15 meters. It would run the 300-kilometer coastline of Tohoku, and be planted with Machilus thunbergii, different kinds of oak trees, cherry trees, and other plants native to the region. The walls of greenery would serve as tide embankments. In nature, it takes 200 to 300 years for trees to form a forest. But, Miyawaki believes an artificially created forest could be achieved in 15 years.

The debris is the shattered remains of homes and offices, and the belongings of so many victims. The wood from the waste would give birth to new woodlands, offering repose for the souls of lost ones. I find Miyawaki's proposal deeply moving. In Japan, tide embankments are usually created by primarily planting black pines; but, on flatlands, their roots remain shallow. By elevating the ground level, as suggested in the plan, the soil would be more aerated enabling roots to burrow into the debris. The crushing tsunami that swept across Tohoku, as well as one generated by the northern Sumatra earthquake in 2010, proved that native trees can endure natural disasters.

At present, none of the governmental blueprints for restoration include Miyawaki's plan. However, it is gaining support, and I feel confident it will be realized in one form or another. How uplifting it would be if artists around the world offered their creative input on this project. The power of art, in my view, would provide both comfort and a connection between people suffering in disaster areas; imagine this great wall becoming a connecting point for people all around the world.

After March 11, there was an enormous influx of young people who came to volunteer for rescue activities, distributing food at emergency shelters, as well as clearing debris. Before the disaster, many of the devastated areas along the coastline had already been hard hit by the lack of young people. Indeed, the number of elderly residents was growing at a faster clip than in other regions of Japan. When the earthquake struck, it literally destroyed their local industries, the infrastructure, their workplaces, their homes, their livelihoods. Their communities were almost completely obliterated. Today, we feel a ray of hope. Eighteen months after the disaster, while there are fewer volunteers, there are numerous projects that have been launched through the goodwill of people to generate new businesses and restart old ones in order to create jobs and rebuild communities. The list of supporters includes experienced businesspeople, as well as less-experienced young people who have a strong desire to be socially responsible entrepreneurs.

After the Great Hanshin-Awaji Earthquake in 1995, there was also a huge influx of volunteers, which caused an array of problems because there was no system for coordinating them. Based on that, the "Law to Promote Specified Nonprofit Activities", which is widely known as the "NPO Law", was enacted. Since then, a growing number of social enterprises, including NPOs, have been launched with the intention of solving problems, like getting businesses back on their feet. Recently, the ruling Democratic Party of Japan has framed policies based on this concept of "New Public Services".

At present, the central government supports 12 NGOs and other organizations that are working to create jobs in communities that were hard hit by the disaster. The objectives include the creation of 600 social enterprises that would host 2,000 interns, whose leadership skills would be fostered. It would provide a network base among entrepreneurs in the drive to generate a new style of business called "the 6th sector of the industry", which rolls agriculture, commerce and industry, and tourism into one. Communities would be created within areas with temporary dwellings for displaced people, which would then lend support for projects, like planting trees for tide embankments.

Entrepreneurs, businesspeople, and students, living in other parts of Japan, could support such enterprises through donations or interning, which would create a stronger volunteer force. New Orleans, which was devastated by Hurricane Katrina six years ago, is said to be on the road to making a solid recovery thanks to the efforts of some two million volunteers and entrepreneurs committed to restoring that city's luster. That reminds us that we have a long way to go and must be patient. By fully backing these budding social enterprises through the power of communication, we will certainly foster new and stronger bonds between people. As seen in the Great Hanshin-Awaji Earthquake, these enterprises will reshape Tohoku, and will eventually reshape Japan.

From the edge of despair, I continue to hope. With this book in my hands, I offer a prayer for hope everlasting.

In the eyes of a man from a disaster rescue team

Tetsuya Abe

Representative of the NPO Tsunami Disaster Recovery Support Center

I had recovered the 15th body when I got a call from Yasushi Handa, asking me to look at his photographs.

I like Handa as a person, which is perhaps why I am drawn to the world framed by his camera. But, to tell you the truth, I don't know which came first: I was impressed by the photos, which caused me to feel an affinity with the man capable of capturing such images, or I was impressed by the photographer, which caused me to view his works with unconditional acceptance. Handa is a passionate, tough, arrogant man; but, he's also a gentleman, naïve, and shy. He is a professional as well as an artist at the same time. Overall, such a personality is endearing.

It was this photographer who implored me on that day to come to Tokyo immediately. He was insistent that I see the photographs he had taken in the disaster areas. He first arrived in the stricken Tohoku region a mere 20 days after the Great East Japan Earthquake. Over the next month, he made several roundtrips from Tokyo to photograph the tragedy before him.

I was dubious. I had arrived right after the disaster to search for survivors, and stayed on to help with restoration, so the harsh reality was something I understood all too well. Why would Handa, who wasn't a news photographer, come to such devastated and dangerous areas?

Whenever there is a natural disaster in Japan or another part of Asia, I'm dispatched to help. I sometimes encounter horrific scenes of death and separation. If the disaster is one specific area, large-scale government-sponsored rescue teams are typically on site within six hours. It's very rare for a nongovernmental rescue team, like mine, to arrive ahead of public officials to launch the hunt for survivors. This time, however, it was different. Every agency in charge of organizing rescue efforts was reeling from the massive scale of destruction, which spanned 800 kilometers of coastline. With the devastation from the quake, the tsunami, and the unstable nuclear reactors at the Fukushima Power Plant, there was no way police, firefighters, and Self Defense Forces could mobilize quickly enough. Even after 48 hours, they had only managed to make it into a few towns.

The air was pungent from the fast decaying fish, extraordinary in number, that had been swept in by the tsunami. The sludge reeked, as did the poisonous chemicals seeping from destroyed tanks. Grain storage silos and other foods began to ferment from the water damage. And then there were the bodies, waiting for loved ones to identify and claim them, which began to emit the putrid smell of decaying flesh. This was the site that Handa had walked into with his camera.

Survivors, still shell-shocked by the overwhelming destruction, could only sit in the silence of sadness at the scene of decay before them. Amongst them, came a photographer to document their state of shock and the vast tragedy. What was his intention and what did he seek to capture with his camera? I had to know.

The news clips, which showed people, homes, and cars being swept away by the tsunami, did not convey the fear and despair of the victims. It was simply a graphic portrayal revealing the destructive force of the tsunami and the fires amidst the screams of people. What had stirred the heart of this photographer? The immense piles of garbage that the media focused on could never stir the moral fiber of a viewer to enter such a wasteland. Why on earth would he stand on such garbage—the treasures and trivia of properties swept away? He later confessed to me that he had watched such news with a sense of ambivalence. He knew entering such areas with a camera was reckless and perhaps ultimately meaningless.

But alas he had reached a decision.

I can easily imagine that by the 20th day his desire to express the tragedy in different terms was burning. Carrying his equipment, with no assistants, Handa entered the devastated areas. But, as he stood before such a horrific landscape, he could not even grip his camera, he said. He stood motionless, unable to do anything. Even this man, with bountiful spiritual strength, could not process the gravity of destruction that the Earth had unleashed. His skill and methodology for manipulating light and composing an aesthetic scene were of no use with this subject matter.

Suddenly, he found himself in the midst of out-of-season snowstorms, which meant there would be no retreat from the devastation. It was like his resolve was being tested by God. Engulfed by the extraordinary stench of death and clouds of limestone dust, which had been sprinkled for sterilization, he was filled with anger, with no one to direct it at. He was a diminished figure without hope. Witnessing the absurd and unfair boundary between life and death, he kept calling out and crying. I could imagine Handa standing motionless, filled with a feeling of helplessness.

Eventually, the wind lulled and the snow subsided. From a rift in the clouds, came the sunlight, helping Handa to recover his senses. He went days in areas that had no water, and slept curled up in his car, trembling with fear. He stood in the midst of the destroyed wilderness, armed with his 65-million pixel camera, which rejected anything emotional. Unabashed, he looked at the dreadful natural state of the scenery. I could envision him frantically shooting 3500 shots, day after day.

I don't think his pictures sprang from an expressionist drive, which is probably a better reflection of his talent, but rather something more central to his instinctive core, causing him to shoot pictures with abandon. With these assumptions and a sense of responsibility as a member of a disaster rescue team, I examined the photographs taken by Handa, my friend.

Standing there, I came to a realization.

Every single random subject can be found in his photos. These are not crafted photos, but rather the actual state of devastated areas, with no element of goodwill and comfort. There is none of the smiles, tears and emotions that the media intentionally seeks out. What lies in Handa's photos is the red-rust-ed, real world that was submerged by saltwater. The sky is amazing ultramarine, because all factories and cars stopped emitting fumes and exhaust. An apricot tree is flowering, robustly releasing the energy conserved during winter. How did he manage to do this? The sorrowful world where our team stood motionless on that dreadful morning in March was here in Handa's works.

What these photos depict is the actual disaster that existed before the government created maps showing a hazard line. Media coverage of the tsunami shows how it literally swallowed all infrastructures, while the earthquake coverage, with aftershocks coming for days on end, simply broadcast what this natural phenomenon looked like. These images don't show viewers what actually happened to the people living there. Of course, news coverage is a necessary tool enabling Japanese in other regions, as well as people around the globe, to know that a tragedy is unfolding. But much of the coverage focused on this extreme event failed to show the complex reality of the suffering. No one captured the realism following the tsunami, as directly and candidly as Handa did.

I had been there for months, so his images should have been familiar to me. But my heart paused because the imagery was too overpowering. It evoked painful memories, like when I was trying to keep my footing in the water as I carried a sick person or a body. It stirred my ire remembering the endless mud we removed in an attempt to clear streets, schools, and temples. I could feel the pain in my hands as I clutched the chainsaw as I tried to cut through the huge driftwood that crushed into houses. The wood was saturated with saltwater, causing the chainsaw to overheat again and again. The only thing I could not feel was the stench.

This was the reality of the disaster; the end of man-made creations through human design. It's all been mercilessly destroyed. If you were to step into this wilderness, you would stand on something that used to be alive. All that's under your foot would crumble. On the streets lined with stores and buildings, you would see no human, hear no sound. You would see what was supposed to be an image on the ocean. These are images of a monumental disaster. They speak the truth.

And I feel ashamed of myself.

His photos made me realize his resolution and determination. He did not go to Tohoku to feed selfish ambitions as a photographer; he went there on a precious mission, as one given by God, by the Earth, to capture the exact state of the disaster. He missed nothing, as he followed his destiny, and his photos will be shared with the world for generations. I confess that I was utterly taken aback when I realized this.

Perhaps life is revealed through disasters and tragedies. Sometimes, it is excruciatingly painful. The people of Tohoku continue to live with this indescribable pain.

Over twenty months have passed since the earthquake, but the elderly continue to grieve the past. The tsunami swept across their land, destroyed their homes, and swallowed every possession they had accumulated. For parents, they grieve the present. The tsunami demolished their cars, destroyed their jobs, and took the lives of beloved ones. What about the children? They grieve the future. It's not that they lost their schools to the ocean water, leaving them unable to gather with friends. When they go home or into shelters, they are surrounded by grownups incapacitated by loss. The children grieve for the grownups. It should not be like this. We must look forward, must move on.

We must go beyond mere restoration and plan with better safety strategies, if we want people to have a sense of hope for the future. It should also be about regaining happiness, because people are burdened by so much suffering. As time goes by, that pain should subside. At some point, people should be able to calmly look back on this disaster and provide wisdom for the future.

When contemplating how to rebuild Tohoku, emphasizing greater emotional peace, we have to think of the children's future. We must imagine what it will be like when these children come of age, assuming leadership positions in society. Let's start at that point and work backwards. Children might be unable to articulate what they want in the future, so let us—the grownups—provide them with a blueprint. That is why we need to think about the future, and create a vision of what's possible. The government and individuals must start contemplating a better social system, based on their own experiences. What has this country, with an advanced civilization and culture, learned from its experiences with this devastating disaster? That question is the starting point for creating a system for the future, and one we will need to revisit frequently.

My friend, Handa, just kept taking pictures. Needlessly to say, if he had paused, the photographs would not exist. Yasushi Handa was an eyewitness of the disaster, who caught its essence in a way that a disaster relief worker, like myself, could never have done.

A step toward restoration

Surrounded by ocean, Japan is truly a hydrophilic country. But the only ideas the central and local governments have come up with are to build a 7.5-meter high breakwater wall along the coastline and to evacuate people to higher ground during an emergency. Shouldn't there be more?

There were wooden homes, built on Oya stone or concrete foundations, which withstood the tsunami in Yuriage and Nabenuma areas in Natori, Miyagi Prefecture. Residents escaped to the second floors and survived. According to tsunami researchers, when the bank subsided because of the earthquake, the surface of the sea rose, and massive energy from the bottom created a pressure wave, which generated the enormous second wave, which became a killer tsunami. We now understand this mechanism. Nonetheless, for those who reside in the area, building a higher and stronger bank is not enough to prevent future disasters. Is everyone going to move somewhere else because of a hazard line set by the government? Can scientists come up with technologies to impede killer waves? The homes that survived were closely examined, particularly the foundations, for 10 months, which gave us data and knowledge to develop a multidimensional disaster prevention plan. Approximately 150,000 people are unable to return to their homes, while 500,000 reside in homes that are barely functional. Considering this reality, we need a more flexible plan that meets a variety of demands.

The plain along the coastline of Sendai City was hit by a 3.6-meter high tsunami. Couldn't we build shelters capable of holding 40 people each that are 7.5 meters tall, 12 meters long, with a width of 6 meters? The foundations would be streamlined in order to withstand both surging and receding waves. The windows, which could be opened and closed, would be made from acrylic used at aquariums so that they could endure strong water pressure. Each shelter would feature an air-conditioning system powered by solar energy; a water supply from a well; independent heat from propane gas; a variable, airtight septic tank for sewage; electric-powered lifts; an engine to produce power when clouds and rain prevented use of solar energy; smoke balls to signal that people evacuated to shelters; life jackets; retort foods and water for 40 people for a period of 72 hours; and inflatable boats for rescue activities. If we had had such shelters spaced 500 meters apart, for a total of 20 shelters on the 15000-hectare agricultural land in the Miyagino and Wakabayashi areas in the Sendai Plain, which aren't on higher land, we might have saved 704 people that day. A person can quickly walk four kilometers per hour, which means covering two kilometers within 30 minutes, one kilometer within 15 minutes. If such shelters had existed, even older people with difficulty walking could have reached the shelters through rice fields, avoiding cracks in the earth. If we estimate the cost of a shelter at 55 million yen each, the cost of 20 would be around 1.1 billion yen. That figure is well below 1% of the total cost of the Super Breakwater Wall off Kamaishi Port, which was destroyed by the tsunami.

Silent tragedy

Stefano Carrer

Correspondent Il Sole 24 Ore

A silent tragedy, a catastrophe accompanied by mute pain. As the weeks turn into months and the three-pronged disaster that struck Japan on March 11, 2011, a disaster unprecedented in history—an earthquake, a tsunami, and a nuclear crisis—becomes more distant in time, in those of us who tried to report those events, what tends to make its way forward is the perception of a loss, rather than the summation of the single images of destruction. Hundreds of kilometres of coastline ravaged by nature's fury, dozens and dozens of towns and cities submerged by the floods, about eighteen thousand people killed or gone missing forever who knows where.

Those of us who for the following months travelled down the whole of the Calvary along the coastal region from Hachinoe to Iwaki cannot recall explicit displays of despair, outbursts of anger, mindless panic. Not a single slur addressed to the emergency services that couldn't avoid being delayed owing to the sheer size of the catastrophe—not a single sign of undisciplined rebellion against the effects of a cruel destiny that suddenly causes you to lose your home and your loved ones. To come across people shedding tears was a purely fragmentary and almost random occurrence: the cry of relief of a woman at last able to embrace her son who had just alighted from the helicopter that had saved him, or the more subdued sobbing of a daughter at the crematorium where she had gone to bid farewell to her elderly father who had died trapped between the walls of his half-submerged home.

My thoughts go back to the inner struggle that I as a reporter had to bear so as not to grow accustomed to the monotonous succession of urban scenarios wrecked beyond imagination: the fact that there was no lamenting made it harder for us as we travelled from one destroyed city to another day after day to be left aghast, almost as if we had entered a paradoxical situation of normality. What astonished the whole world was the composure of a whole population before the most heartbreaking adversity, roughly summed up with the word "stoicism" and undoubtedly the fruit of a specific history and culture, also expressed in everyday and routine ways. For instance, the long orderly line of people waiting, on a cold morning two days after the earthquake, at the entrance to the only supermarket that promised it would open in the inland city of Kesennuma. The foreign observer simply assumed there would be free distribution of food and other staples. After all, houses and banks had been destroyed and aid still hadn't arrived, with the exception of the very first emergency services. But no: people were expected to queue up as well as to pay, without even being sure that once their turn had come they would find something left on the shelves. How could anyone have criticized that mother with her daughter in her arms if she had suddenly lost control and tried to jump the line to get to a bottle of milk, paving the way to uncontrolled looting? But instead, just silence and orderliness. These are the things that are hard to forget, such as the fishermen's boats that had ended up on the roofs or the intermittent fires at the fuel depots.

Also etched in our memory are minimalist episodes, in some cases paradoxical, ones that are hard to imagine in other countries, such as the one involving three bank employees who, before their half-destroyed building, tried to find a place to put a notice bearing a warning written with a marker: "We apologize to our customers but all banking activity has been suspended". It would be mistaken to interpret this simply as bureaucratic obtuseness. Also unforgettable are the heroic stories told with the tone of normality, such as the one about the fisherman from Ishinomaki who pointed to the boats that were still intact and explained how they were saved: right after the earthquake struck, when they realized the tsunami was heading their way and would soon reach them, they quickly set sail so that in a half hour they could be at sea and thus safe. But it is also a reporter's duty to let others feel admiration for the evacuees' level-headedness, without running the risk of painting a semi-idyllic picture, breaking down the tragedy into a series of single events.

There's always a downside. We needn't necessarily admire the conditioned response that keeps people from raising their voices, at all levels of society. No doubt certain cases of bureaucratic obtuseness made the emergency services less efficient, especially during the first few days. The foreign journalist would check his or her permit to use the motorway or get fuel (even just a few litres) with guilty feelings knowing that private trucks still couldn't do so, and no solution had yet been found to the dramatic fuel shortages as a result of some obscure law on the obligation to keep certain stock levels divided by territory (which kept early supplies from arriving from the south of the country). Even in a country that is doggedly preparing to deal with catastrophes—aware that the problem is not if but when they will happen—not everything clicked perfectly when faced with the severity and sheer scope of the cataclysm. We must always take care not to generalize.

Even in Japan, after all, there are people who raised their voices, perhaps unheeded at the time, but who contributed to future improvements in the public safety services of a country that traditionally knows how to give its best and be very efficient—under every circumstance—especially when all the parameters are clear, but less so when the terms within which one can operate are unknown (i.e. during the earliest phases of an emergency). In other words, Japan is not a country of miracles, even if many circumstances end up being like a near miracle. Starting from the fact that after the earthquake in Tokyo, you couldn't see a single broken glass or bent traffic light: proof of the excellence of the country's construction technology and a compliance with the strict laws that other countries can only envy, countries where 16th-century buildings can withstand an earthquake, whereas others built just a few years before collapse on their inhabitants.

As for the reconstruction process, there were some who expected things to move faster, especially after having seen the page in the *Wall Street Journal* purchased by the Chinese authorities to show how the post-earthquake reconstruction in Sichuan was completed in an incredibly short amount of time, thanks to a top-down approach that minimizes the time between the decision-making and the actual implementation. Obviously, it is a question of an unrepeatable mechanism where the State comes up against the limits of a developed democracy, in the complex relationship between central authority, territorial bodies and local demands. Clearly, priority was given to repairing the infrastructures, while putting off the toughest decisions like that of where and how to rebuild the towns. The matter is close to being unsolvable: abandoning the traditional villages on the seashore to rebuild in areas that are more sheltered (which is what the government wants) risks changing the features of the ancient fishing villages forever, and erasing the traditional social life, while rebuilding everything the way it was before means prohibitive costs for safety infrastructures, which among other things might not necessarily be efficient, what's more in areas already affected by depopulation.

In any case, the funds allocated for the reconstruction measures are helping Japan to enjoy high growth rates for its gross domestic product this year, among the best rates of the advanced countries. This is something we might observe with a twinge of misplaced envy. In some European countries the consequences of the sovereign debt crisis are comparable to the damage caused by one or several tsunamis, as has been pointed out by a number of economists. But there isn't the slightest chance that even a robust set of public measures to stimulate the economy will offset the long-term effects of the financial tsunami.

The ancient whisper

Tetsuo Yamaori

Scholar of Religious Studies

1. Prologue

On March 11, 2011, I was in Kyoto. I was stunned watching what was unfolding on the TV broadcast: turbid waters sweeping fiercely through a densely built-up downtown area. Long ago as a child, I had walked those streets.

Kamaishi, located along the Sanriku coastline in Iwate Prefecture, was a city of life and energy, echoing with the sounds of hammering from a major iron mill—a symbol of reconstruction in postwar Japan. When the war ended, I was living in the nearby city of Hanamaki. I recall getting on the train and getting off at the end of the line, going over Sennin Pass, to walk to downtown Kamaishi. Watching the water gush through the city, I knew its inhabitants had been overwhelmed by its unrelenting force.

When the Miyagi earthquake struck in 1978, I was in Sendai in a room on the 9th floor. I felt as though I were floating, almost like a state of seasickness; but, I wasn't in danger. In January 1995, when the Great Hanshin-Awaji Earthquake hit, I was living in a suburb on the western side of Kyoto. I was startled as books tumbled from shelves, but the tremor quickly subsided. The earthquake and tsunami that ripped through the Tohoku region were far more dreadful. It defies description.

It's the type of disaster that is said to happen only once a millennium, which reminds me of a passage from *An Account from My Hut,* by Kamo no Chomei, who wrote about his experiences when a major earthquake hit the capital of Kyoto in 1185. Over 800 years ago, he described the arbitrary hand of destiny canceling out the lives of countless people through earthquakes, typhoons, and famine. "Dozens of men and women died ... We don't know how many people starved to death". His assessment reveals the pitiful conditions following the earthquake. He wandered the streets and sighed as he tallied the body count at close to 42,300.

From beginning to end, what Kamo no Chomei saw was a world overflowing with dead bodies. Surrounded by such horror, we can assume that he understood that life is undeniably uncertain. Perhaps we are now reliving the age described in *An Account from My Hut* and *The Tale of the Taira Clan*, also written 800 years ago. That notion haunts me.

> Even if the world becomes chaos
> As mountains fall apart
> Oceans dry up
> How should I hatch
> A plan to betray my Lord?

This tanka poem was written by Minamoto no Sanetomo, the 3rd shogun of the Kamakura feudal government, who was a contemporary of Kamo no Chomei. The young shogun's poem reflects the agonies of his soul as he laments the constant political struggles. Recalling the pathetic undertone of this Japanese-style poem, I cannot help but think "how should I hatch a plan to betray" my country? I pray this country survives, as the mountains crumble and the ocean dries up.

We hung our heads in despair, as we contemplated the vast number of dead and the ferocious power of nature. Media reports intensified by the minute, as individual body counts turned into estimates of the mass number of deceased. The pendulum would swing again, as individuals were culled from the piles and identified. There were countless numbers of "corpses soaking in the water", reads a poem by Otomo no Yakamochi, and countless numbers of "corpses fleeced with grass" strewn over mountains and fields. I pray that the souls of the departed—every single one of them—leave their bodies, and soar up high, to be enshrined in the mountains and forests of the country.

2. Two myths and the strategy of an uncertain life

The earth shook violently and released a massive tsunami that engulfed the land, causing the islands of Japan to be tossed about like tiny boats. Next, the fires and explosions came from nuclear power plants, the energy yielded from nuclear fission. Since that fateful day, our sense of control was obliterated. The islands of Japan seem to sit atop a gunpowder warehouse.

March 11, 2011 is the date that seems to proclaim the beginning of an age of uncertainty. I have a gut feeling it was merely a preliminary disaster before a wave of tremendous diastrophisms and extraordinarily violent weather in the future.

I am not trying to be an alarmist; it's just that the havoc of March 11 made me recall the mythical stories of ancient literature.

The two stories are *Noah's Ark*, which everyone knows, and *Three Carts and the Burning House*. The former is from Genesis in the Old Testament, while the latter is a parable from Chapter 3 of the Lotus Sutra, a sacred Buddhist scripture.

These are stories, with growth rings, which have been handed down for generations, spanning two and three thousand years. They can be categorized as myths, or ancient folklore. *Noah's Ark* is a story about water, while the parable is one about fire. The March 11th tragedy, which continues to unfold in front of us, is also about water and fire. The sudden burst of the Earth's massive energy released these two elements, which in turn created a pool of deep angst due to the horrific suffering.

Let's begin with *Noah's Ark.*

God saw that the people of earth were leading corrupt and wicked lives. In a fit of anger, God decided to destroy them all along with the earth.

Noah however was the exception. He was a righteous man, living according to the laws of God, so God granted him survival and instructed him to build an ark, which would carry him, his wife, their three sons and their wives, two of all creatures—male and female—and food.

Seven days later, the floodwaters came. It rained for forty days and nights, wiping away every living thing, with the exception of those on the ark.

The floodwaters subsided after a hundred and fifty days, and the ark came to rest on the mountains of Ararat. Noah built an altar, and made burnt offerings. God blessed Noah and his sons, instructing them to be fruitful and replenish the earth.

By following the will of God, the story tells how and why Noah and his family were spared. In essence, their rescue boat saved those who brought forth the world we have today.

Now let's turn to *Three Carts and the Burning House.*

There was a wealthy man in the country who had an enormous but dilapidated home. One day, a fire broke out, setting the old house ablaze.

Unaware of the fire, the man's children remained in the house, happily playing with their toys. Their father called for them to come outside immediately, but they paid no attention to him.

The wealthy man had a thought. He placed three toys in front of the house gate: a beautifully decorated ox cart, a sheep cart, and a deer cart. He called to them again, saying he had unusual treasures for them.

Hearing this, the children leapt to their feet, pushing and shoving each other to catch a glimpse of the precious vehicles. The wealthy man succeeded in rescuing his children and gave them all real carts with white oxen.

Here, a man uses three toy carts to rescue his children from danger. In the end, they find their rescue boat in the form of carts with white oxen. It's a story in which everyone is rescued. And if the man hadn't noticed the flames, they would have all perished.

These stories predated the Christian era, and can thus be called myths, or ancient folklore.

After the earthquake and the ensuing crisis at the Fukushima nuclear power plant, I heard the call of these two ancient stories, whispering their continued relevance and overturning my perception of what constitutes modern history.

When these two stories first appeared, there were those who understood that man's destiny was linked to water and fire. We should recognize this.

For example, Socrates and Plato, Buddha and Christ, Lao-tzu and Kung-tzu, were among such people. They contemplated the basic questions of life: what is man? What is the world? They guided people, through easy words and stories, on how to escape human folly and its madness.

These philosophers lived between the 8th century BC and the start of the Christian era. It was a highly unique and epoch period, which is why German philosopher Karl Jaspers referred to it as the Axial Age.

The great thinkers of the Axial Age contemplated the meaning and the ramifications of most hardships and tragedies that human beings would later face.

Let's return to the two stories.

Noah's Ark is unequivocally a story of survival. It provides a blueprint for escaping a disaster, with instructions for building the most suitable boat to flee on. Indeed, the depiction of the survival strategy is picturesque.

This survival story is pivotal in the histories of both Jewish and Christian civilizations. It reveals the idea of God's chosen ones, and is echoed in the theory of evolution. Indeed, it is part of the foundation that guides Western ideas and underpins Anglo-Saxon civilization. A genealogical table of political and economic theories advances and expounds upon this survival strategy.

In modern times, the strategy of survival is played out in advanced medical practices, such as brain death and organ transplants, as well as in the philosophy that underpins the theory of sustainable development, which has a major role in environmental issues. In short, behind these modern-day techniques and theories lurks the notion that only a select group will survive while others die.

In other words, it's a theory of selection based on the rescue boat and the sacrifice of others. Modern humanism expresses it more kindly in what might be termed the greatest happiness for the greatest number.

So what about *Three Carts and the Burning House*? At its essence, it says that the world we live in is a burning house, and if we fail to realize this, we will all perish. Indeed, if we don't heed the call to escape the flames, we will eventually be engulfed by them.

Life is transient, as expressed by three Buddhist principles: nothing on earth lasts forever; what has physical form will eventually vanish; a human lives and dies. Within this context, the story says we should quickly flee from the transience of the burning house. If one sees the fire, one can escape using the cart with a white ox. If one fails to see the flames, one dies.

We could call it the transience strategy. Apparently, Buddha and Lao-tzu viewed it as such, with no one escaping the hand of death. There was no rescue boat for the select few because all were destined to live and die. We are all on a ship called "the burning house of transience", which means we live together and die together. That's the core concept underlying the transience strategy.

It may sound dark; it may sound pessimistic. But it can also be viewed in a positive light in the sense that people, through sheer energy and will, are driven to reconstruct and regenerate society.

It means that chaos has more fundamental power and more sustainable energy than cosmos, which is the concept of order. It places chaos at the forefront, diminishing the power of cosmos to determine selection. Western thought, with its notion of survival of the fittest, leans toward cosmos, while the Asian transience strategy leans toward chaos as a mechanism to protect ourselves. It creates a dichotomy between two civilizations: those pro-cosmos and those pro-chaos.

Let me add one more thing.

The survival strategy that sprang from Judeo-Christian culture has produced many fruits for all civilizations. Japan too has enjoyed immense benefits on each of its islands. That path to prosperity was clear.

But, frankly speaking, this survival strategy has also generated deep angst, because it fails to reconcile the gap between those who survive by jumping on the boat and those left behind. The more that the progress of civilization is based on the survival strategy, the greater the tension and fear we feel between the pull of life and death. In other words, the advancement of society through the survival strategy breeds a malaise of tension and fear.

In contrast, the transience strategy found in the *Three Carts and the Burn-*

ing House ameliorates the inherent anxieties and tensions that arise in a civilization based on the survival strategy. In this sense, the transience strategy seems to function as a pacifier and balance to anxiety, like a karmic effect on society.

We are facing the aftermath of the greatest disaster that we've ever experienced, and are thrown into endless despair. Under these circumstances, these stories speak to my heart. Indeed, myths and ancient stories offer infinite wisdom and insight. In modern times, we should learn from them.

3. Three Scientists: Torahiko Terada, Kiyoshi Oka, and Tetsuro Watsuji

As I contemplate the greatest earthquake and tsunami to strike in the last 1,000 years, as well as the perilous nuclear power plant crisis that followed, I recall the words of Torahiko Terada and Kiyoshi Oka.

Terada, who conducted a survey following the aftermath of the Great Kanto Earthquake in 1923, was a physicist who was attributed with saying the following famous quote: "Natural disasters strike when people forget the previous ones". He wrote an essay titled *The Japanese View on Nature* in 1935, which could be considered his final statement since he died later that year. In it, he discusses how Japan has been threatened by natural disasters for thousands of years.

Largely due to the ever-present threat of earthquakes and typhoons, he wrote that Japan's natural environment is inherently unstable. When nature ran wild, Japanese hung their heads, resigned to its fierceness and their inability to counter its force. People tried to derive wisdom from the power of nature, crafting a means to cope with it and prepare for future disasters.

That effort grew over time, creating a way of life among Japanese that naturally fostered a deep sense of "natural transience", he wrote. My understanding of it is that people began to hear God's voice and sense the spirits inhabiting nature. Imagine a physicist hanging his head before nature, and listening to the call of natural transience. He elaborated on transience, noting that it was rooted in Japan before the arrival of Buddhism, which I find noteworthy.

The other man, Kiyoshi Oka, was a mathematician who created fundamental theories governing several complex variables, which altered the international world of mathematics. For that achievement, he received the Order of Culture. In his later years, Oka led a life of self-imposed solitude in Nara Prefecture in order to devote himself fully to his studies.

In 1965, Oka spoke with Hideo Kobayashi, a leading 20th-century literary critic, on the theme "Constructing Humans". I found parts of their discussion on the fate of natural science astonishing.

In Oka's view, the king of 20th-century science, theoretical physics, had brought about tools of "destruction". The obvious examples were the inventions of the atomic and hydrogen bombs. This science, from his viewpoint, had failed to yield anything to subplant these destructive creations. Moreover, theoretical physics and other branches of natural science had focused on "mechanical manipulation", which he deemed uncreative.

Oka was criticizing the overemphasis on the development of engineering technologies, which can be seen today in such pursuits as genetic manipulation. In the dialogue, he was critical that those in natural science could not even recreate chlorophyll. Who can challenge the veracity of Oka's comments?

The advancement of scientific technology has been a great boon to mankind. Nonetheless, what those two farsighted leaders insisted on in their closing years resonates with me: transience is natural and profound, and science has limitations. Reading between the lines, I hear their call to question the arrogance of science and technology.

I'd like to revisit the views of Torahiko Terada, along with the philosophy and research of Tetsuro Watsuji. These two intellectuals were contemporaries, and analyzed Japan through the window of nature, covering a trajectory of thousands of years. They sought to identify unique natural elements in Japan in comparison with the West. Both men had a tremendous impact on the views of generations of Japanese.

Interestingly, Terada and Watsuji had different insights on the ferocity of nature. In Terada's essays from *Natural Calamity and National Defense* and *The Japanese View on Nature*, both written around 1935, he included the following points: the more civilization progresses, the more violent natural calamities became; Japan was far more exposed to the threat of earthquakes, tsunami, and typhoons than the West; and because of its particular experiences with nature, science in Japan developed according to experiential knowledge in an attempt to adapt to nature, as opposed to trying to conquer it. This explained why science and other areas of study pursued different tracks when compared with other nations.

In addition, the Japanese attitude was to obey the laws of nature and to adjust to the climate. Terada concluded that this coincided with the concept of transiency in Buddhism. Through the experience of countless calamities, be it earthquakes, storms or floods, Japanese developed a sense of "natural transience", as earlier referred to.

Watsuji approached the topic differently in *Climate and Culture*, which was also published in 1935. His comparison of the pastoral climate and culture of the West in contrast to Japan's monsoon climate and culture is well known.

Curiously, Watsuji, in his examination of Japanese climate conditions, only addressed typhoons and monsoons, with no mention of earthquakes, which were central to Terada's writings. At the time he wrote, he most certainly would have had vivid recollections of the Great Kanto Earthquake of 1923; nonetheless, not a word on earthquakes.

According to Watsuji, Japan's climate and culture had the duality of tropical and frigid zones, which generated heavy rain and heavy snow, as well as seasonal routines and abruptness, which fostered a sense of emotional endurance and upheaval. Such peculiarities of climate, he argued, cultivated a lifestyle of receiving and submission. "Quiet, violent passion" and "combative indifference" were paradoxical descriptions he attributed to the Japanese, due to typhoons.

Intriguingly, in expounding upon emotional dualism, Watsuji discussed the Buddhist influence on Japanese regarding the paradoxical idea that the pursuit of earthly desires is a pure aspiration to enlightenment. He saw dualism as a pivotal influence on Japanese family issues as well. Between a man and a woman, a husband and a wife, and a parent and a child, Watsuji maintained there were conflicting pressures between selfishness and sacrifice, which gave birth to the ethic of mercy.

Terada and Watsuji obviously had different opinions. While they both examined the same subject, they approached it differently. As a natural scientist, Torahiko Terada emphasized earthquakes and attributed the emotional framework of Japanese to Buddhist transiency. In contrast, Tetsuro Watsuji, who approached it more logically, focused on typhoons and the importance of the morality of mercy, a guiding principle among Japanese.

Though the differences are great, the commonalities are important and should be noted. Both viewed Japanese science as more adaptive and focused on coping with problems, as opposed to Western science that was aggressive and focused on conquering nature. How should we restore and revive the islands of Japan, which were seemingly cracked at the core by this latest disaster? We should tackle this burning question, with a clear view of the analysis provided by these two scholars.

4. Epilogue

The Tohoku region bore the brunt of the powerful earthquake that shook the country on March 11, and the region continues to suffer. The echoes of their agonies continue to reverberate across Japan.

It's as though their pain and suffering seep to the surface, enabling me to hear the soft, ghost whisper, with an Iwate accent, of Kenji Miyazawa, a deceased author from that prefecture. In a nostalgic melody, I hear his words.

Miyazawa was born in 1896, just two months after the Meiji Sanriku Great Earthquake, which had a magnitude 8.2. The great tsunami that followed swept away 22,000 people. Four days after his birth, the Rikuu Earthquake, with a magnitude of 7.2, struck directly beneath the boundary between Iwate and Akita prefectures, killing hundreds more.

On March 3, 1933, about six months before Miyazawa passed away at the age of 36, the Showa Sanriku Earthquake, with a magnitude of 8.1, hit, killing an estimated 3000 people. In addition to that, the Tohoku region suffered poor harvests and severe famine between 1930 and 1934. It was within that backdrop that Miyazawa wrote his masterpiece titled *The Life of Gusko Budori.* Clearly, the passion and anguish he poured into that story came from his life experiences.

The story revolves around Gusko Budori, who was born into a family of woodcutters in Ihatov, a fictional name, derived from Iwate. After a severe winter, his family was torn asunder by the ensuing financial crisis. It was a childhood deeply scarred by natural disasters, including drought and volcanic eruptions. Gusko eventually becomes an engineer at Ihatov's volcano bureau, where he is able to mitigate the damage of volcanic eruptions and fertilize soil by creating artificial rain. Even so, one problem remains: how does one protect farmers from the severity of cold? He finds his answer in the volcano, which he decides must erupt. Everyone can be evacuated prior to the explosion, except the person who flips the switch; that person must perish. Gusko decides to sacrifice himself. With the eruption, temperatures immediately rise, freeing everyone from the tyranny of the cold.

It's a story in which self-sacrifice brings relief. But, in his *Outline of the Essential Art of the Peasant,* Miyazawa wrote, "One cannot achieve personal happiness, until everyone is happy". That was the world view of Miyazawa, a man of strong convictions. And, to put it another way, the world cannot achieve happiness until every person achieves it. In that context, how do we understand the destiny of that one person, Gusko Budori, who volunteers to die? Did he achieve personal happiness, as Miyazawa implied was possible? An enormous quandary is rooted in his message.

When I think of those engulfed in a struggle for life in the disaster areas, including those inside the nuclear power plants, Miyazawa's words resound gravely. It poses urgent and serious questions that strike at the heart of who we are.

The Tohoku region is now burdened by suffering.

Photographs of the Sublime: Y. Handa's great work

Hideki Kuwajima, Ph.D.

Associate Professor of Aesthetics, Hiroshima University

1. The Historical Sublime: "Non-representational" Tohoku

When I first saw Yasushi Handa's photographs of the Higashi-Nippon Dai-Shinsai (Great East Japan Earthquake) in 2011[1], I was instantly struck by the similarity of some images to the cityscape of Hiroshima after August 6, 1945. Though the former event is completely different from the latter, these two resemble each other in the devastated landscape resulting from a painful and tortured event in human history. Hence I will discuss Mr. Handa's work only from a view of the problem of "aesthetical" perception, or "representation", of a historical event. Afterwards referring to some disasters in the past, such as Hiroshima (in order to explain a philosophical concept of the "historical sublime"), I am not involved in any political and religious judgment of the good and evil in my essay.

Philosophically speaking, the atomic bombing of Hiroshima cannot be perfectly represented in our imaginations because it was a historical event that defies description. In other words, it was a real incident beyond imagination. The contemporary American philosopher Berel Lang called it the "historical sublime," referring to the Kantian thought. From that, we might say "we cannot create any poetry or art in general after Hiroshima", recalling the famous words on Auschwitz by Theodor Wiesengrund Adorno. This passage seems to have a double meaning: one depends upon the "savage," or inhumane, nature of scientific technology put to ill use through nuclear weapons, the other upon the historical sublime mentioned above[2]. The peak of our modern civilization, either in the creation of artwork or in the development of technology, ceased with corrupt and malicious events, like the Holocaust and atomic bombings, while the events beyond our imagination exist within a framework seemingly impossible to reproduce, or "represent," in equivalent images or forms.

Strictly speaking in terms of the "aesthetics" of representation, a kind of philosophy of our sensibilities, like the representation of the events in Hiroshima or Auschwitz, we cannot perfectly describe the entire event of the extraordinary earthquake and tsunami on March 11, 2012 in Tohoku, the northeast region of Japan. Of course, the catastrophic scenery before our eyes resulting from the earthquake and tsunami was caused not by human evil or our misuse of scientific technology but by the natural or geological mechanism intrinsic to our planet, Earth. This is why hereafter I examine the scenery of Tohoku, post March 11, 2011, from a view of the "historical sublime" ruled by Mother Nature (not based upon some kind of political and religious position at all). In what sense can Mr. Handa's photographs represent an event that is not easy to describe due to its ingenerate character of over-perception? In my concluding remarks, I will illustrate how his artwork is a good example of a "photograph of the sublime."

2. The Magic of Handa's 65 Mega Pixels: Images beyond Our Eyesight

The most important aspect of Mr. Handa's pictures is closely related to the state-of-the-art camera: His magic "65 mega pixels." It is the art of high-resolution images that is executed by this talented photographer. What kind of vision can Mr. Handa create, or represent, by using this hyper-focused technology?

There seems to be two types of highly artificial effects in his work.

One is the ability to produce a highly magnified image, which presents an extraordinarily clear picture. A very spacious "tableau" emerges before viewers. This vast expansion of one photograph, even if it is impossible to produce in reality, overwhelms our senses, particularly the sense of seeing. The motif of Mr. Handa's work is not abstract. Even so, his photography might affect us the same way that the work of Barnett Newman, a famous American Abstract-Expressionist painter from the 1950s, can, as with such paintings as *Vir Heroicus Sublimis.* Thanks to the photographer's use of this hyper-focused technology, his works are capable of exciting our imaginations, just like we might feel standing in front of a huge, flat canvas painted by Newman, which allows us to extend our visual experience. In fact, Mr. Handa's photographs could be viewed as artificial or super-realism rather than naturalism (In this context, we might regard "super-realism" as a kind of "romanticism").

The second artificial effect is the sense that Mr. Handa's delicate digital photographs seem to embody an ancient notion that "gods reside in detail". In examining his works, we could naturally focus on the abundance of painful scars carved into the ground of Tohoku. The ability to plunge into the possible philosophical insights generated by this detail is equal to a "contemplation," or "theoria," put forth by Aristotle. The Victorian art critic and philosopher John Ruskin once employed this term in one of the volumes from his renowned series, *Modern Painters,* in defense of the artwork of the English painter, Joseph Mallord William Turner (In my first book in 2008, I illustrated the close relationship of Ruskin's geological interest with the aesthetical idea of the sublime)[3]. Our insight, which is drawn "downward" into the earthly world post-disaster, is capable of bringing us into the deepest level of contemplation. What is left is debris, or the carcass of all that previously existed. However, when we stare at the texture of the devastated landscape in detail, we first cast our eyes downward, deeper and deeper, onto and into the ground. Eventually, through this sudden upside-down visual process, we can have the "deepest" and most advanced insight "upward" toward what is heavenly.

Our contemplation of the painful, but "artificial," scenery captured by Mr. Handa could enable viewers to enjoy a kind of sublime, soul-elevated feeling. Then, prompted by the art of the photographer, we could access one supreme form of "representation of the impossible disaster." With this, there emerges the historical sublime.

3. My Memoir, or Resonance with the Devastated Landscapes in Our History

On March 11, 2011, I was with two academic friends at a meeting for the "Society for Studies of the Sublime," which was held in Yamaguchi, located on the most western part of mainland Japan. That evening, the bullet trains bound for Osaka and Tokyo were either delayed or cancelled. I managed to get back home to Hiroshima by midnight, where my pregnant wife was waiting for me. When I left Yamaguchi, I was filled with worry about my relatives living in my hometown, which is on the eastern part of Japan (not in the most damaged parts of Tohoku). Sitting in the safety of the "Far West," I called over and over again to no avail. Phone lines were dead.

The situation reminded me of my experience in the early morning hours of January 17, 1995, when the Kansai (Kobe, Osaka, and Kyoto) region was rocked by a massive earthquake. I was a graduate student at Osaka University when the Great Hanshin Earthquake hit. I was stunned by the sounds emanating from the earth and the force of the quake that jolted everything up and down. Kobe, a prominent port city, was completely destroyed, though no tsunami swept through it. The contemporary Japanese novelist and peace activist, Makoto Oda, a self-described "co-writer" and translator of the work of the ancient Greek teacher of rhetoric named Pseudo-Longinus, discussed and revised the original concept on the basis of his observations of the damaged and devastated landscape of the Kobe area (Oda harshly speculated that the quake damage and the resulting fires were perhaps the result of government negligence).

Let me tell you another story. In April 2004, I was offered a professorship at Hiroshima University, so I moved from Osaka to Hiroshima, which is located in the more western part of Japan. I had no relatives there. However, as is often the case with young strangers, I had a "boy-meets-girl" encounter, which resulted in me marrying a woman from Hiroshima. Sheis among the youngest of second-generation A-bomb victims. She is a liberal woman in politics, and recognizes as herself to be a descendant of them, working as a staff writer at a local newspaper company for the peace-buildings in the world.

I was affected by my wife and Hiroshima itself. At my university, I have since given a regular lecture on a drama (a kind of love comedy) centered on the prosperous future of a ceratin young female survivor after Hiroshima; it was written by Hisashi Inoue and titled *Chichi to Kuraseba* (It was translated into English by Roger Pulvers and published as *The Face of Jizo*). My perspective of the atomic bombing in Hiroshima has also been influenced mainly by my long interest in the aesthetical and philosophical category of the sublime in a broader sense (not in a political and sentimental factor). Now I find a philosophical concept of the "impossibility of representation, or perception" as one of the most important elements of the sublime. My academic focus on the sublime in general, from the "non-representality" of Great Nature to that of Hiroshima, resulted in the publication of my first book, *Suko no Bigaku* (Aesthetics of the Sublime), which was released in May 2008.

My book drew attention, which resulted in the creation of academic followers. I mentor several students, including some aged, "mature" ones originally from Hiroshima, who are deeply interested in the problem of the representation of Hiroshima, or the aesthetics of the devastated landscape of the city. I have recently conducted the monument tour with a few of them around August 6, the memorial day.

From April to August 2012, the first half of the semester in the Japanese academic year, I inaugurated a primary theme in one of my graduate school classes: "Devastated Landscape and the Sublime: Lisbon in 1755, Kobe in 1995, and Tohoku in 2011."

Hence, I will tell you that when you seek a way to represent the disaster in Tohoku on March 11, 2011, you should look back at the history. If you don't, you will be at a complete loss. Mr. Handa's photographic collection on the disaster in Tohoku resonates strongly with the landscapes of the "representation of the impossible disaster," such as Hiroshima.

May all the dead, all the victims, and all living things in the world, live long!

Postscript

After my writing this essay, I had the opportunity to meet Mr. Handa in Tokyo on August 31, 2012. He discussed how the history of repeated disasters, such as great earthquakes and tsunami, has fostered a certain "gentle" resignation among those living in such regions. He suggested a comparison to the stories compiled by Kunio Yanagida in *Touno Monogatari* (The Tales of Touno, Iwate). The earth's carcass, containing the dead and living things in Tohoku, are all equivalent under Mother Nature. Mr. Handa explained that the present work would also include pictures taken inside portions of the 20-kilometer zone from the centre of the "secondary" disaster after the earthquake and tsunami, which were recently reopened to the public. This creates another sense of the shifting reality surrounding the devastated Fukushima Dai-ichi Nuclear Plant in Tohoku. It makes me suppose that this Handa's collection will resonant even more with another. This is why, I think, the present photographic work of Mr. Handa displays two different dimensions: one is a horrible but "gentle" face of the "20 days after" the earthquake and tsunami in the greater coastlines of Tohoku and the other is a quiet but "apocalyptic" face of the "1 and a half years after" the disaster in Fukushima.

[1] See the Japanese version of the book featuring the photographs of Mr. Yasushi Handa (born in Kyoto, 1955-): *20 Days After*, Tokyo: Yoshimoto Books, March 2012. The works such as "Rikuzentakata, Iwate prefecture" (*Ibid.*, p. 35, Plate: No. 18) and "Minamisanriku, Motoyoshi, Miyagi prefecture" (*Ibid.*, p. 78, Plate: No. 40) particularly remind me of the devastated delta-scape of Hiroshima just after the A-bombing in August 1945. The motif of the latter, the ruined Minamisanriku-cho Town Hall, is now a kind of sacred memorial, or cenotaph, among the locals. There was one heroic staff member who kept calling for people to evacuate until she was swept away by the huge tsunami, which barreled in exceeding the height of the roof. It could become a symbolic building like the A-bombed Dome in Hiroshima.

[2] Hideki Kuwajima (born in Gumma, 1970, Associate Professor of Aesthetics and Art Philosophy at Hiroshima University), *Suko no Bigaku* (Aesthetics of the Sublime), Tokyo: Kodan-sha, May 2008, pp. 187-235. I discussed here "American Technological Sublime" and "Possibility of the Representation about Hiroshima, August 6, 1945."

[3] *Ibid.*, pp. 130-159. I strongly argued that one of the most important elements in the Aesthetics of the Sublime should be a geological phase in natural science in the 17th and 18th centuries. Then, I created the term "geological aesthetics." Genealogically we might trace the origin of this even back to the "Irish-Celtic Sublime" (that is also the technical term I created) theorized by Edmund Burke.

Seeds of hope from the abyss of disaster

Satoru Wakabayashi

Director of Nerima Art Museum, Tokyo

Yasushi Handa and I first crossed paths 20 years, when I was working in the world of advertising and he was shooting fashion and sets for advertisements. He was young, bursting with energy, and his photos exuded that. His images had a distinctive texture and depth that uniquely unveiled the inner quality and essence of whatever was being photographed, be it a person or inanimate object. The higher the quality of the object, the more magnificent it would seem when viewed by his lens. When working together, I had to pay close attention to what I put in front of him; everything had to be high quality, had to have a substantive story to tell. Even the models needed to have quality of character and lives filled with passion and purpose.

After I left the ad industry for a position in the art world, I ran across Handa's work from time to time. But one day in July 2011, I looked up to find him in my office. "I want you to take a look", he said, as he spread out the photos now contained in this book. He had hastily returned to Japan following news of the March 11 disaster. He'd been in the United States, shooting pictures of iron structures—part of a project he's pursued in recent years in between ad jobs. It was day 20 after the disaster, when he decided to pick up his 65-million pixel camera and head to the disaster areas.

I hesitated to make an immediate comment; but, one thing was clear: his photos struck at my core, at a visceral level, causing me to feel tremendous anguish. It called to mind something I had read by the sculptor and poet, Koutaro Takamura (1883-1956), in an essay titled *The World of the Tactile,* that our tactual sense is the most primitive and basic of all our senses. He argued that superior art—whether painting, photography, music, or any other form—was capable of tapping into that deep-seated, primal state.

After showing copies of the photos to a young, female colleague whose hometown was Ofunato, one of the hard hit areas, she asked to go home. It took her a week to return to work, but she wasn't really there. Her mind was far away, as she struggled to make sense of nature's power to strip her town and its residents of all that made it "home". The photos had triggered this oppressive realization, which now weighed heavily upon her heart and soul. Yes, Handa's photos unveiled the unbearable pain of loss and misfortune.

In the Heian period, Saicho (766-822), who started the Tendai sect of Buddhism in Japan, taught that all living things, including plants and other insentient objects, have the inherent potential to attain enlightenment. The Chusonji temple, located in Hiraizumi in Iwate Prefecture and designated as a UNESCO World Heritage Site, is a Tendai temple believed to date from 1105, which was built and expanded over the course of a century under three generations of samurai from the Fujiwara clan, beginning with Fujiwara no Kiyohara, his son Motohira, and grandson Hidehira.

The temple was built to house the souls of samurai killed in battles, including enemies, which rocked the region of what is now called Tohoku in the latter half of the 11th century. The temple houses the Amitabha, the celestial Buddha said to reside over the Pure Land in the West.

In Kyoto, Chionin temple houses the renowned painting called "Amida Nijugo Bosatsu Raigozu (The Descent of Amitabha and Twenty-Five Attendants)", which depicts Amitabha and 25 Buddhist saints descending from heaven on a fast-moving cloud to save all living things and bring them to the Pure Land. In Handa's photographs there are no people; but, in each image I can visualize the 25 Buddhist saints descending to help all living things find their way to salvation. Yes, even the far-strewn piles of debris could be rescued from the pain of this disaster.

Not everyone initially looked that closely at the photos. When Handa brought the series to Japan's most prestigious photography museum to see if they'd be interested in displaying them, they declined, saying it would be more appropriate to show the works in a gallery setting alongside other photos of the disaster taken by other photographers. When the museum later hosted a solo exhibition of photos from the disaster by a prominent photographer in the art field, the hint of bias became clear. Thus, when Skira Editore, Europe's most highly regarded publisher of art materials, decided to publish Handa's work in a book, it was affirmed that his photos are not merely a documentary of the disaster but a showcase of haunting photographs capable of speaking to the world on a variety of levels.

Nonetheless, I questioned my own reaction, wondering if my judgment was skewed by my personal relationship with him or by my sensitivity to earthquakes. Was my colleague emotionally overwhelmed because of the power of Handa's photos or because of the brutal imagery of her hometown in ruins? If the latter had been the case, then any photograph would have had the same effect.

To check myself, I decided to compare photographs of the disaster taken by 18 renowned photographers in the art world. Variations in quality aside, each series revealed a central theme, such as "The Power of Nature and the Calm after the Storm", "The Hint of Life", "Restoration Work alongside Rescue Work", "Restricted Zones near the Nuclear Plants", "Families in Despair and in Recovery", and "Hometown: Past and Present".

Handa's work, on the other hand, defied classification. He entered the disaster areas well ahead of any photographer from the art world. Camera in hand, he recorded the aftermath of the disaster in its full magnitude. Images capture so much detail, yet are devoid of thought given to how and what those images might represent to an audience. The photos suggest a sense of urgent and impulsive energy to record every fragment of the calamity. And those gruesome details are magnified by the power of a 65-million pixel camera. But is it art? How can any tragedy, particularly one inflicting such widespread misfortune, be called "art"? Do we showcase the photos in a book because they capture one of the largest natural disasters in the history of man, or because they encapsulate a universal theme found in philosophy and art?

Alas, viewers must draw their own conclusions based on their own individual reaction. I witnessed a colleague wither in despair as she processed Handa's images of the damage done to her hometown. I, on the other hand, felt tremendous emotional turmoil, which caused me to recall images and aspects of Buddhism. These photos have the ability to affect each of us, which is why they can be termed "art".

Japanese have learned to bend with the force of nature, while Westerners seem intent on finding ways to confront and control it, as suggested in Handa's photos featured in *Iron Still*, the tentative title for another book to be published by ADP in Japan. But even iron bends when hit with the full force of nature. It makes me wonder if we've used elements of nature to build the right things. Putting these books side by side, perhaps there's an answer to be found. Perhaps Handa, whose eyes captured the essence of such images, can lend greater thought and meaning to this dilemma. What can an artist tell us to help us better understand our world? Are there fundamental themes that beg to be explored? What does Handa wish to say?

Sometimes artists are driven by sheer impulse, which can border on recklessness. As viewers, we're challenged to discover what drove them. It might be a universal theme, like "Pain and Suffering", or something more particular to Japan, like "Elements of Buddhism". In the grand scheme of things, Handa's photos seem to ask all of us to question whether our civilizations are creating things meant to stand the test of time, the test of nature.

I'd like Handa to turn his focus away from the iron structures, such grand symbols of civilization, toward a different horizon. Perhaps there is something to be gleaned from *Guns, Germs, and Steel: The Fate of Human Society*, by Jared Diamond, an American author and scientist, who traces the development of civilizations through the influence of environment and geographical features. What more can he tell us through his photos? What underlying story has yet to be told? Is there enough depth and lucidity that these photos could speak to future generations?

"Even if the world ends tomorrow, we shall plant an apple tree", wrote Takeshi Kaiko (1930-1989), an author I hold in high regard. No matter what happens, we have to hold on to hope for what the future will bring.

Perhaps this book contains the seeds for tiny apple trees, waiting longingly to be discovered and planted by viewers. I hope my colleague will plant her own apple tree and see it bloom, inspired by whatever moved her heart and soul so profoundly.

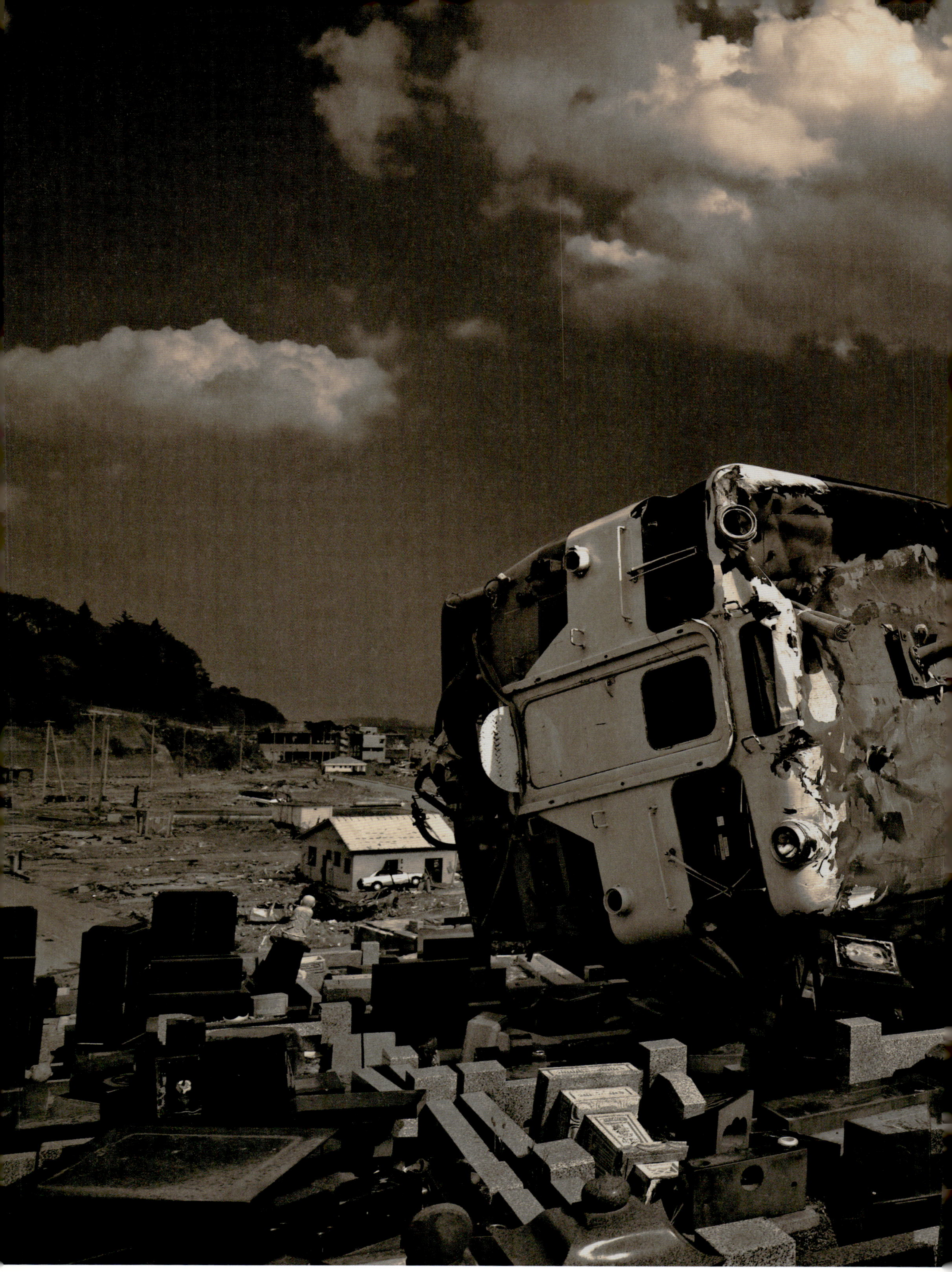

This train is on top of a cemetery around 30 meters above sea level.
Onagawa Cho, Ojika County, Miyagi prefecture

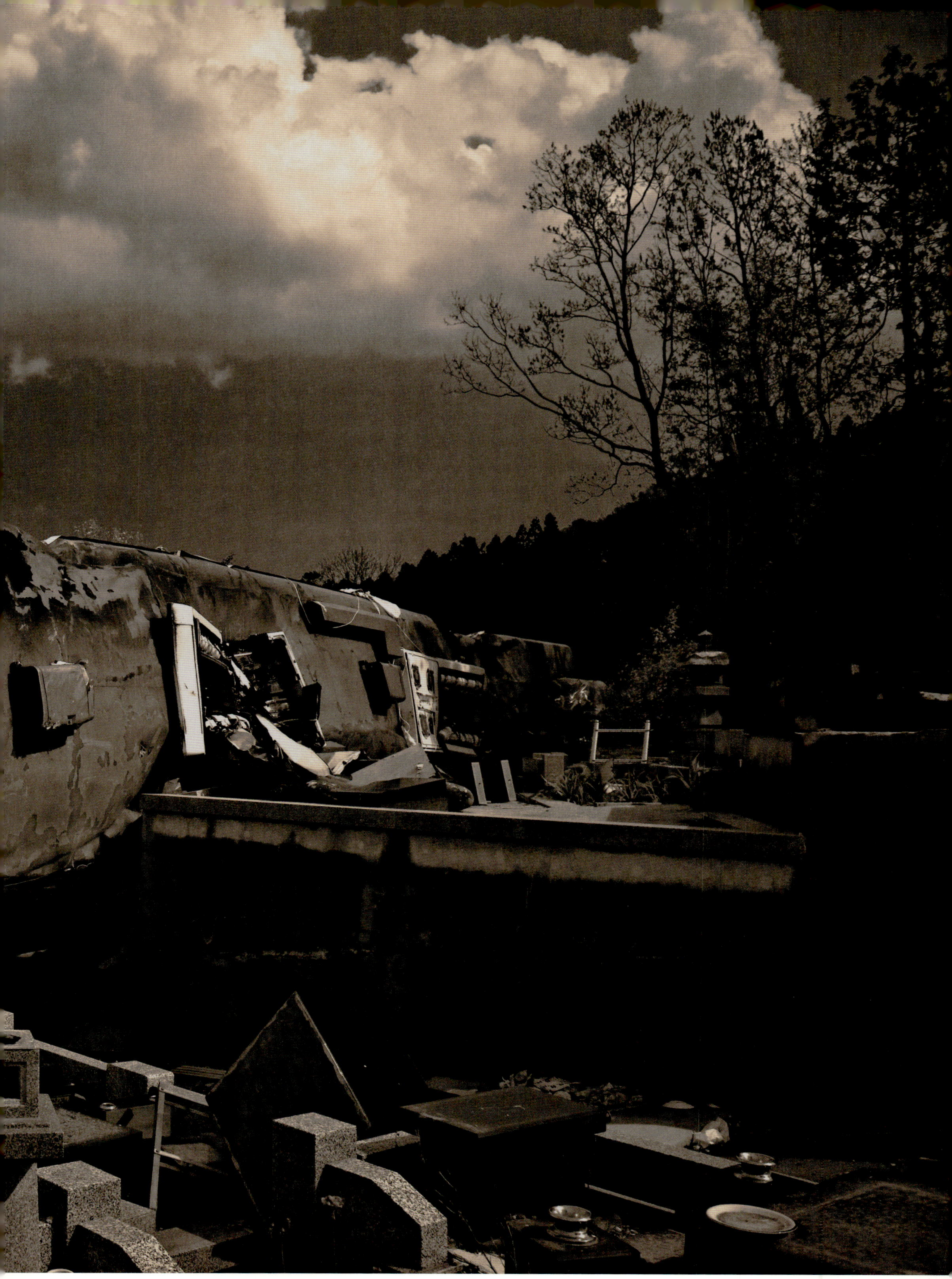

Pages 54-55. The top story of a business.
City of Kesennuma, Miyagi prefecture

Pages 56-57. A collapsed boutique.
City of Kesennuma, Miyagi prefecture

Pages 58-59. Remnants of a building.
City of Rikuzen Takata, Iwate prefecture

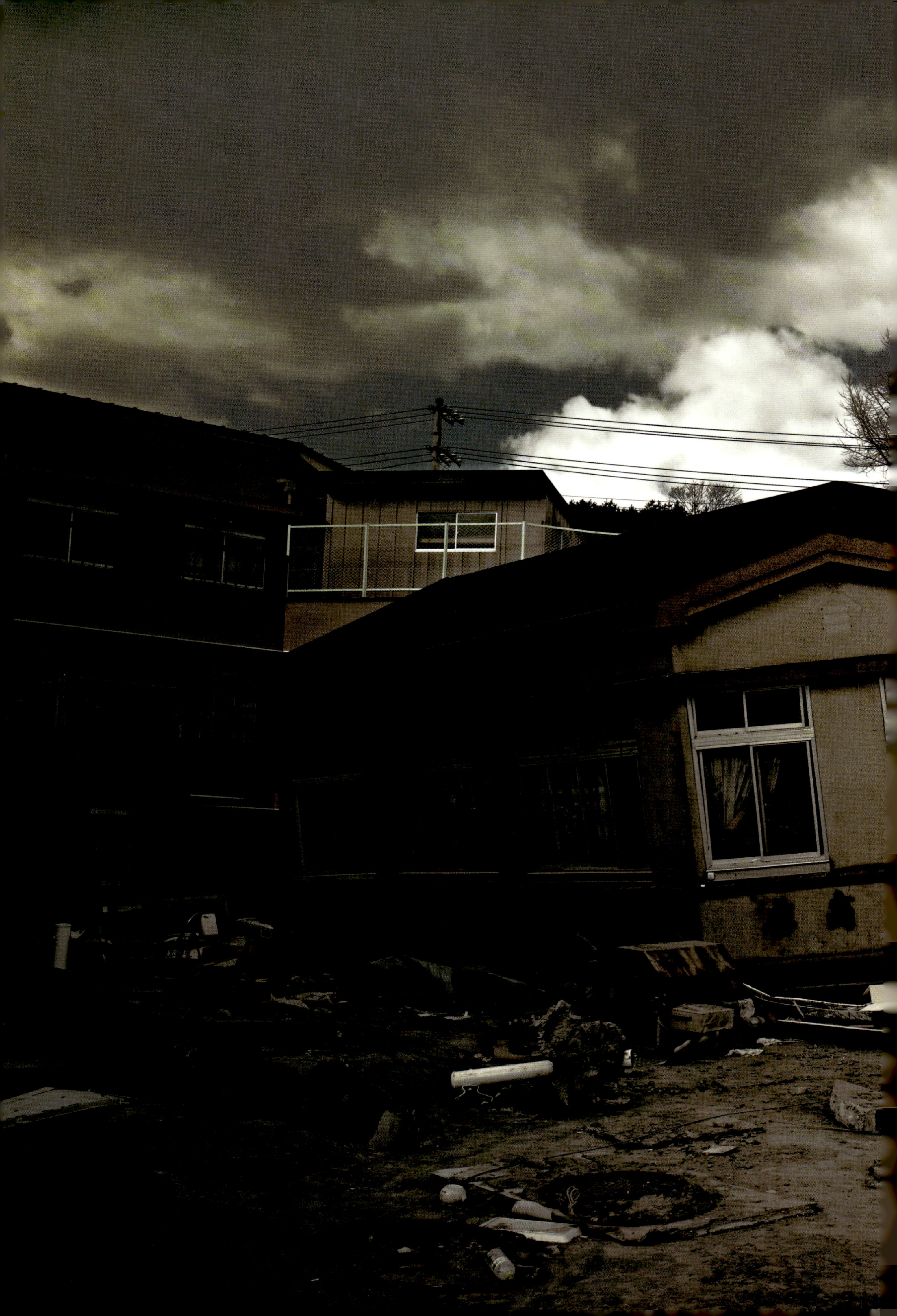

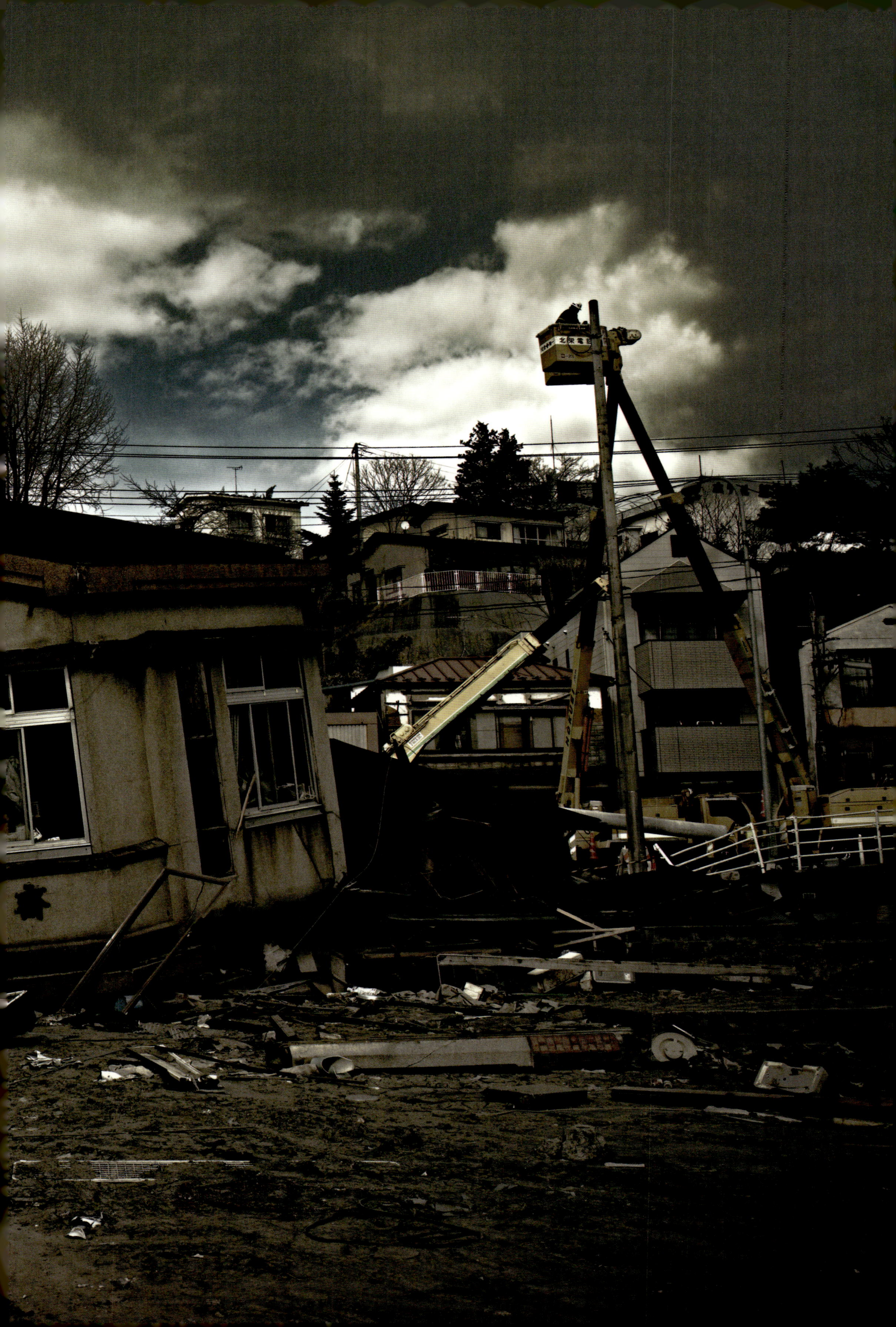

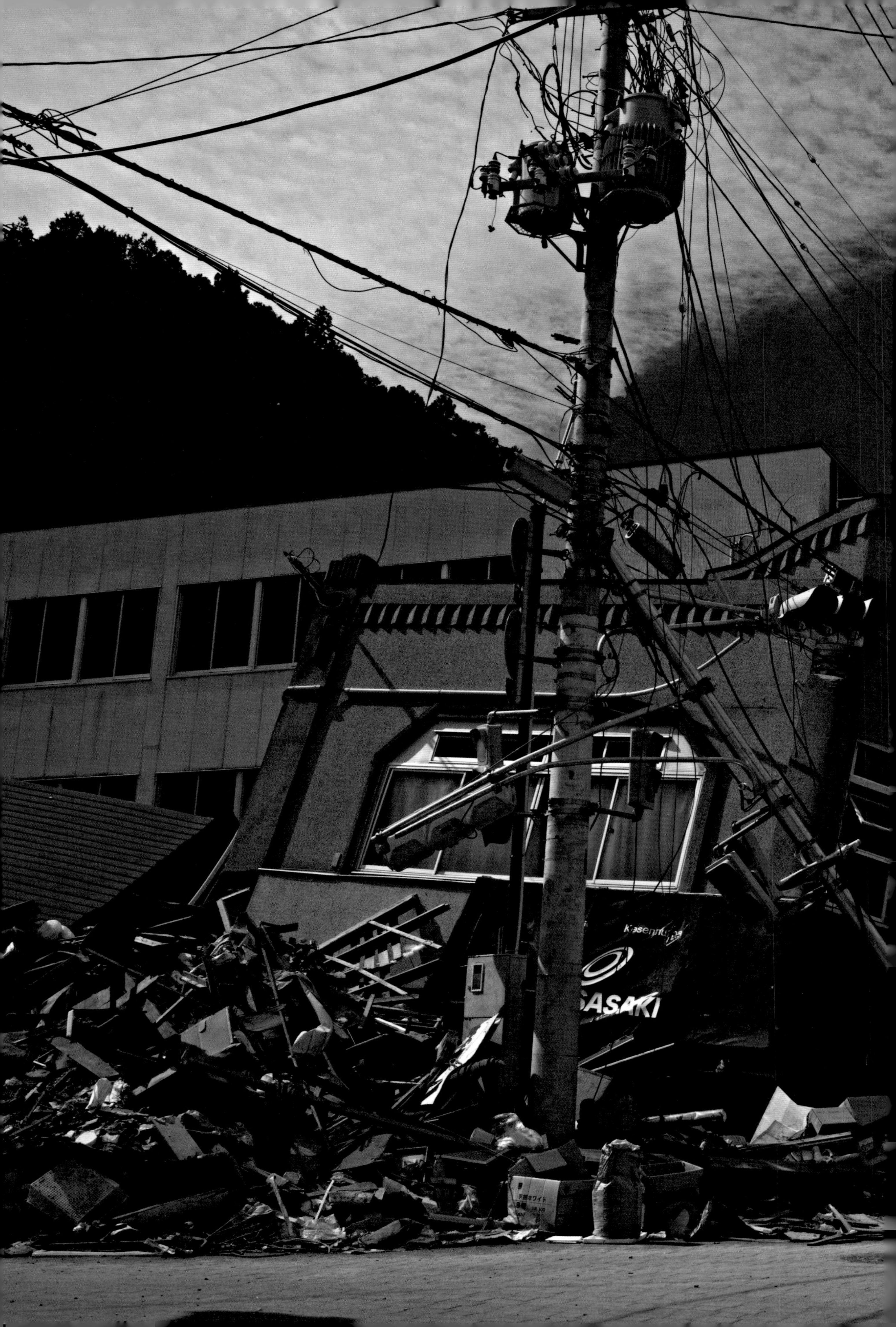

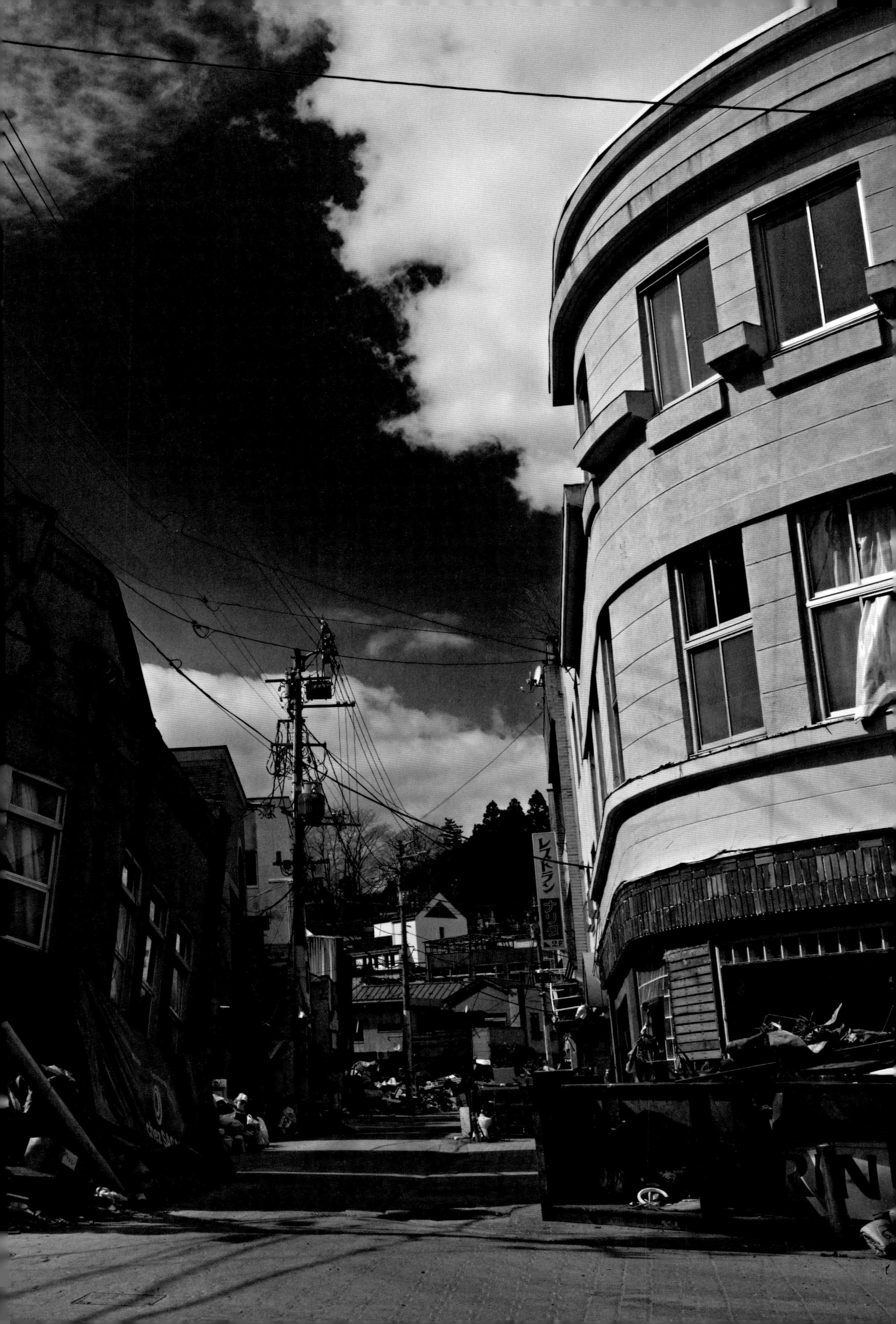
レストラン
ナリタ
2F

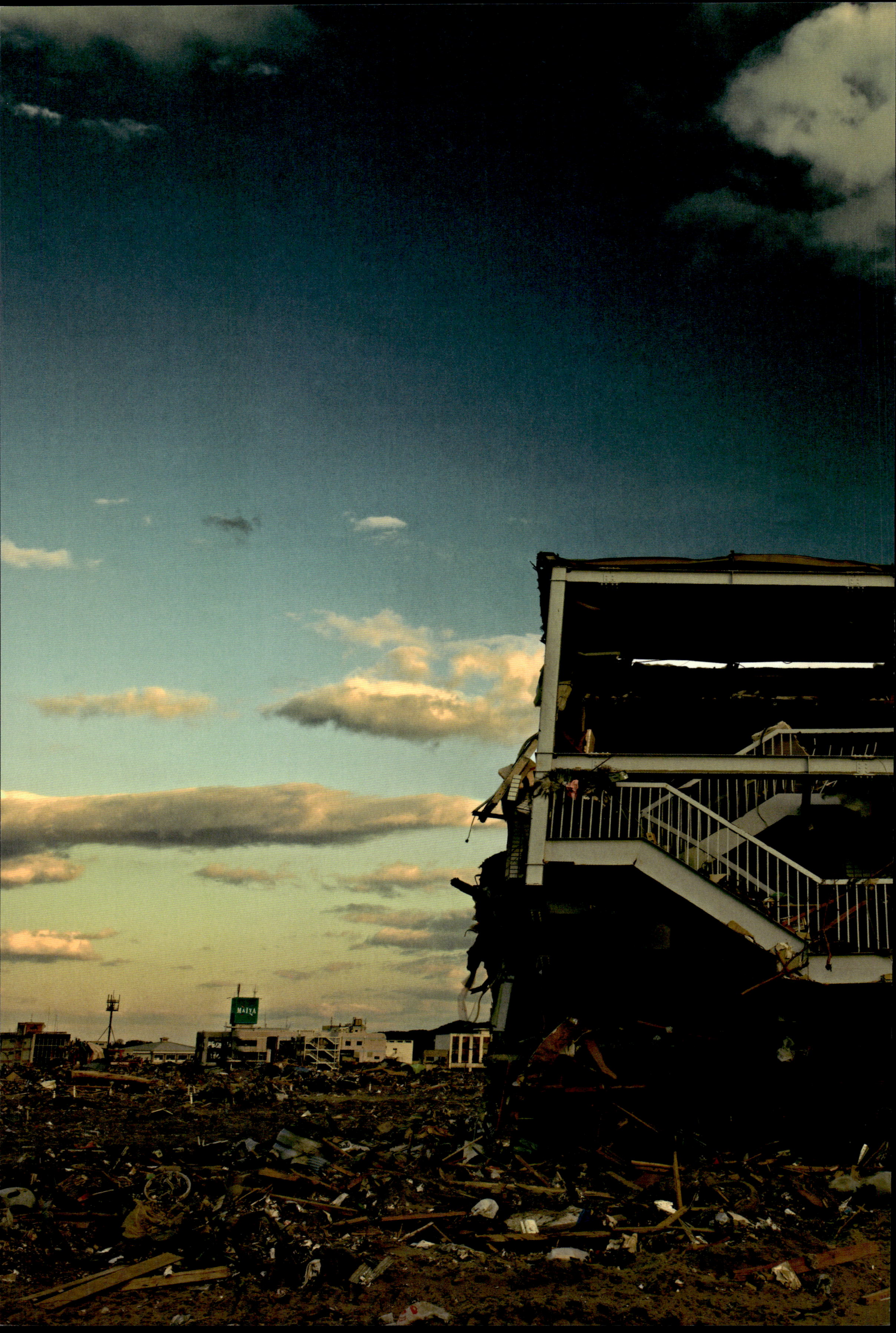
MAIYA

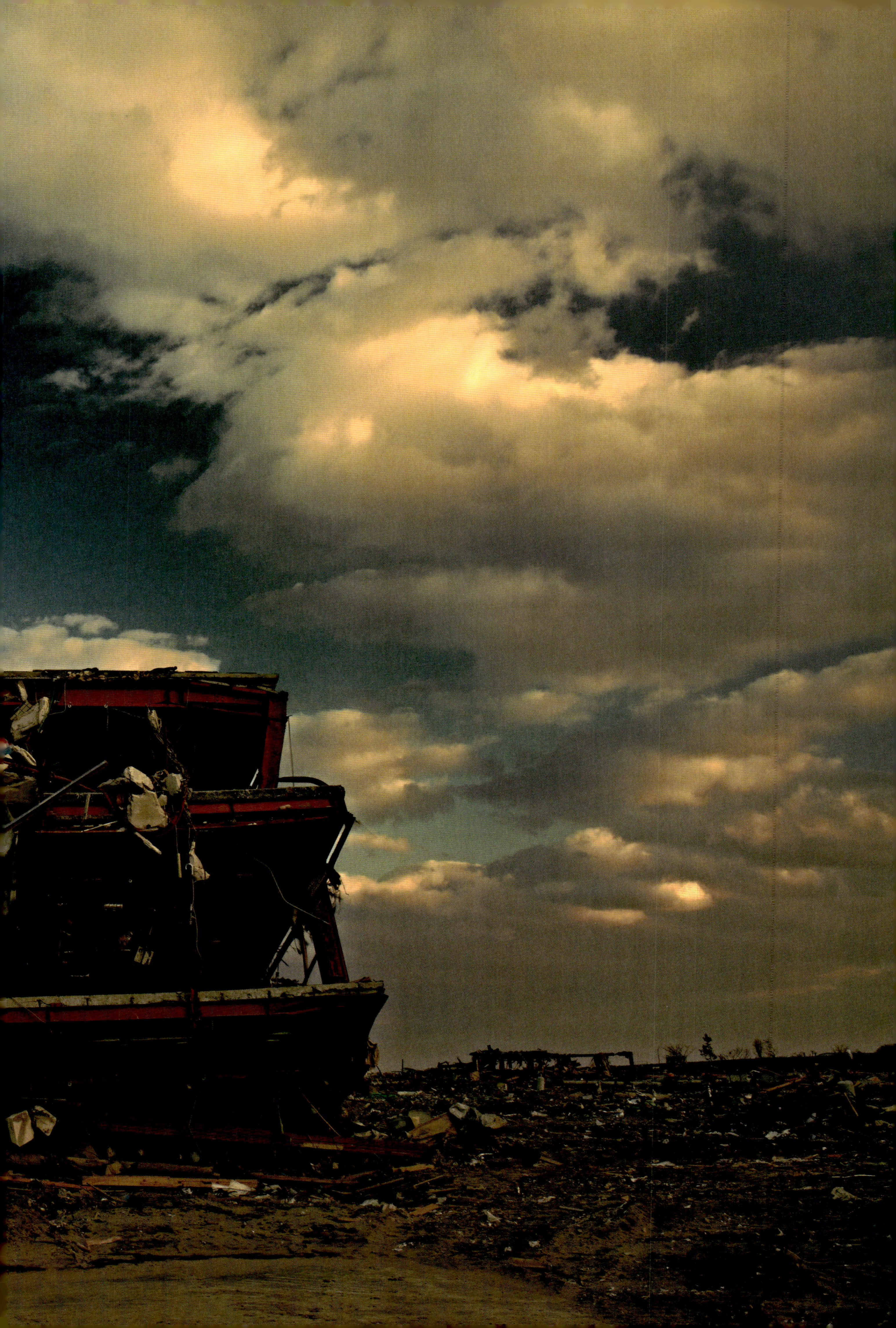

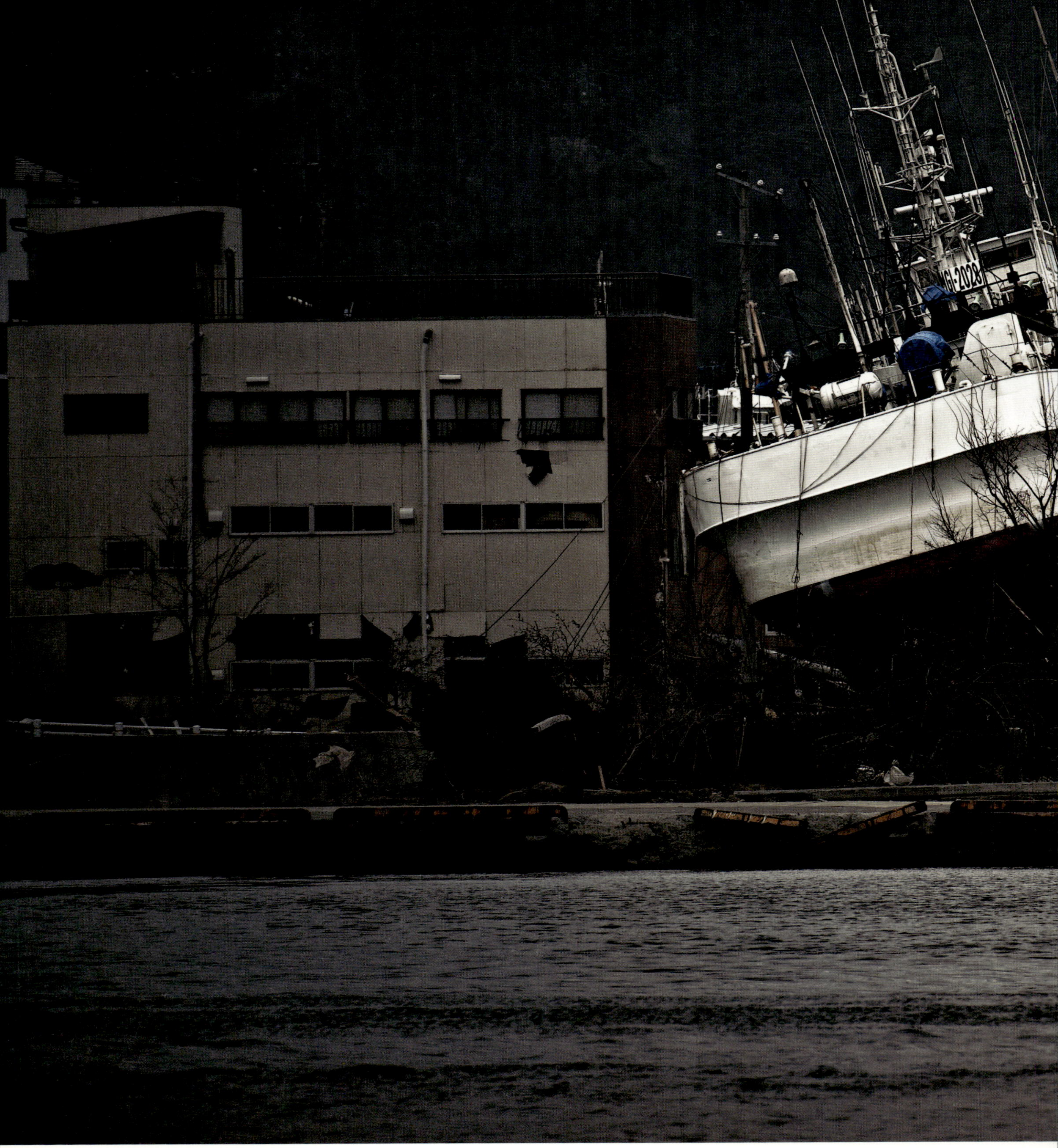

City of Kesennuma, Miyagi prefecture

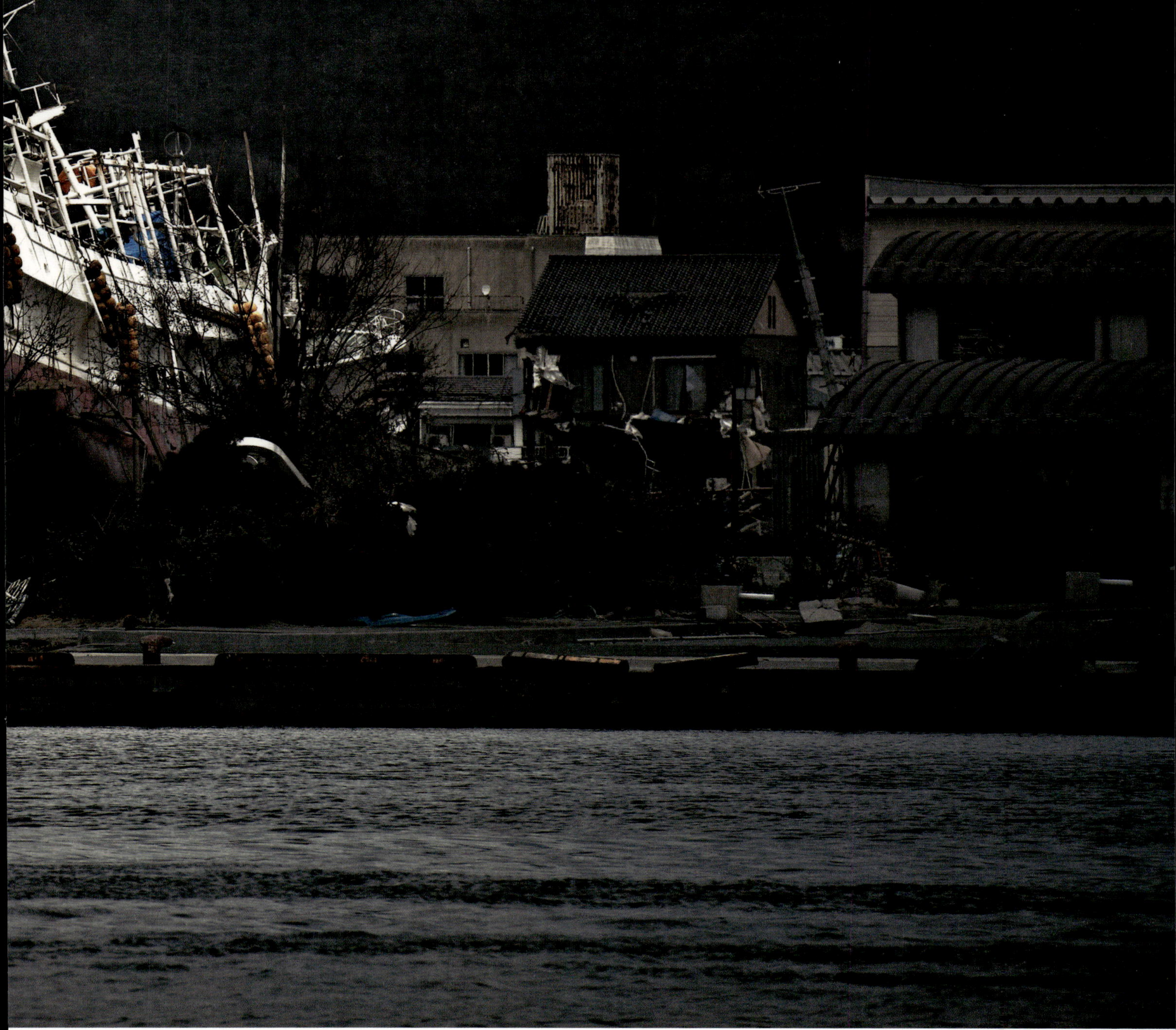

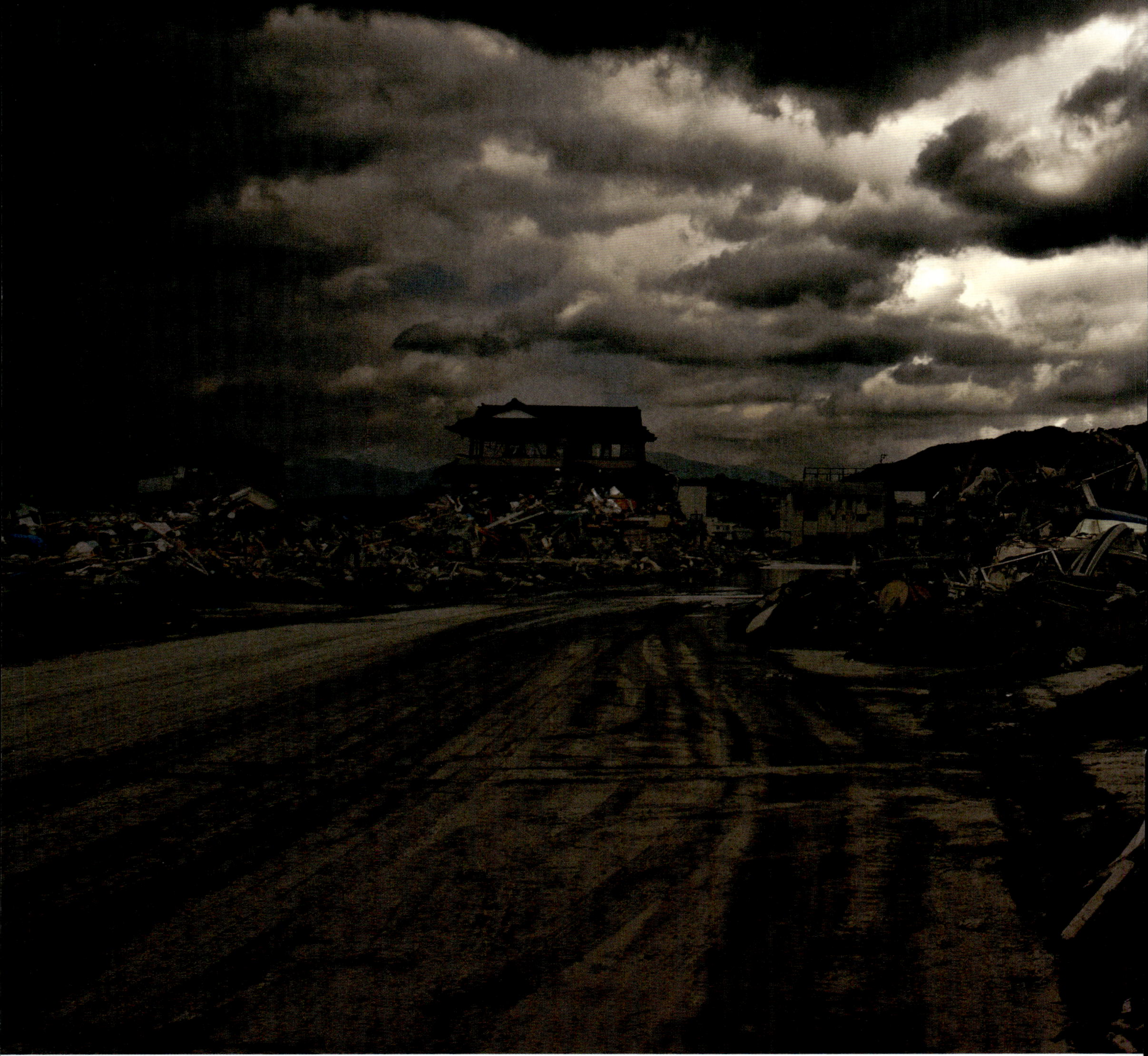

A Red Cross vehicle.
City of Kesennuma, Miyagi prefecture

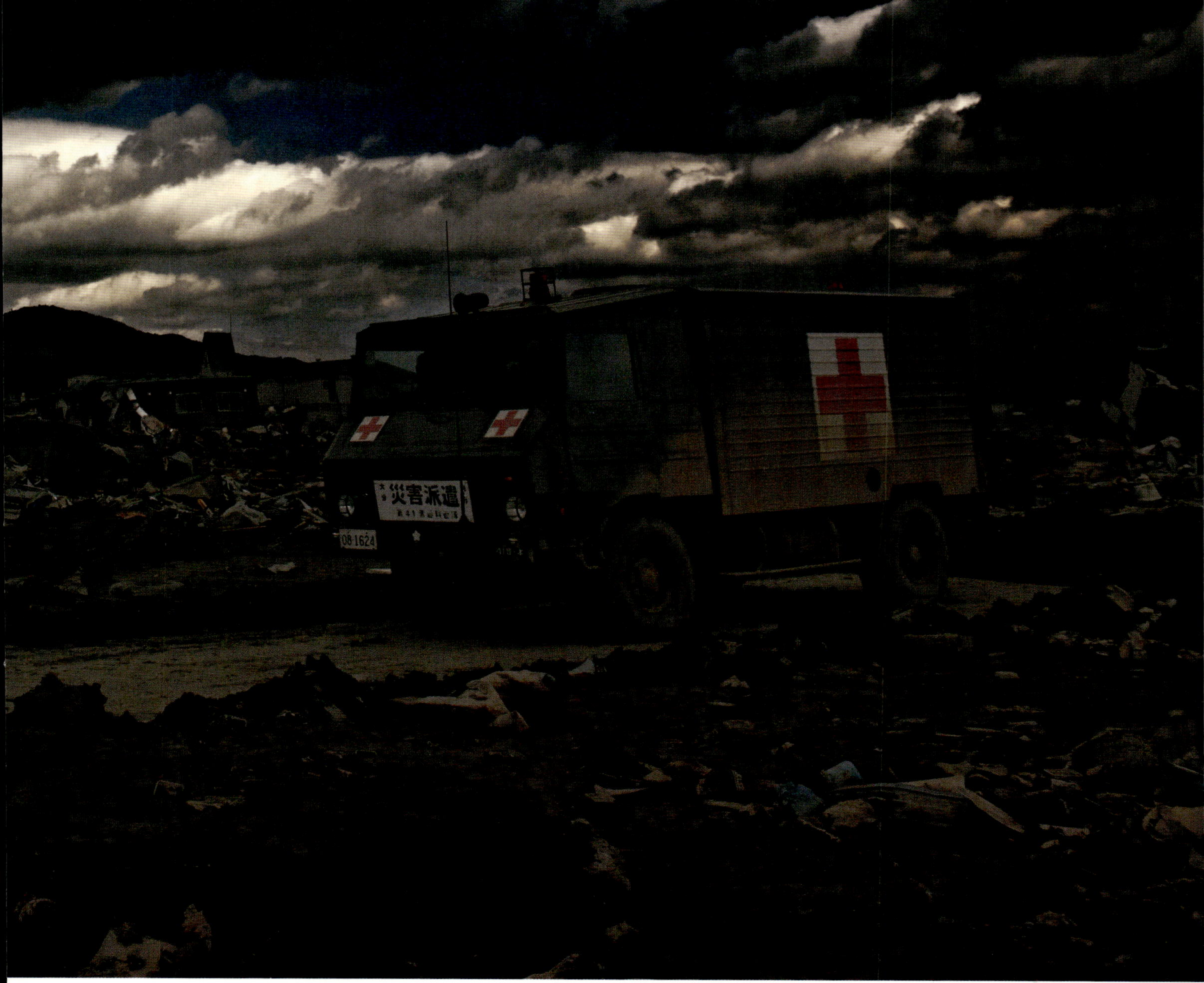

災害派遣
08 1624

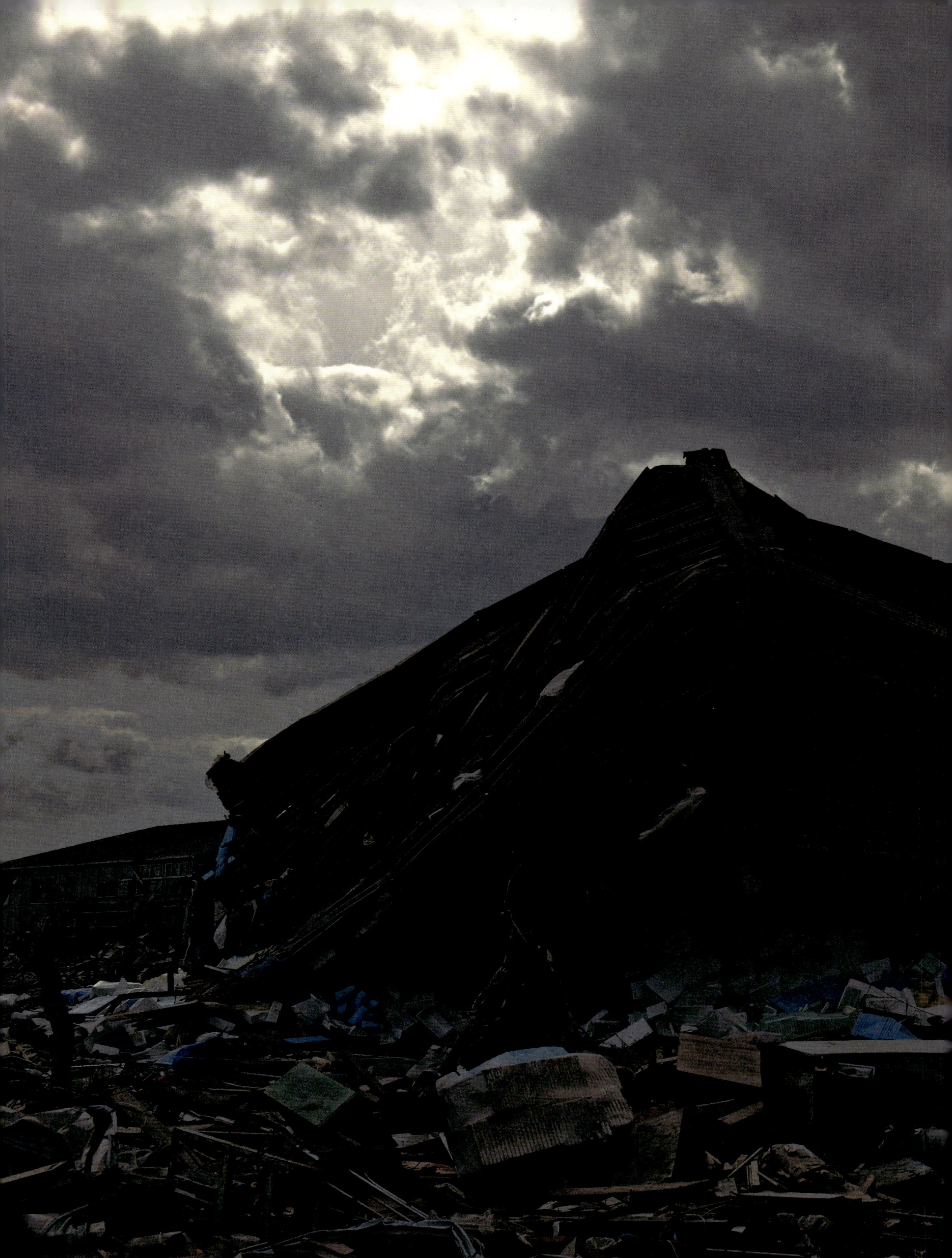

A seafood processing plant.
City of Kesennuma, Miyagi prefecture

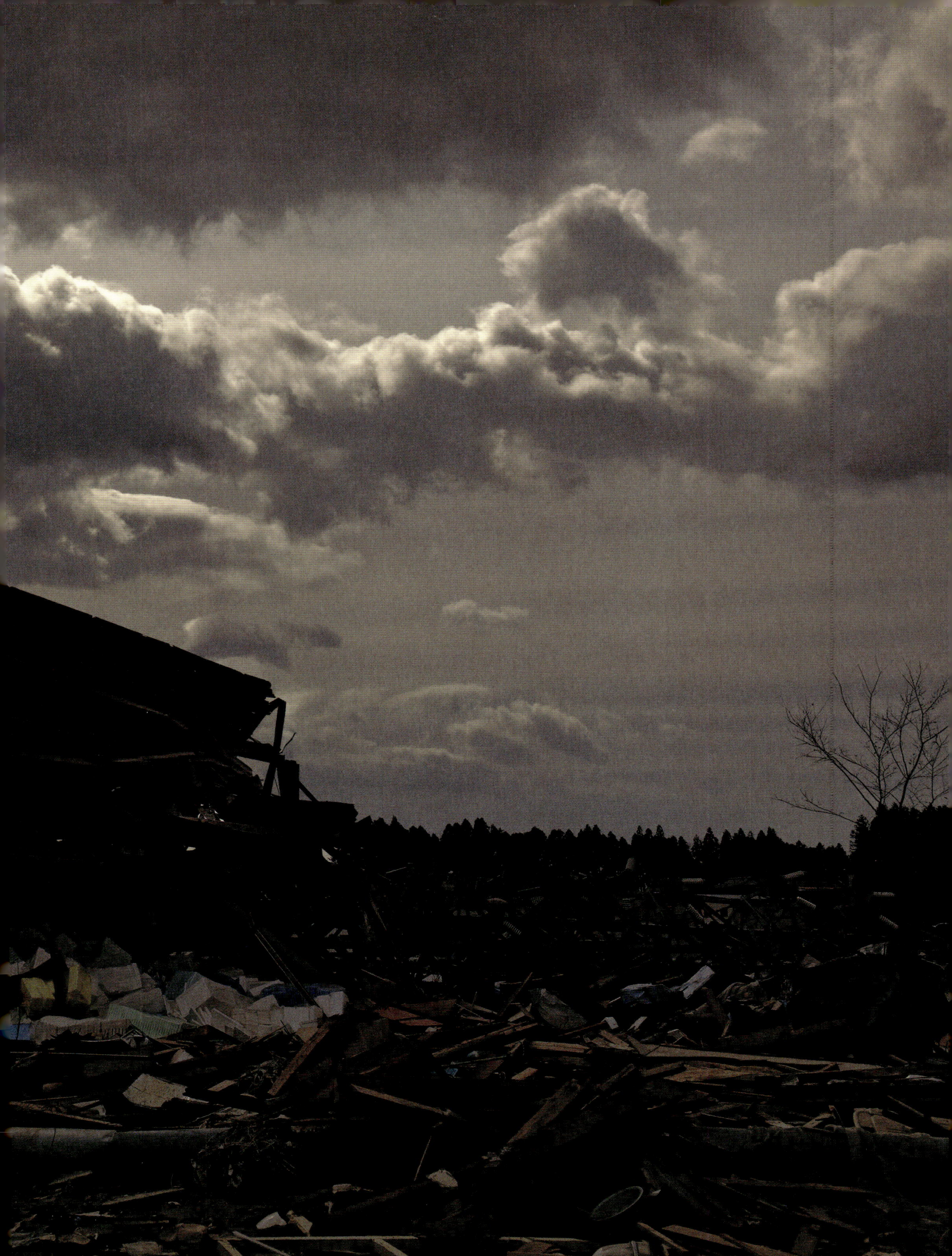

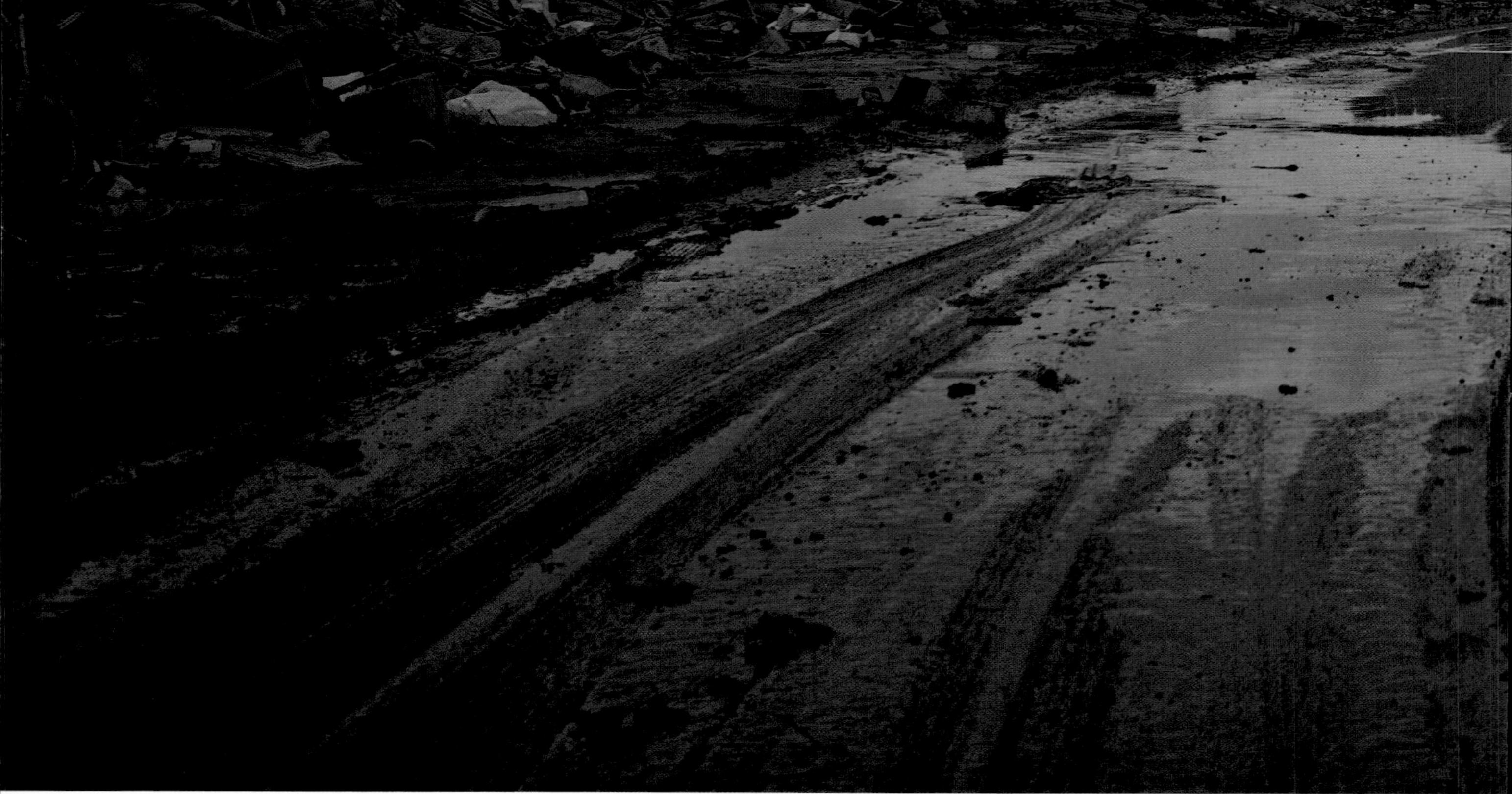

City of Kesennuma, Miyagi prefecture

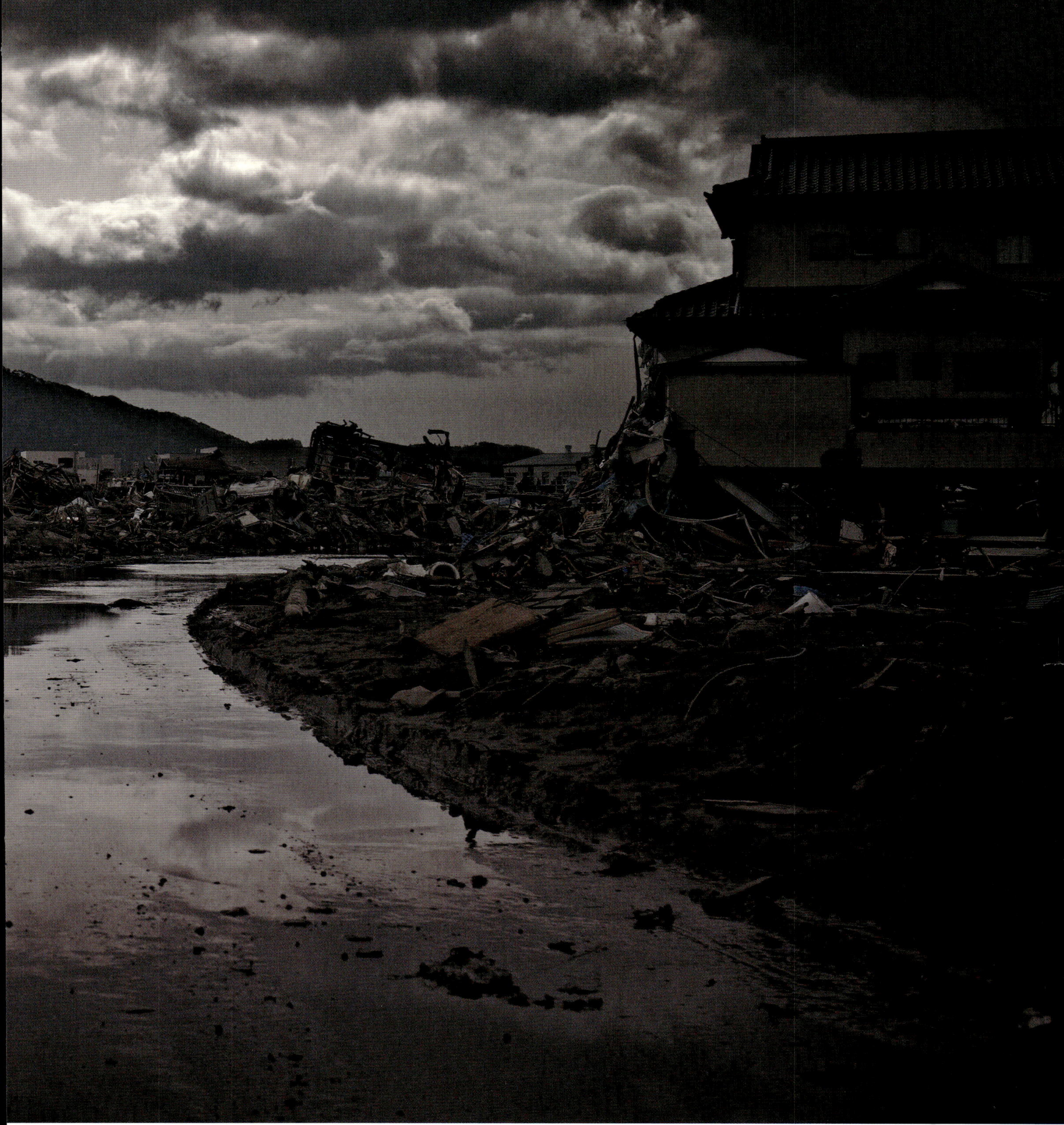

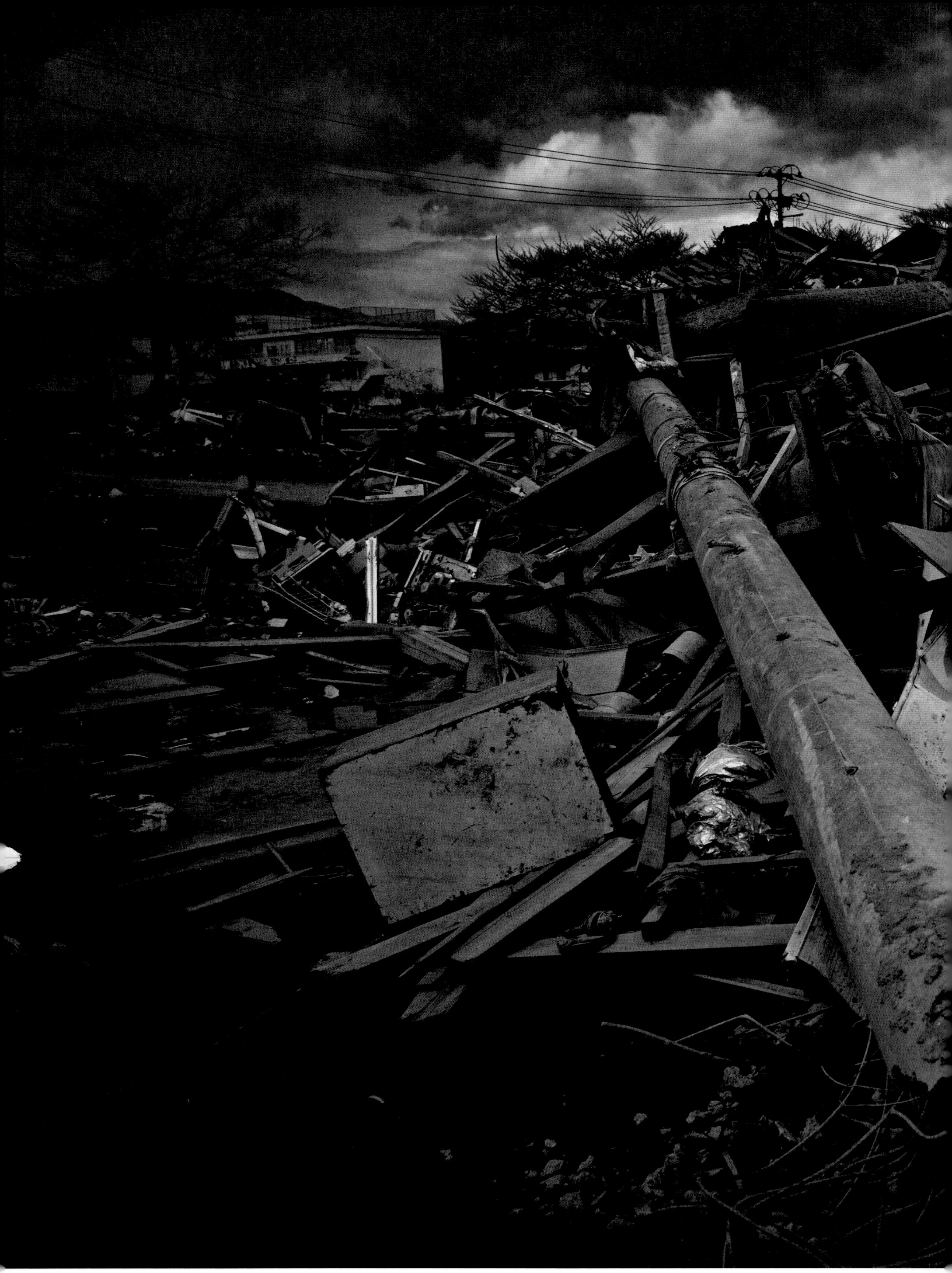

City of Kesennuma, Miyagi prefecture

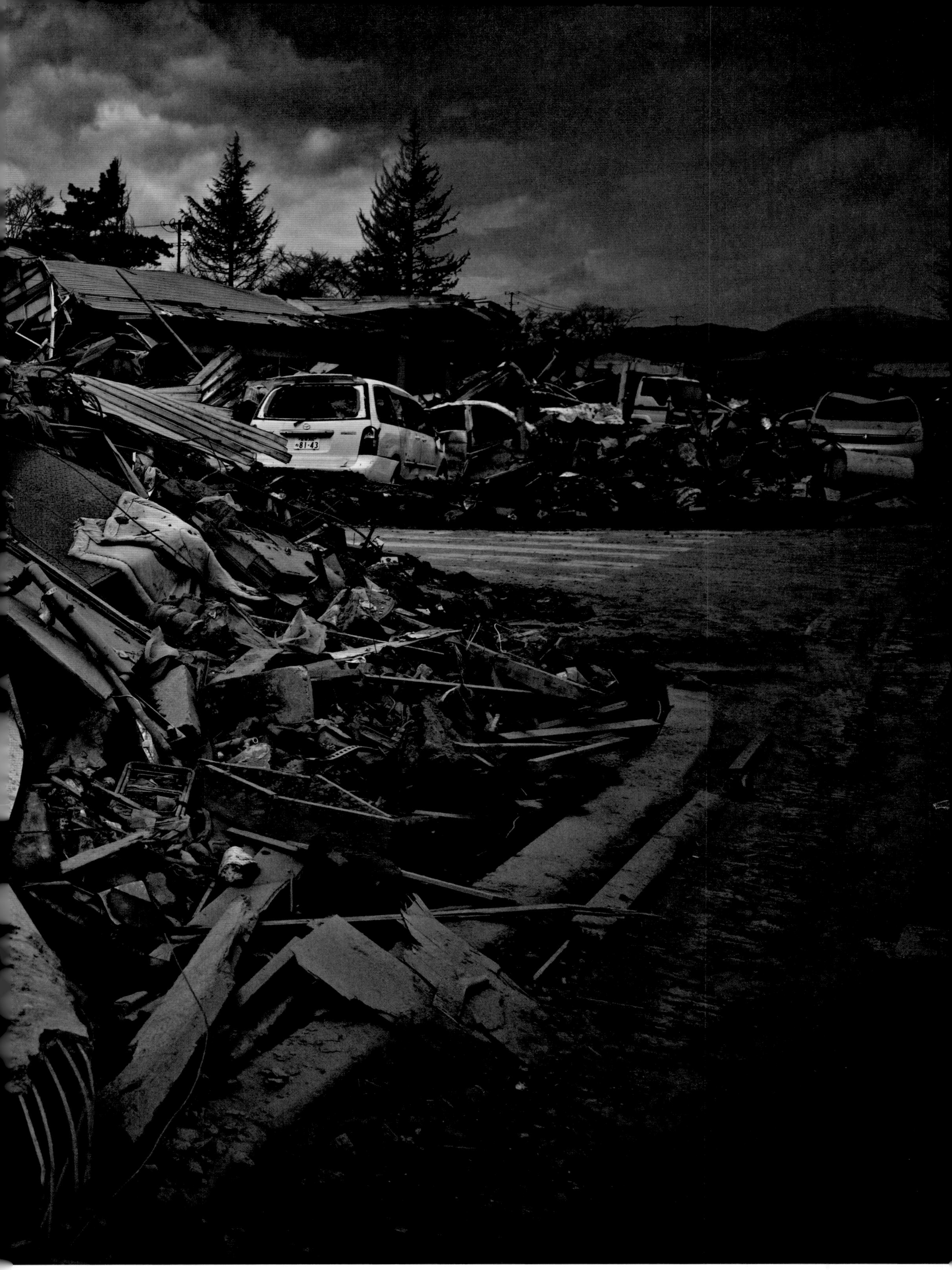
81-43

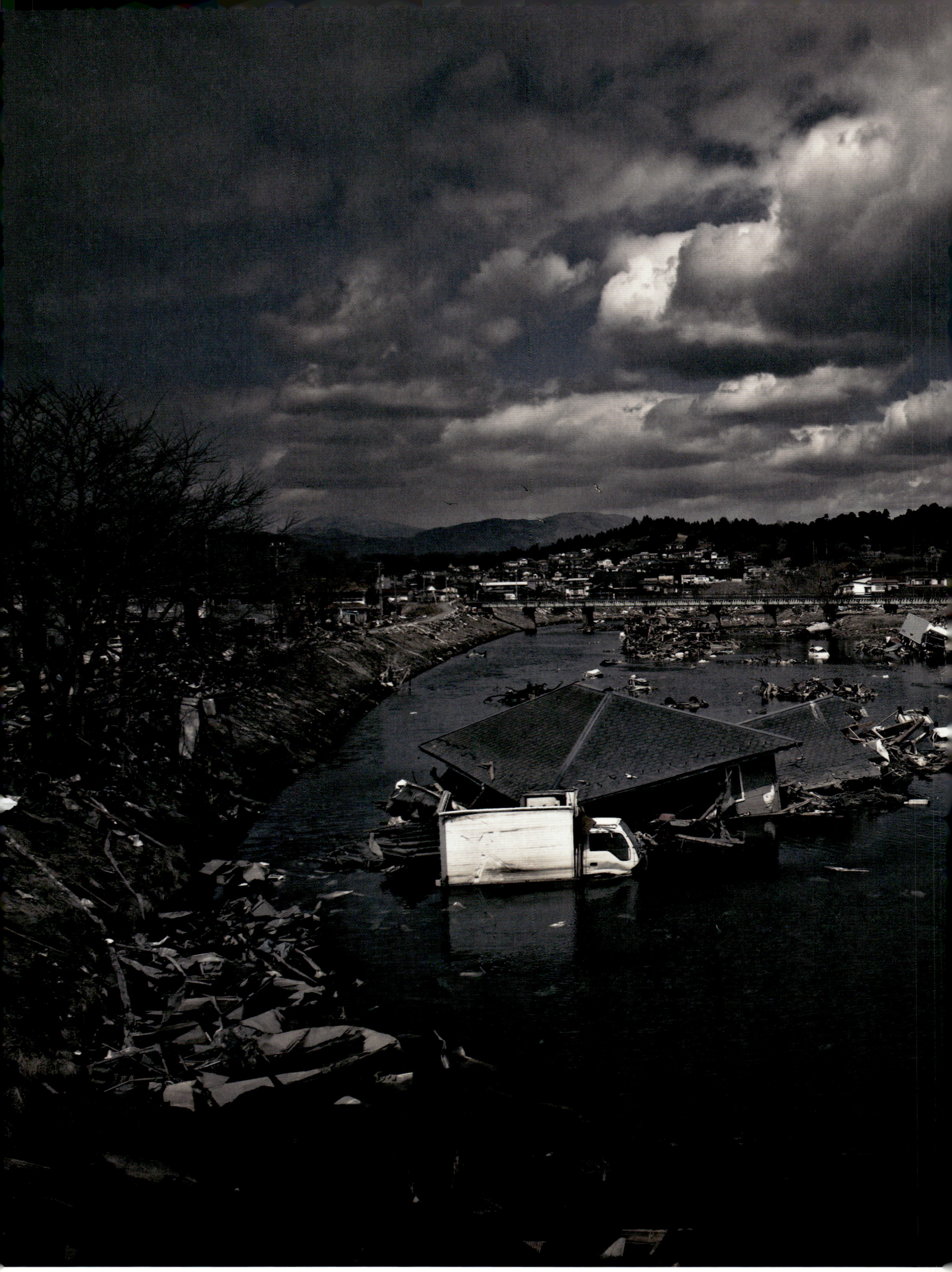

Debris in the Shishiori river.
City of Kesennuma, Miyagi prefecture

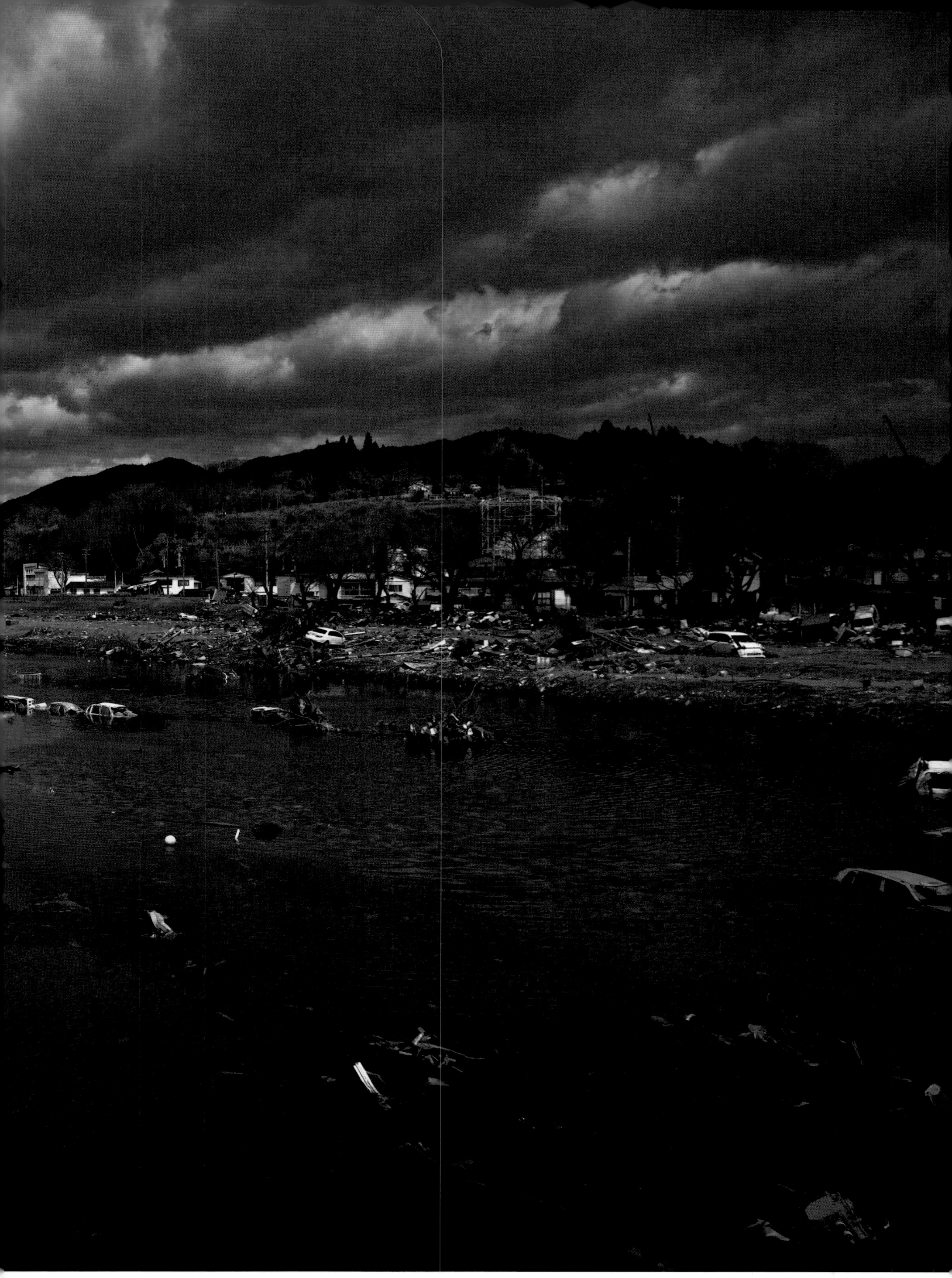

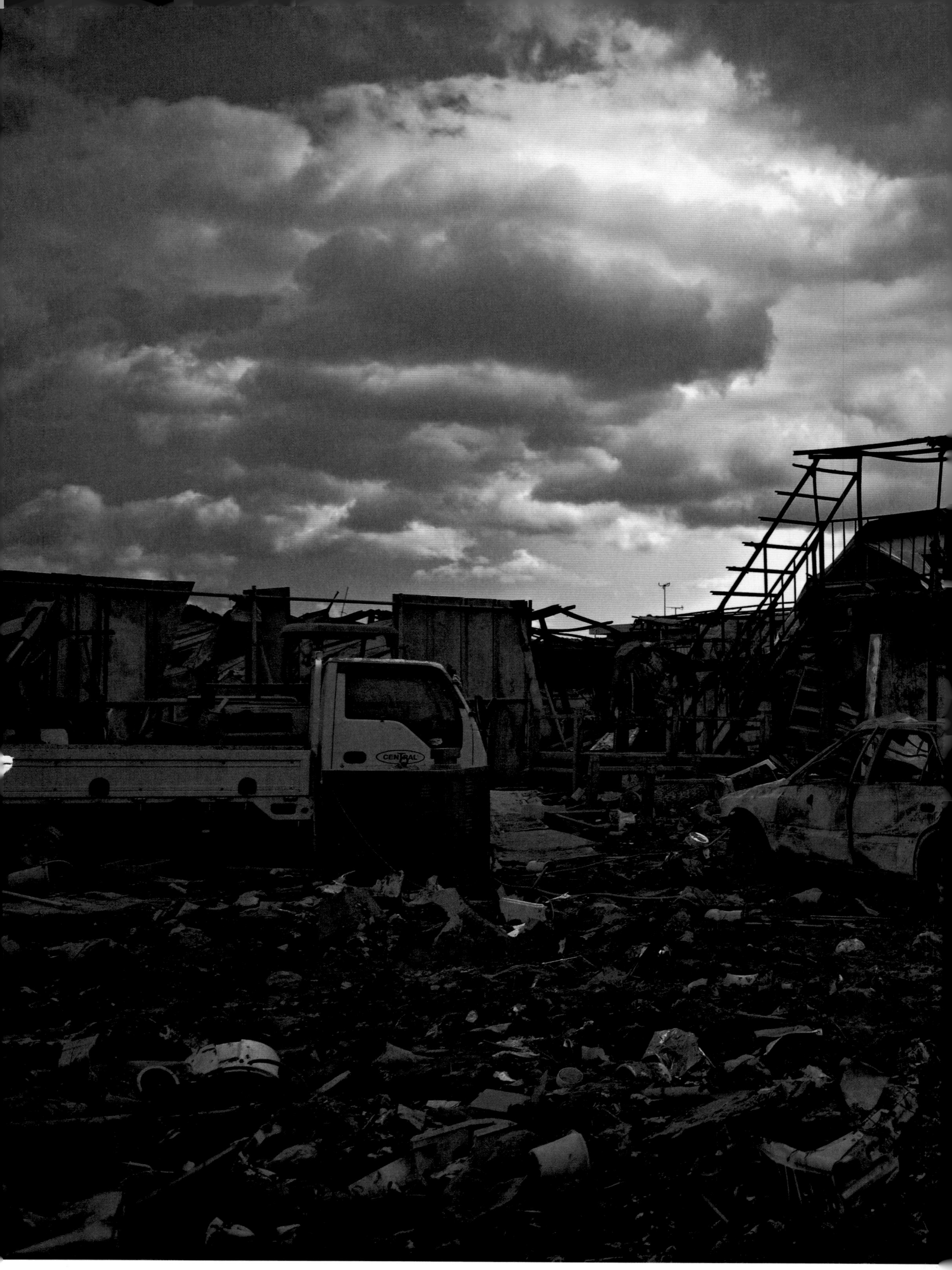

Fire damage after the tsunami.
City of Kesennuma, Miyagi prefecture

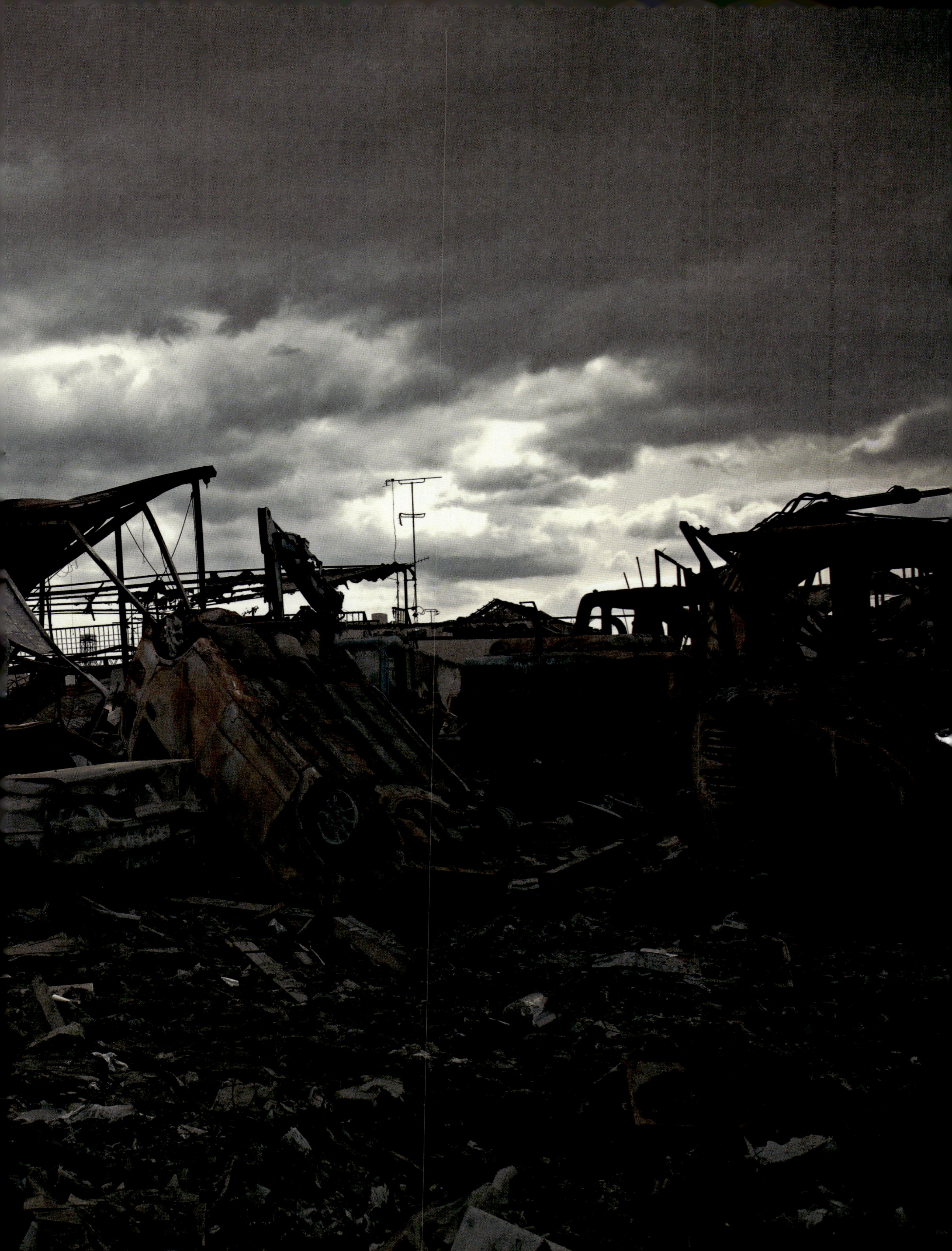

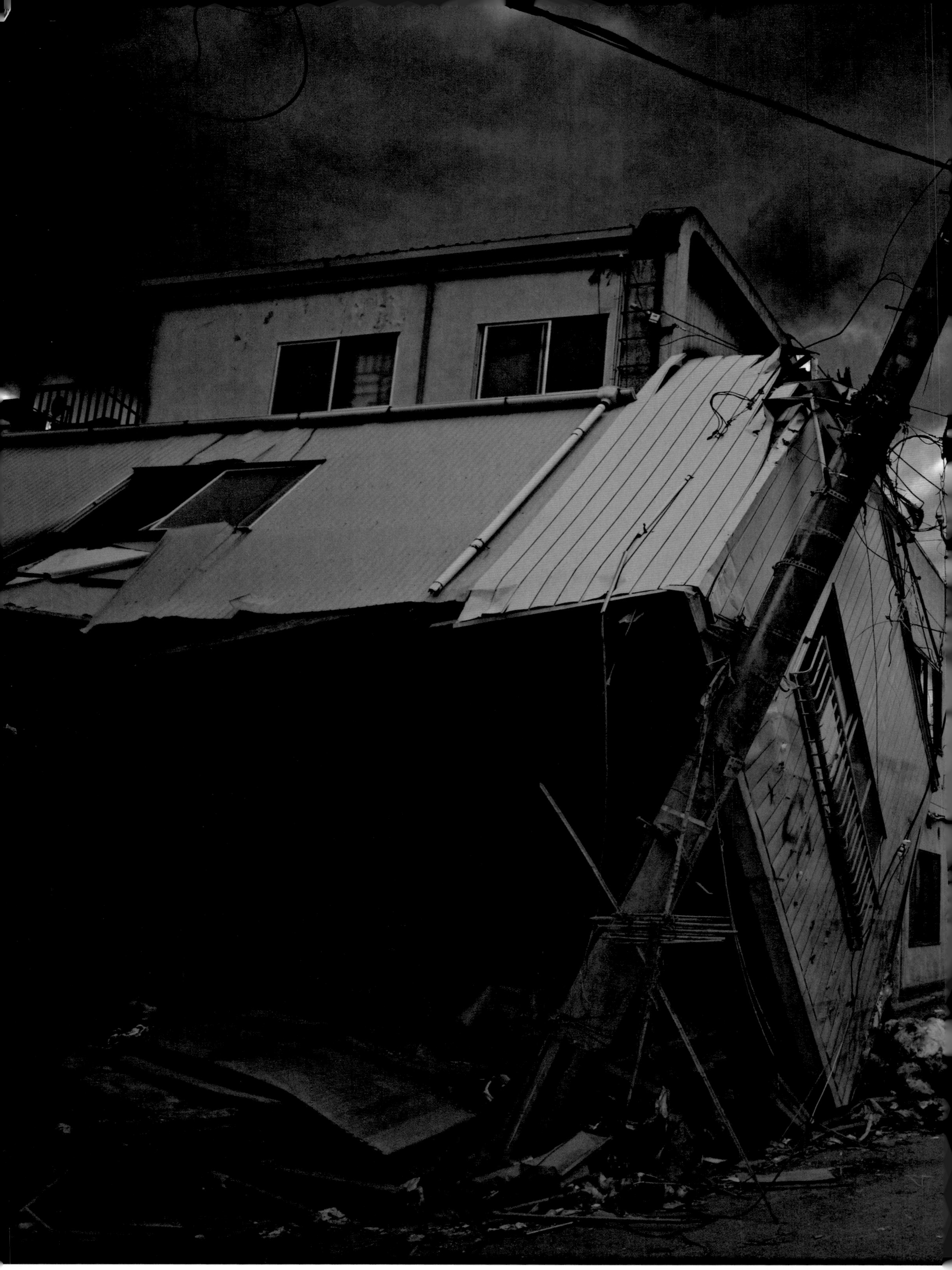

City of Kesennuma, Miyagi prefecture

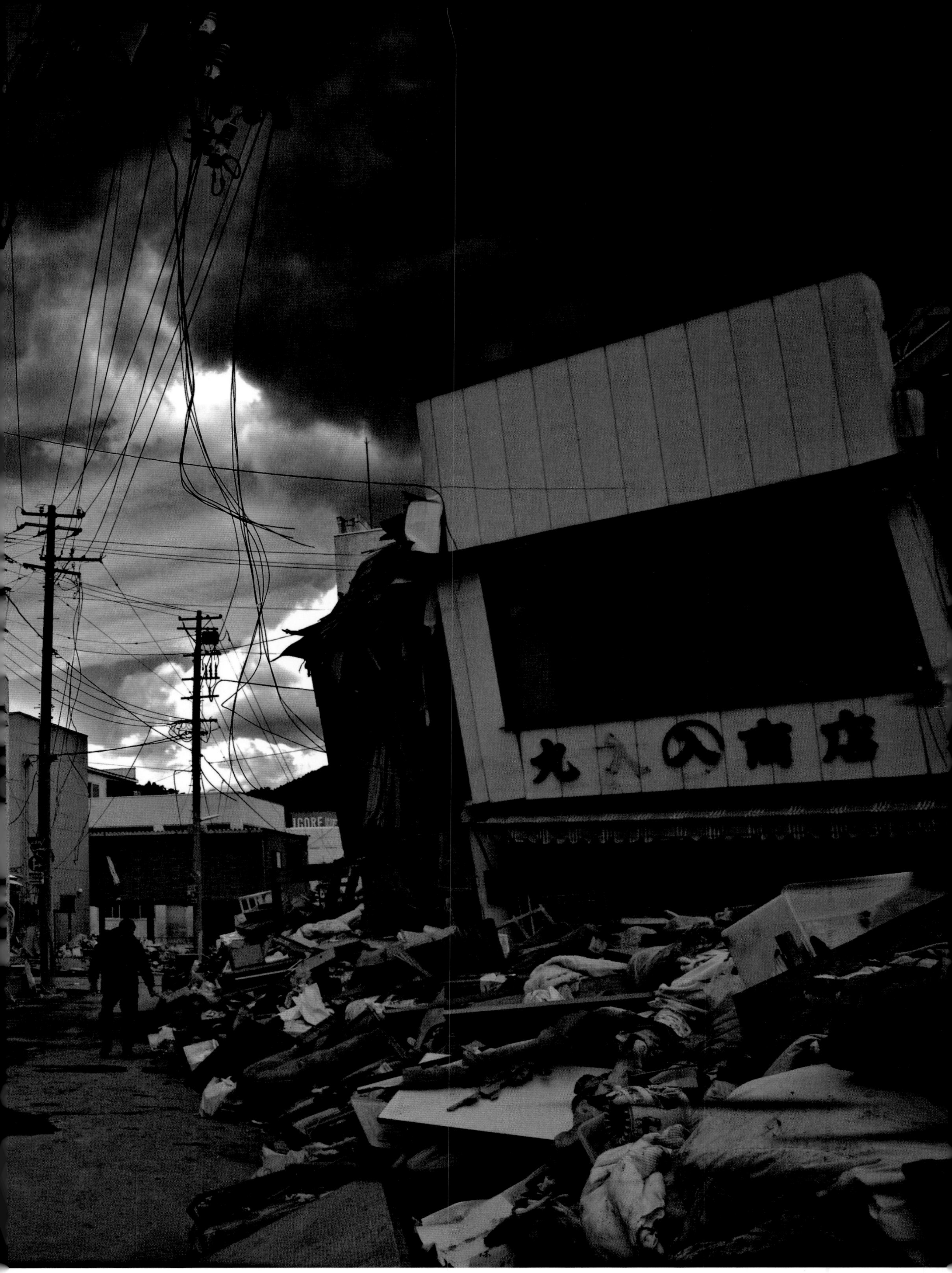
丸
商店

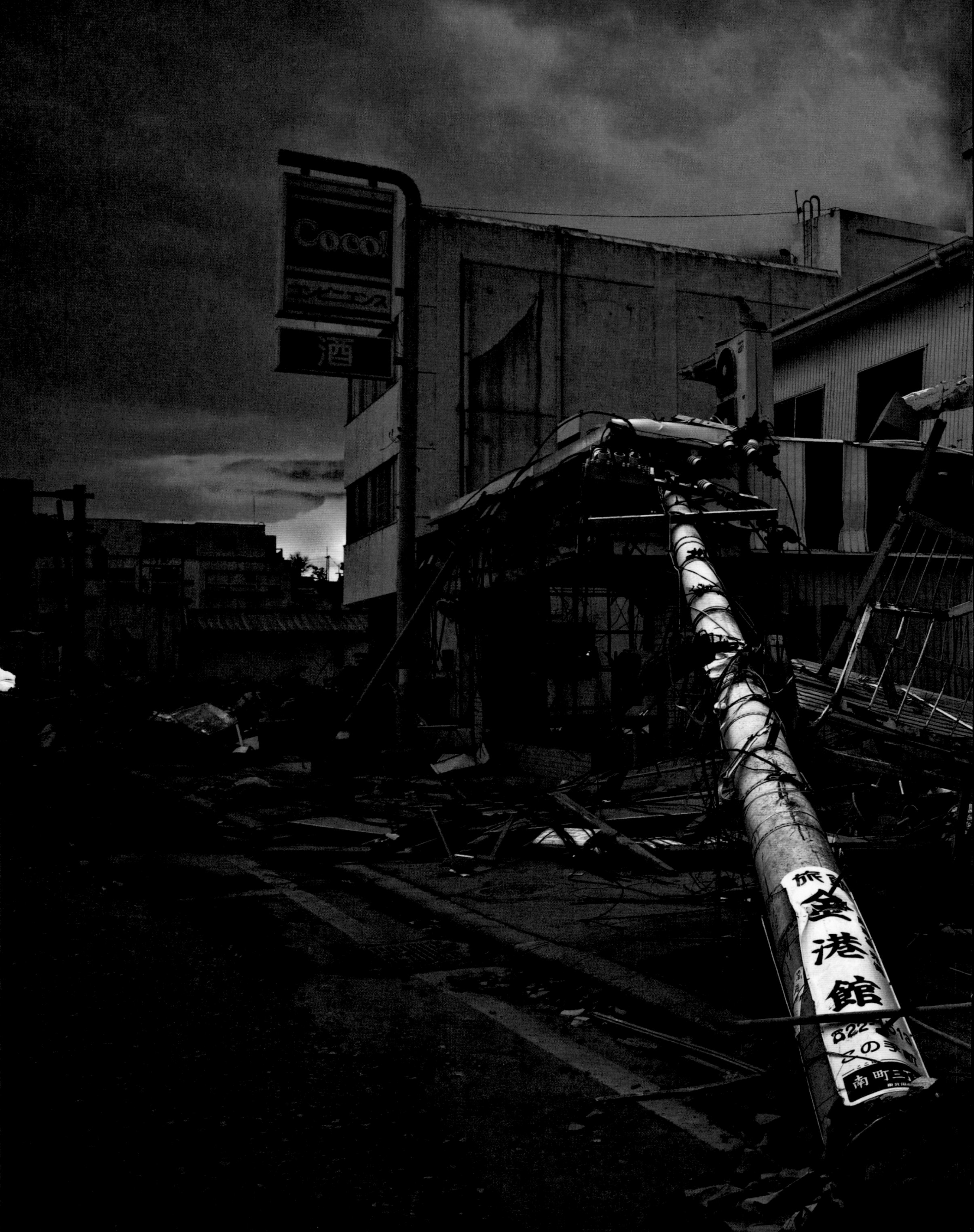

City of Kesennuma, Miyagi prefecture

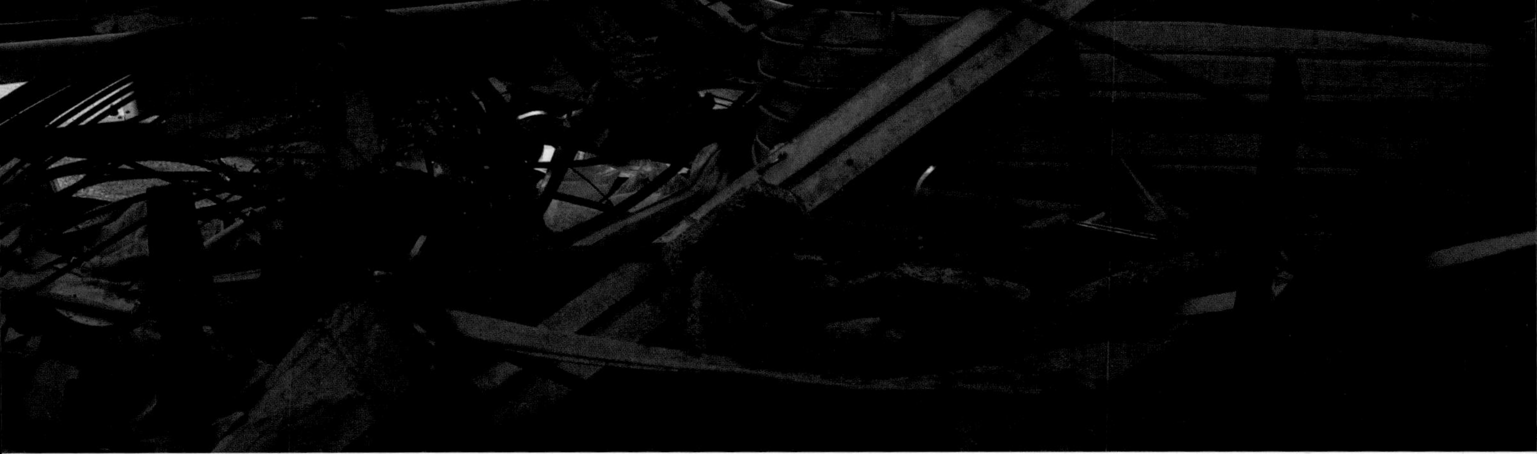

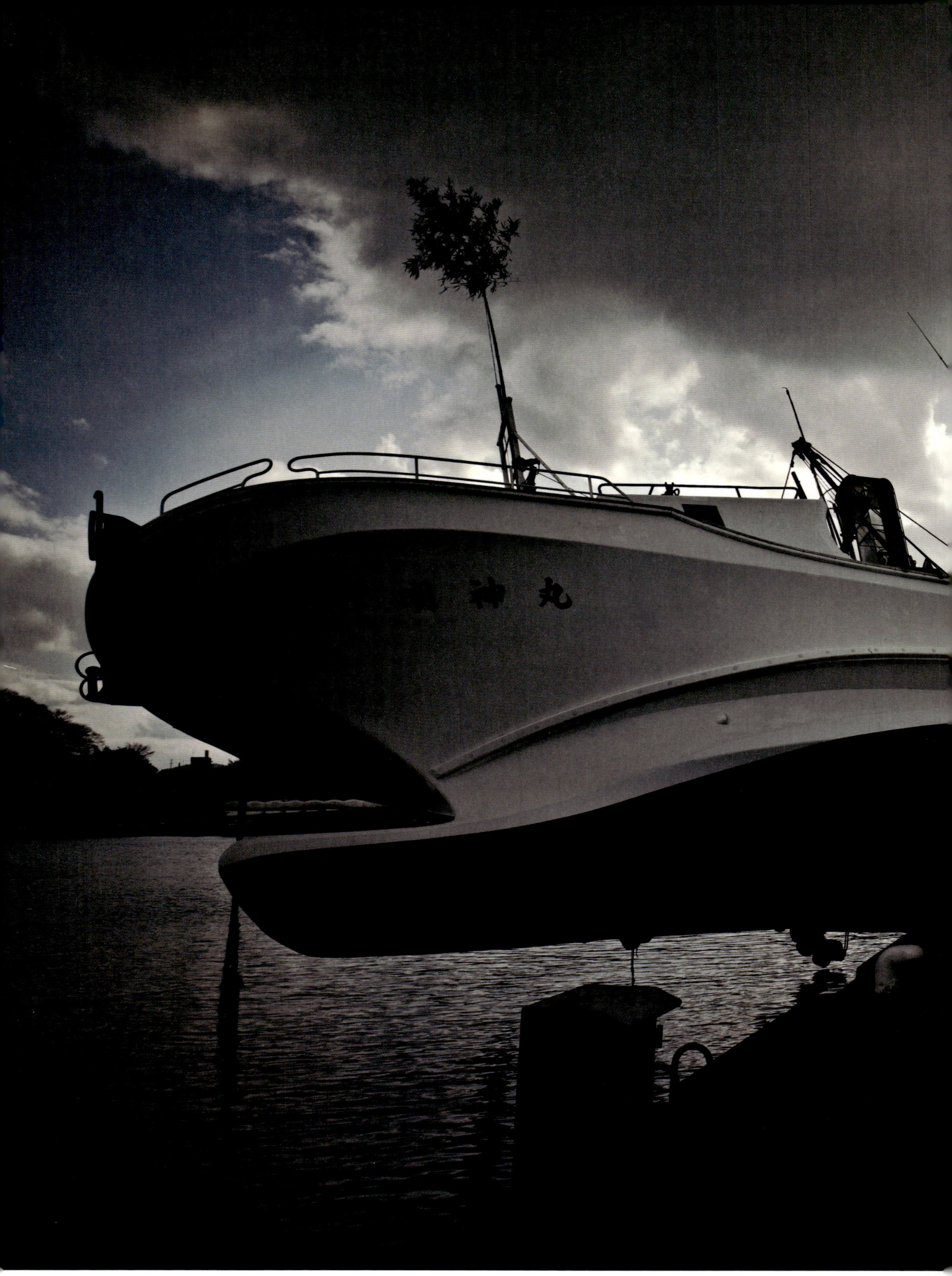

A stranded fishing boat.
City of Kesennuma, Miyagi prefecture

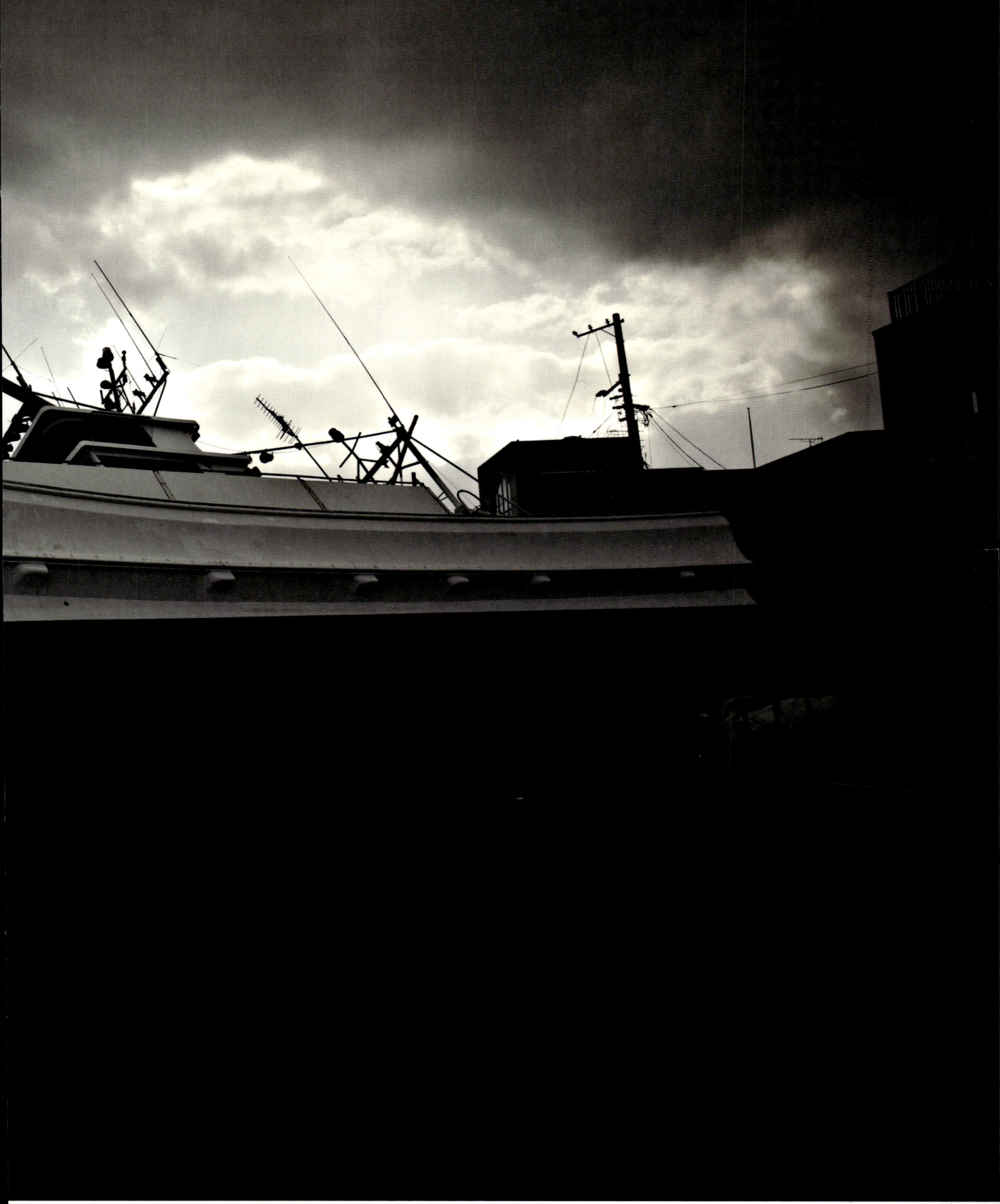

Pages 80-81. The remaining top story of the headquarters for the famous sake brand Otokoyama. City of Kesennuma, Miyagi prefecture

Pages 82-83. A long range tuna boat. City of Kesennuma, Miyagi prefecture

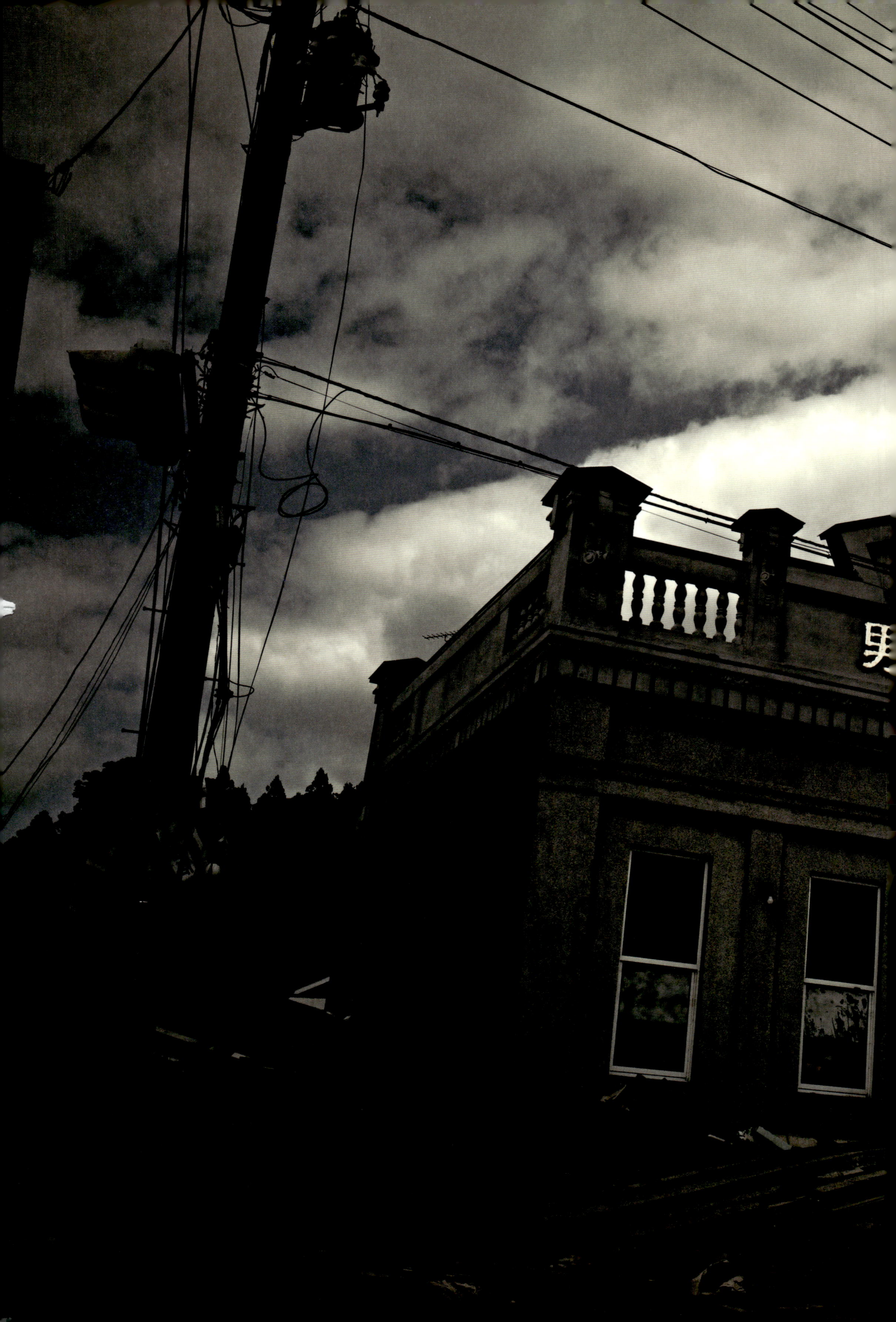

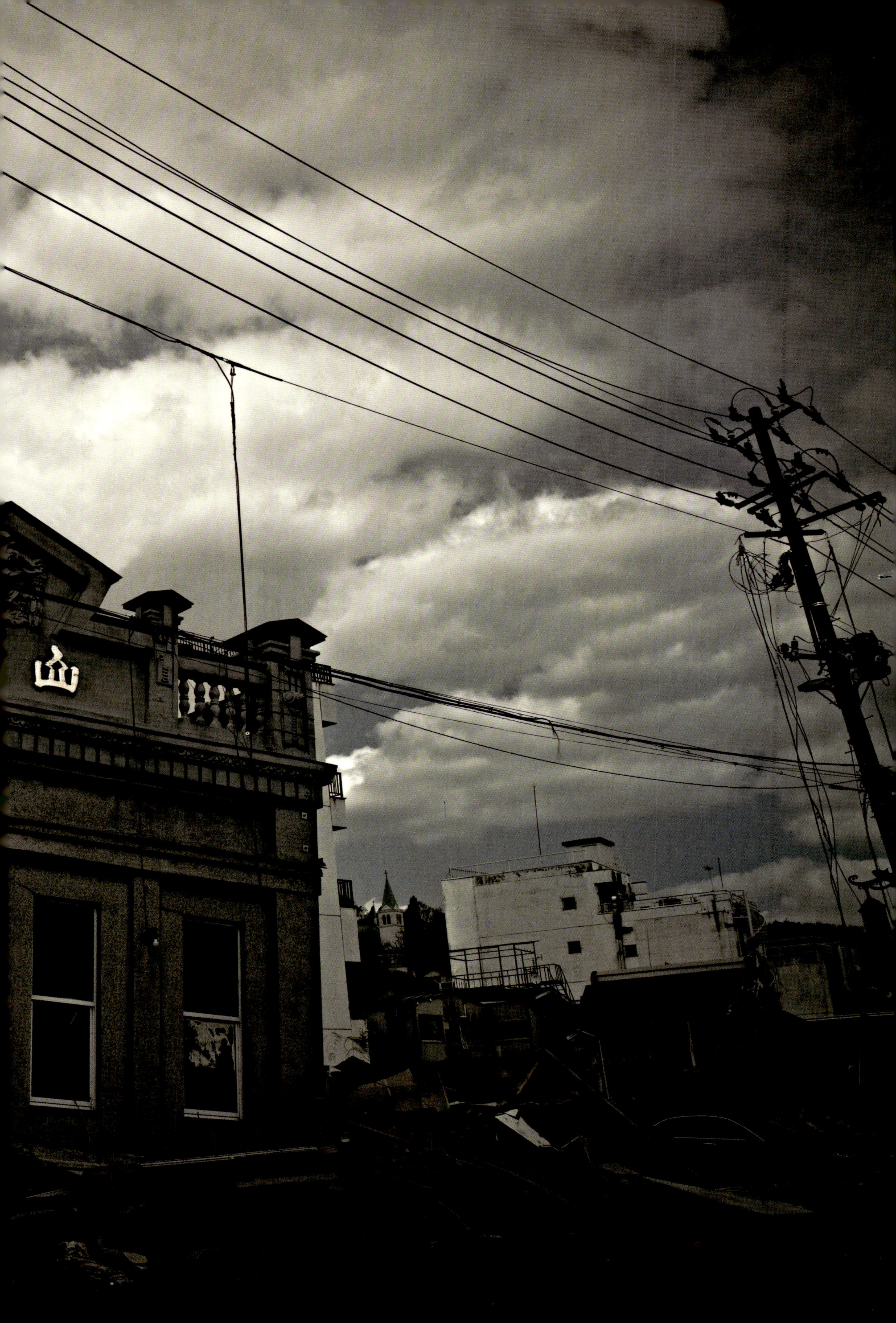
山

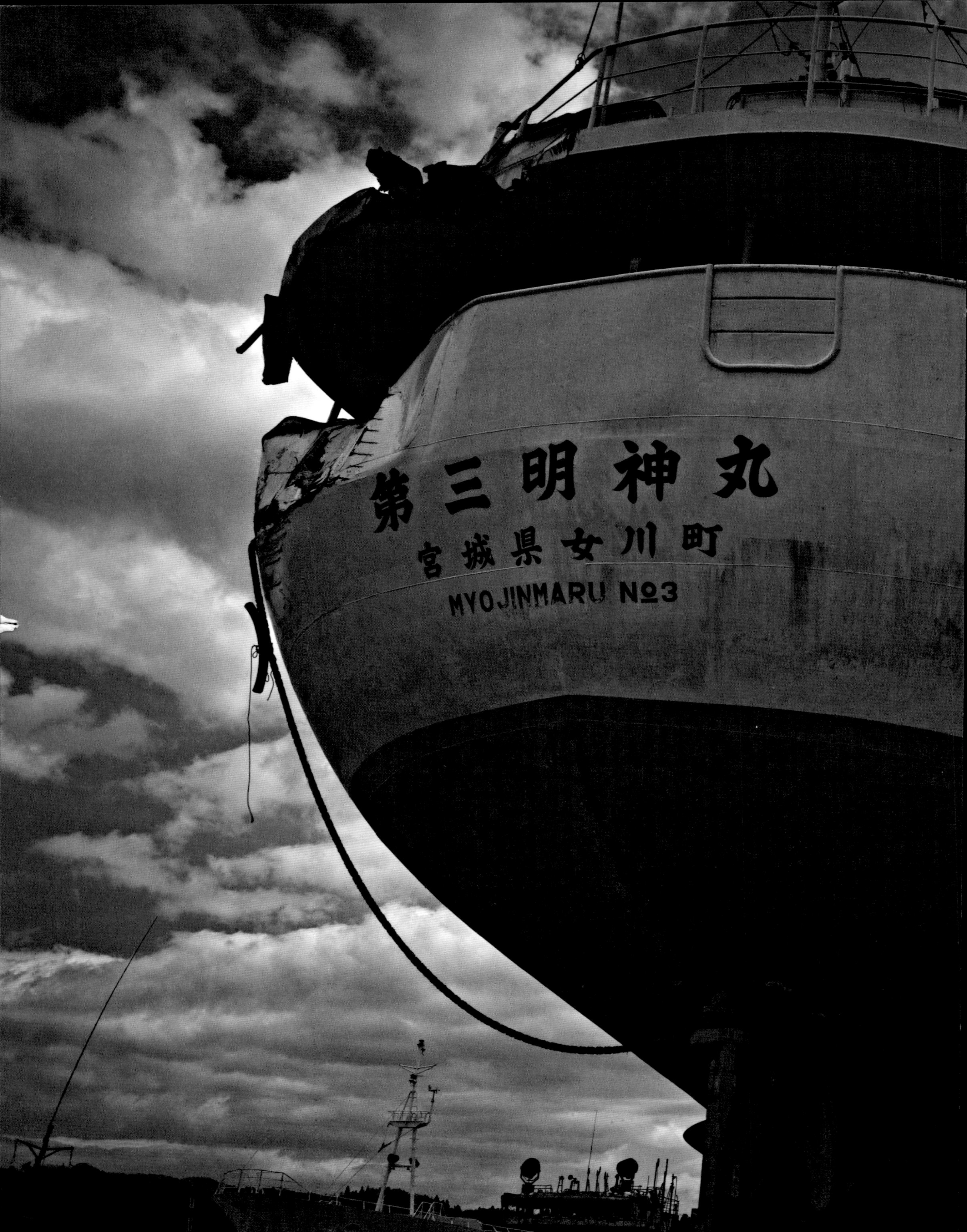
第三明神丸
宮城県女川町
MYOJINMARU No3

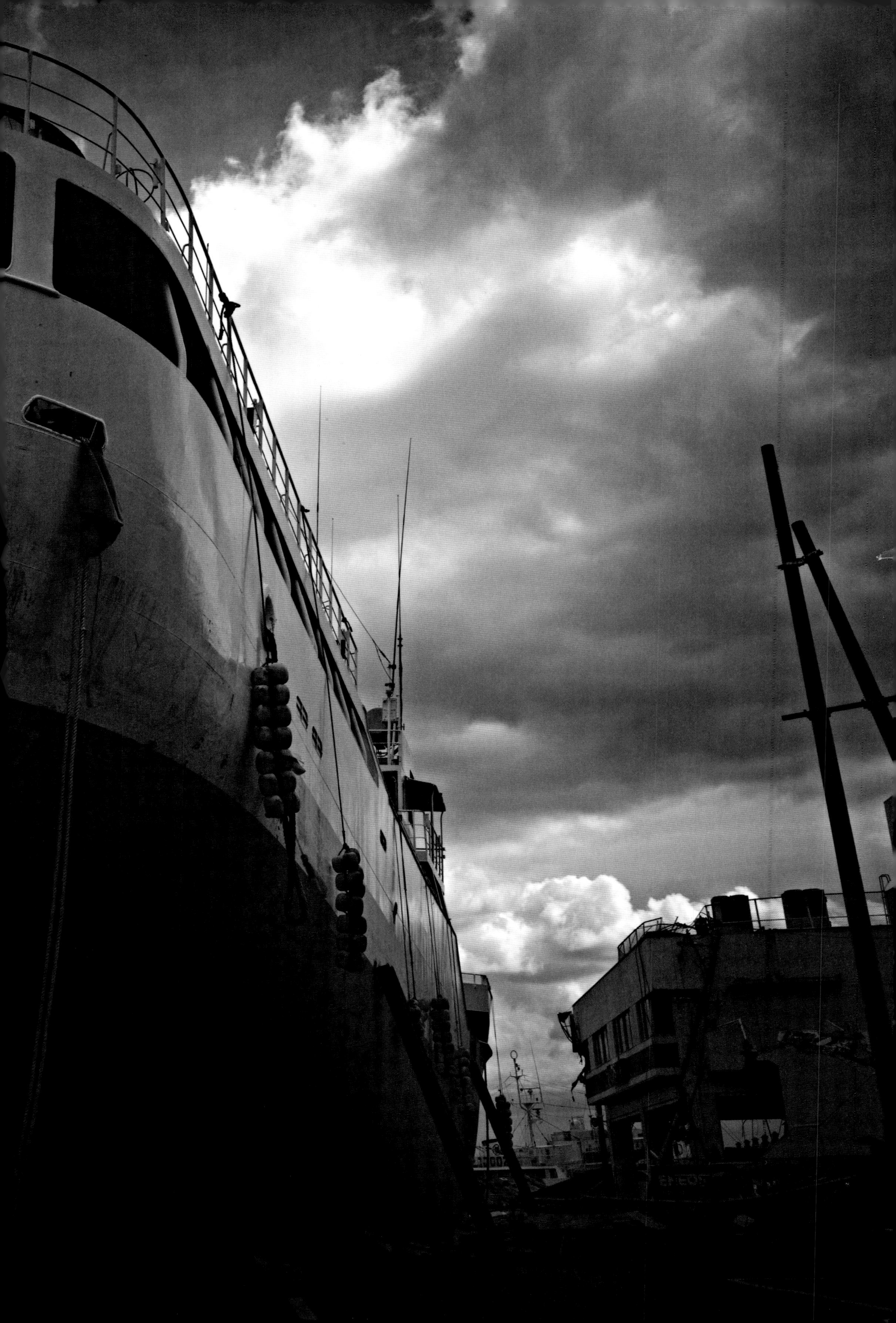

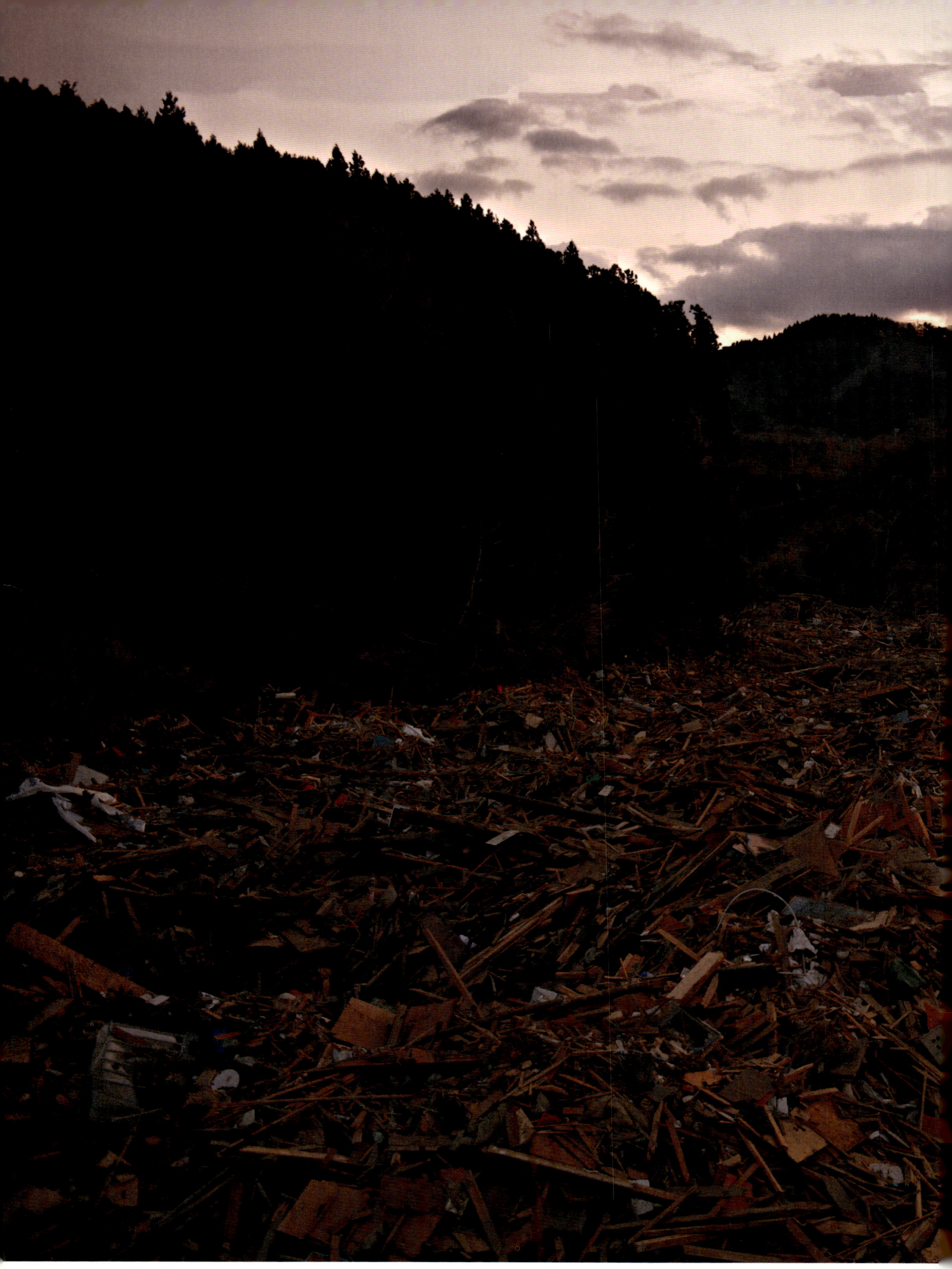

The remains of the residential area.
City of Rikuzen Takata, Iwate prefecture

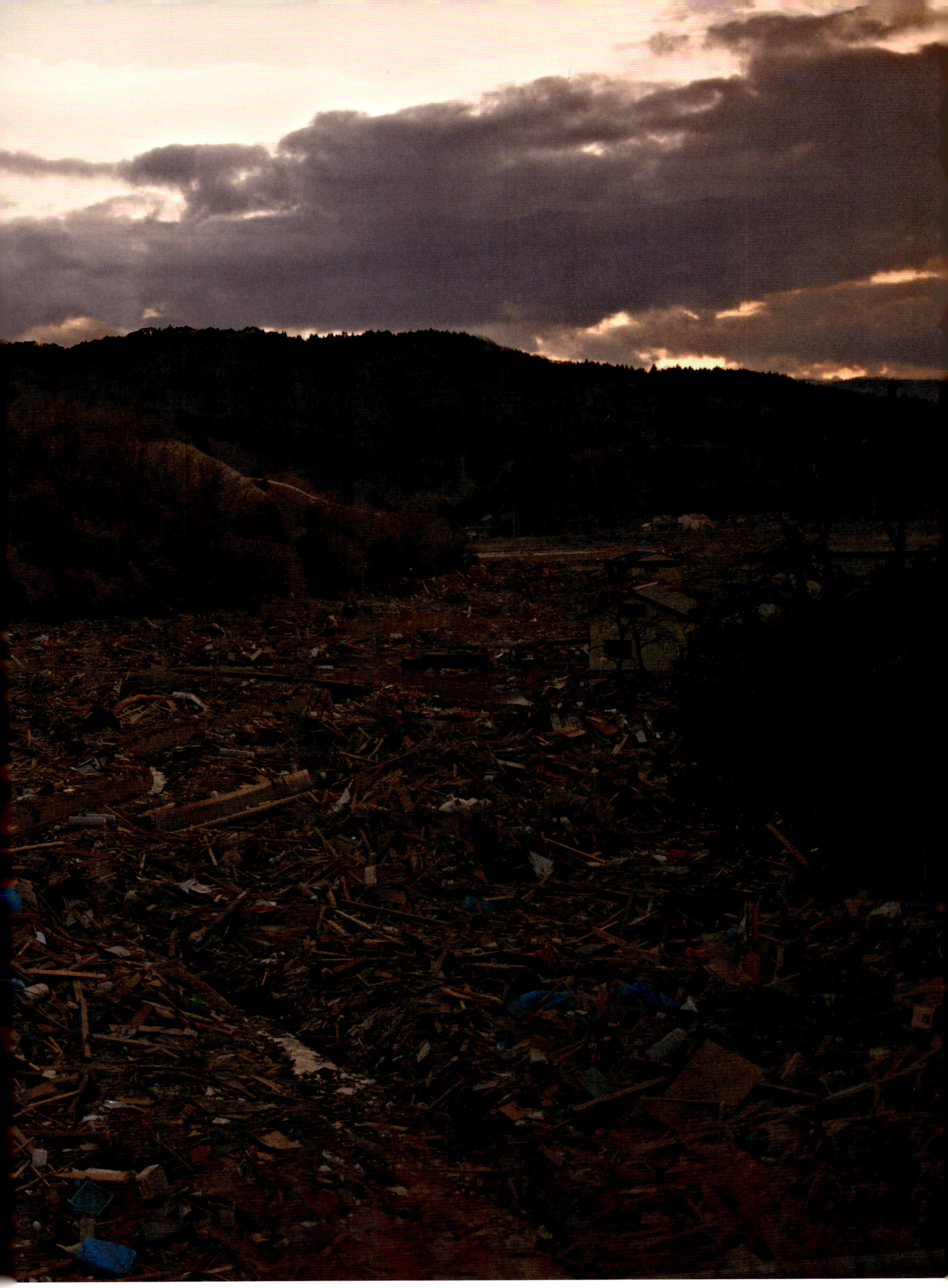

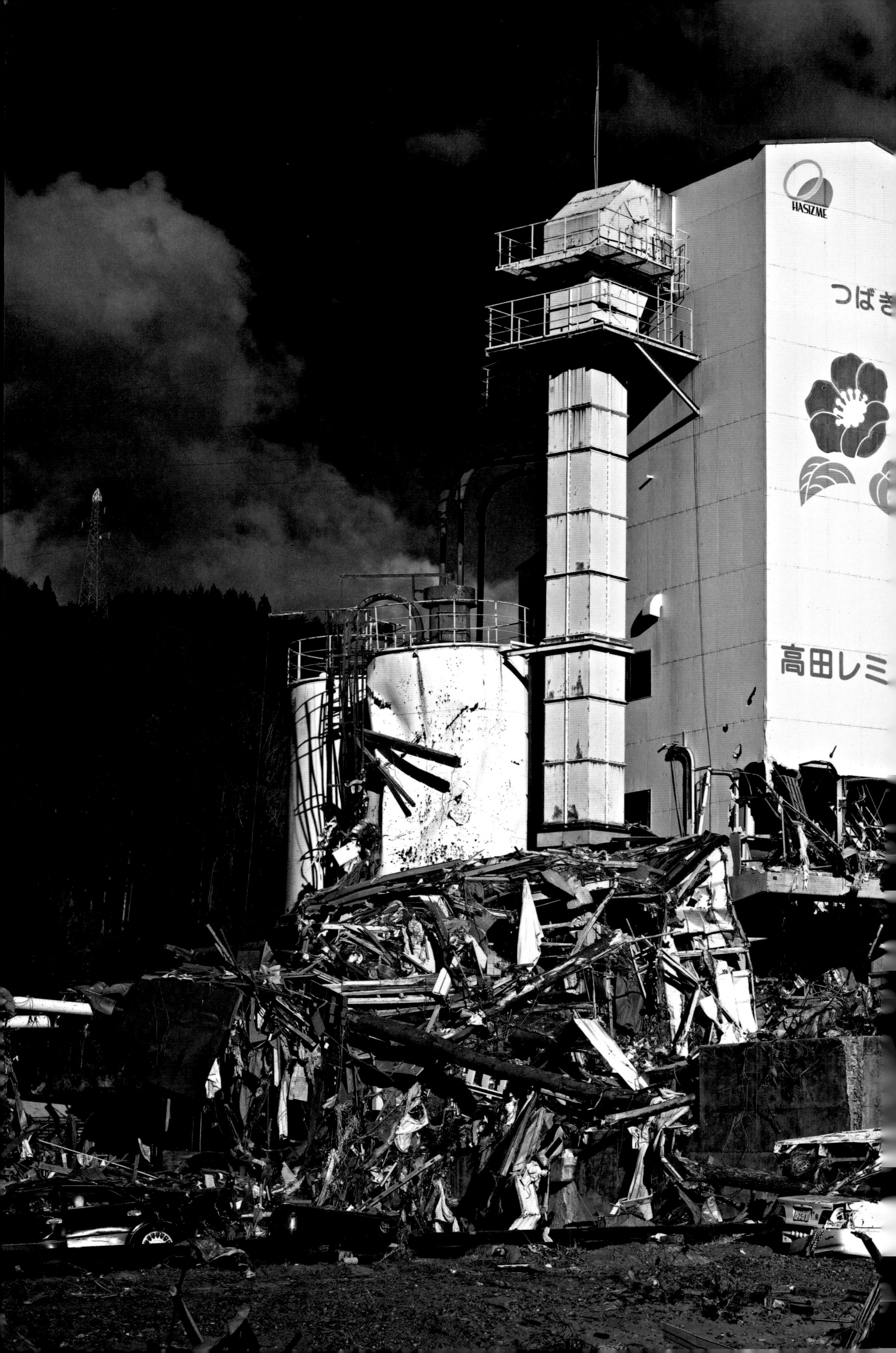
HASIZME
つばき
高田レミ

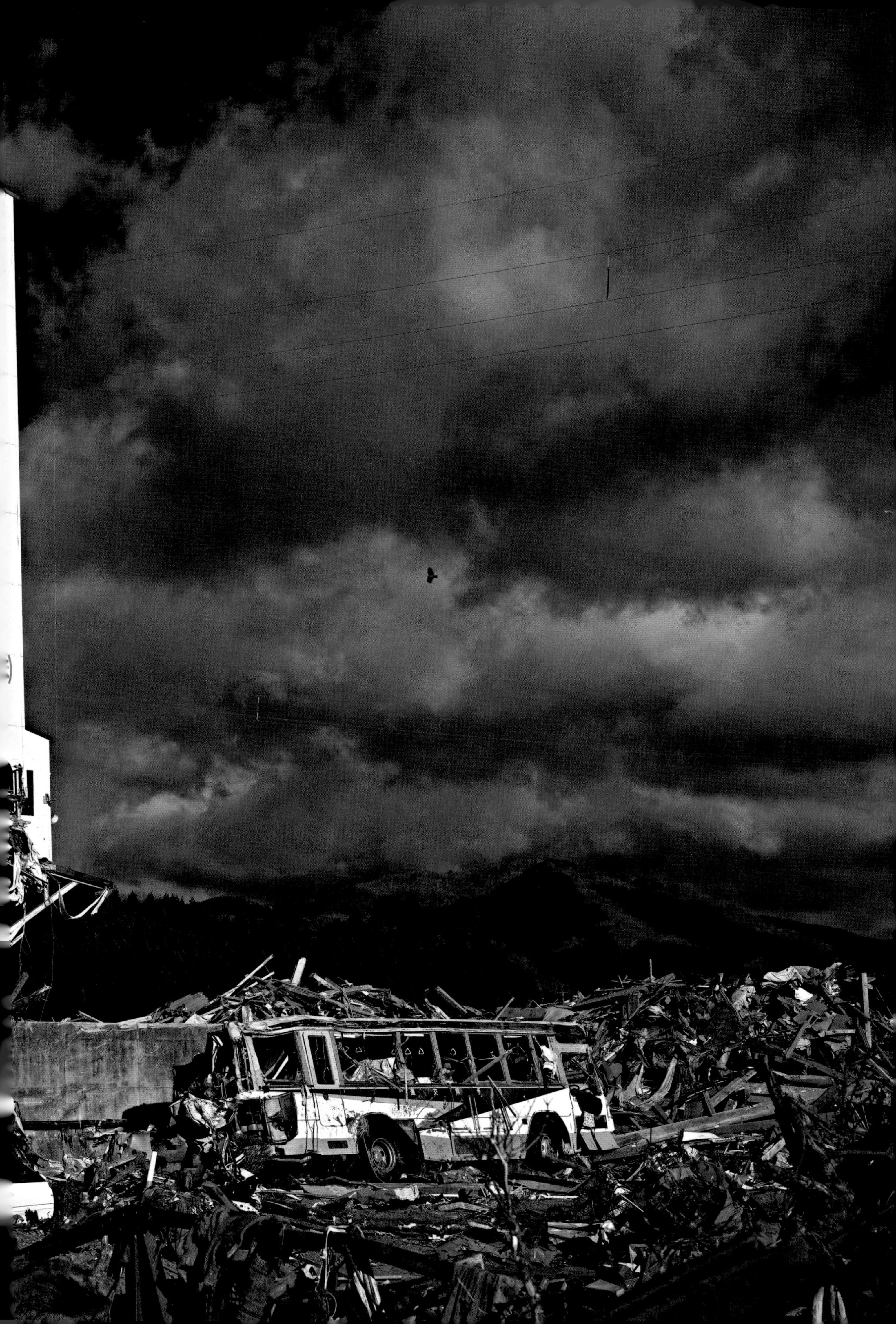

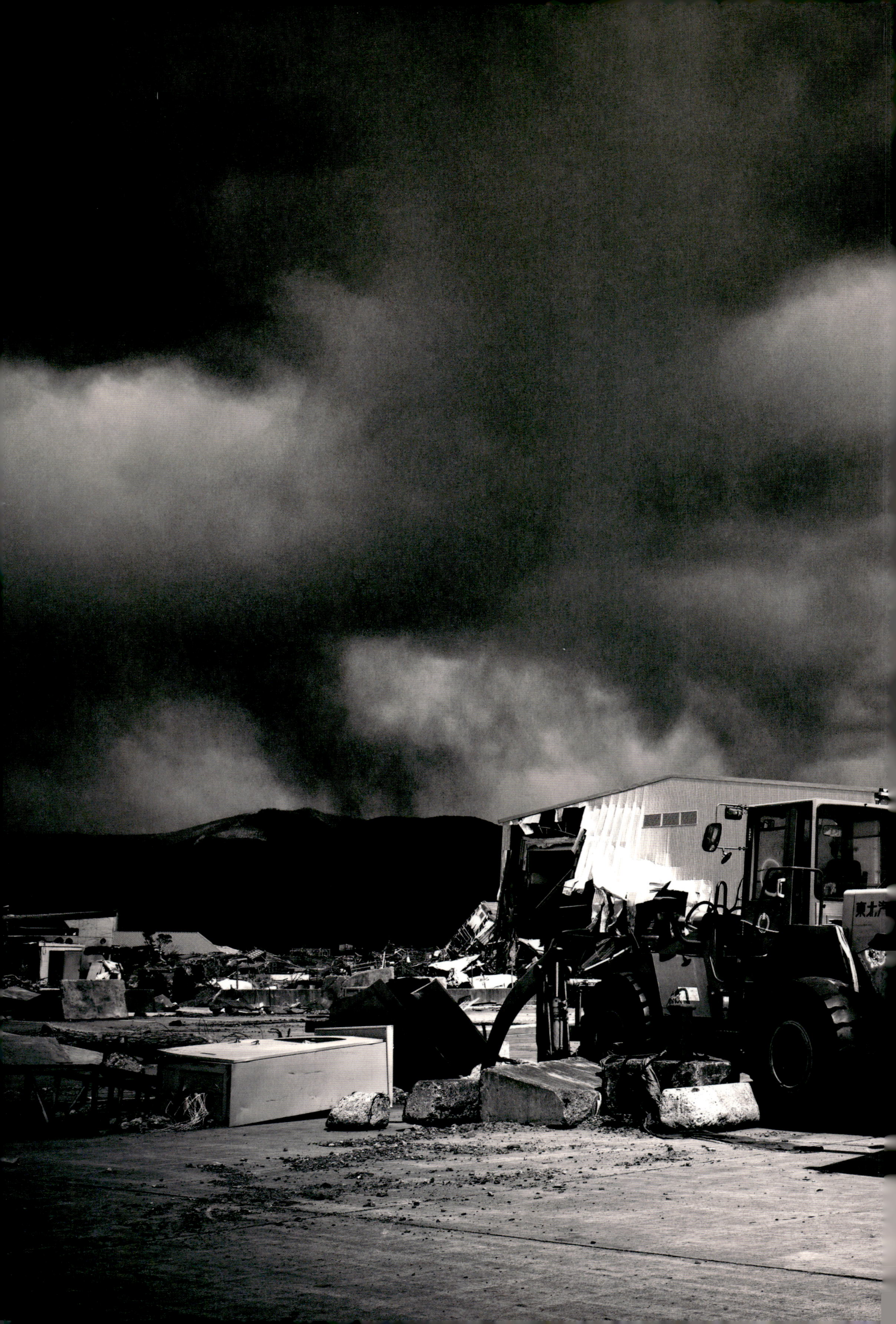

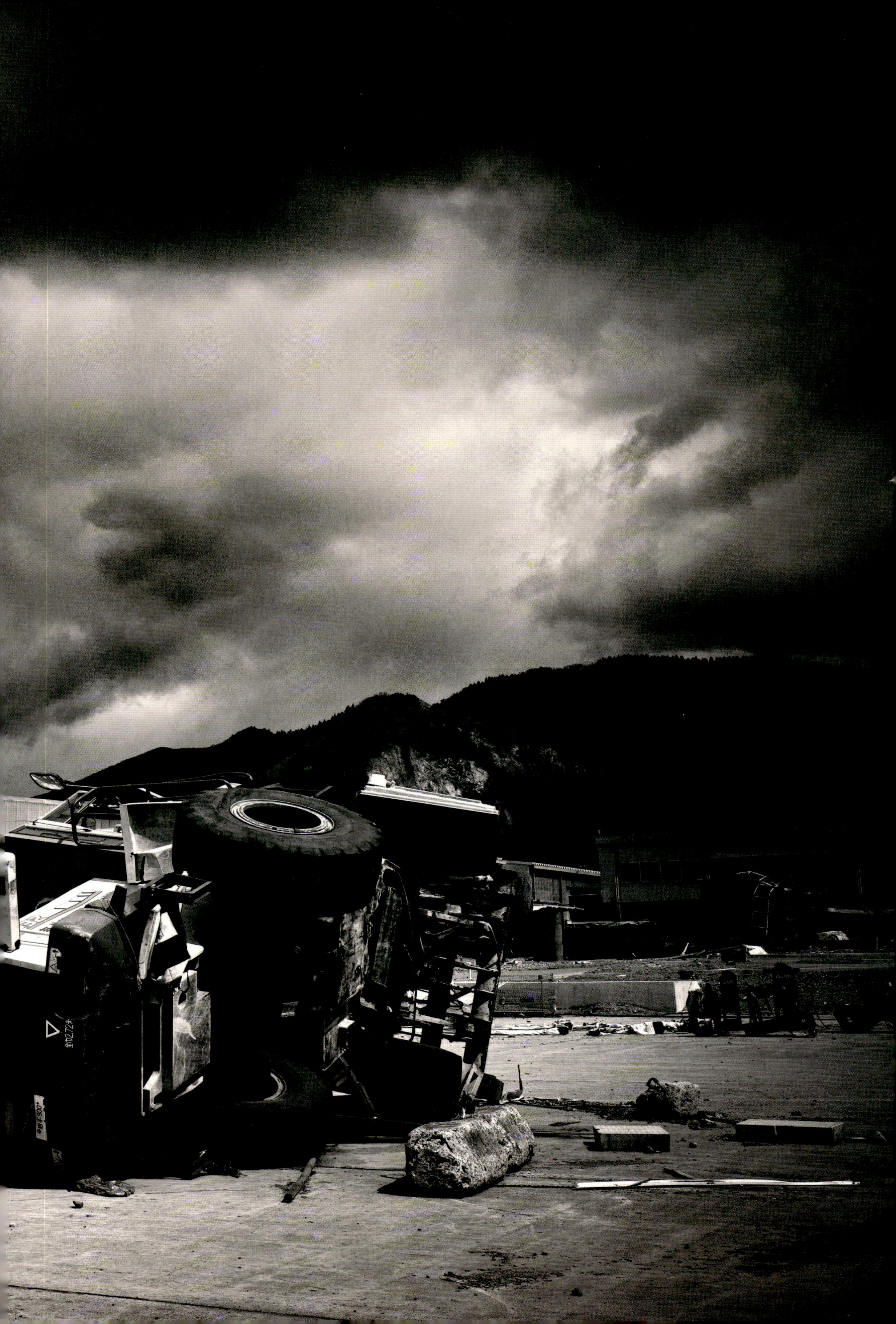

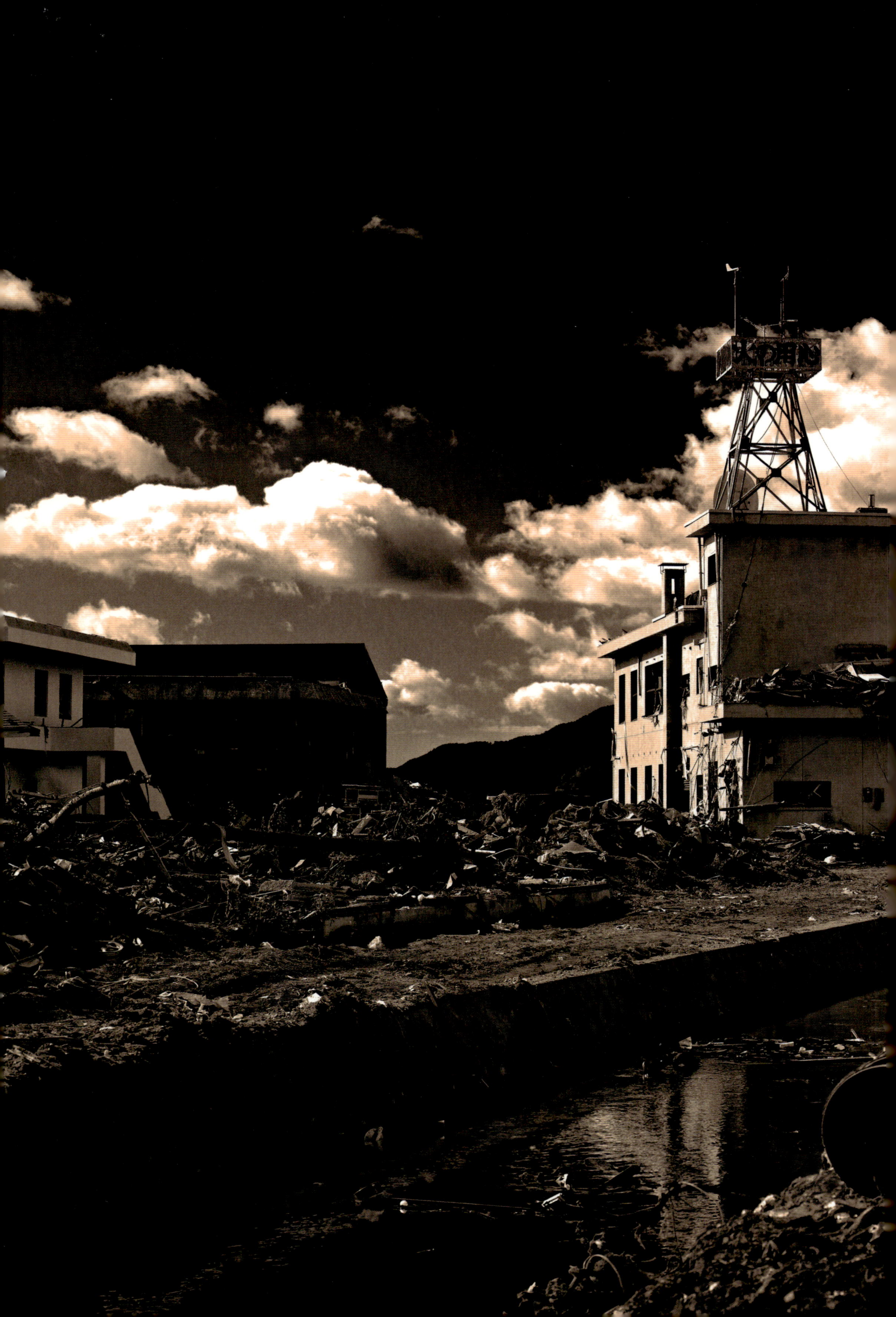

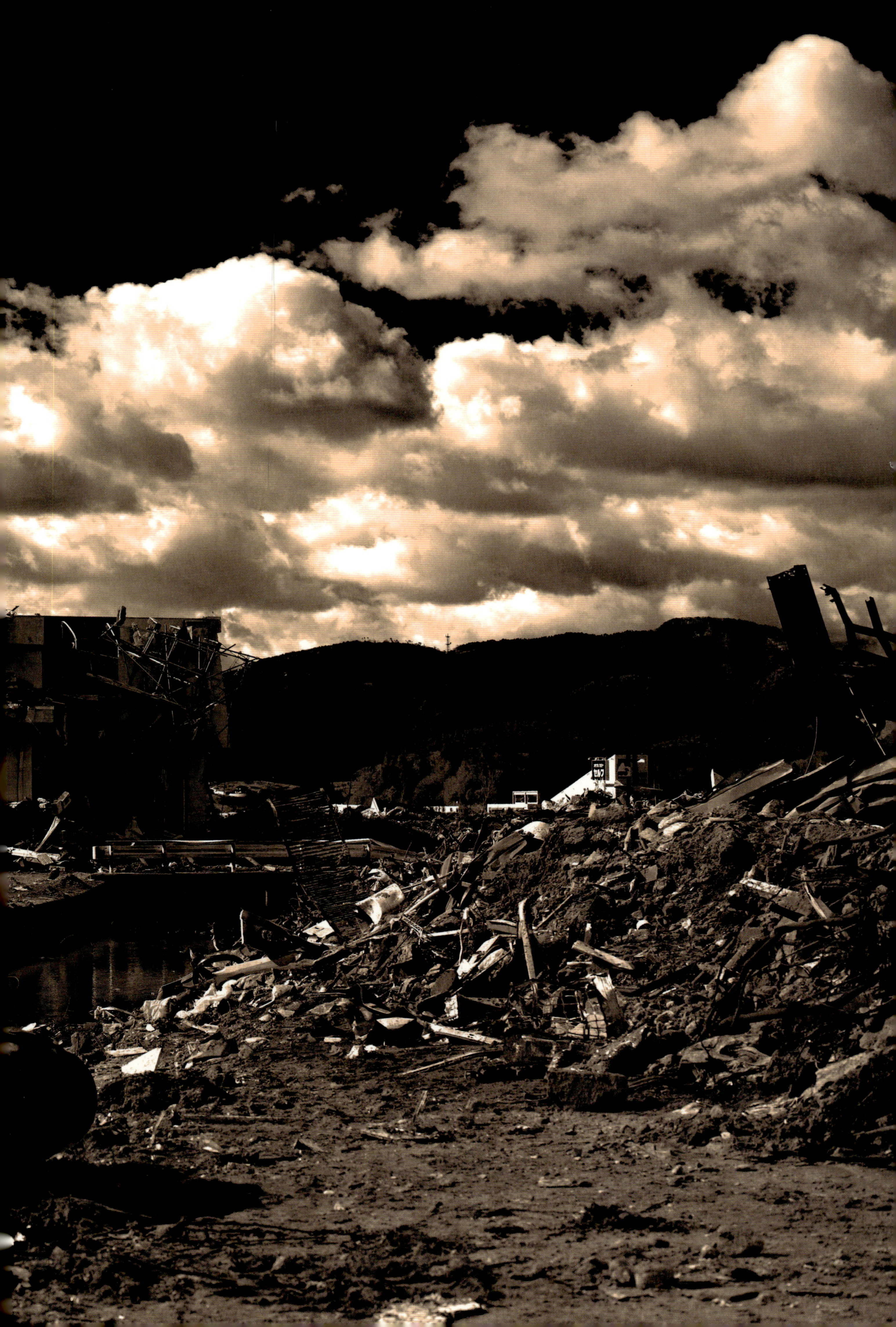
セルフ

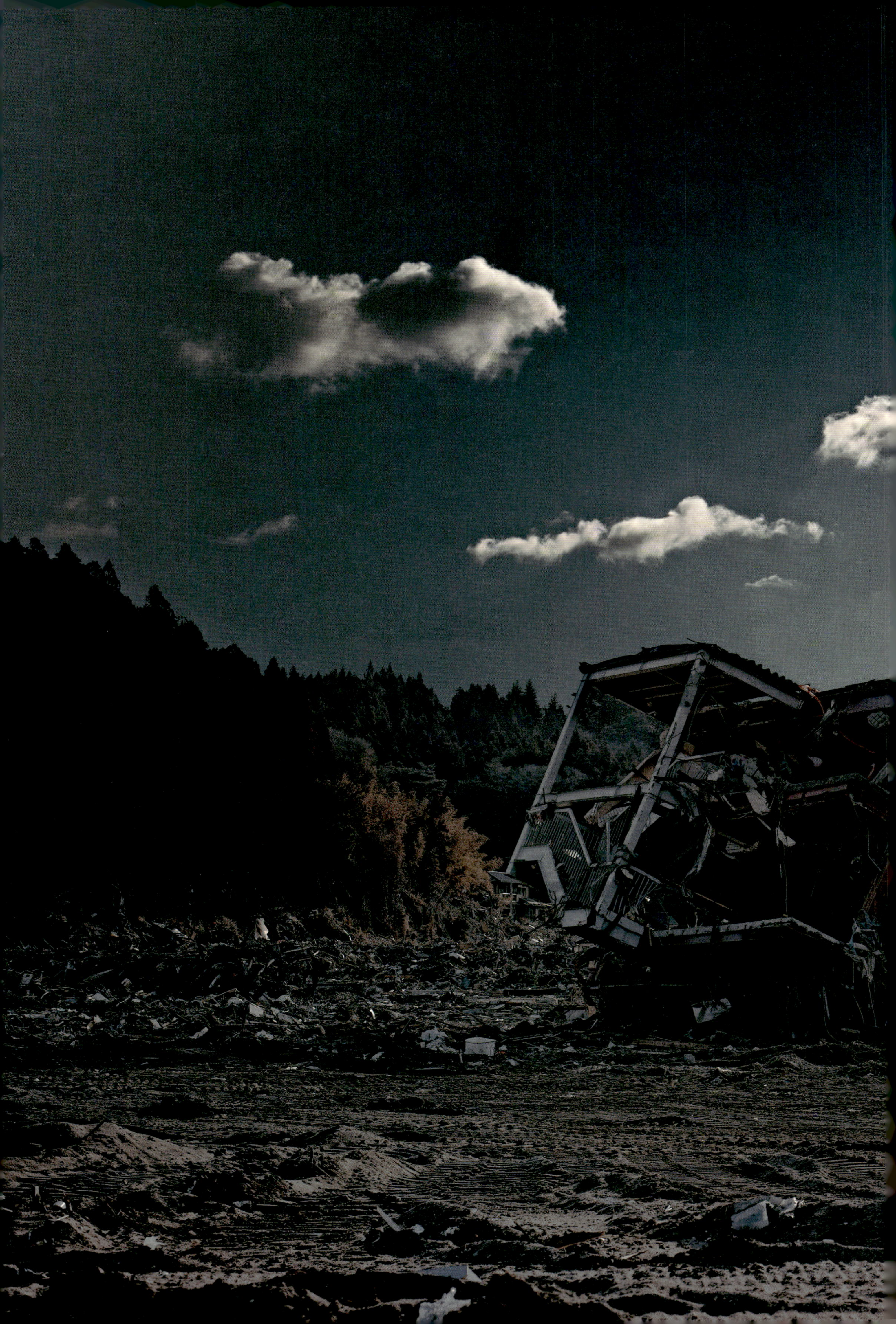

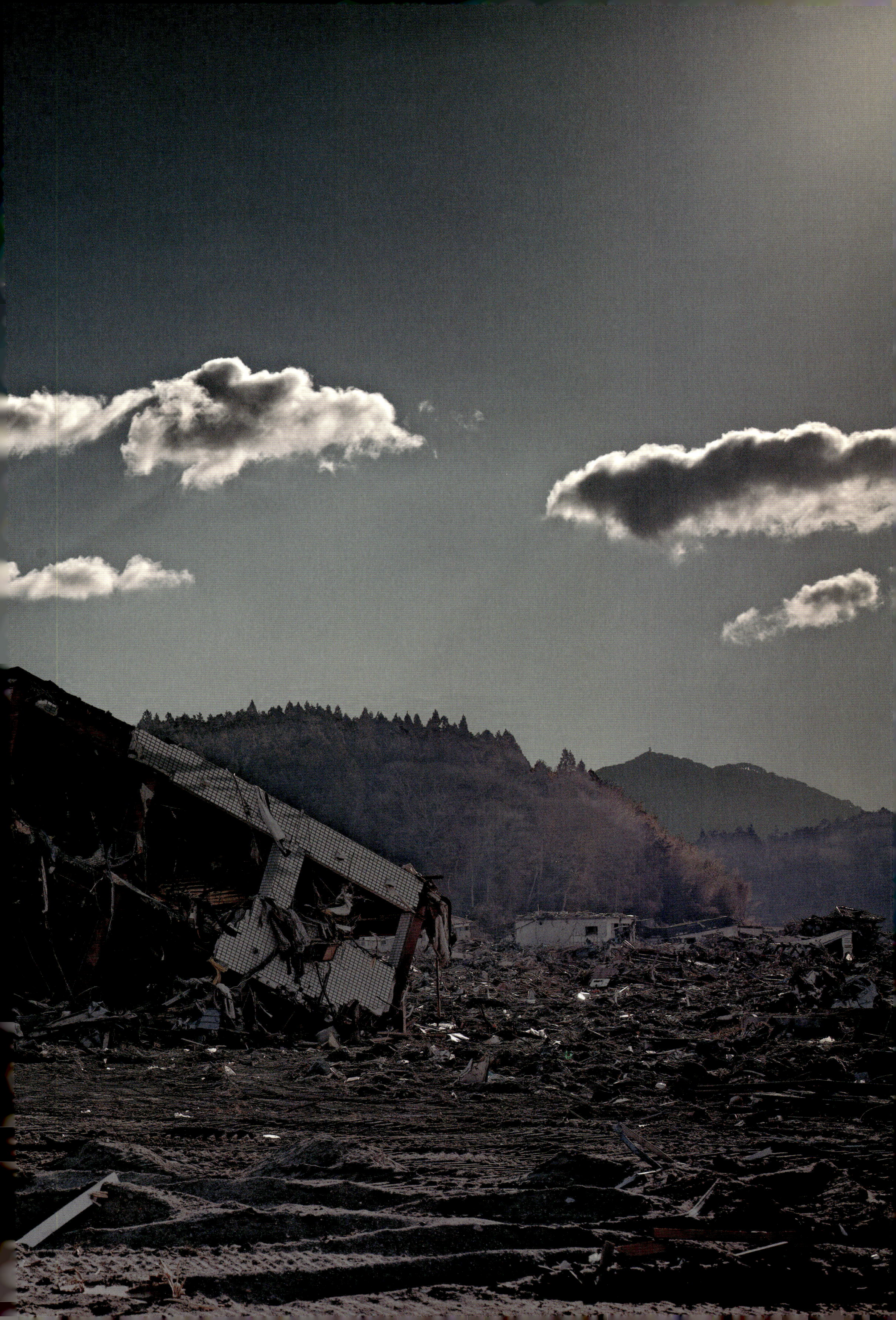

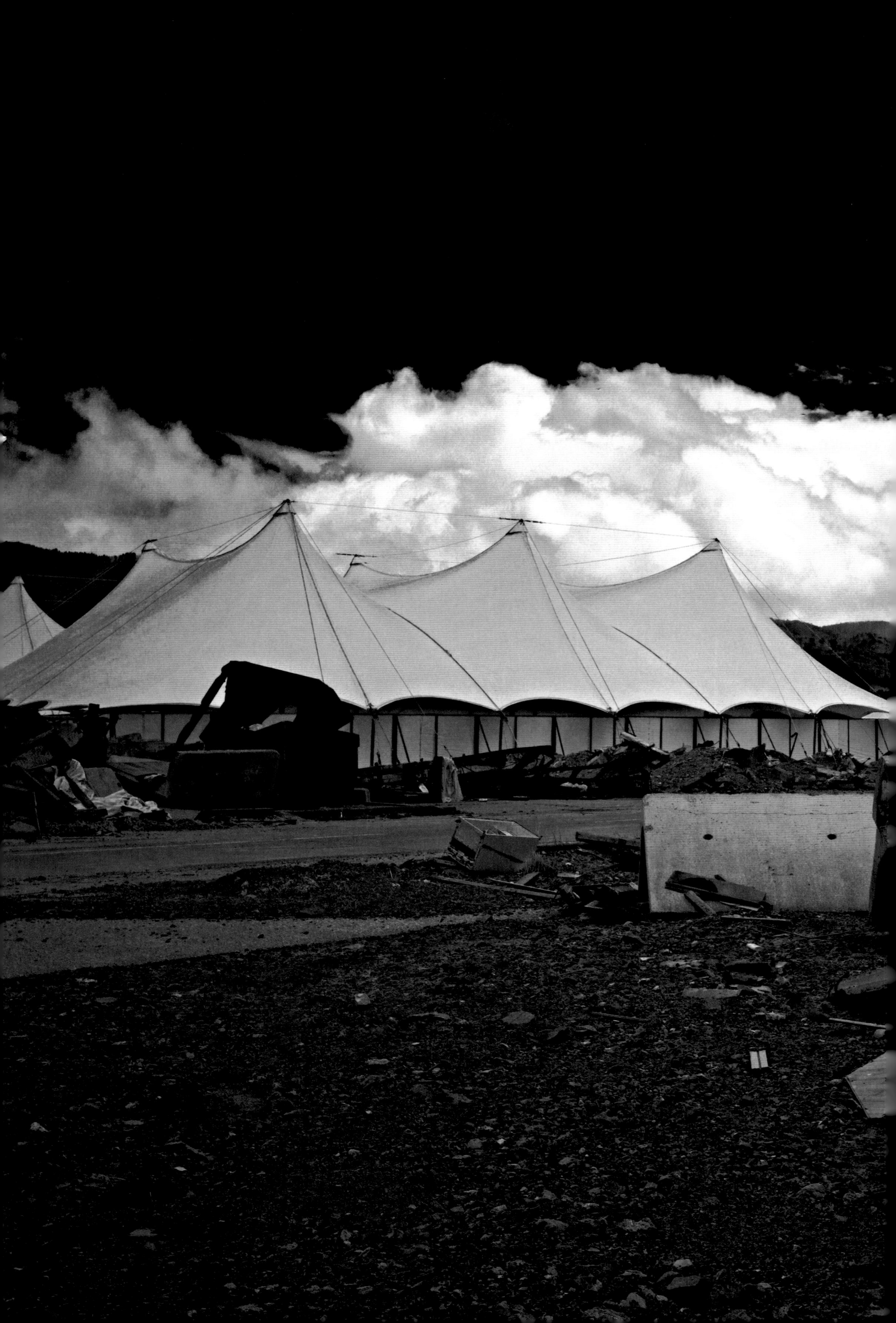

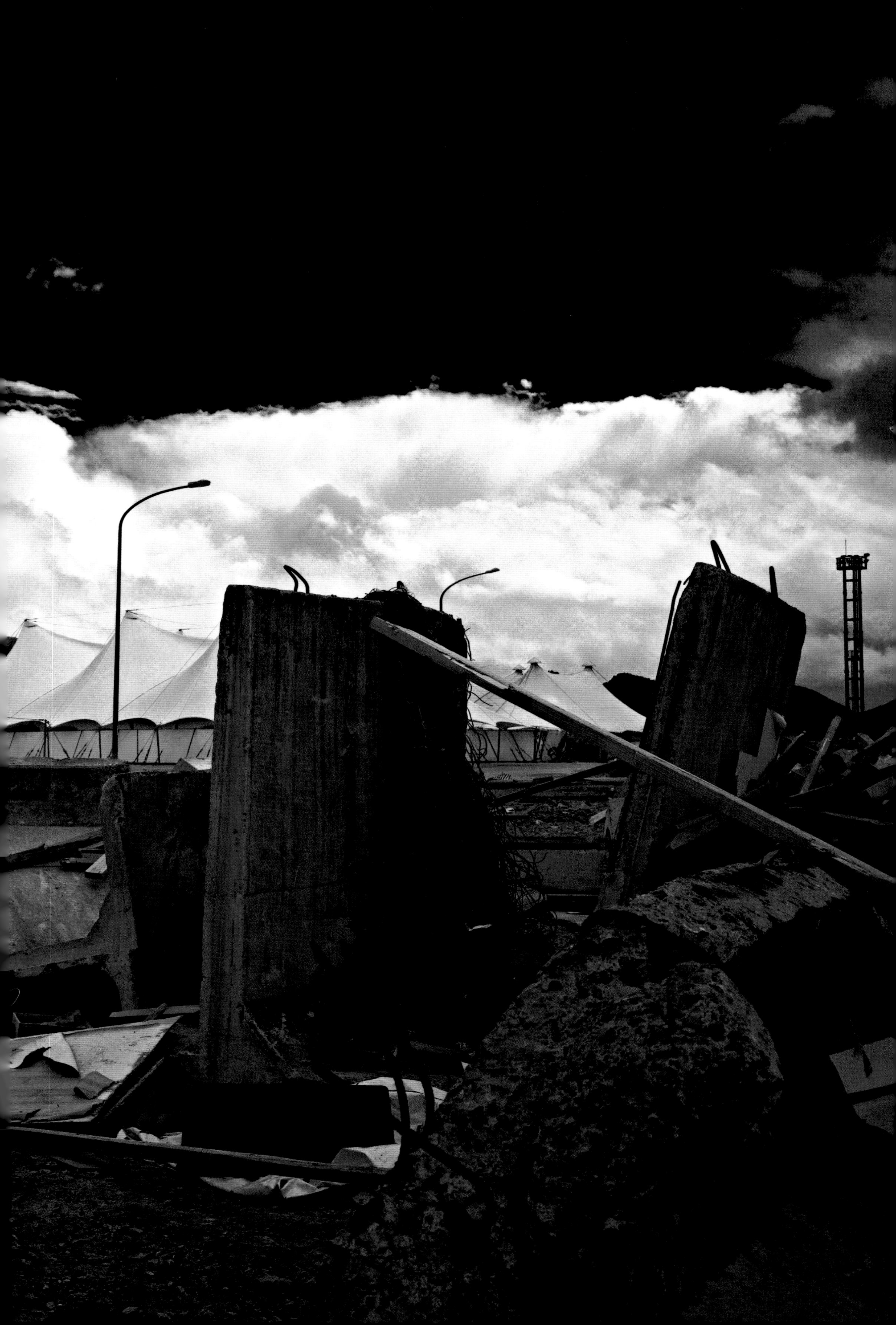

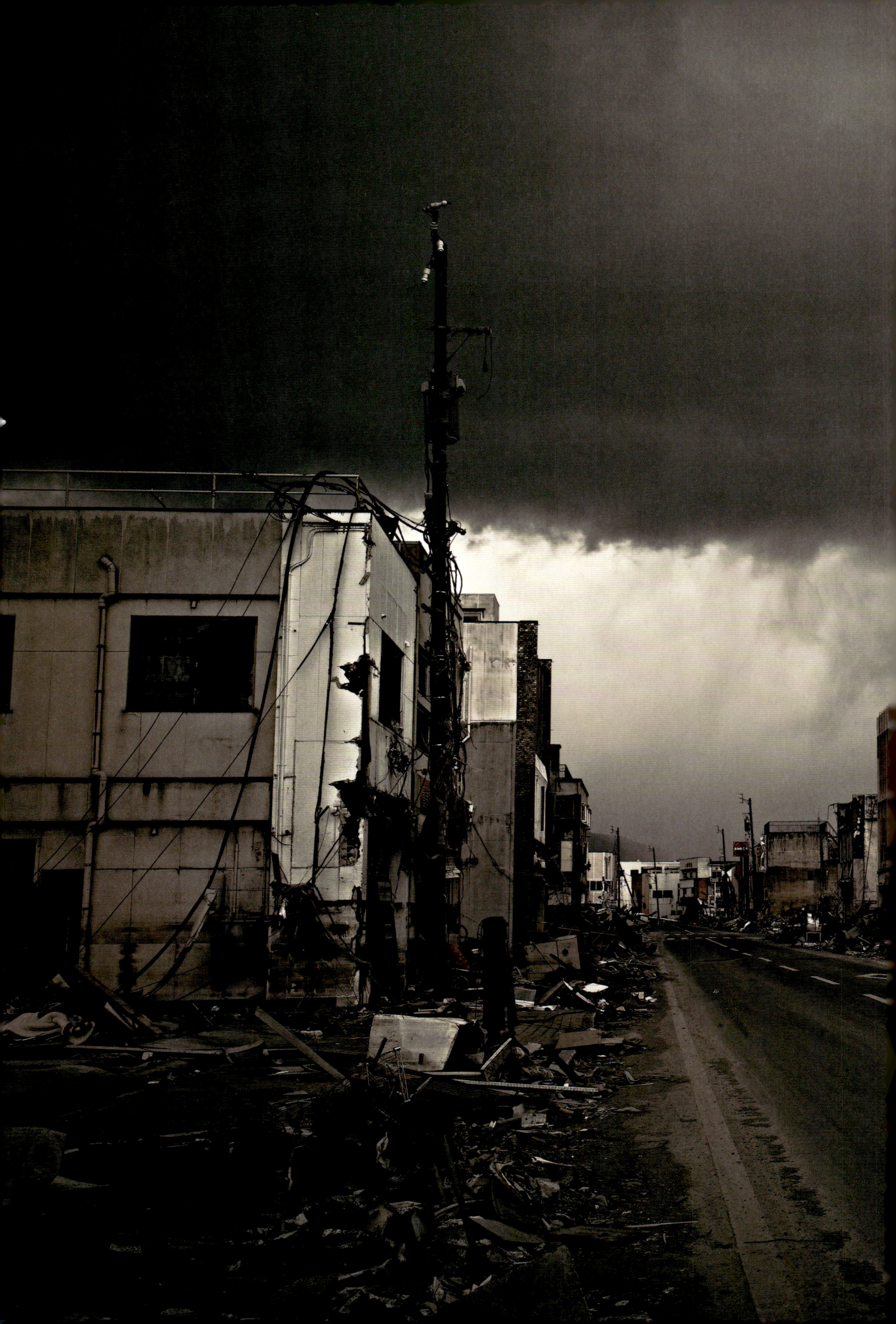

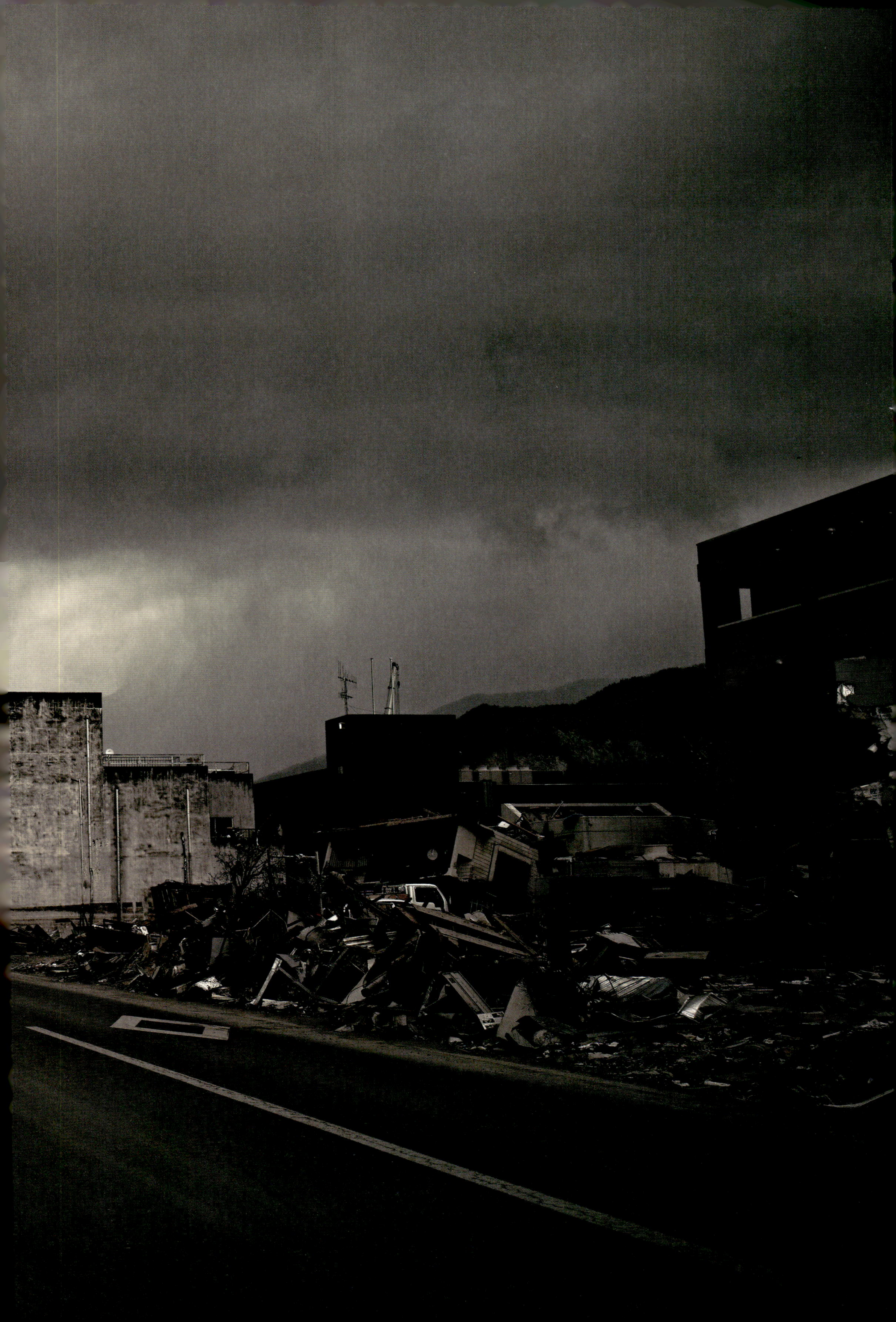

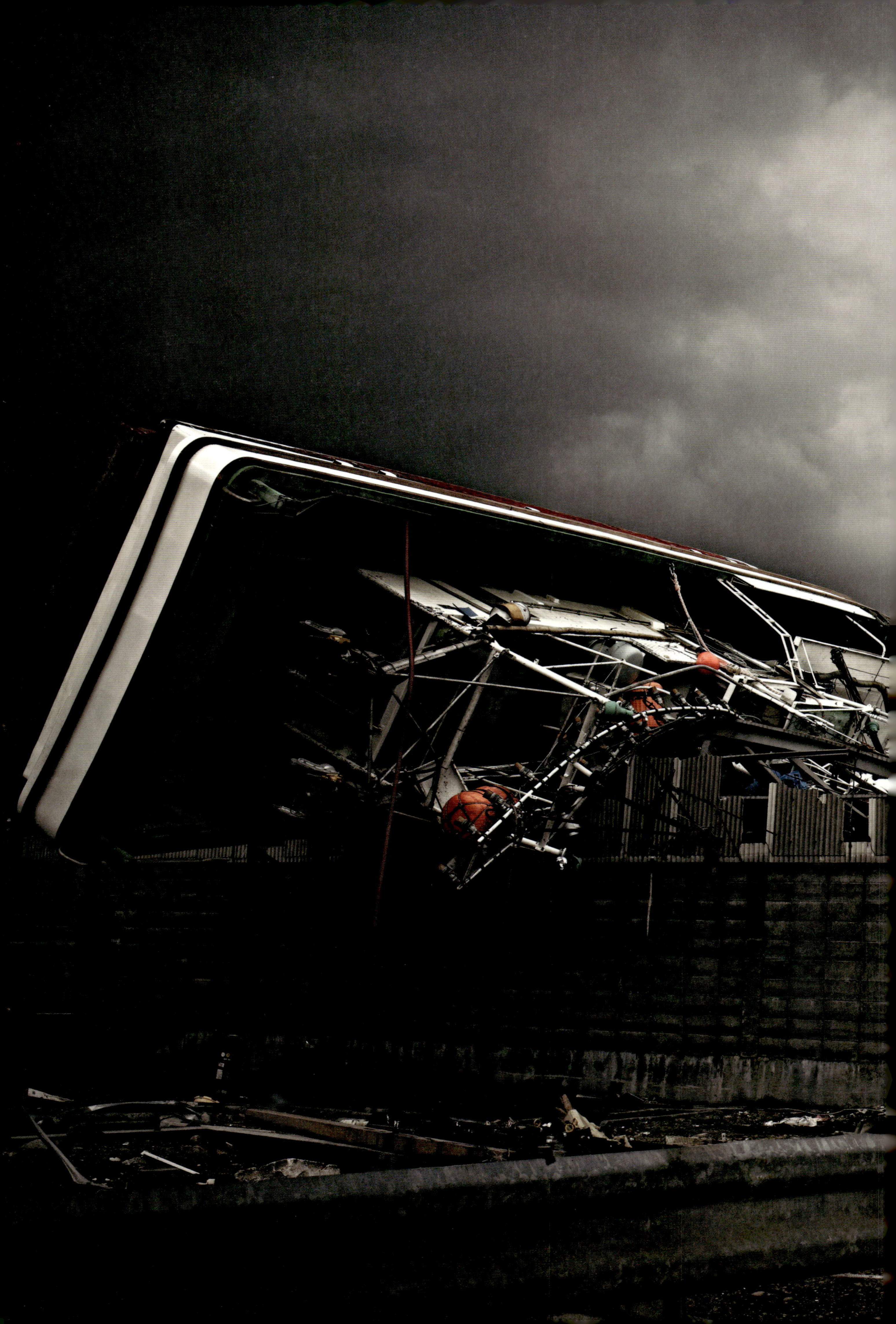

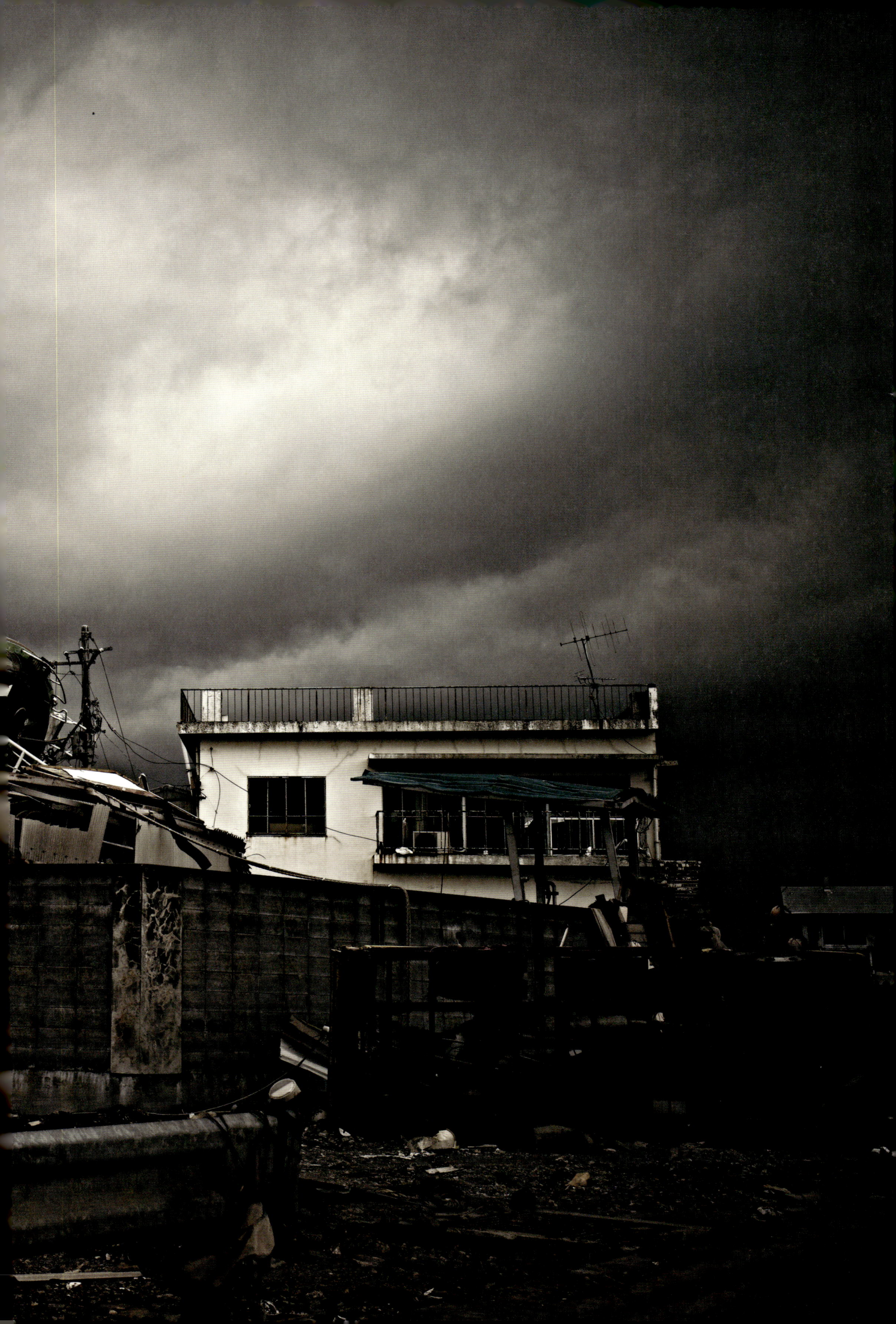

Pages 88-89. A rice granary.
City of Rikuzen Takata, Iwate prefecture

Pages 90-91. Fork lifts.
City of Ofunato, Iwate prefecture

Pages 92-93. A fire department.
City of Rikuzen Takata, Iwate prefecture

Pages 94-95. A building deposited
by the tsunami.
City of Rikuzen Takata, Iwate prefecture

Pages 96-97. Underwater sea walls
in front of tents for enshrining dead bodies.
City of Ofunato, Iwate prefecture

Pages 98-99. City of Ofunato, Iwate prefecture

Pages 100-101. A fishing boat on top
of the second floor.
City of Ofunato, Iwate prefecture

The cracked and peeled foundation posts
warped by the phenomenon of earthquake
liquefaction.
City of Ofunato, Iwate prefecture

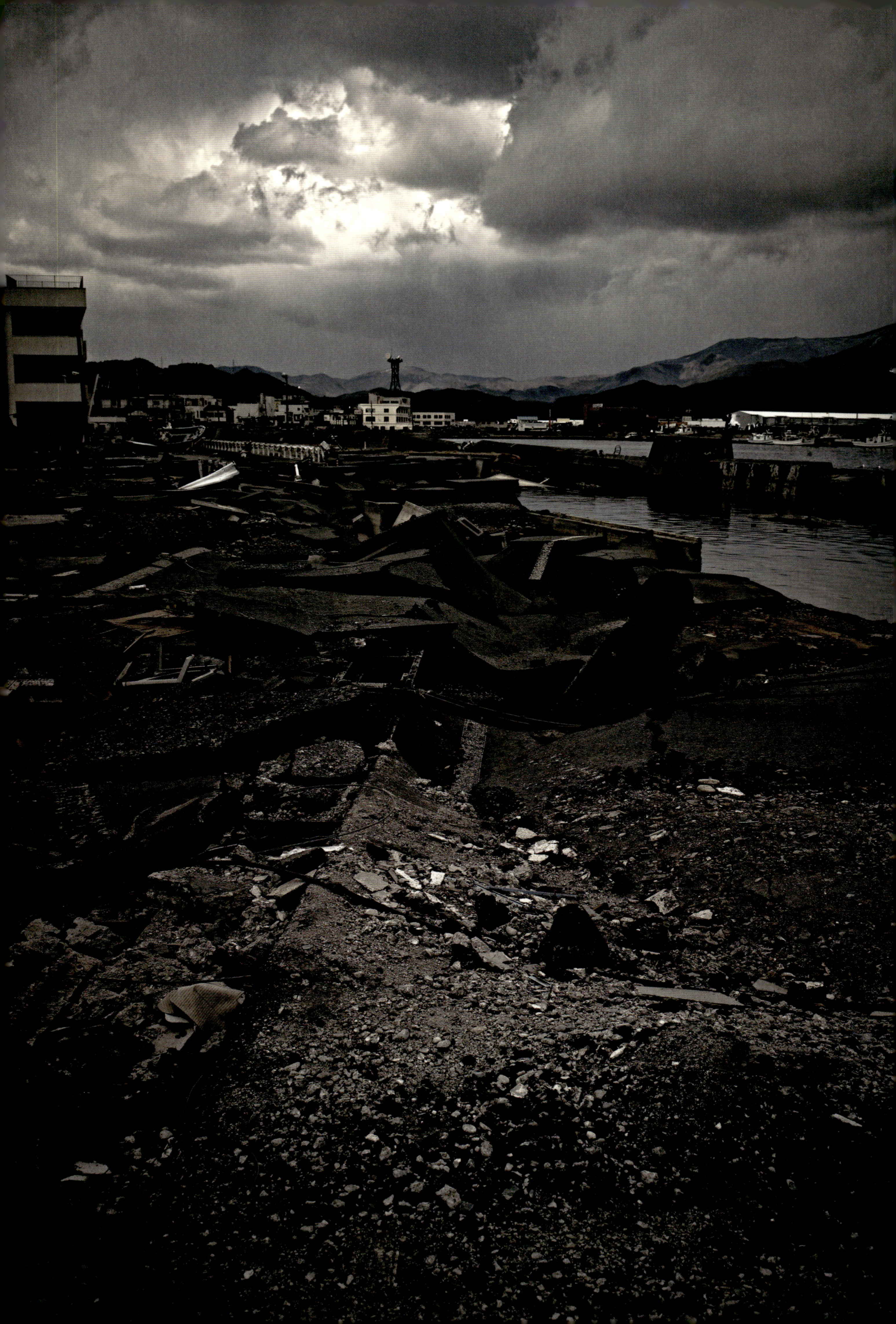

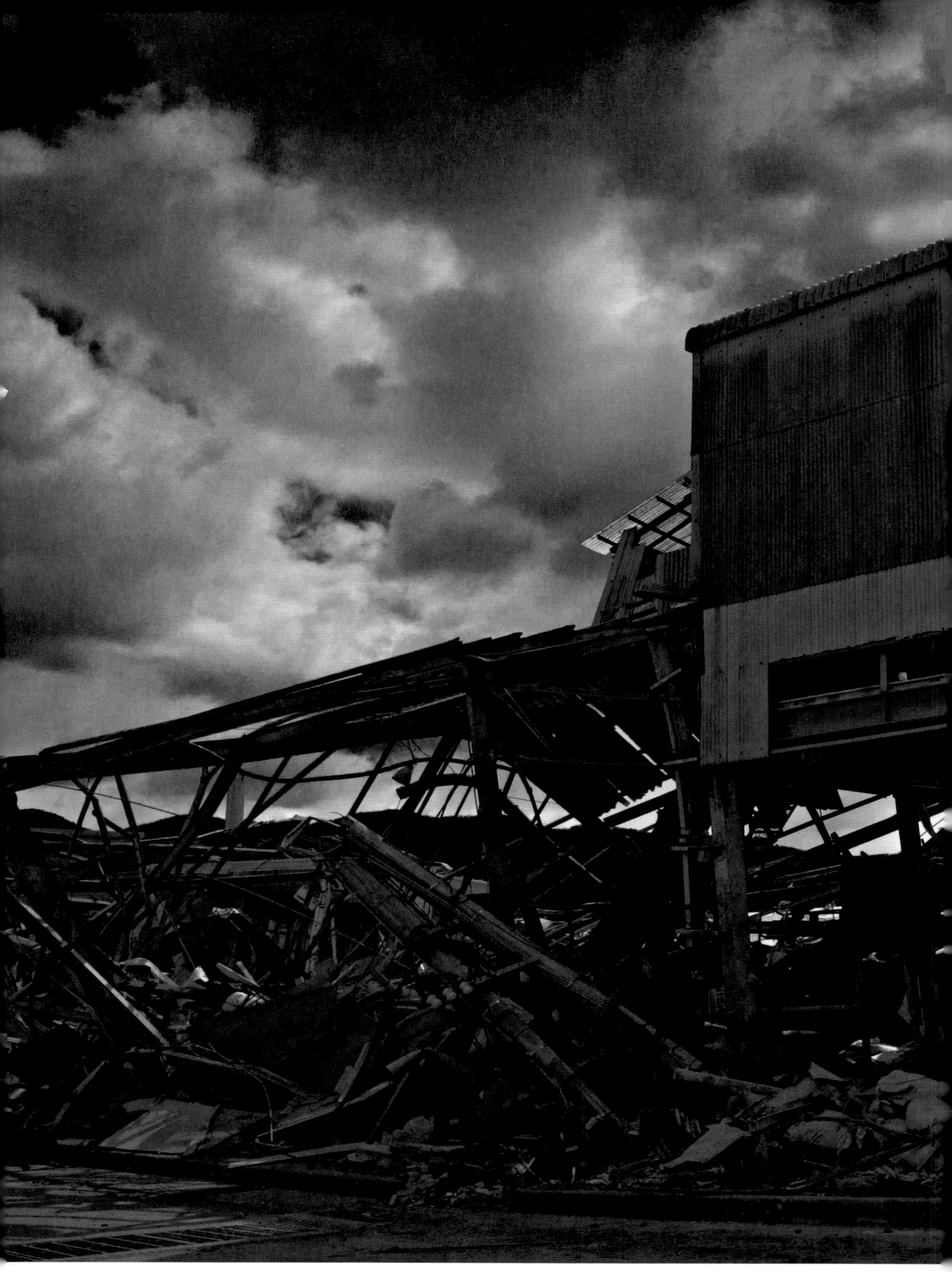

A fishing business.
City of Kesennuma, Miyagi prefecture

Pages 106-107. Shin-Nippon Steel Factory.
City of Kamaishi, Iwate prefecture

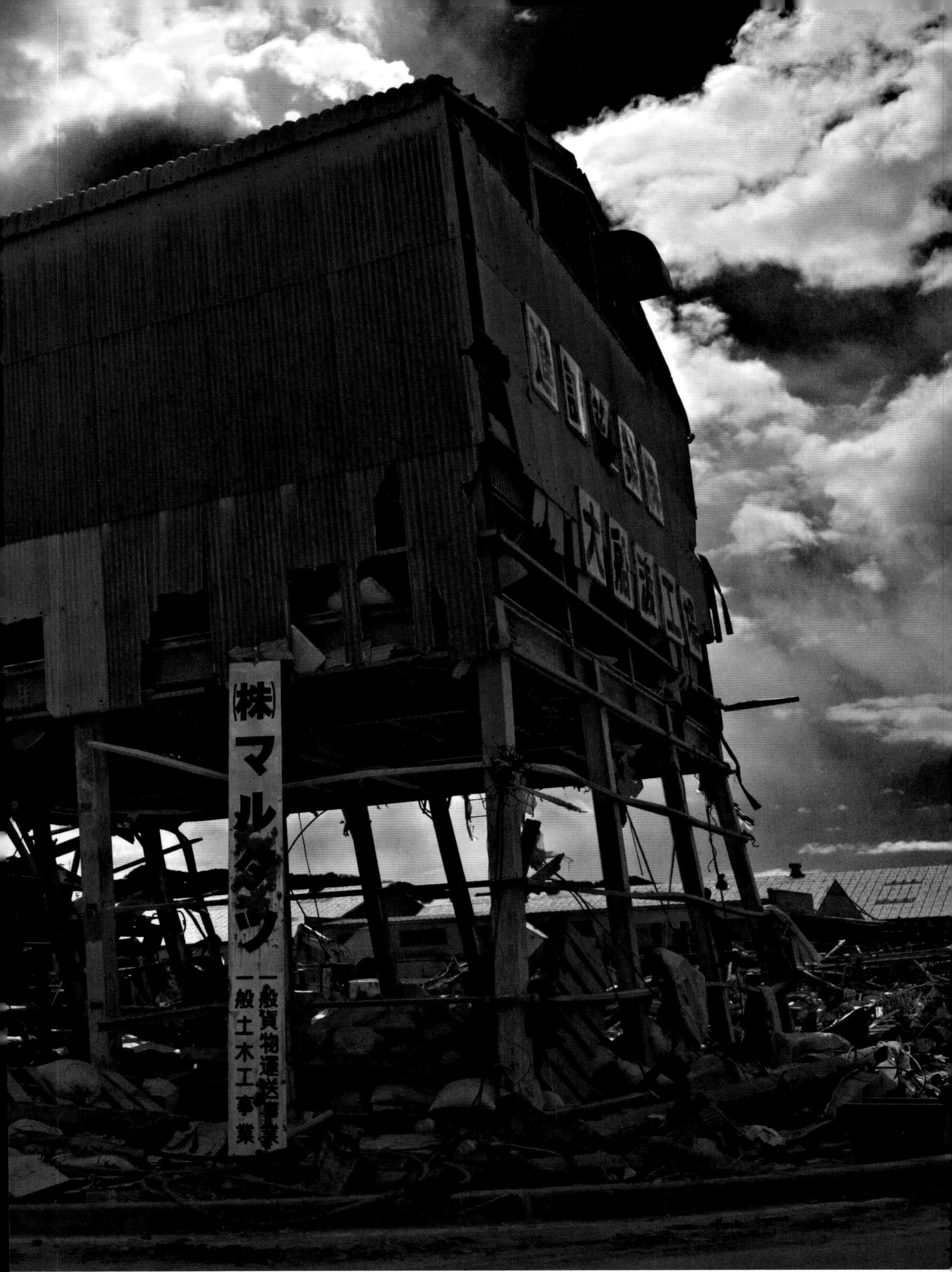

Pages 108-109. Shin-Nippon Steel Factory.
City of Kamaishi, Iwate prefecture

Pages 110-111. The middle of town.
City of Ofunato, Iwate prefecture

Pages 112-113. The city center.
City of Ofunato, Iwate prefecture

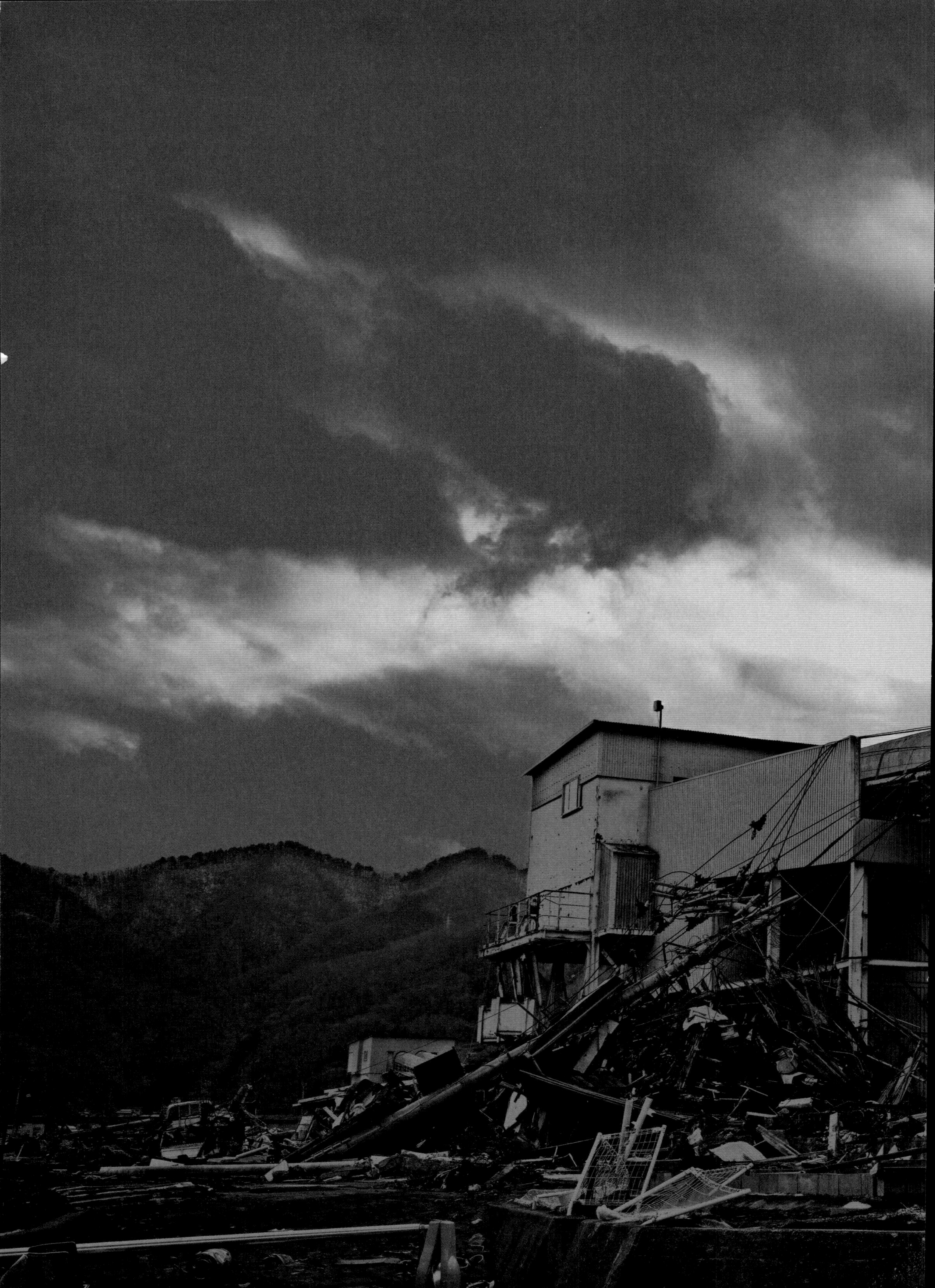

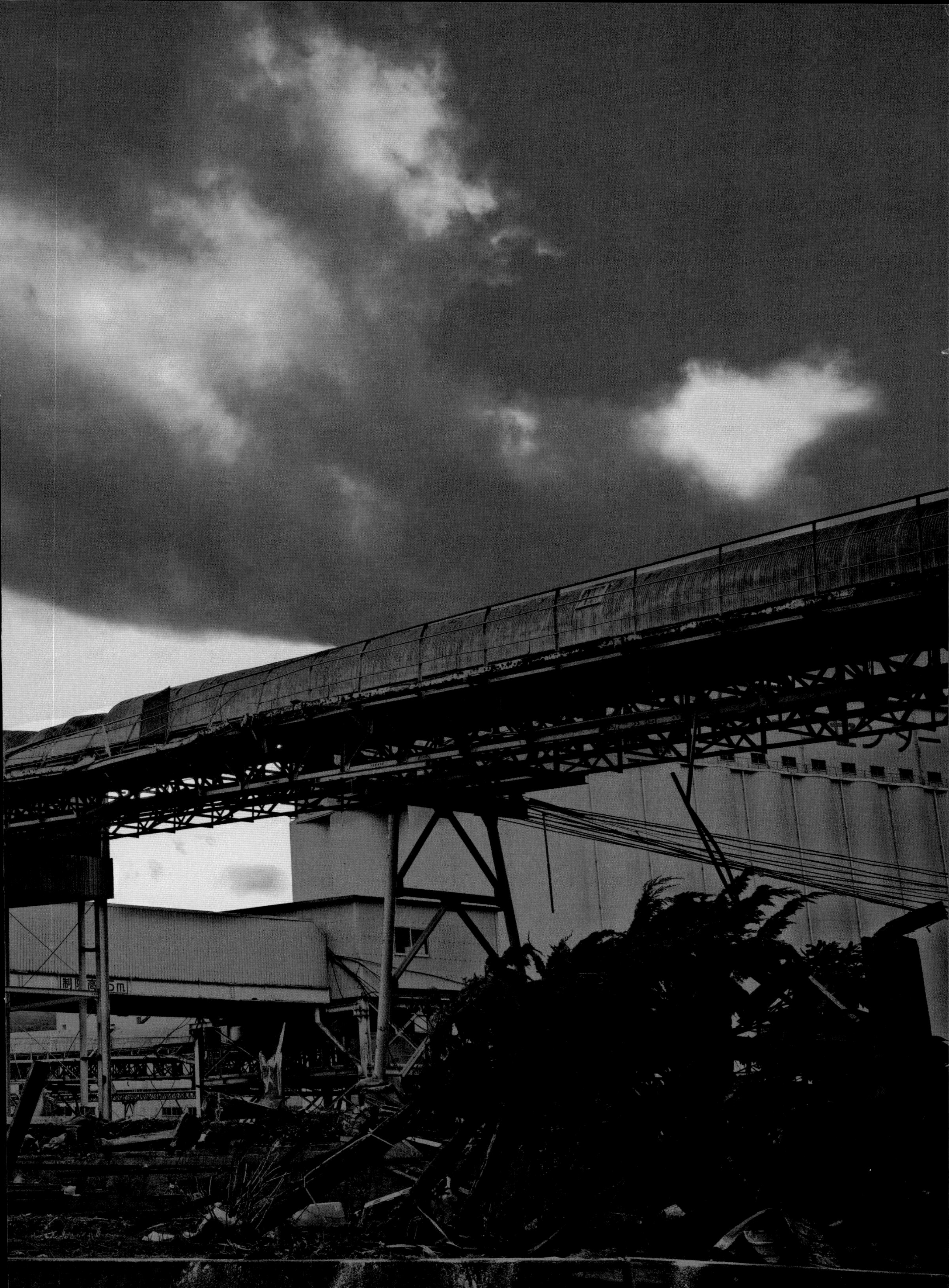

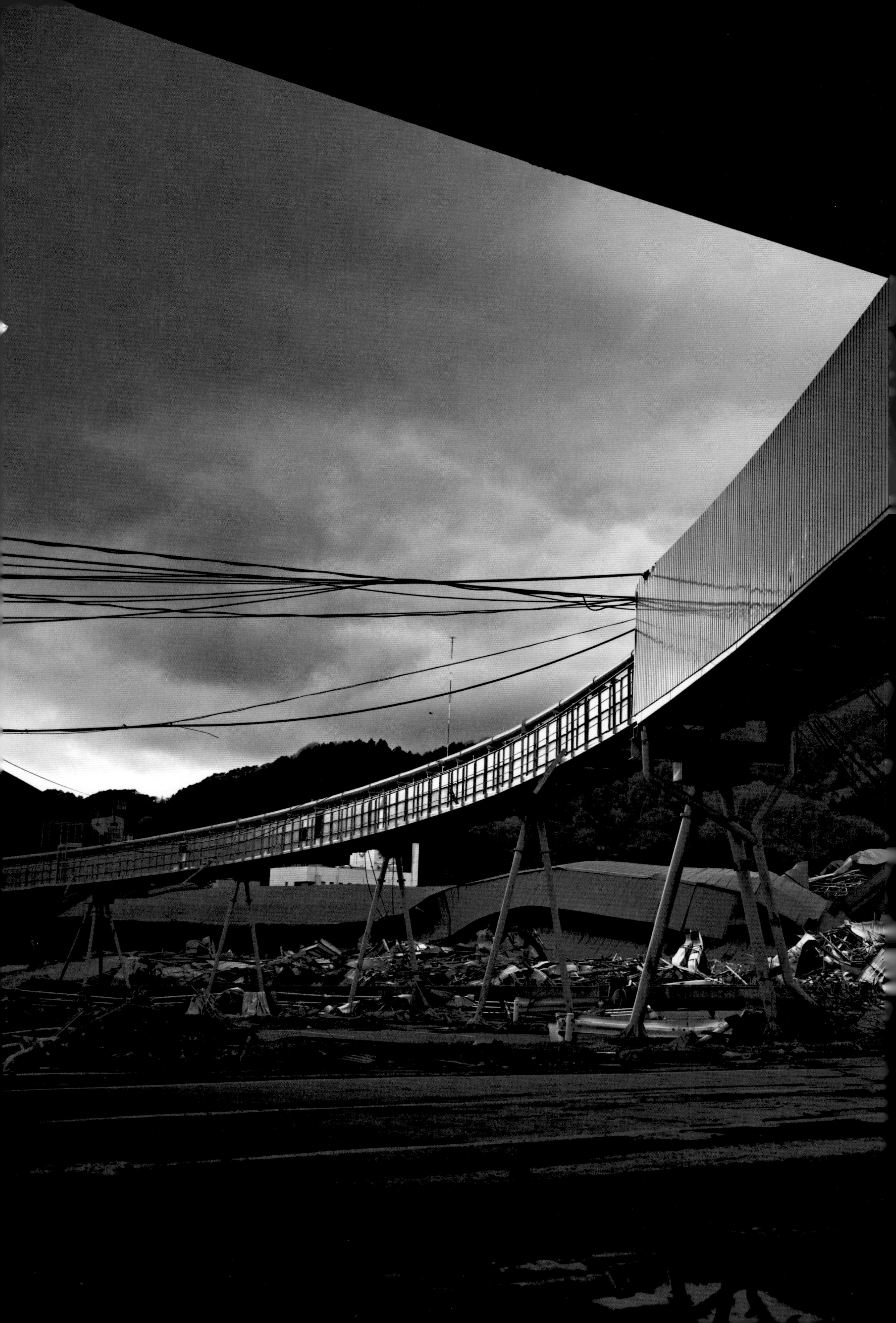

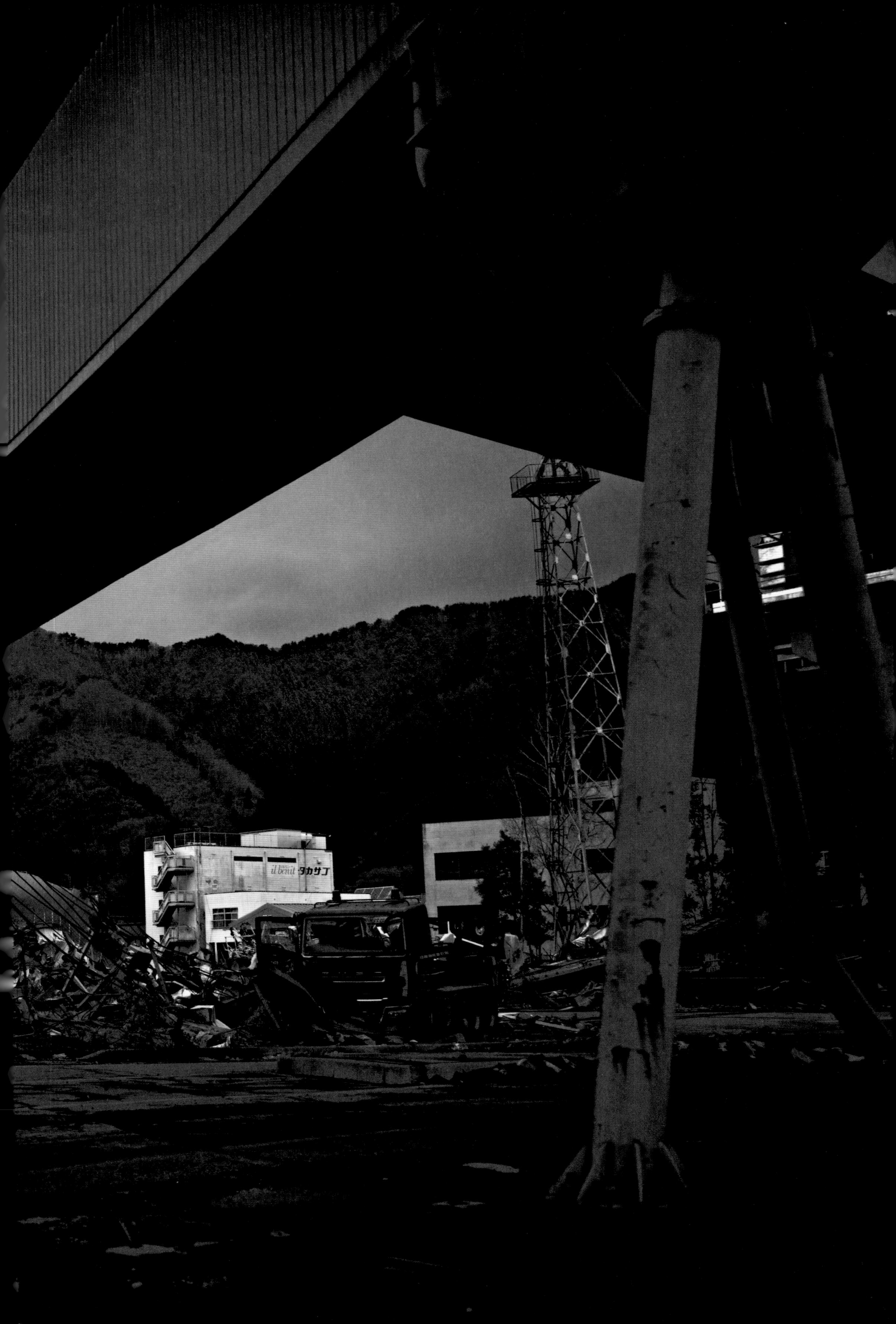
il benit タカサゴ

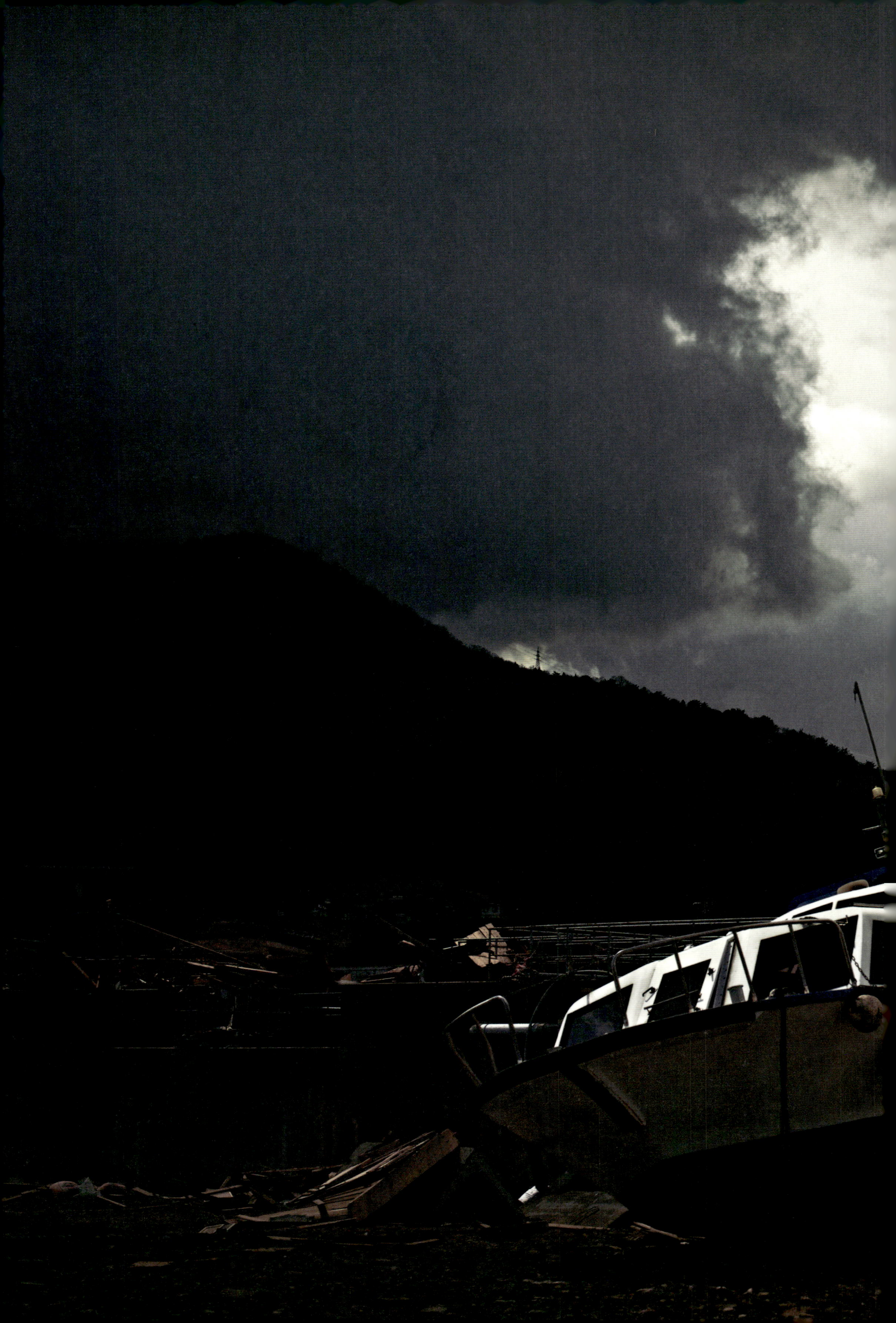

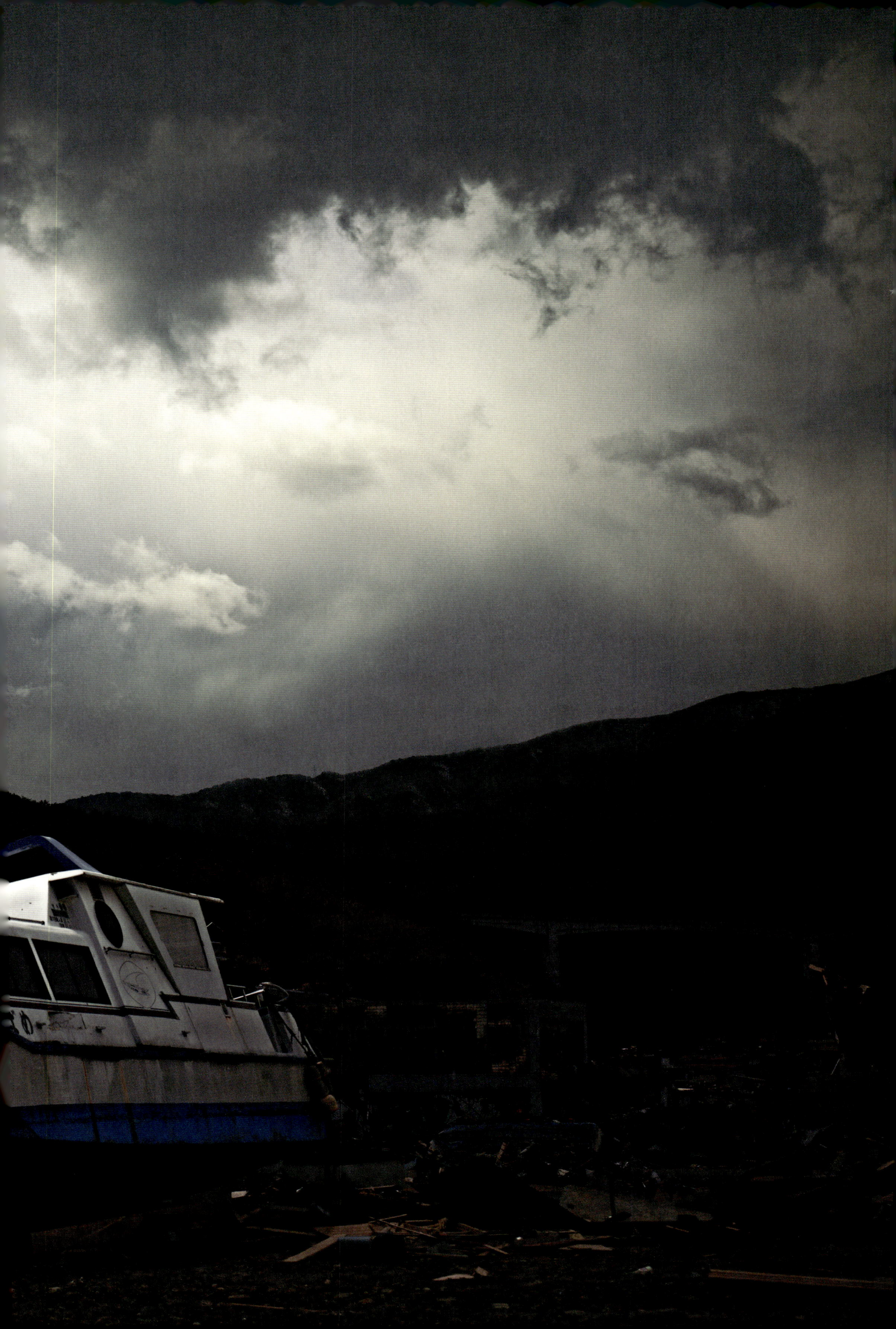

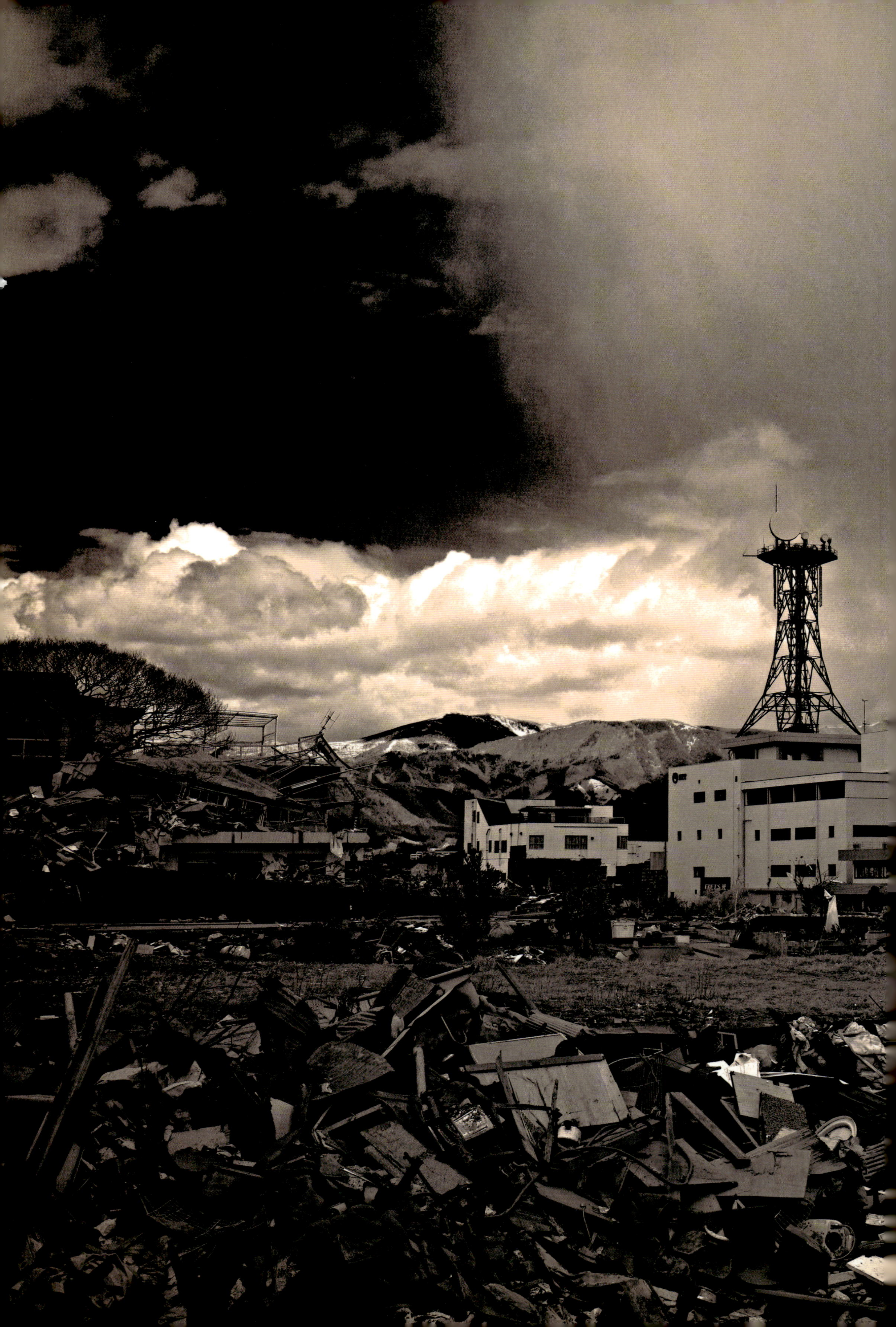

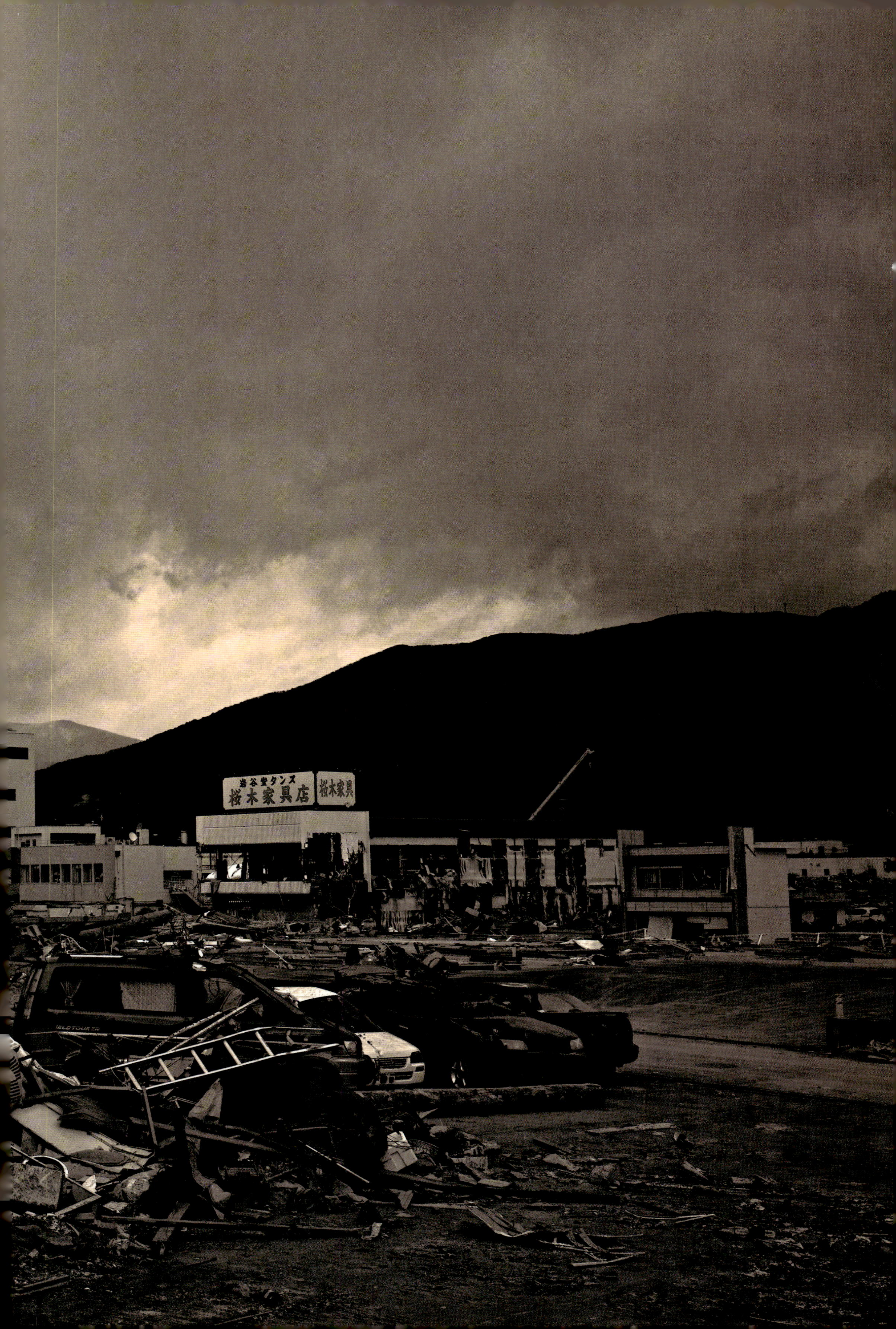
岩谷堂タンス
桜木家具店
桜木家具

Underwater sea walls tossed up from the tsunami.
City of Ofunato, Iwate prefecture

Pages 116-117. City of Ofunato, Iwate prefecture

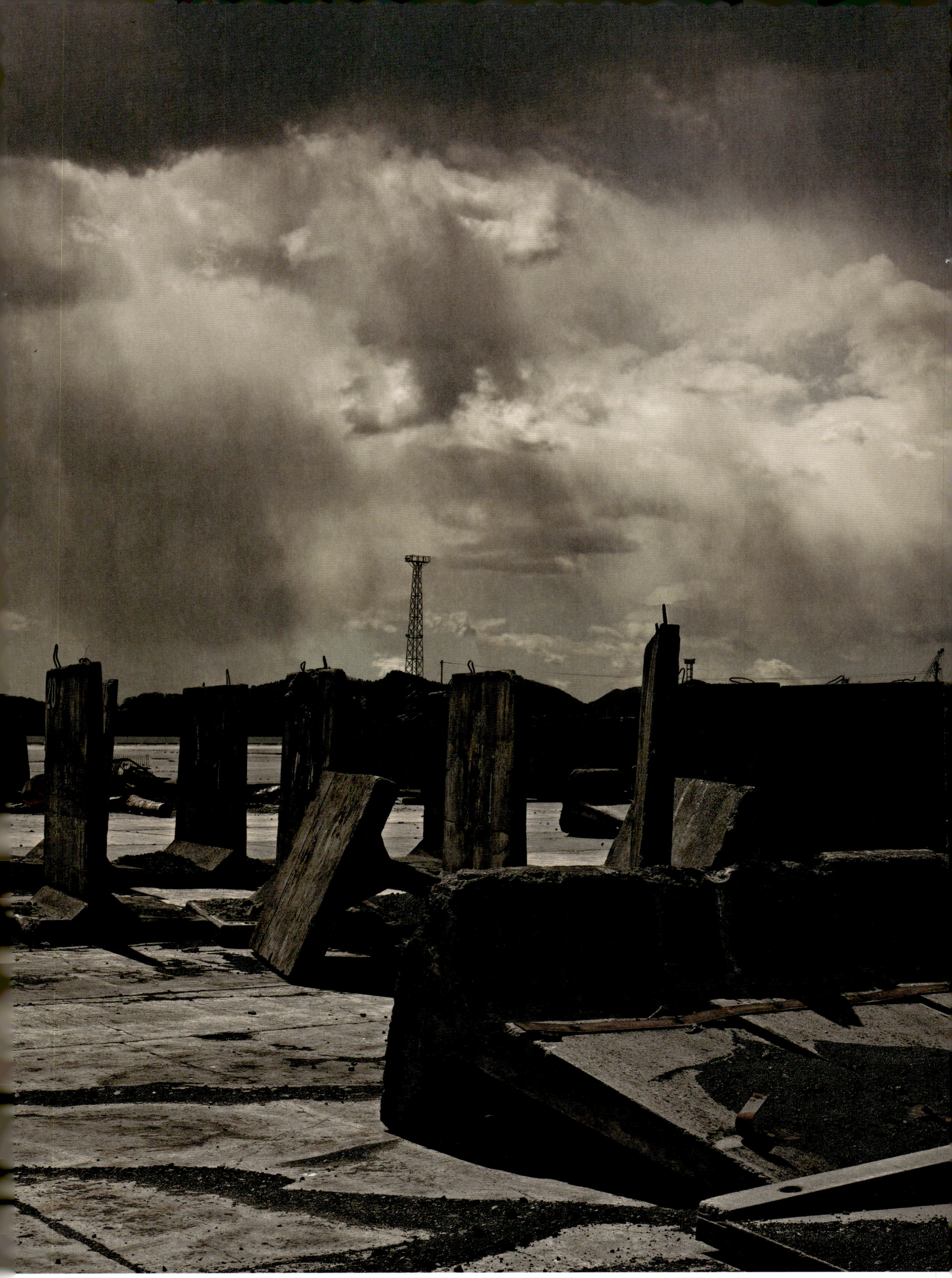

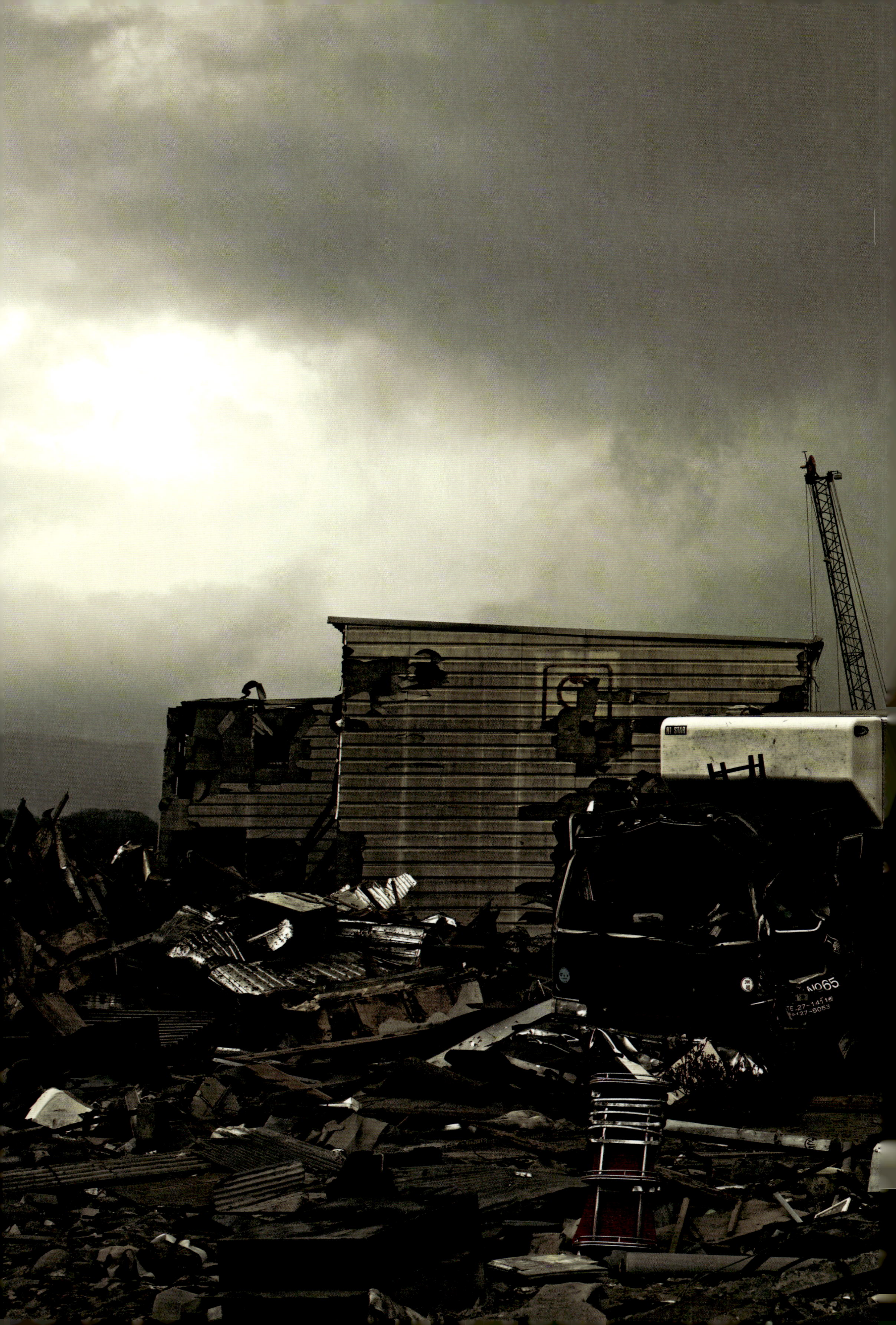
HI STAR
NO65

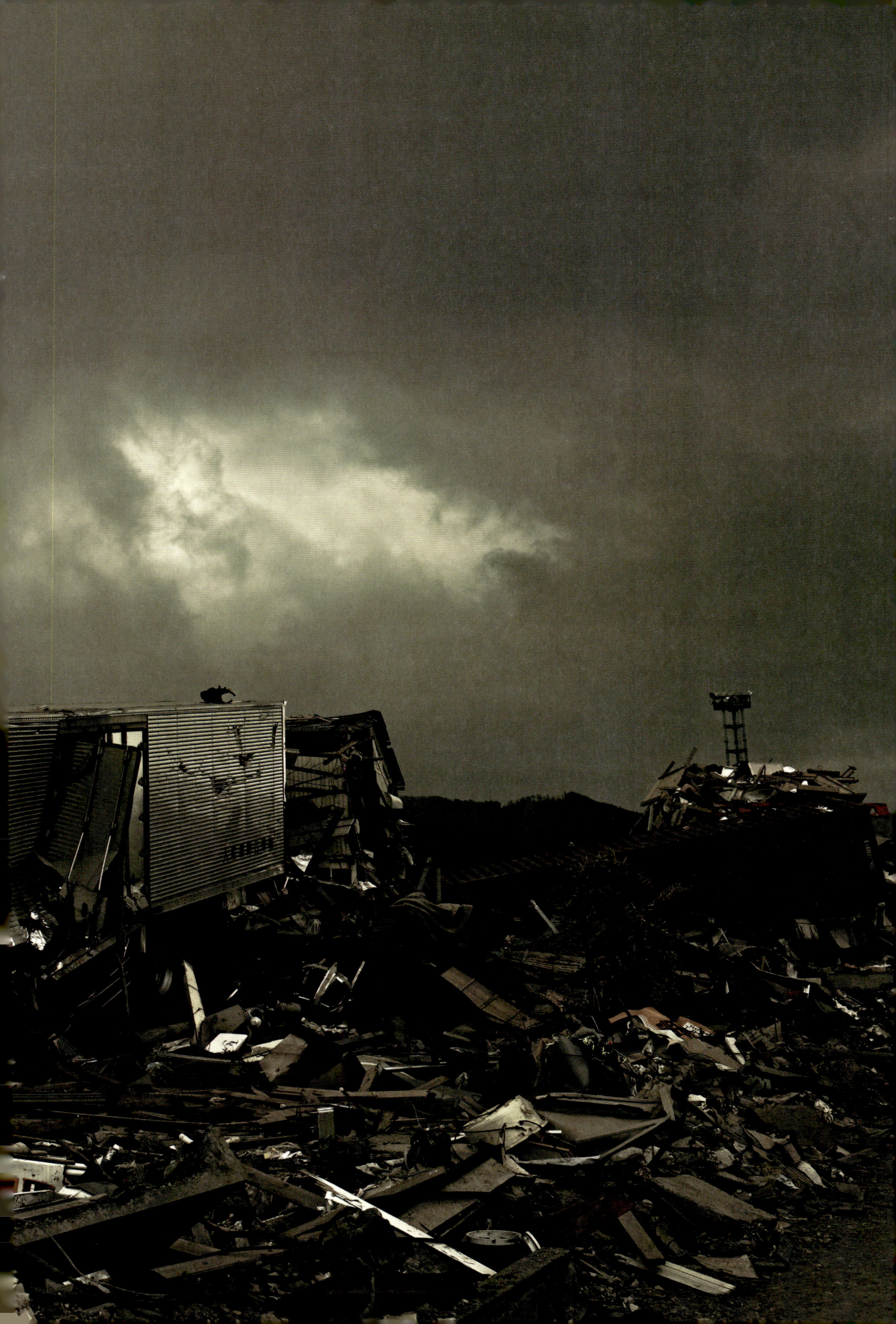

This river turned black from ocean sludge.
City of Ofunato, Iwate prefecture

Pages 120-121. The shopping district.
City of Ofunato, Iwate prefecture

Pages 122-123. Military transports in the center of town.
City of Ofunato, Iwate prefecture

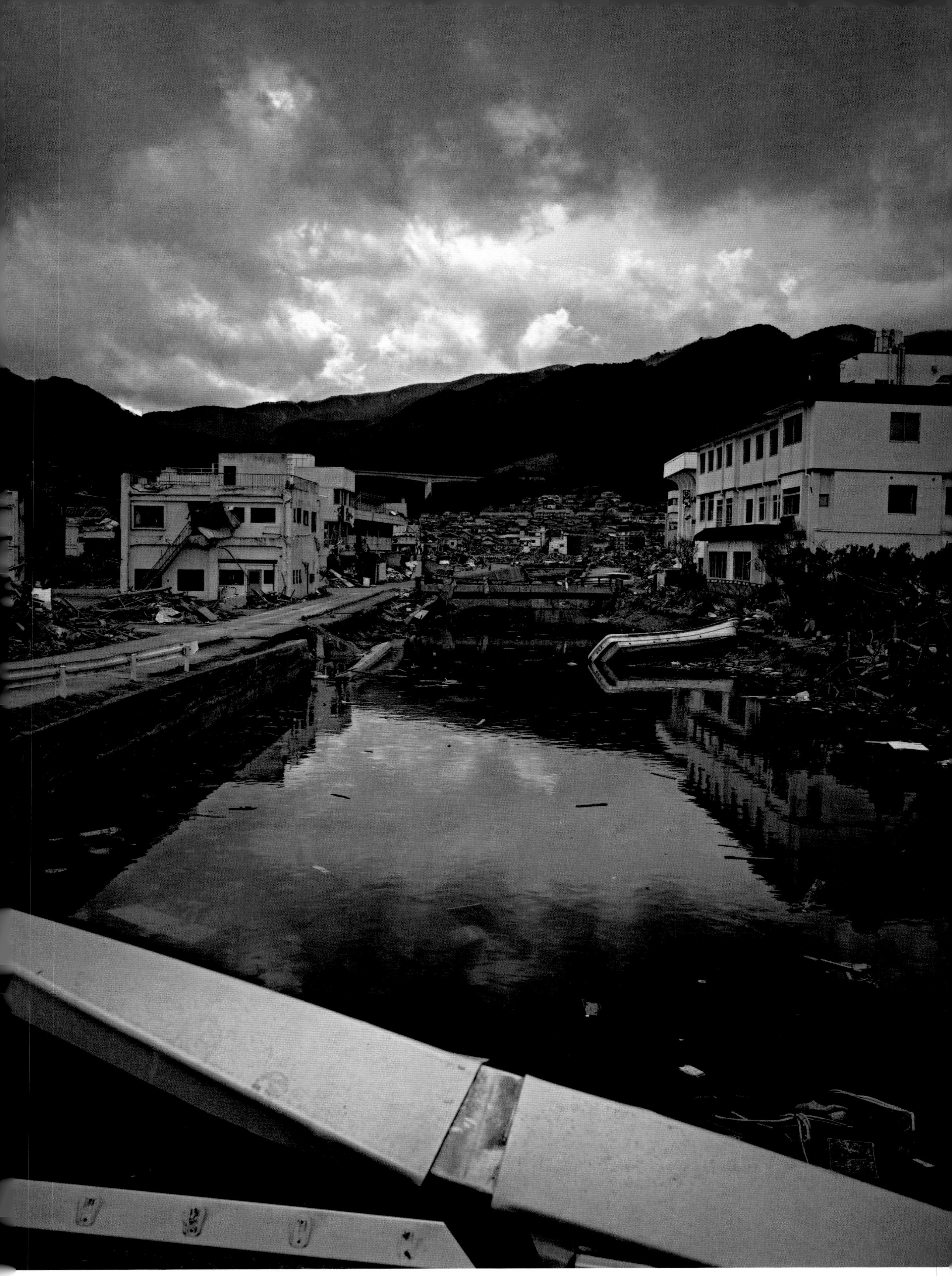

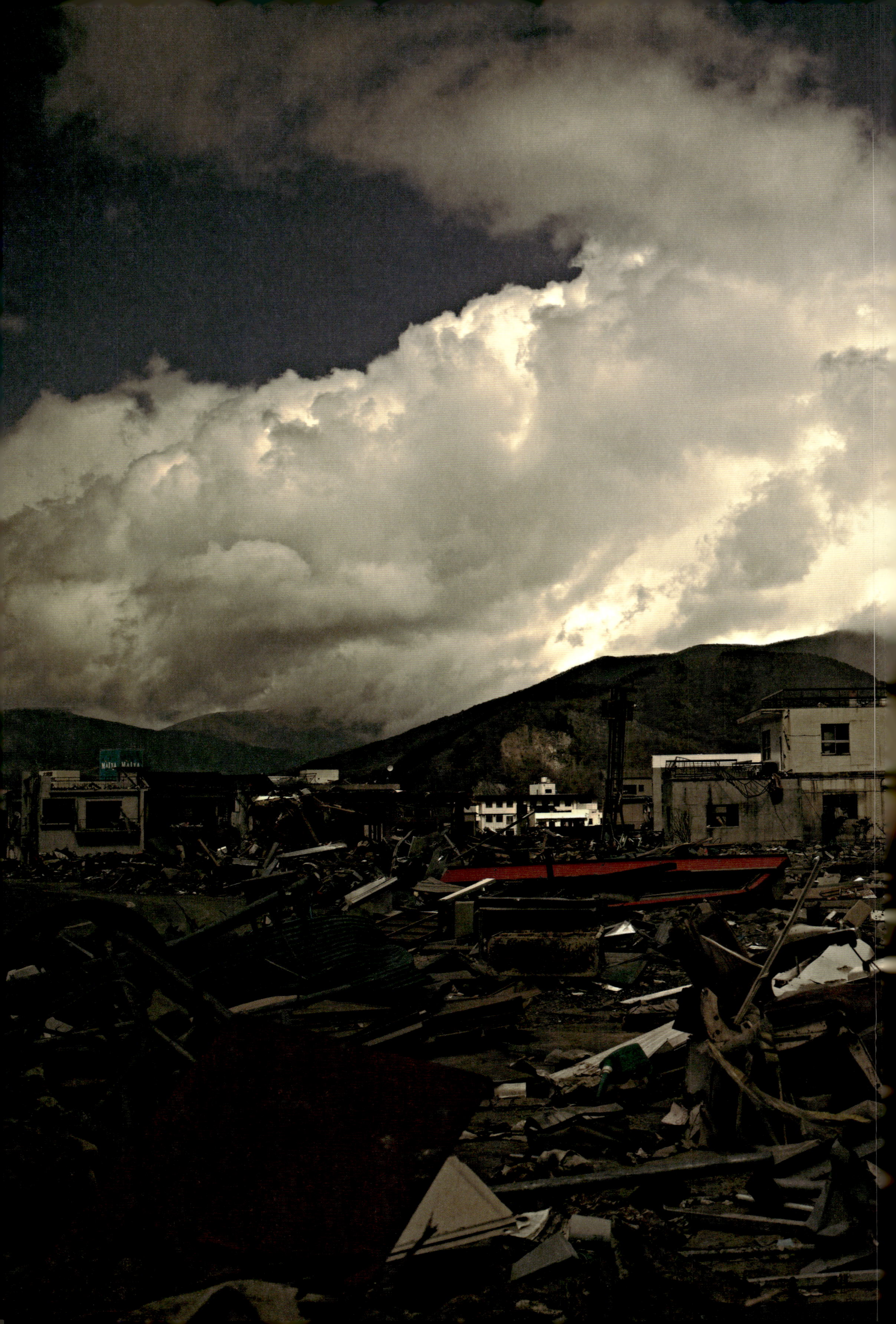
MAIYA MAIYA

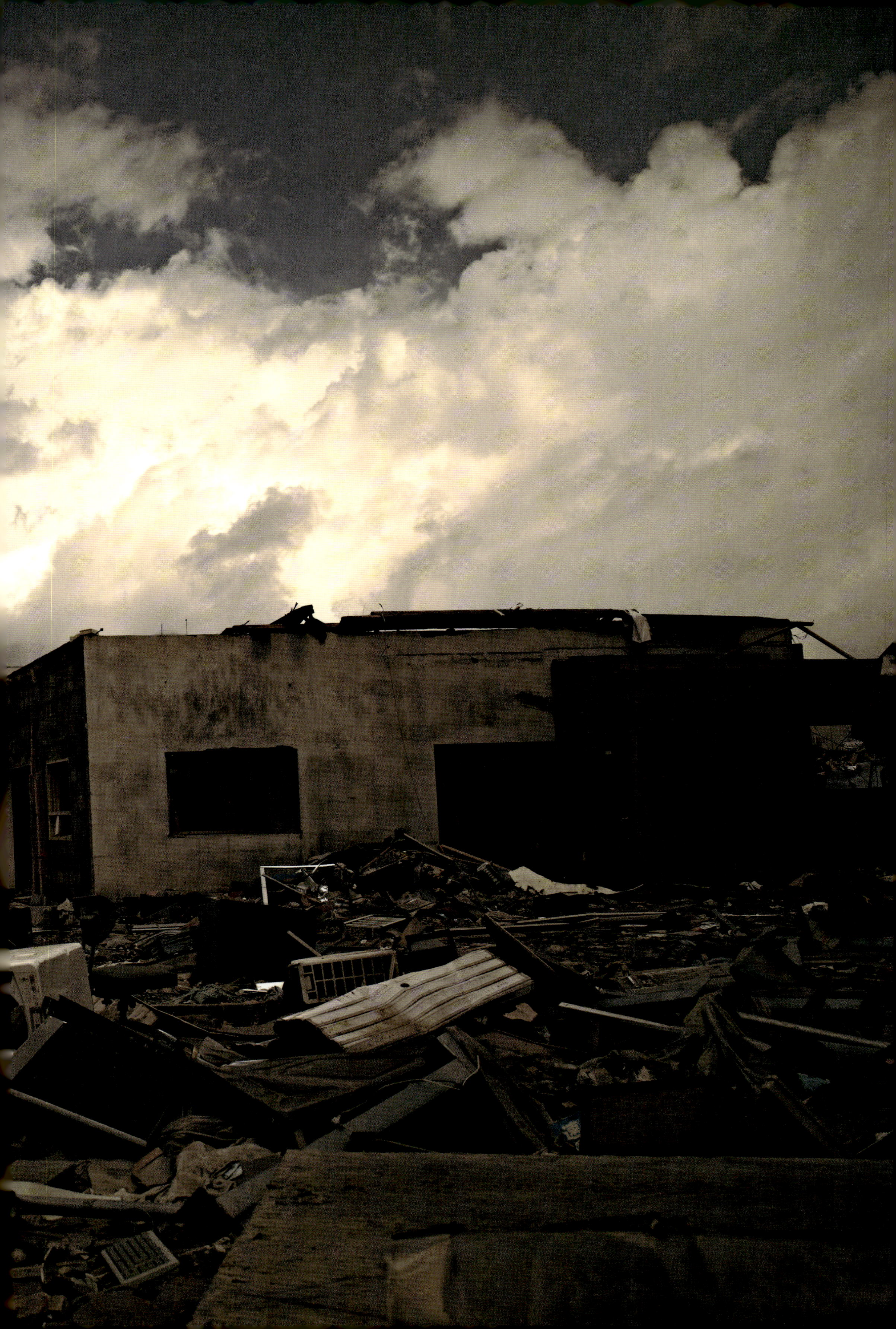

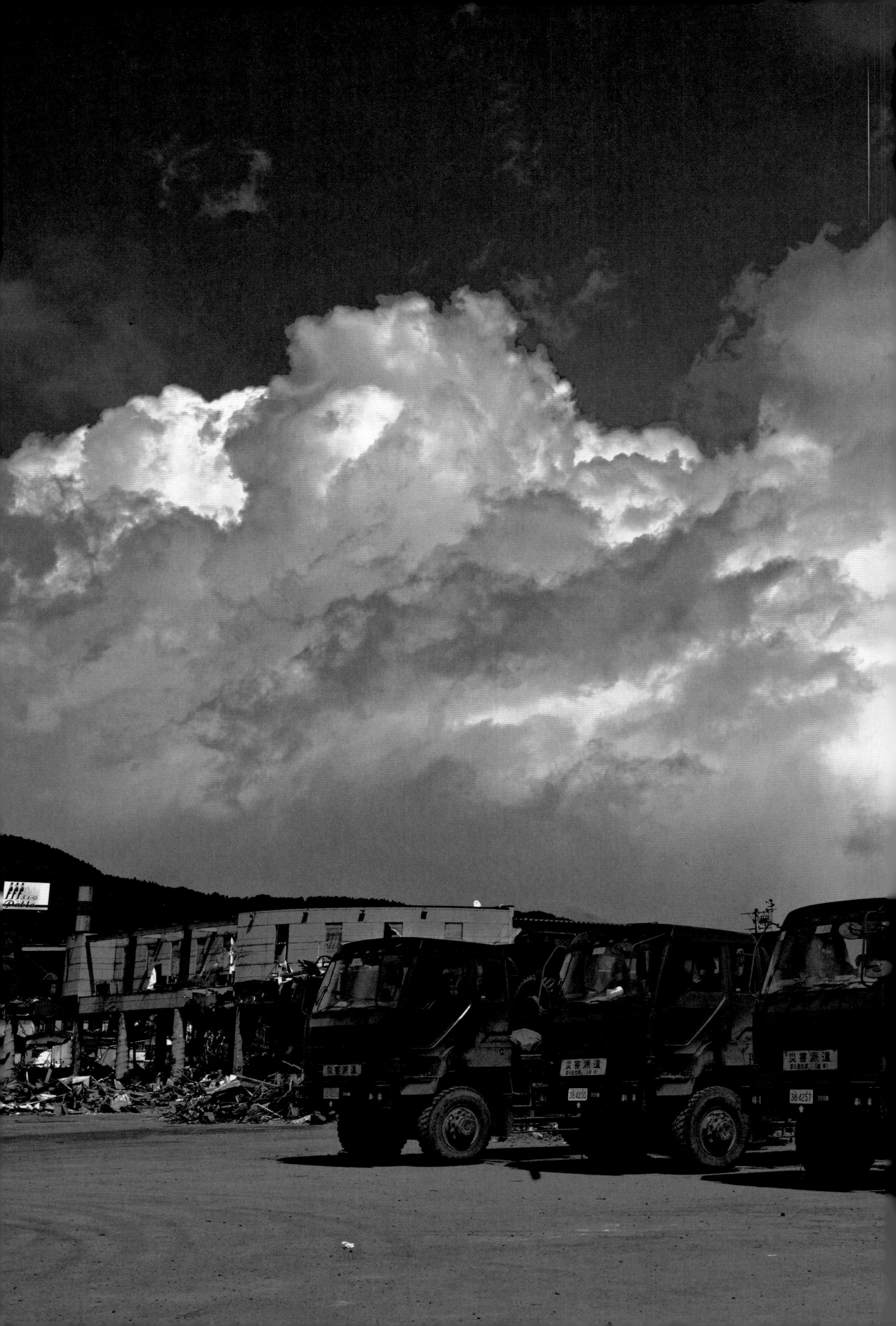
災害派遣
災害派遣
38 4200
災害派遣
38 4257

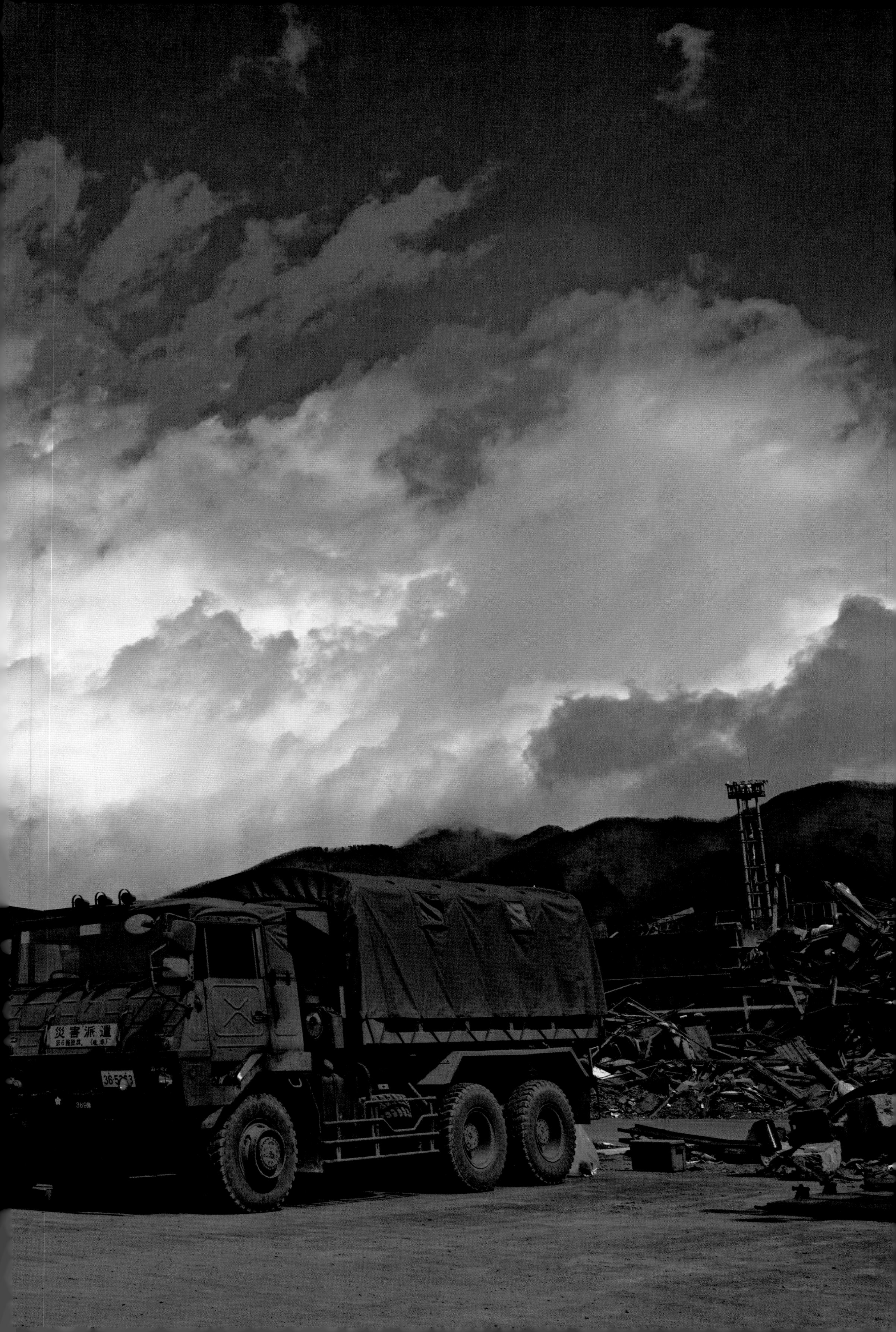
災害派遣

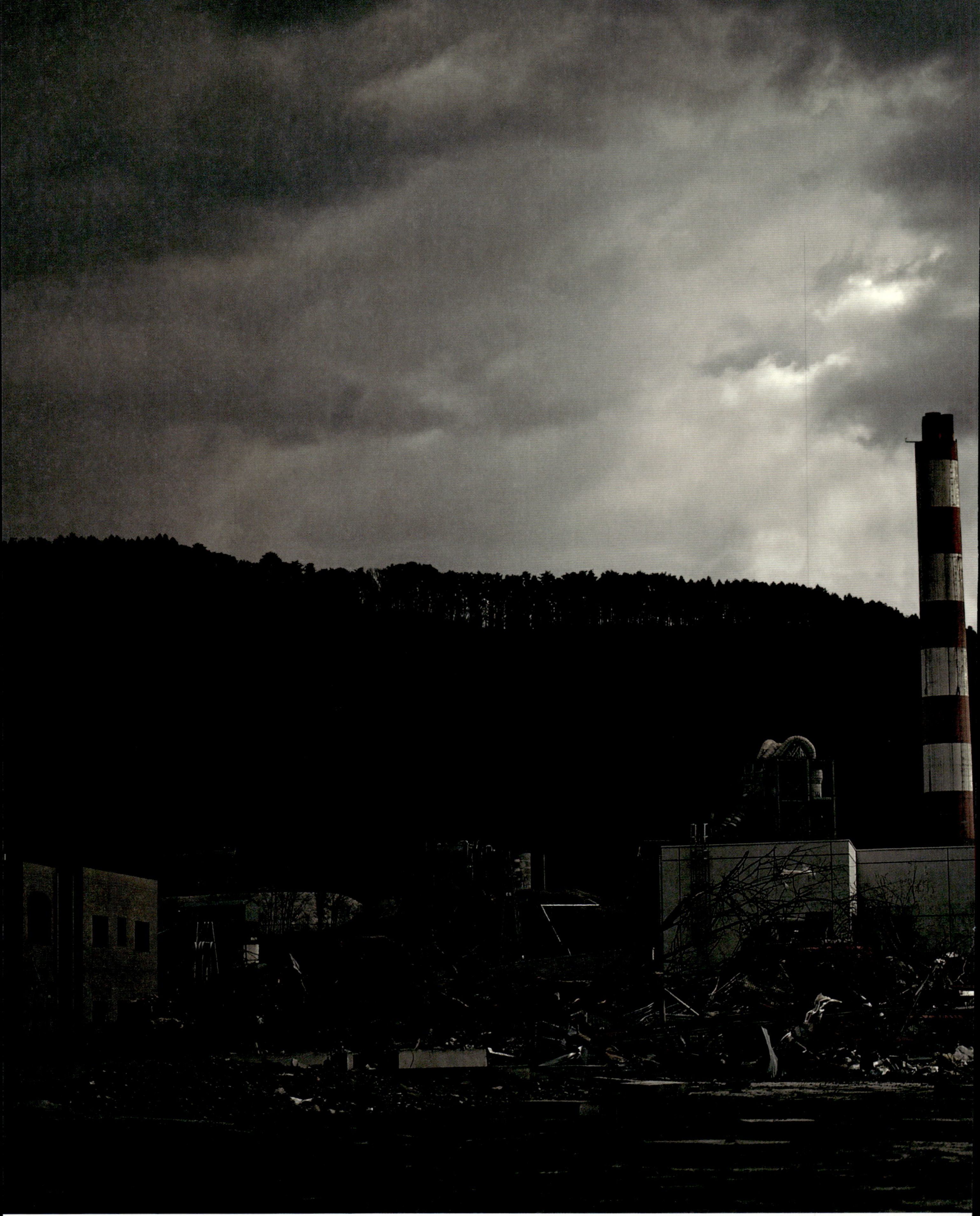

City of Ofunato, Iwate prefecture

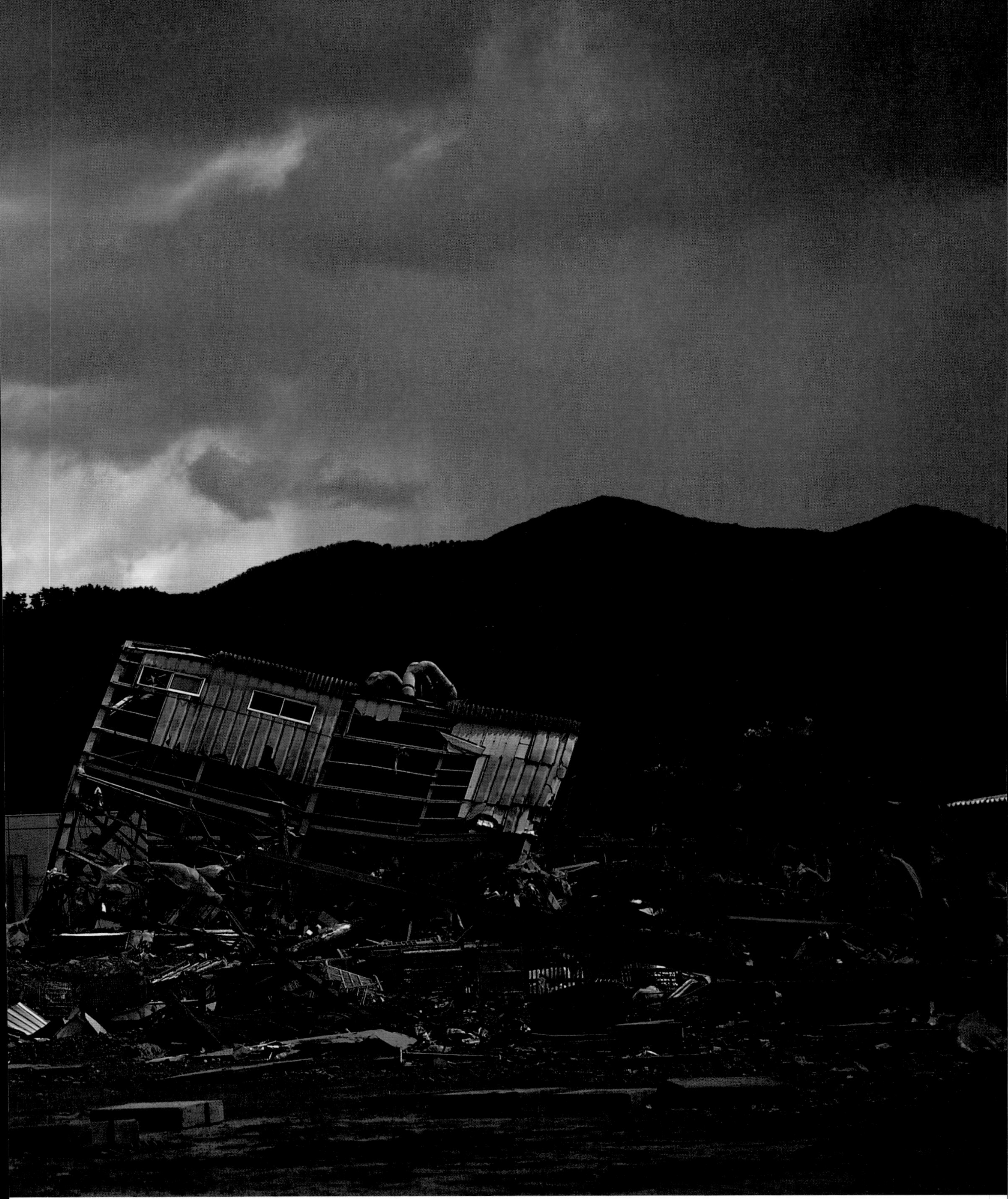

A truck and a building.
City of Rikuzen Takata, Iwate prefecture

Pages 128-129. The city center marked by small posts demarcating where corpses were located.
City of Rikuzen Takata, Iwate prefecture

Pages 130-131. The devastated city with a spared church in the background.
City of Kesennuma, Miyagi prefecture

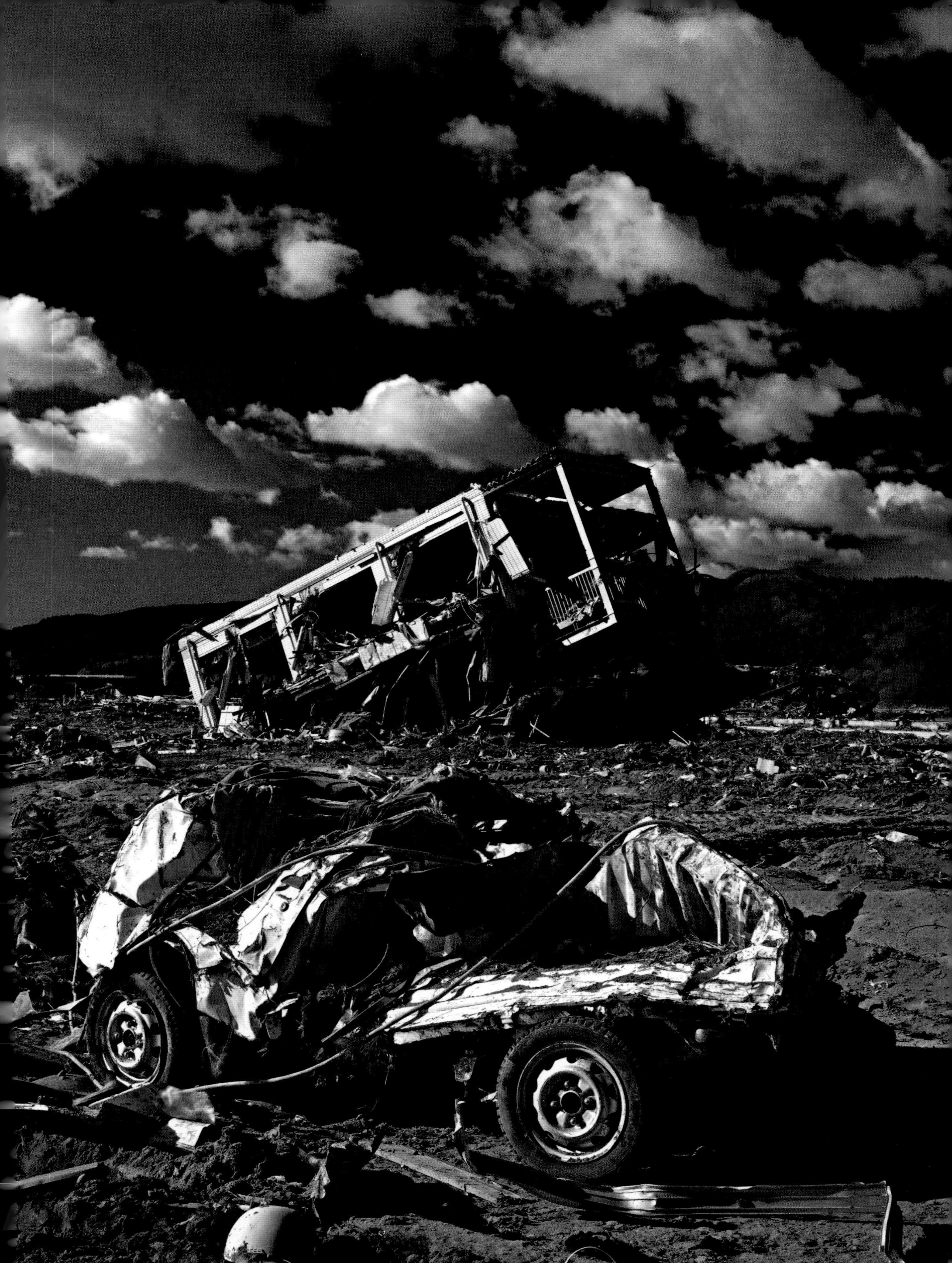

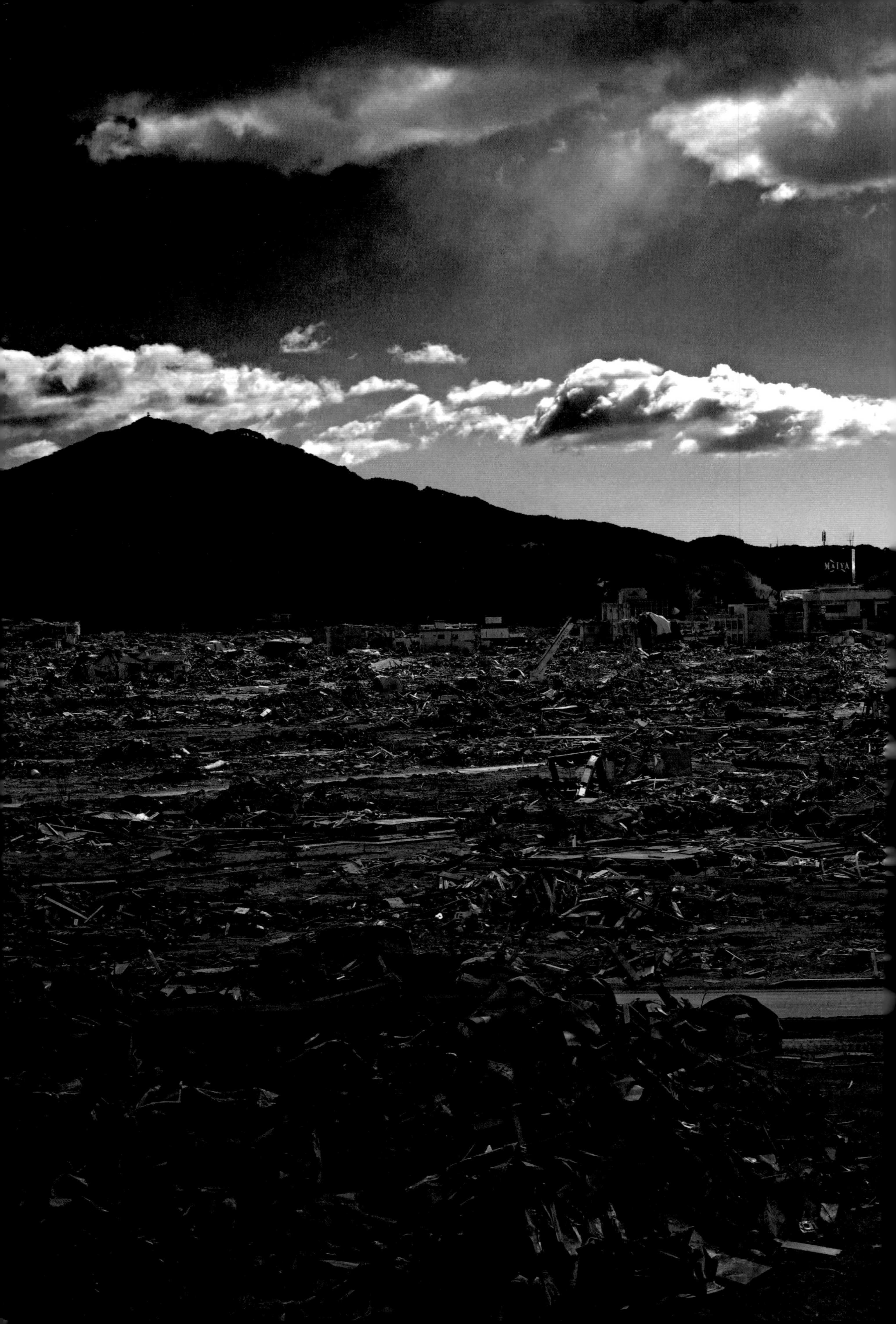
MAIYA

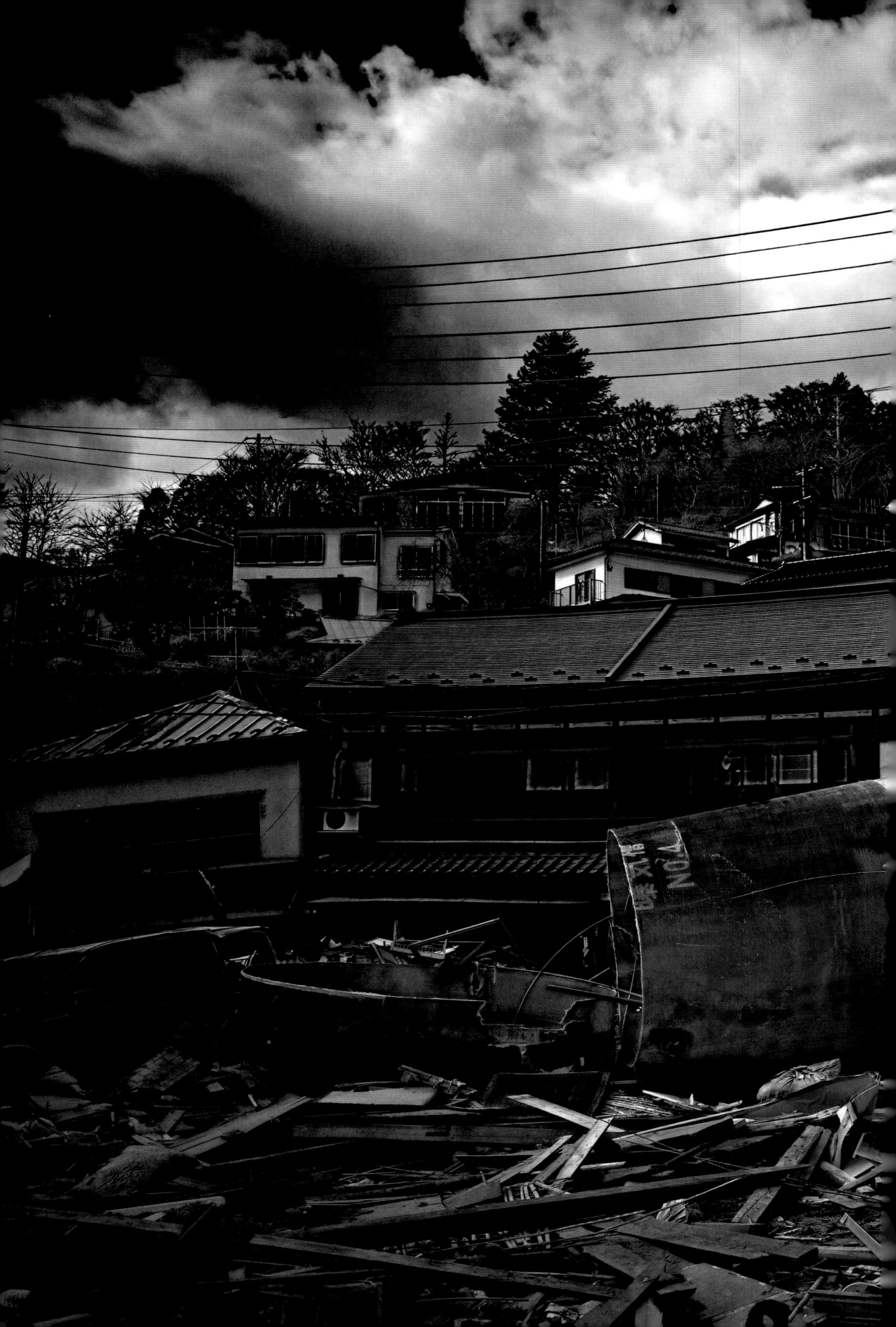
NO.4

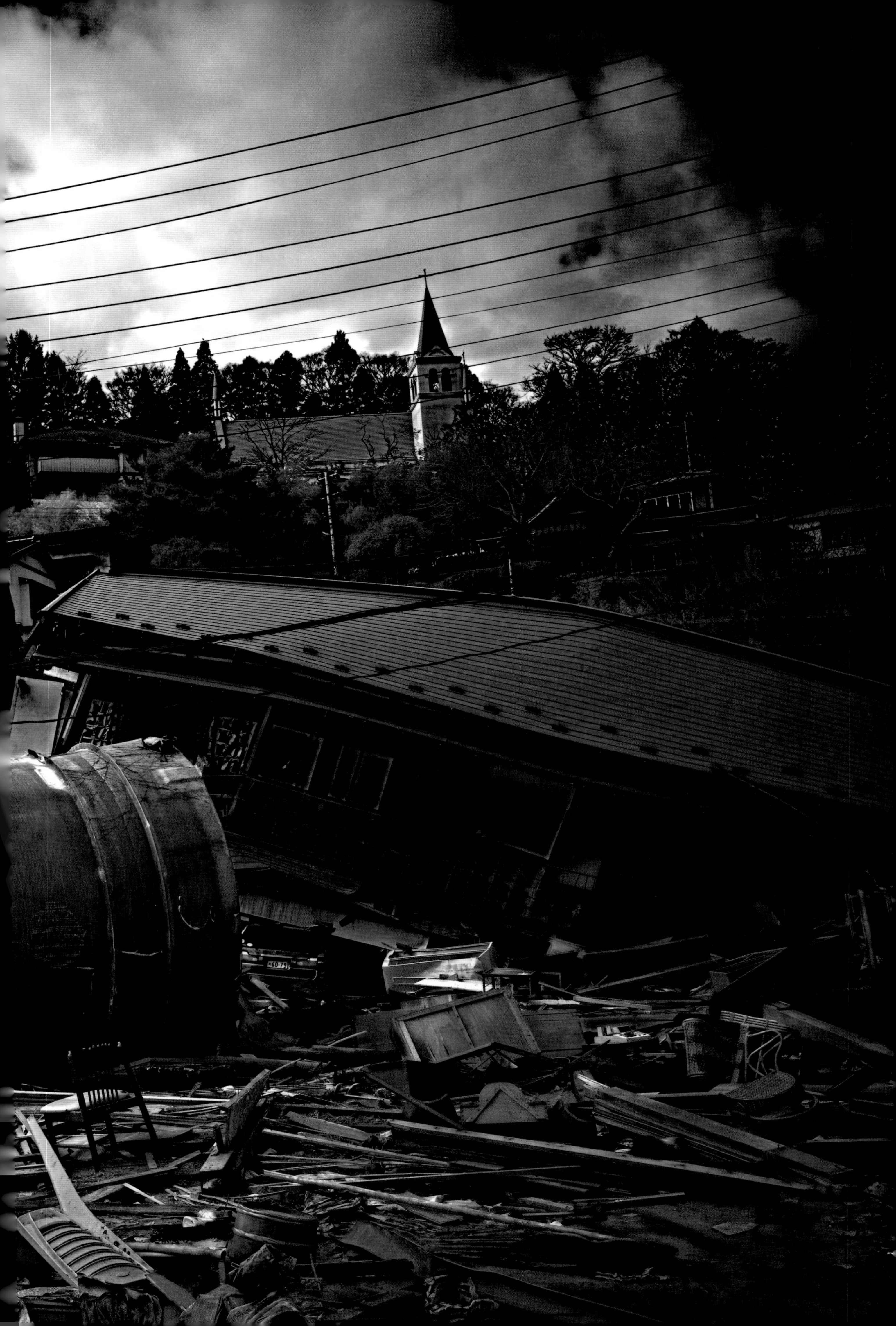

The final borderline of the tsunami.
City of Rikuzen Takata, Iwate prefecture

Pages 134-135. The exposed foundation of a toppled police station.
Onagawa Cho, Ojika County, Miyagi prefecture

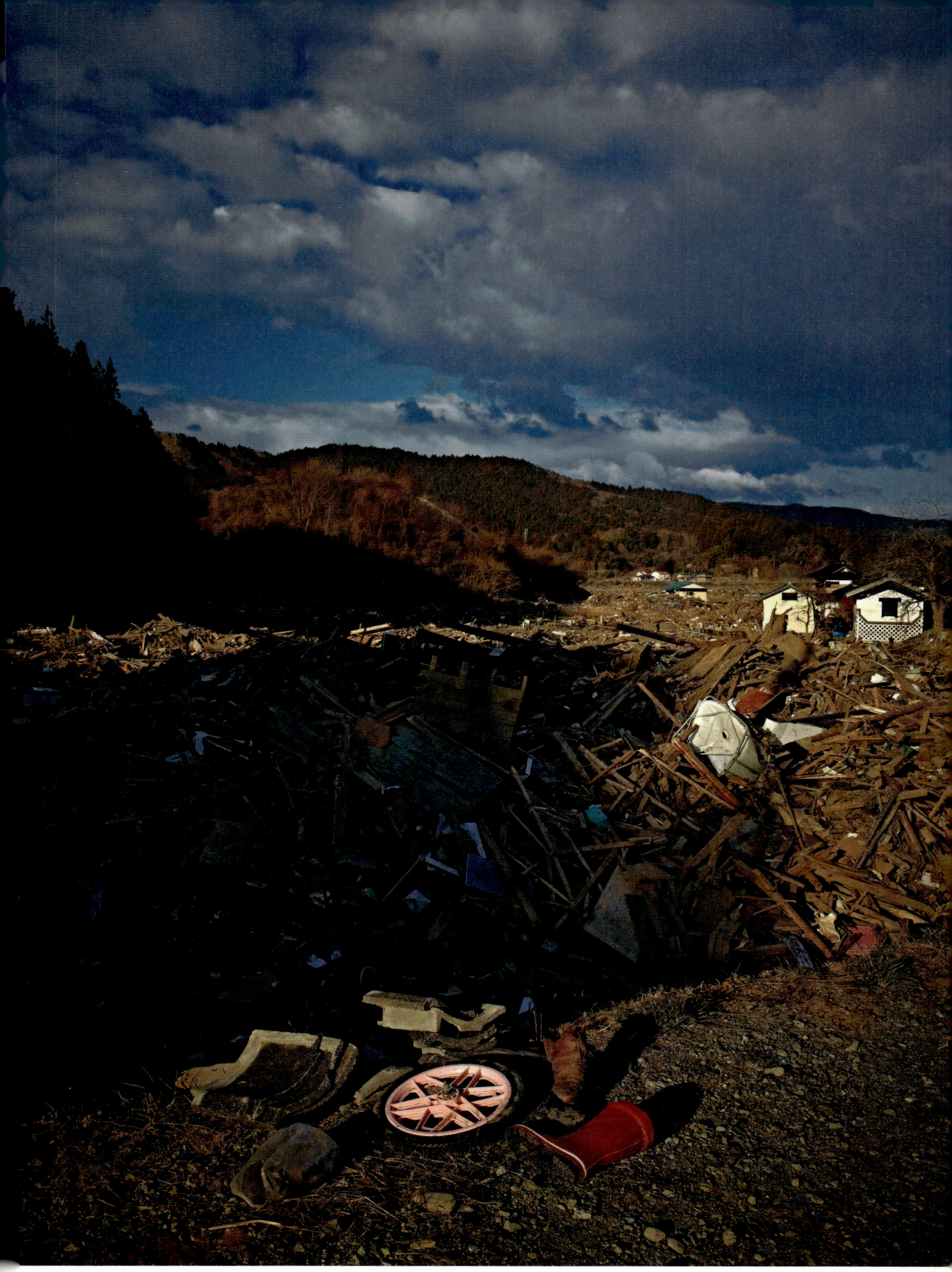

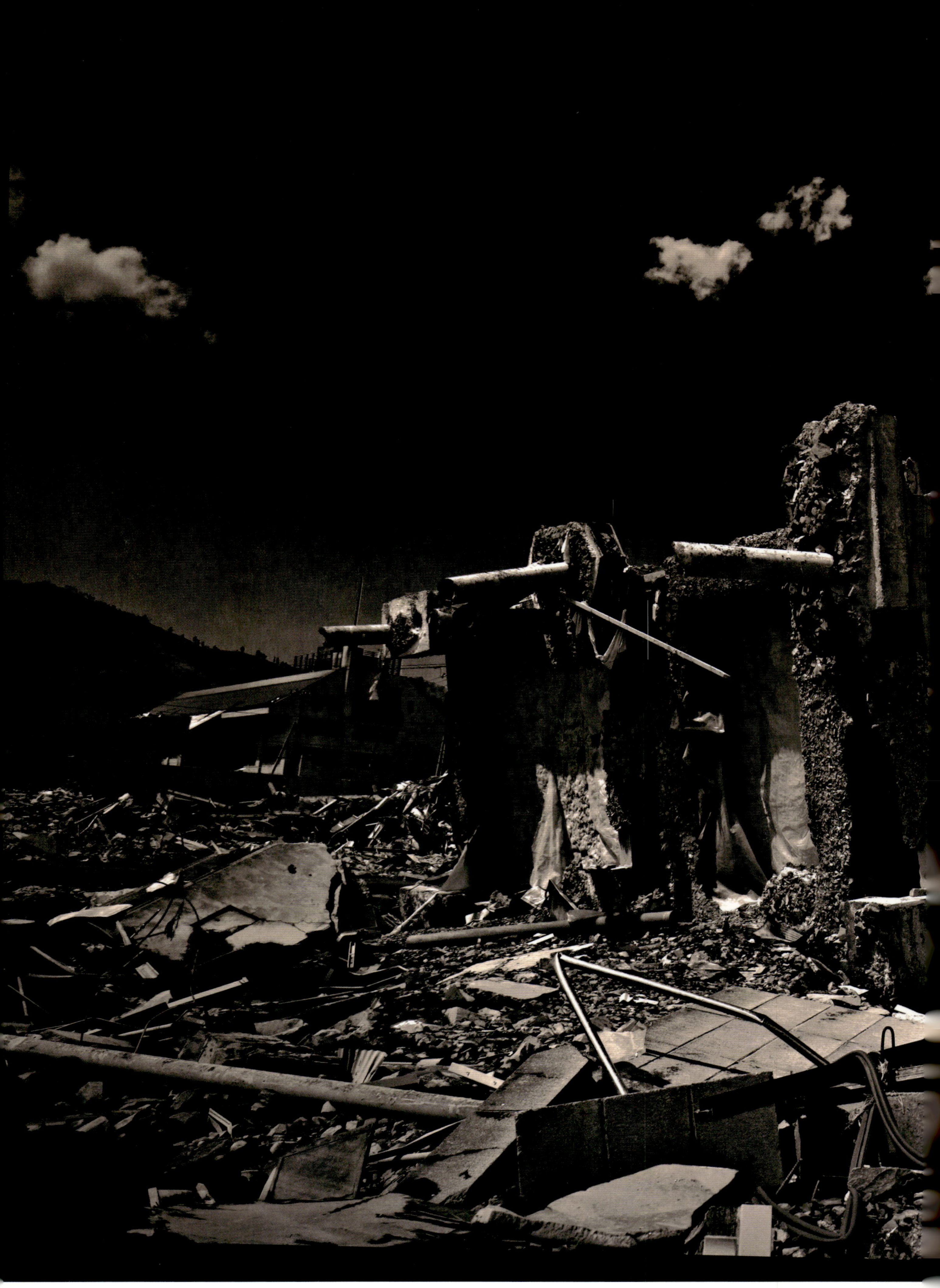

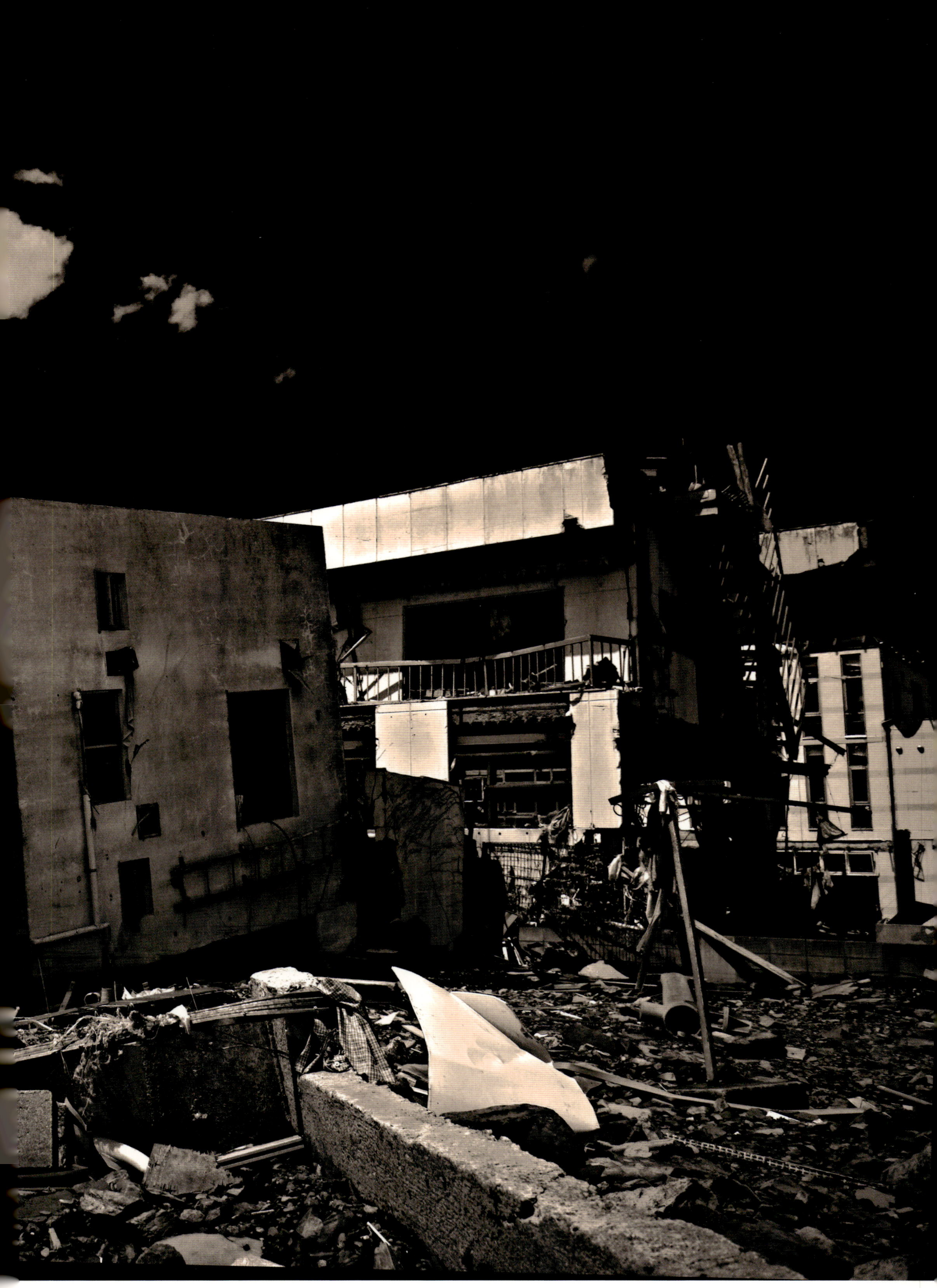

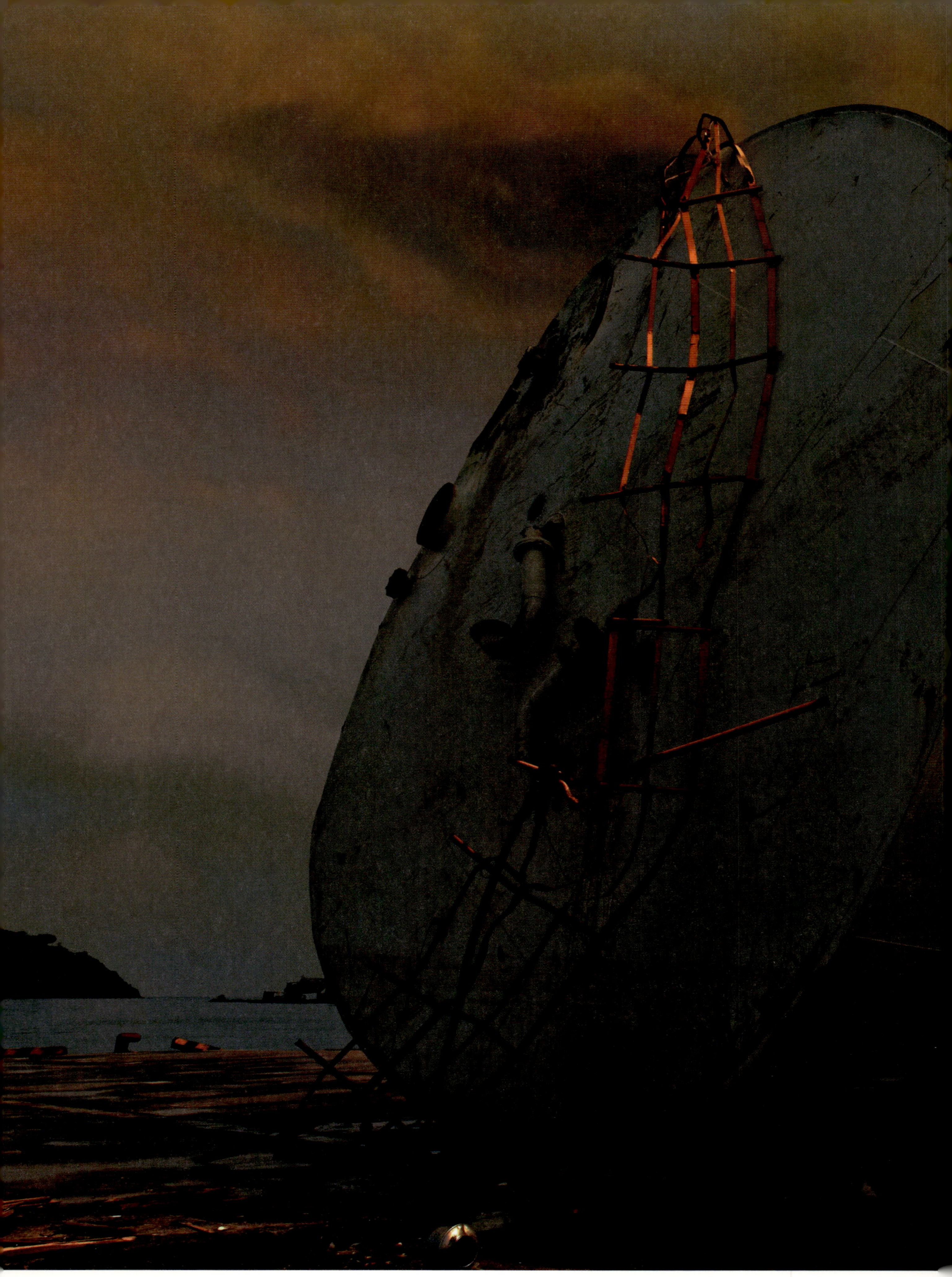

A ship fuel tank.
Onagawa Cho, Ojika County, Miyagi prefecture

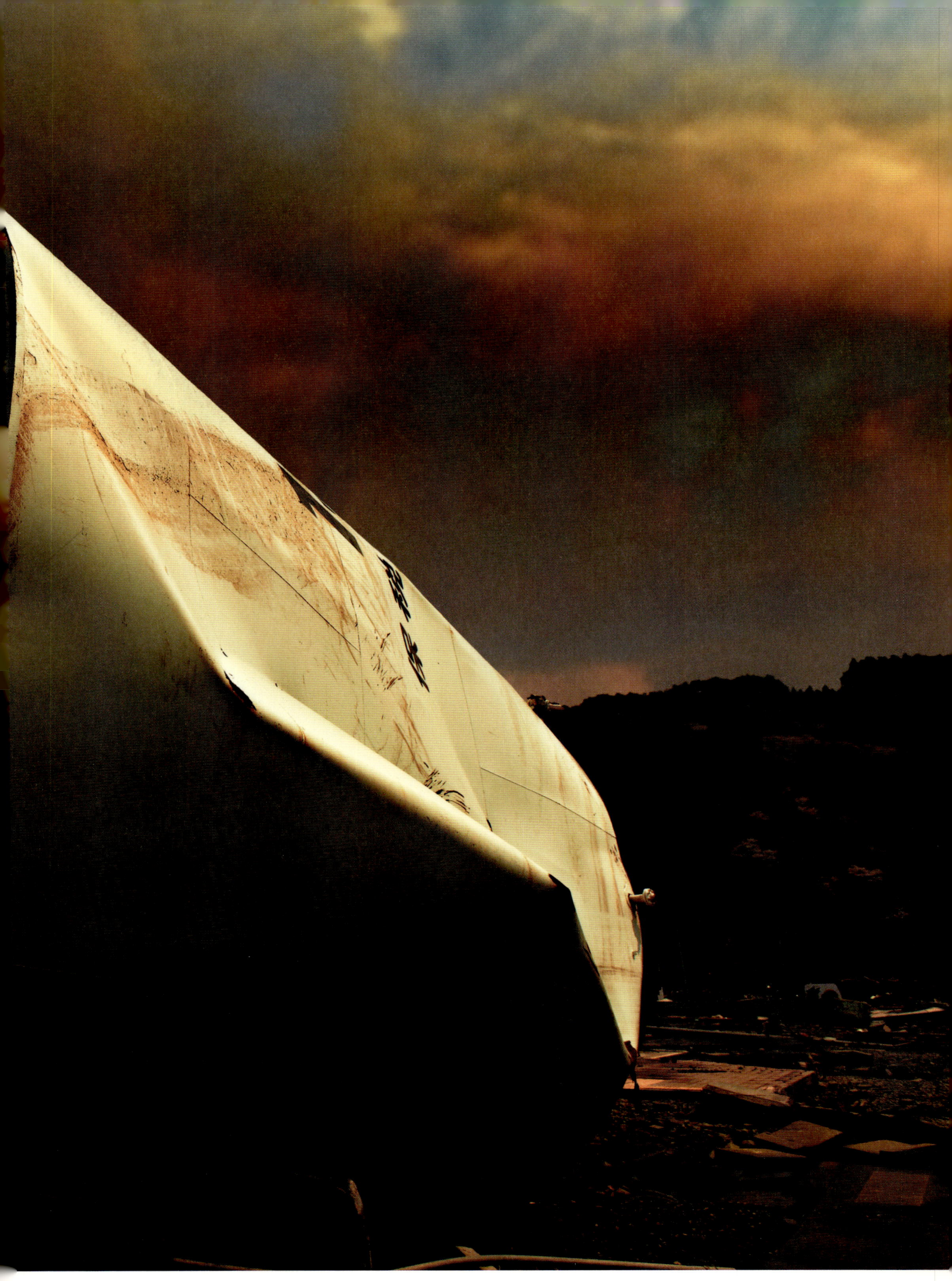

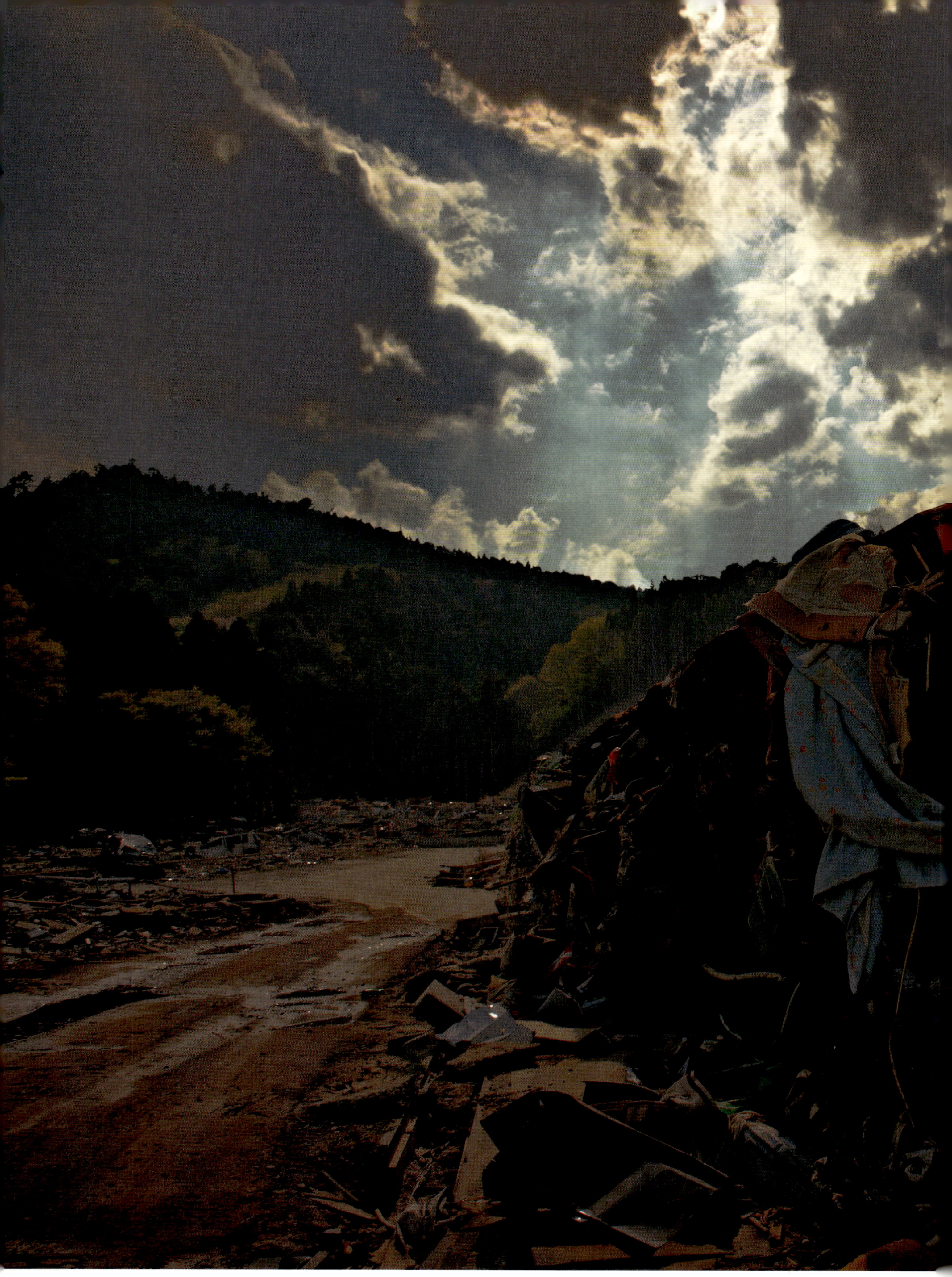

This train is halfway up a mountain.
Onagawa Cho, Ojika County, Miyagi prefecture

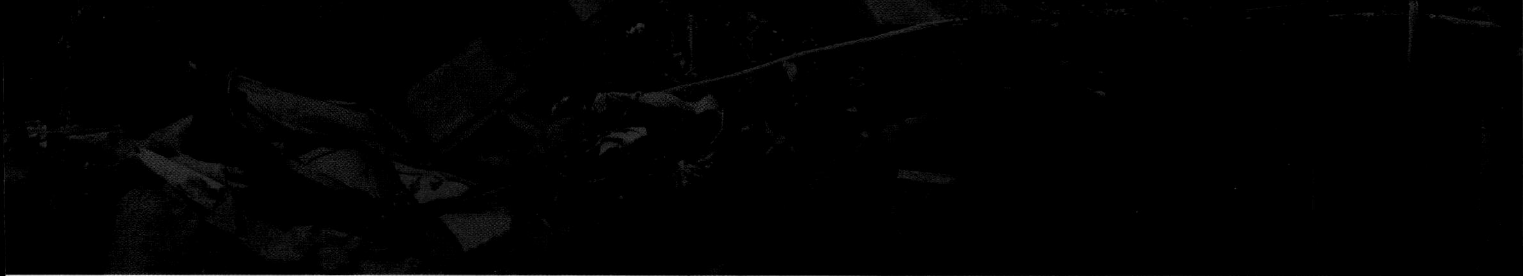

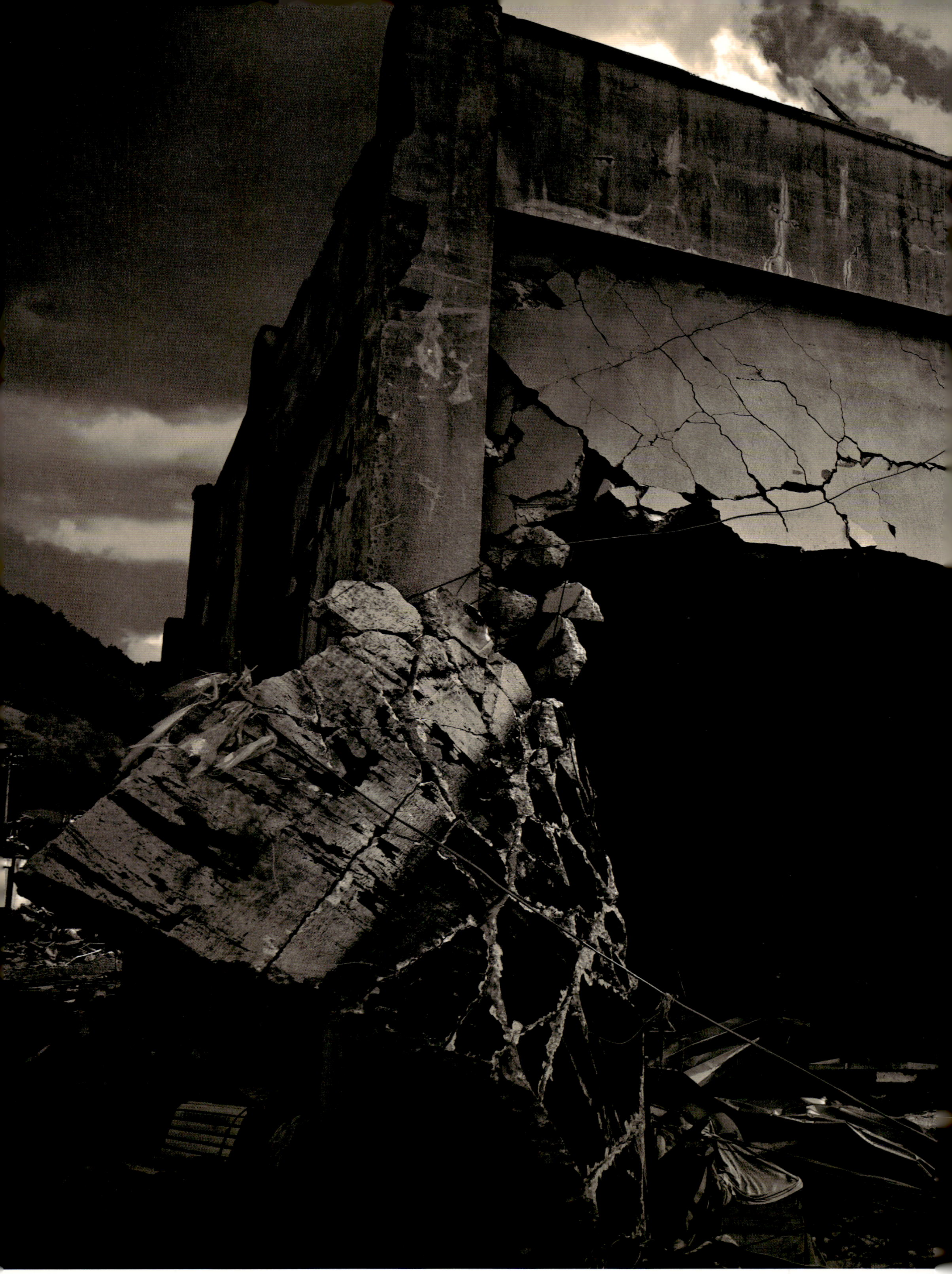

Wave damage to 50 cm thick concrete.
Onagawa Cho, Ojika County, Miyagi prefecture

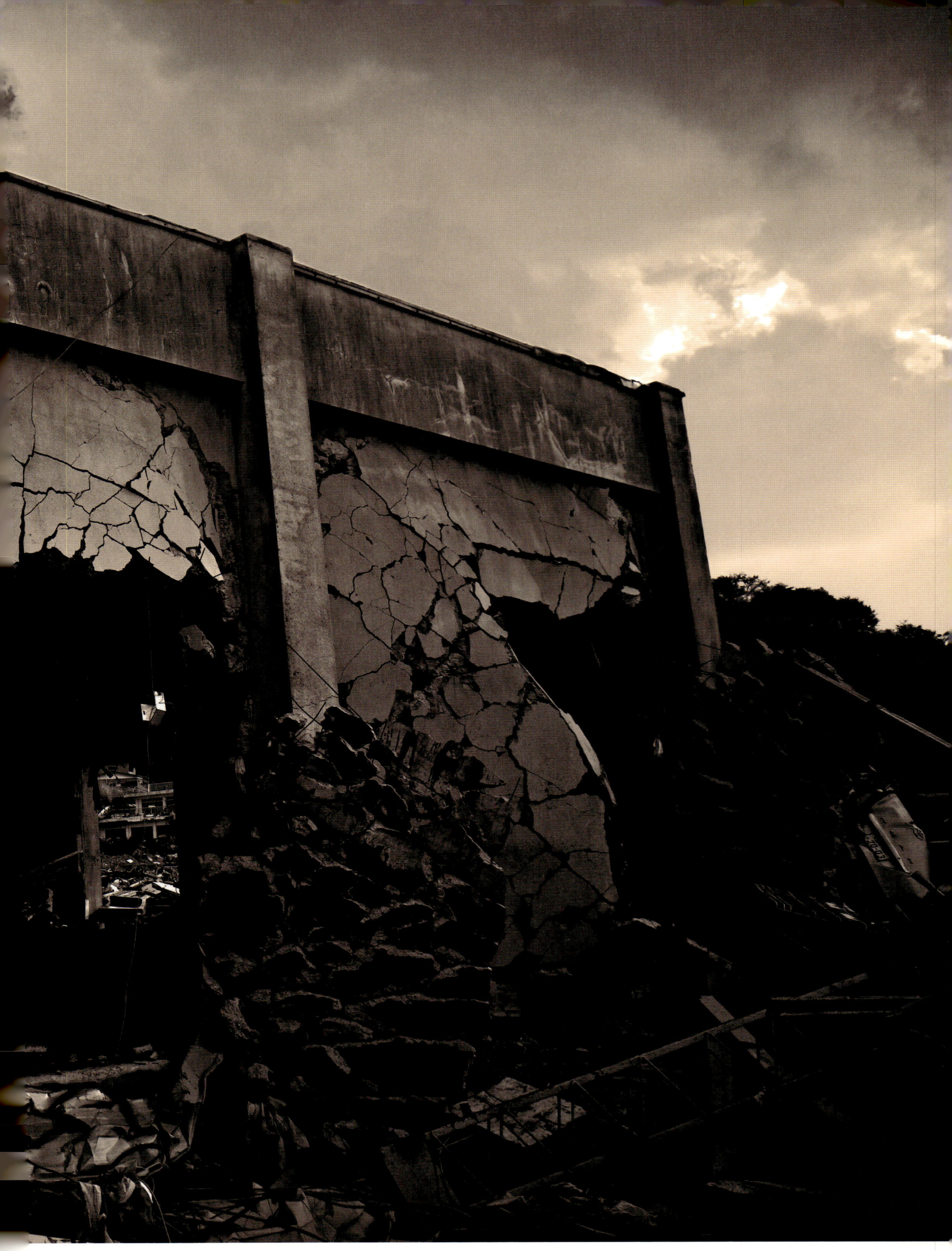

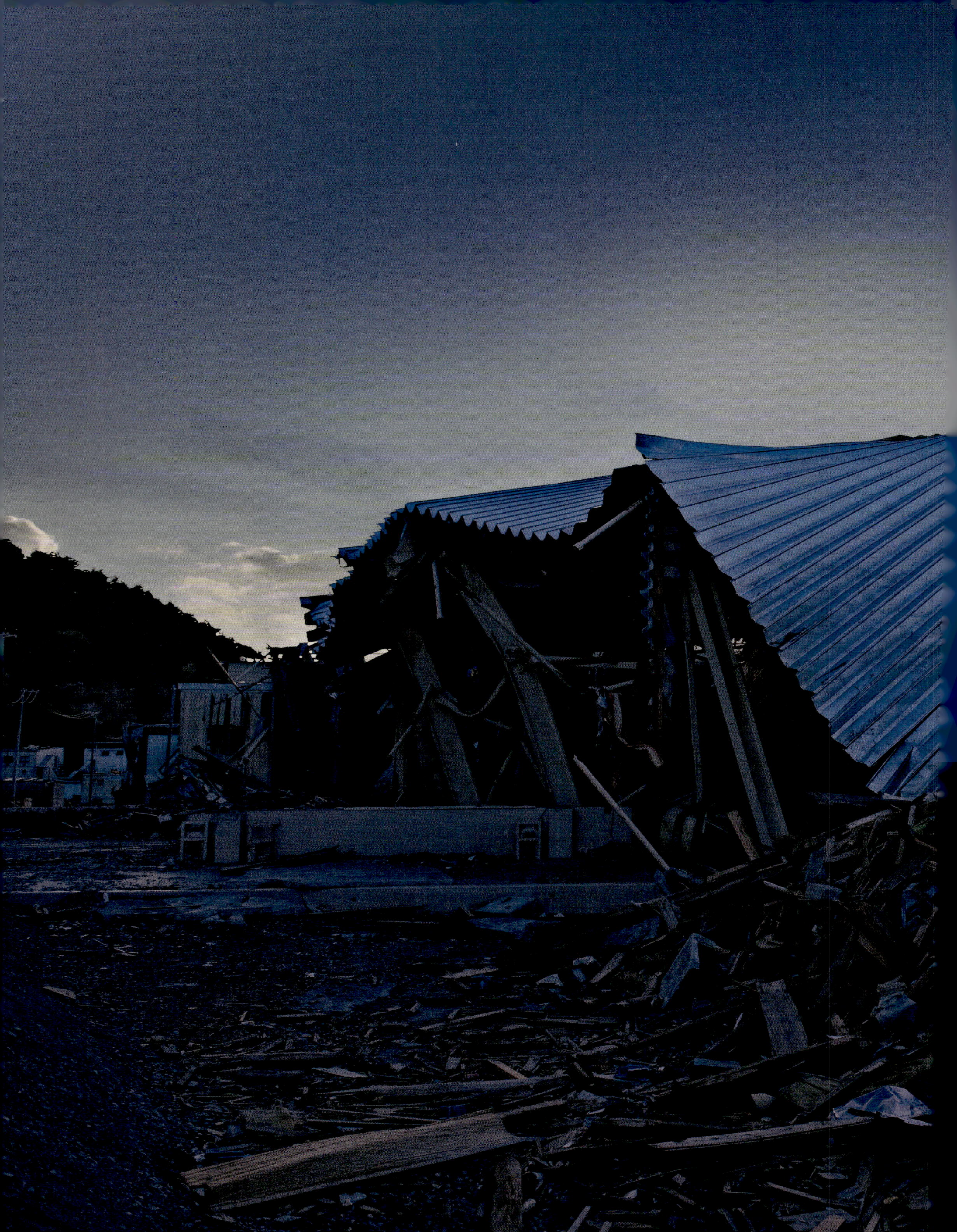

A factory.
Onagawa Cho, Ojika County, Miyagi prefecture

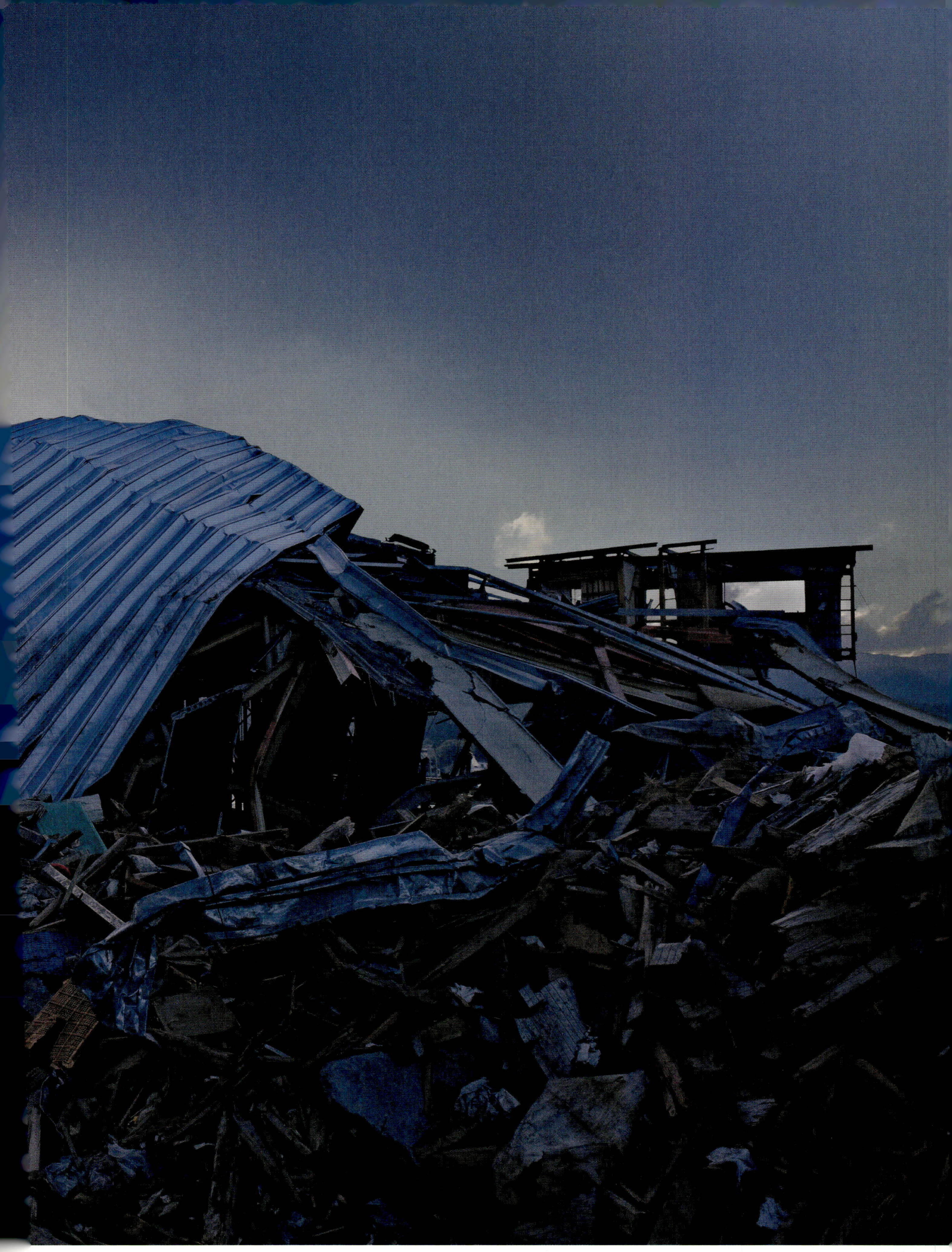

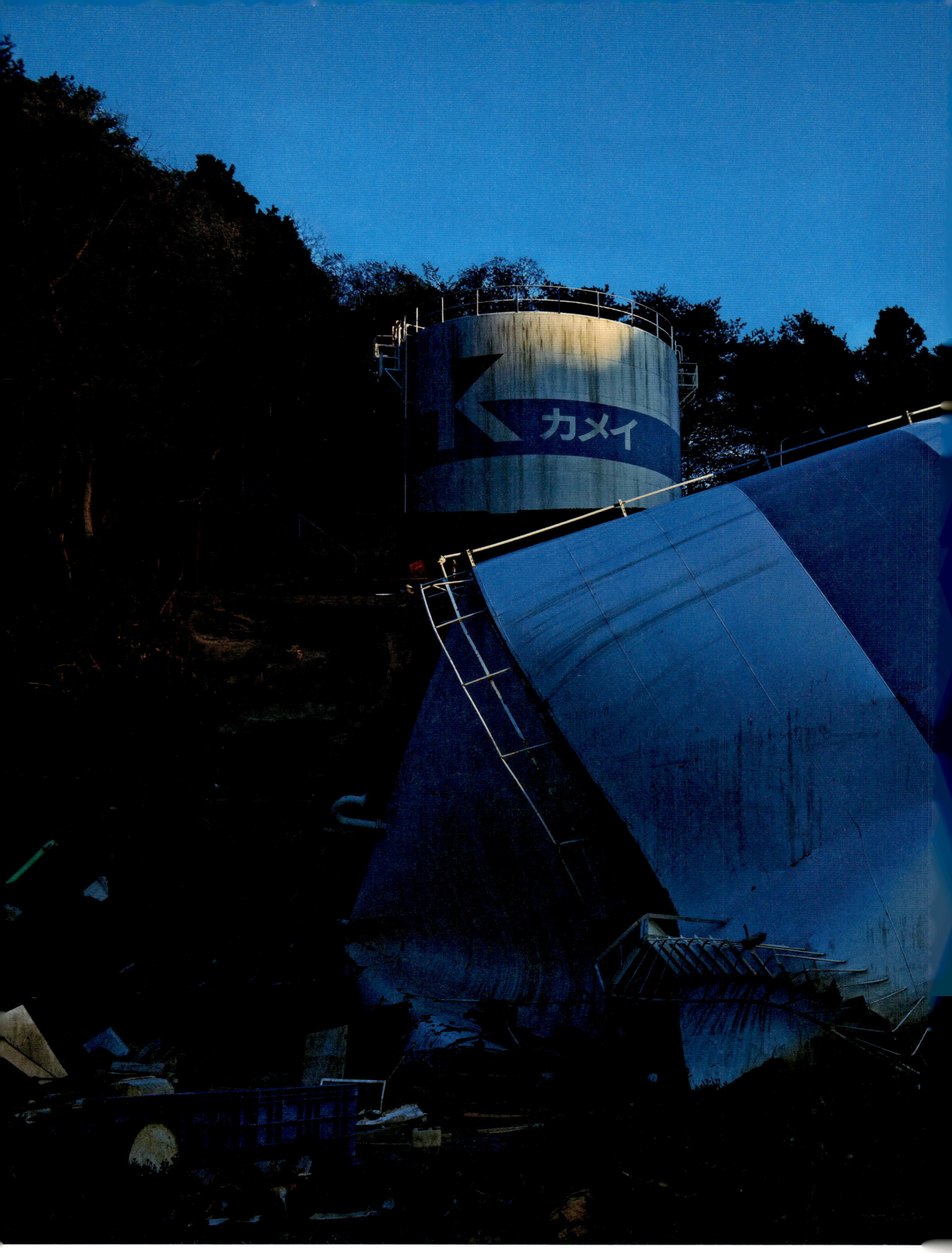

Ship refueling tanks.
Onagawa Cho, Ojika County, Miyagi prefecture

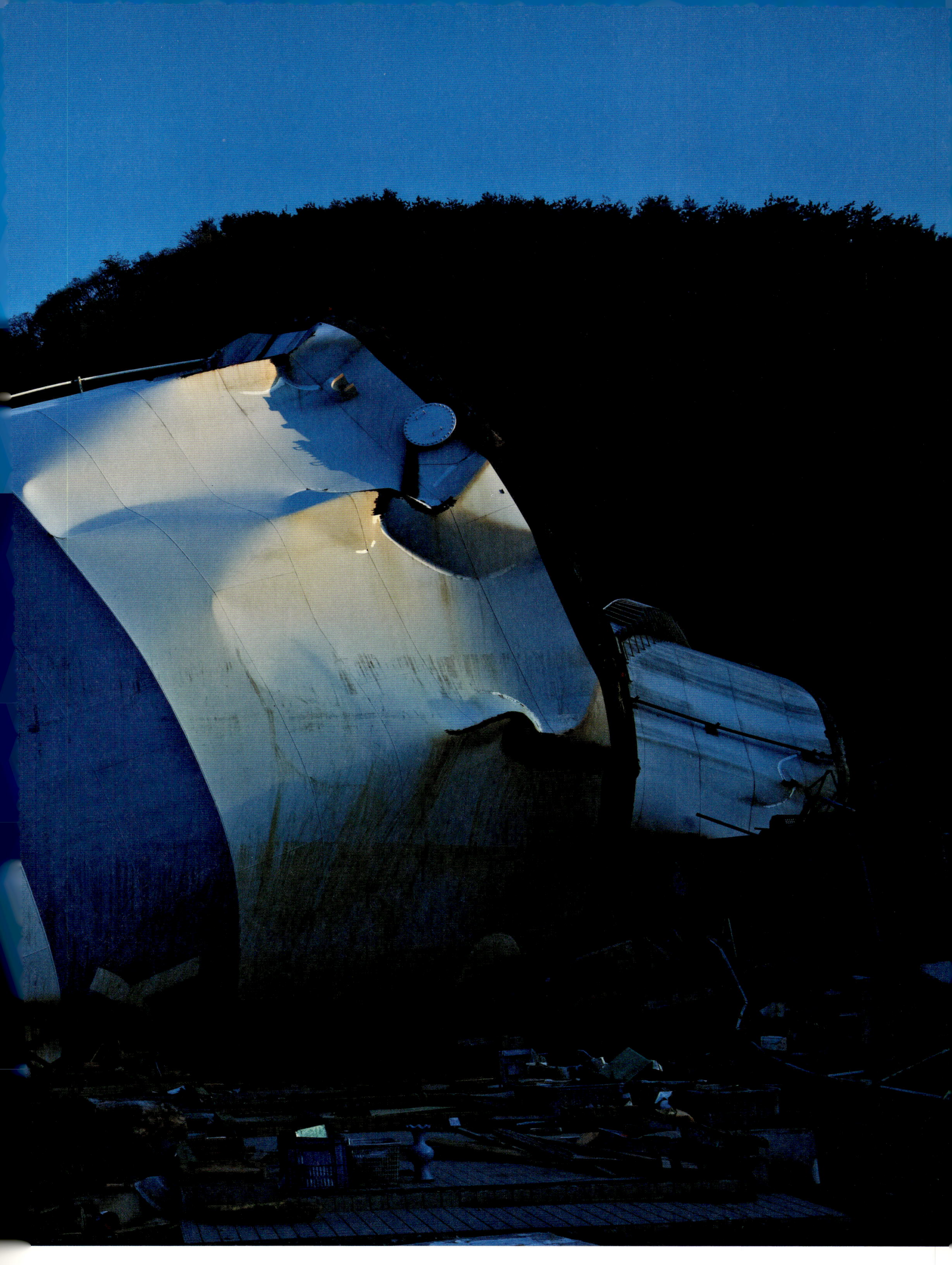

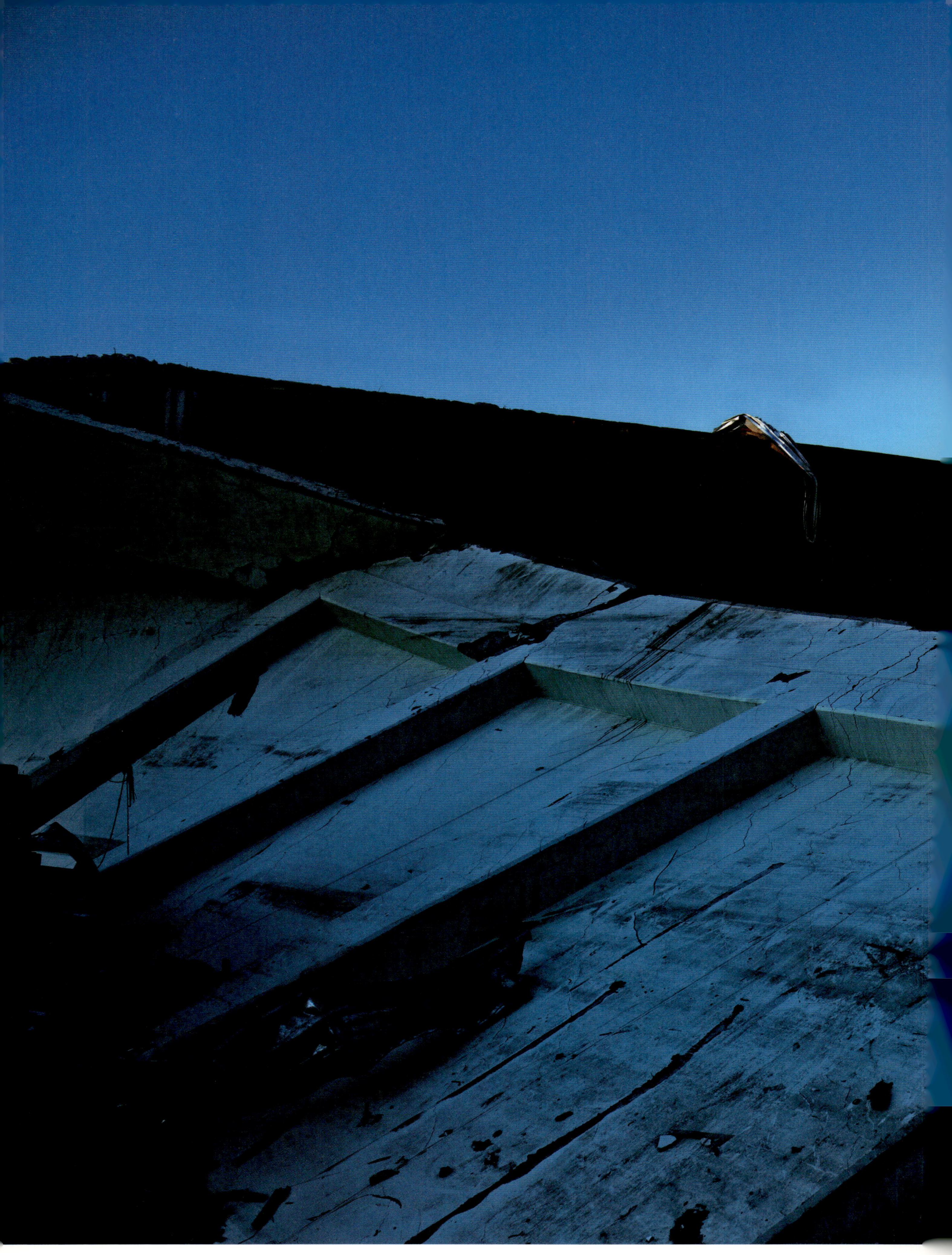

A collapsed warehouse.
Onagawa Cho, Ojika County, Miyagi prefecture

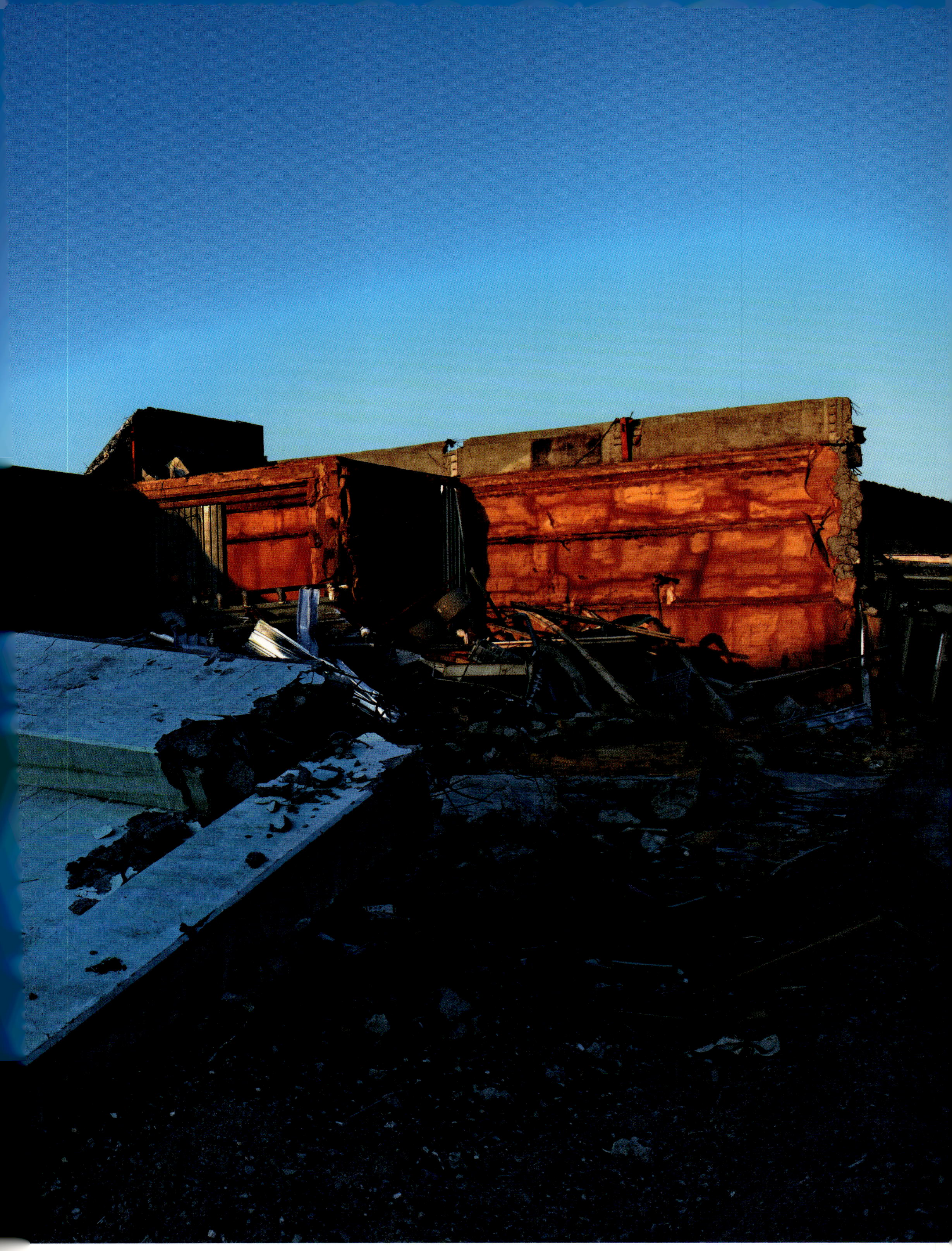

Onagawa Bay, next to Onagawa Nuclear Power Plant.
Onagawa Cho, Ojika County, Miyagi prefecture

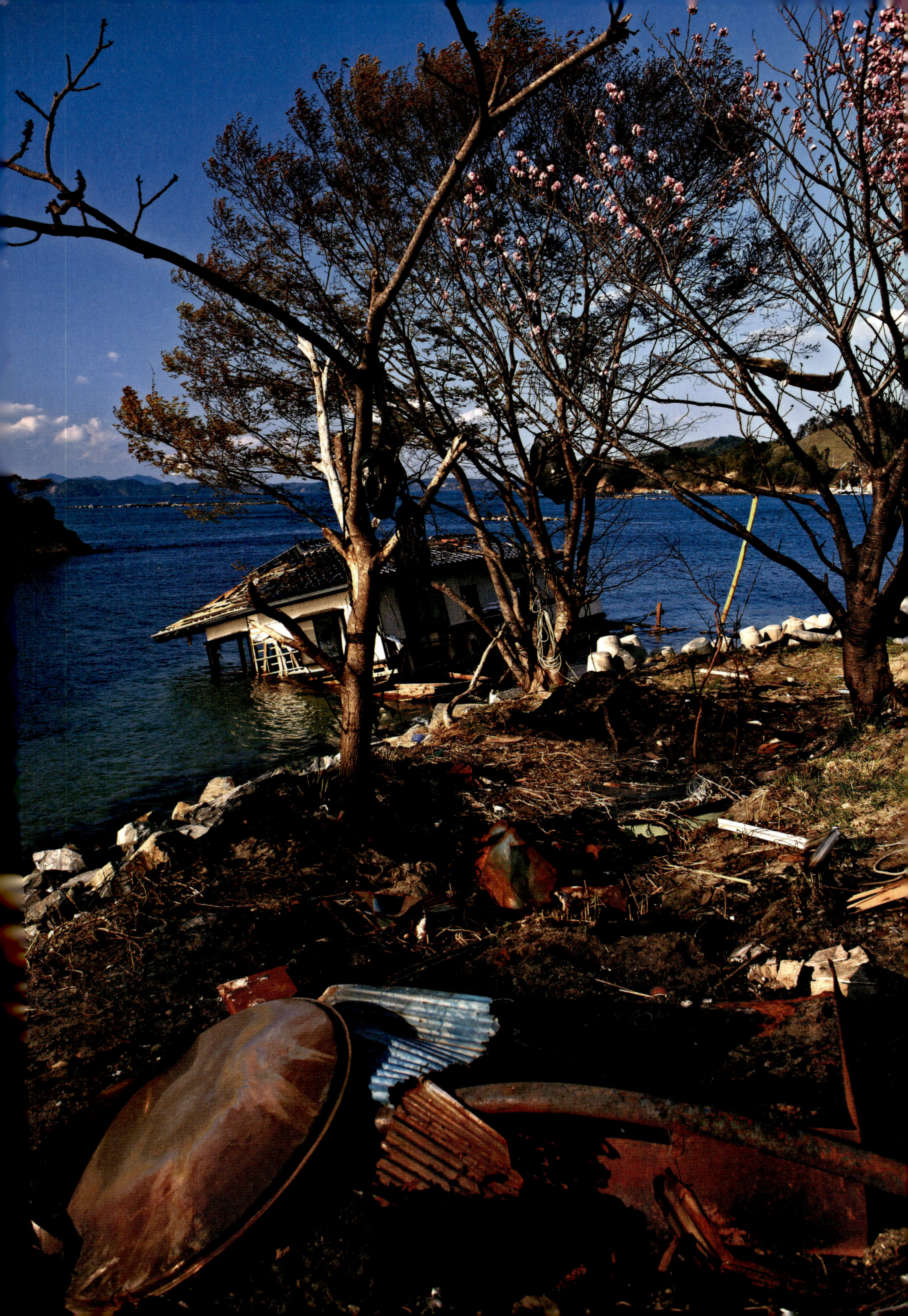

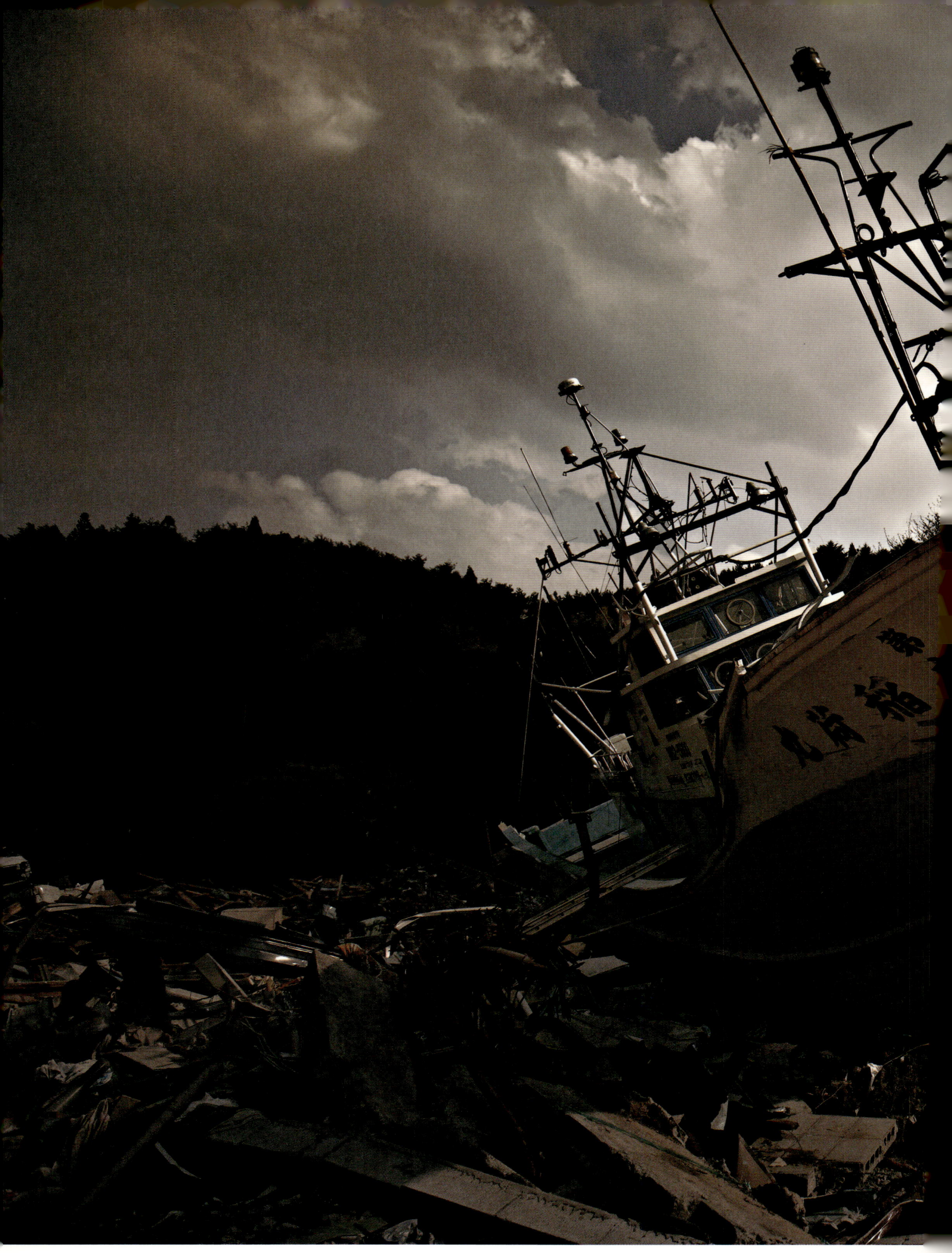

Kilometers from the ocean and halfway up a mountain.
Onagawa Cho, Ojika County, Miyagi prefecture

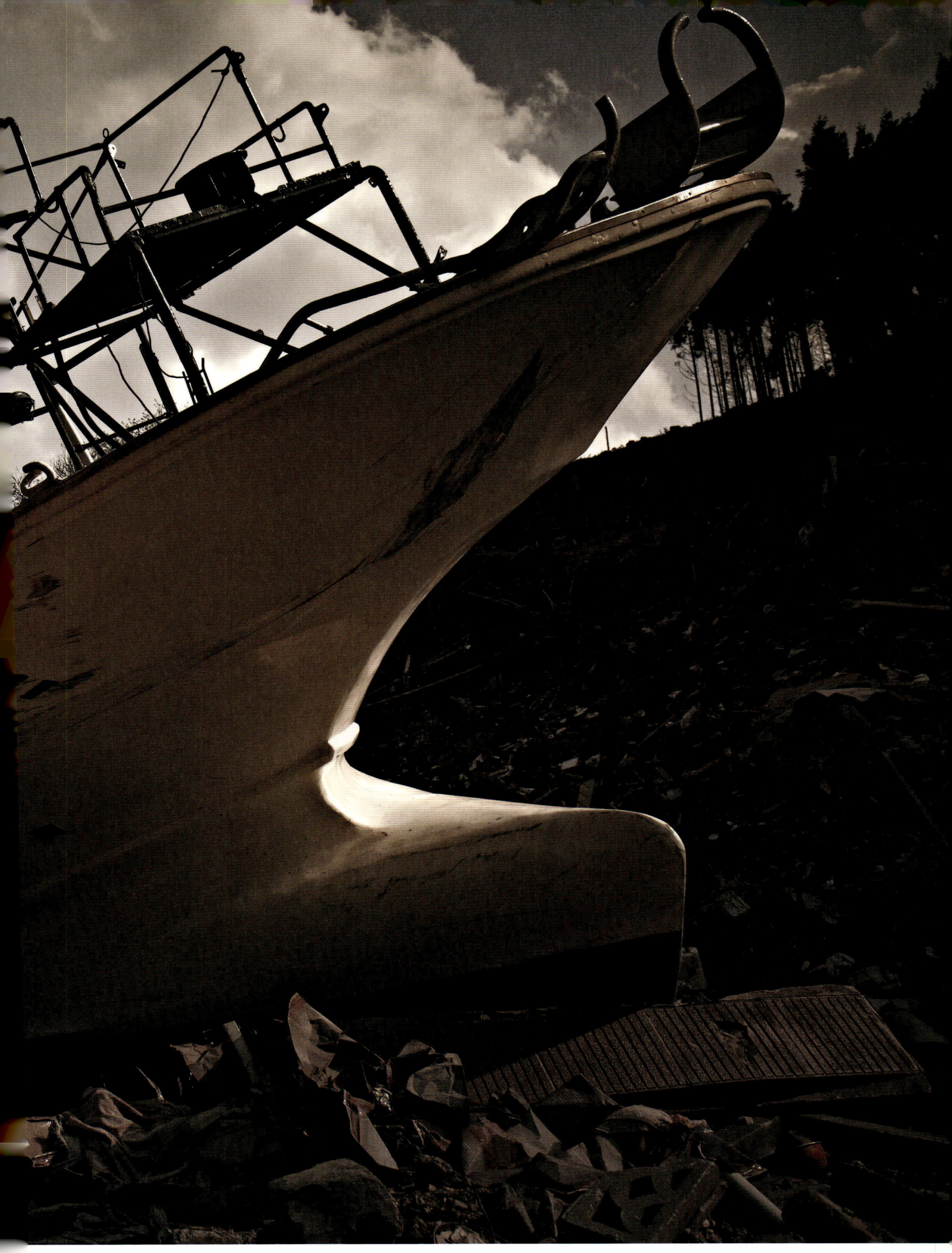

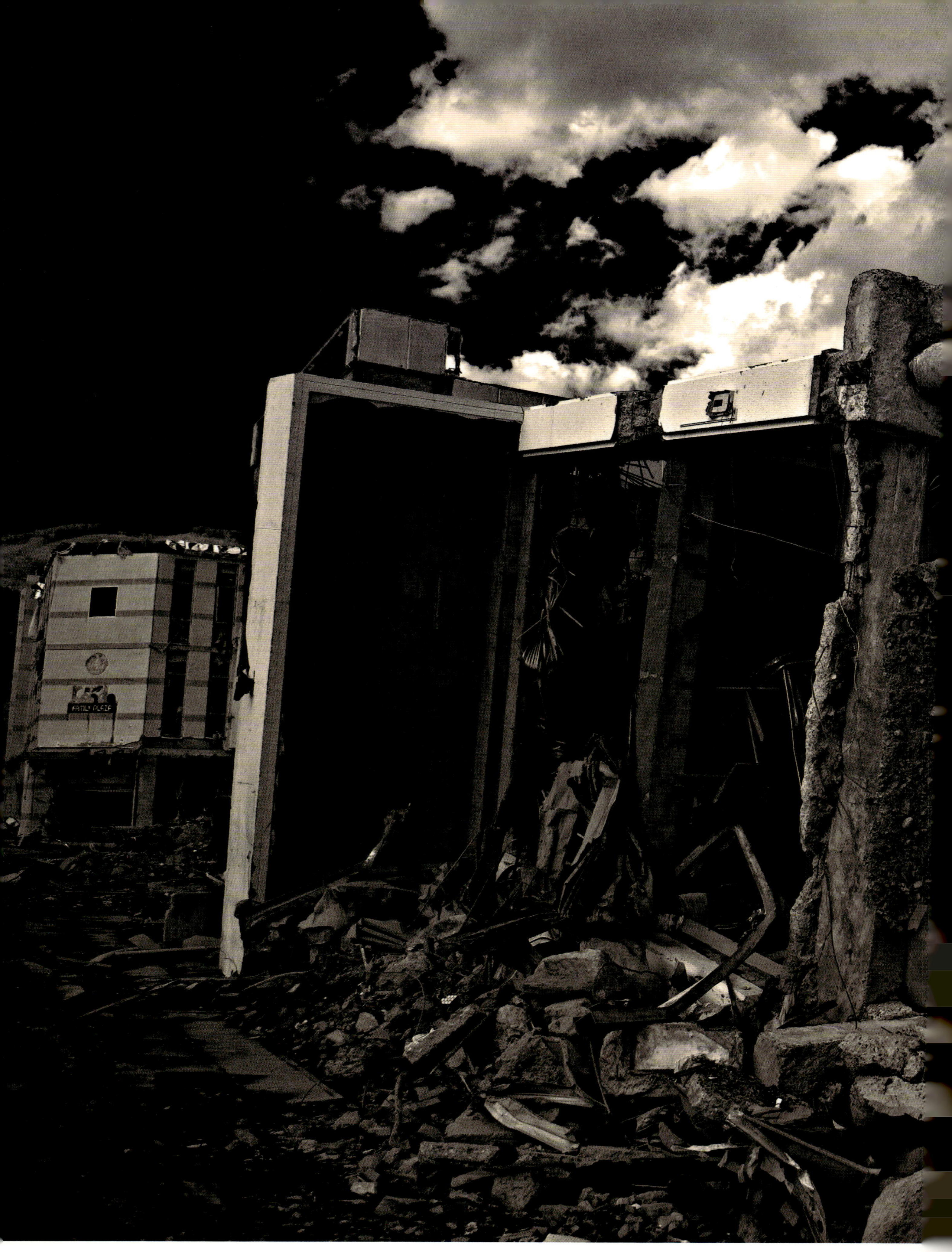

A toppled police station with its exposed foundation posts.
Onagawa Cho, Ojika County, Miyagi prefecture

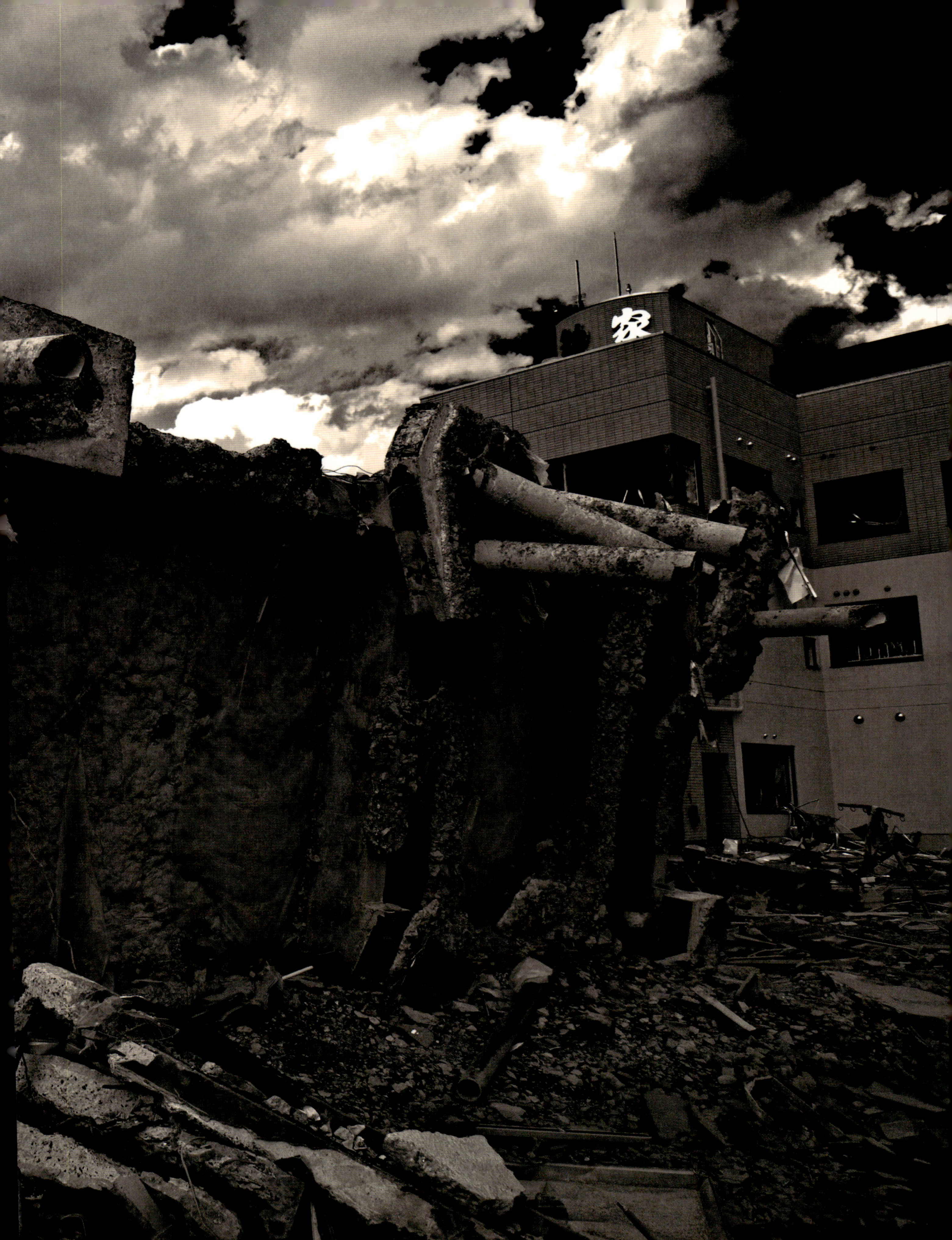
家

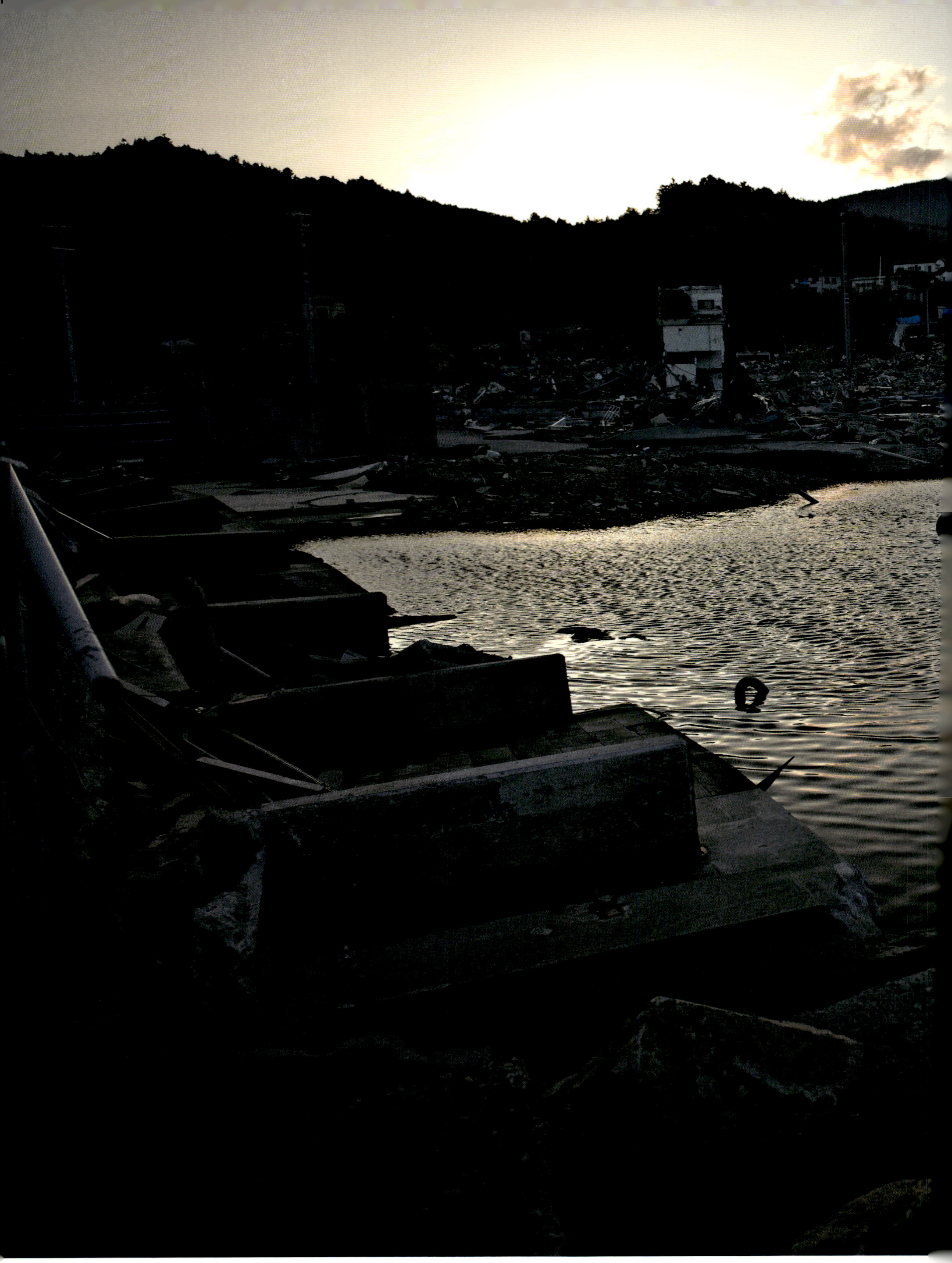

The city center at high tide.
Onagawa Cho, Ojika County, Miyagi prefecture

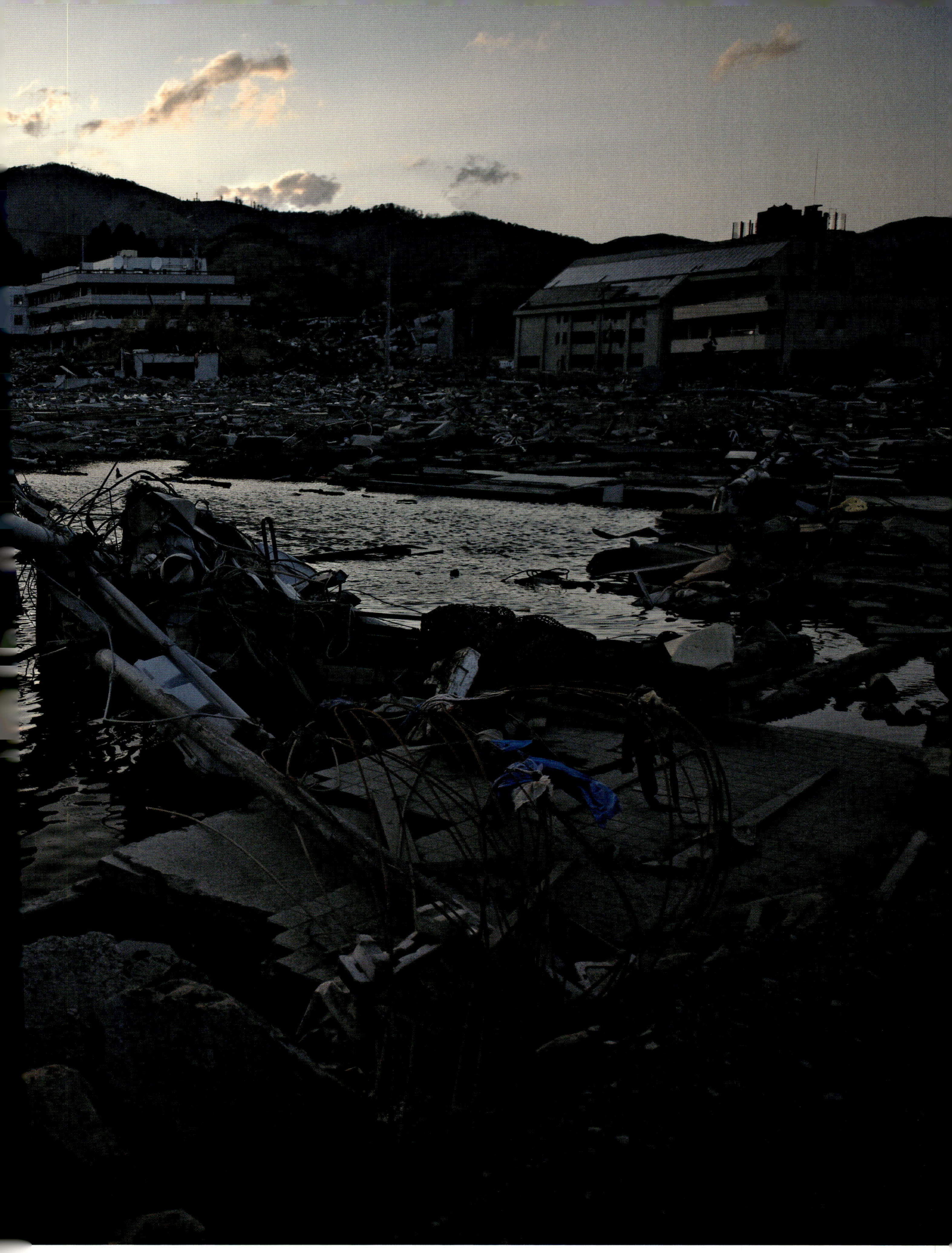

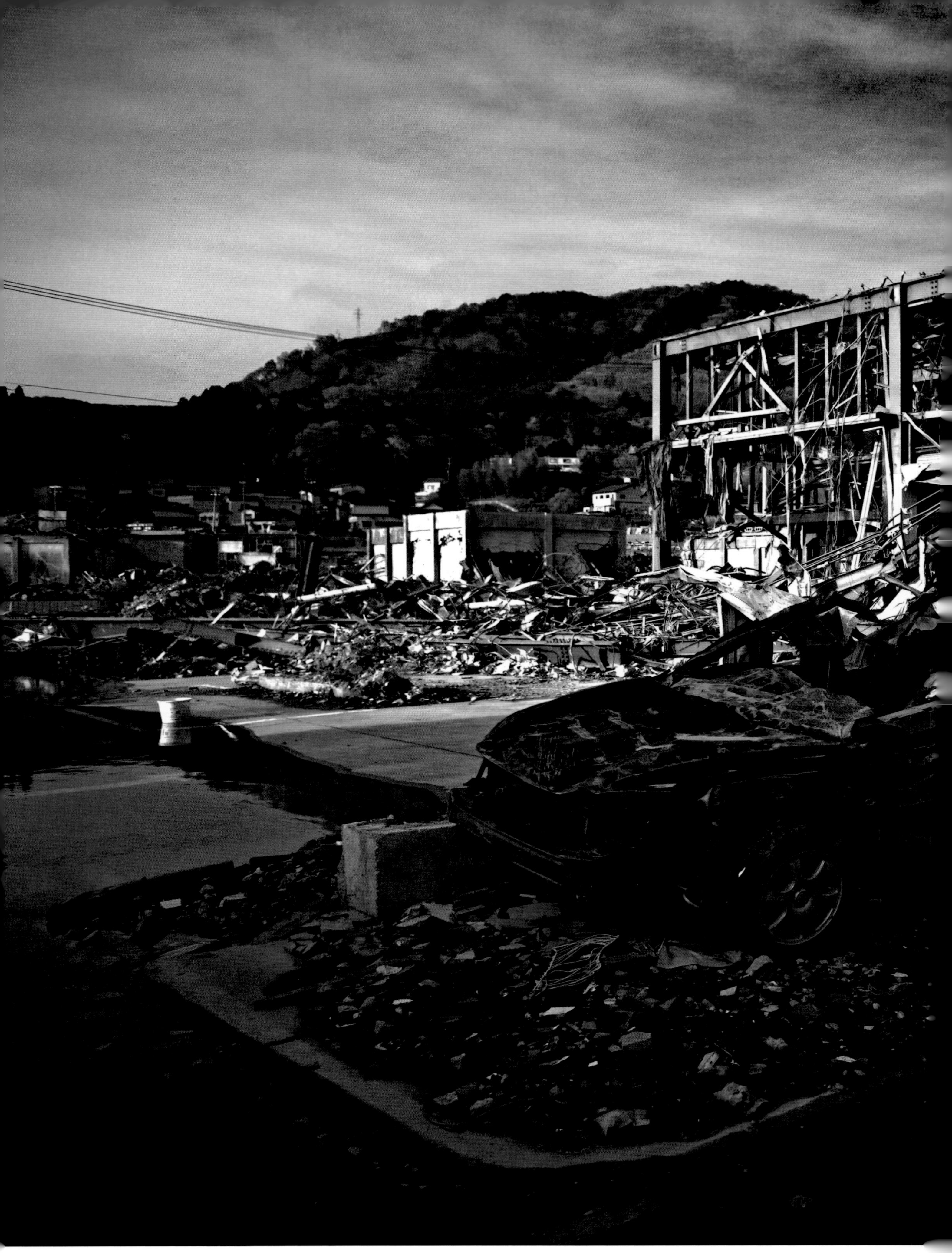

The city center at high tide.
Onagawa Cho, Ojika County, Miyagi prefecture

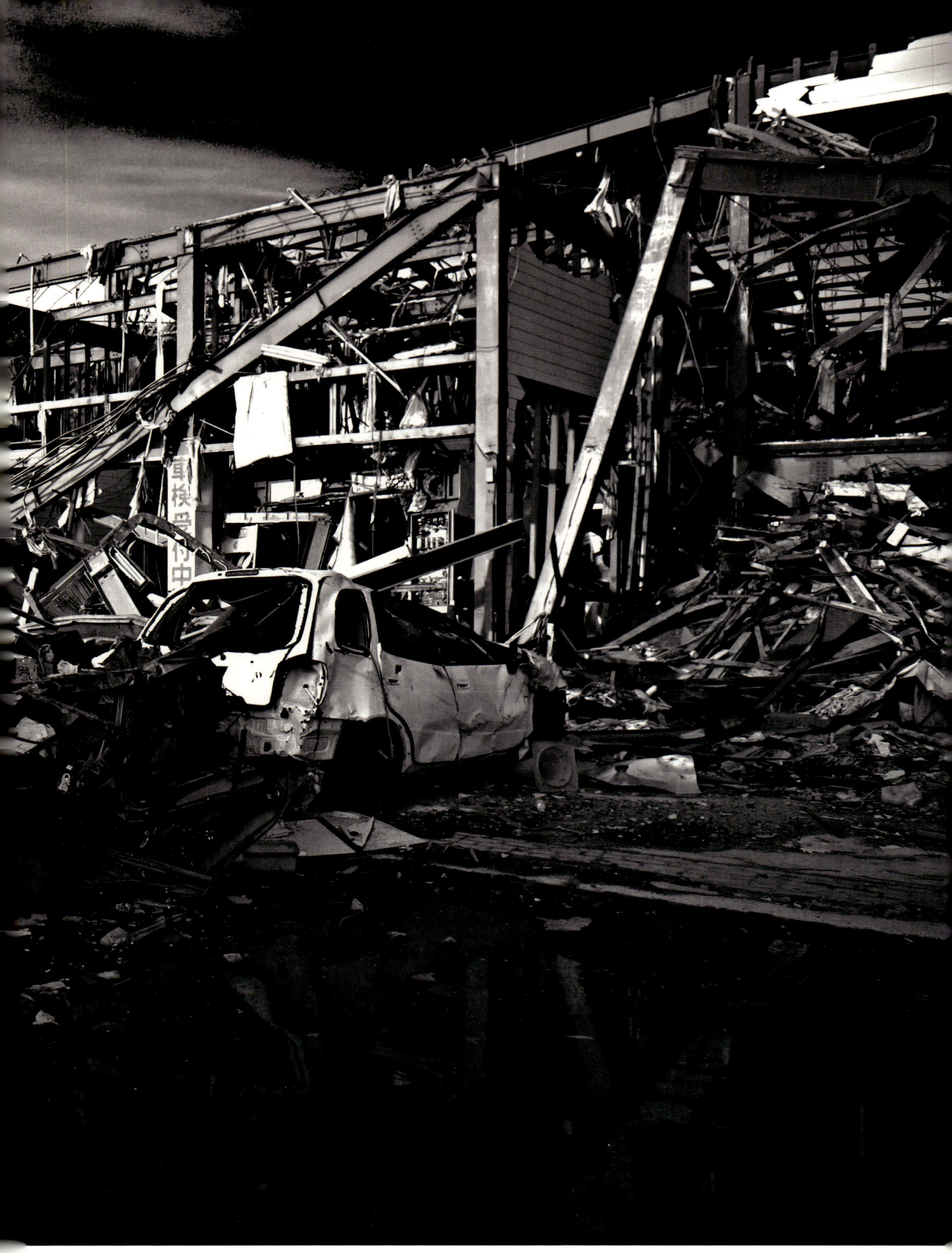
車検受付中

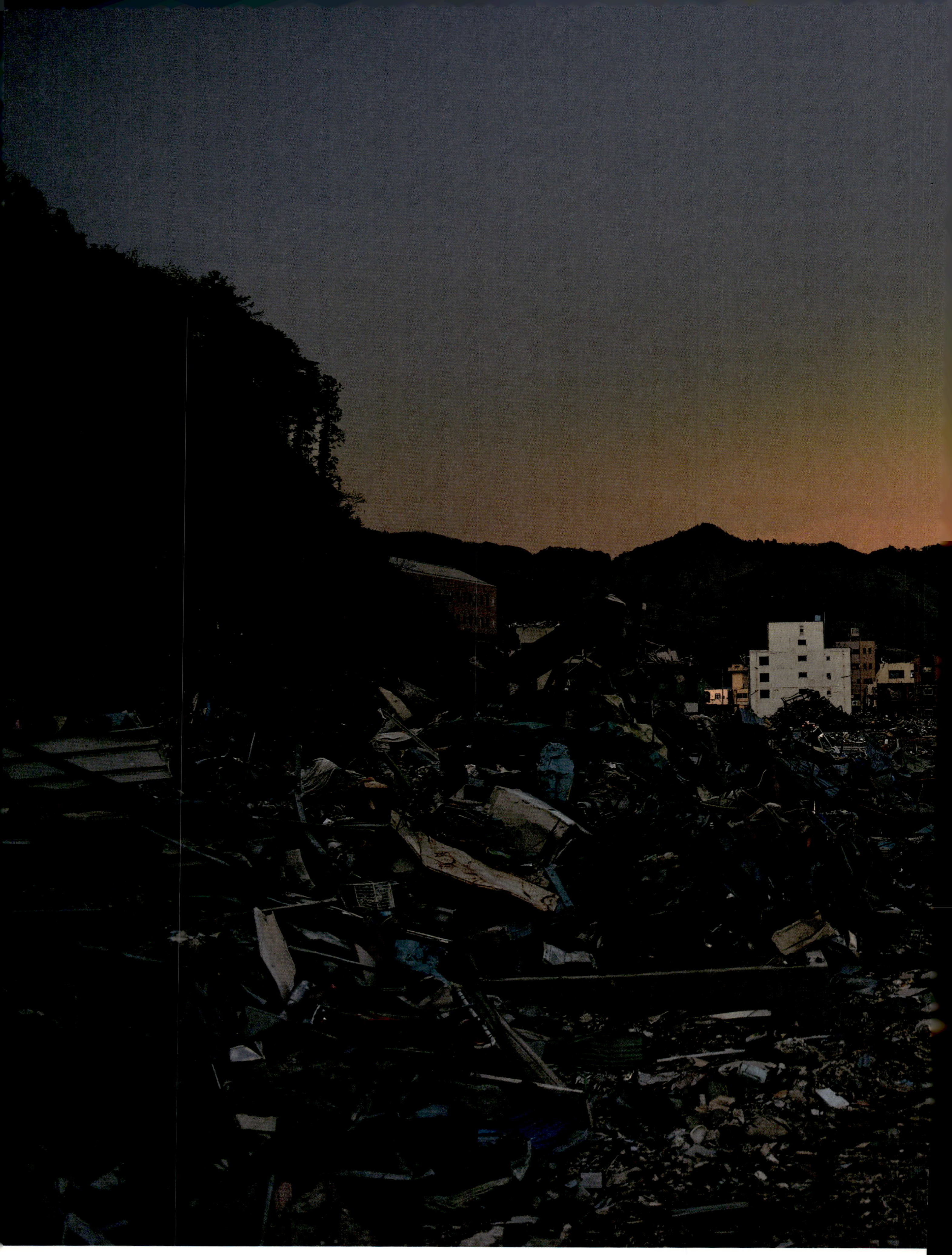

Onagawa Cho, Ojika County, Miyagi prefecture

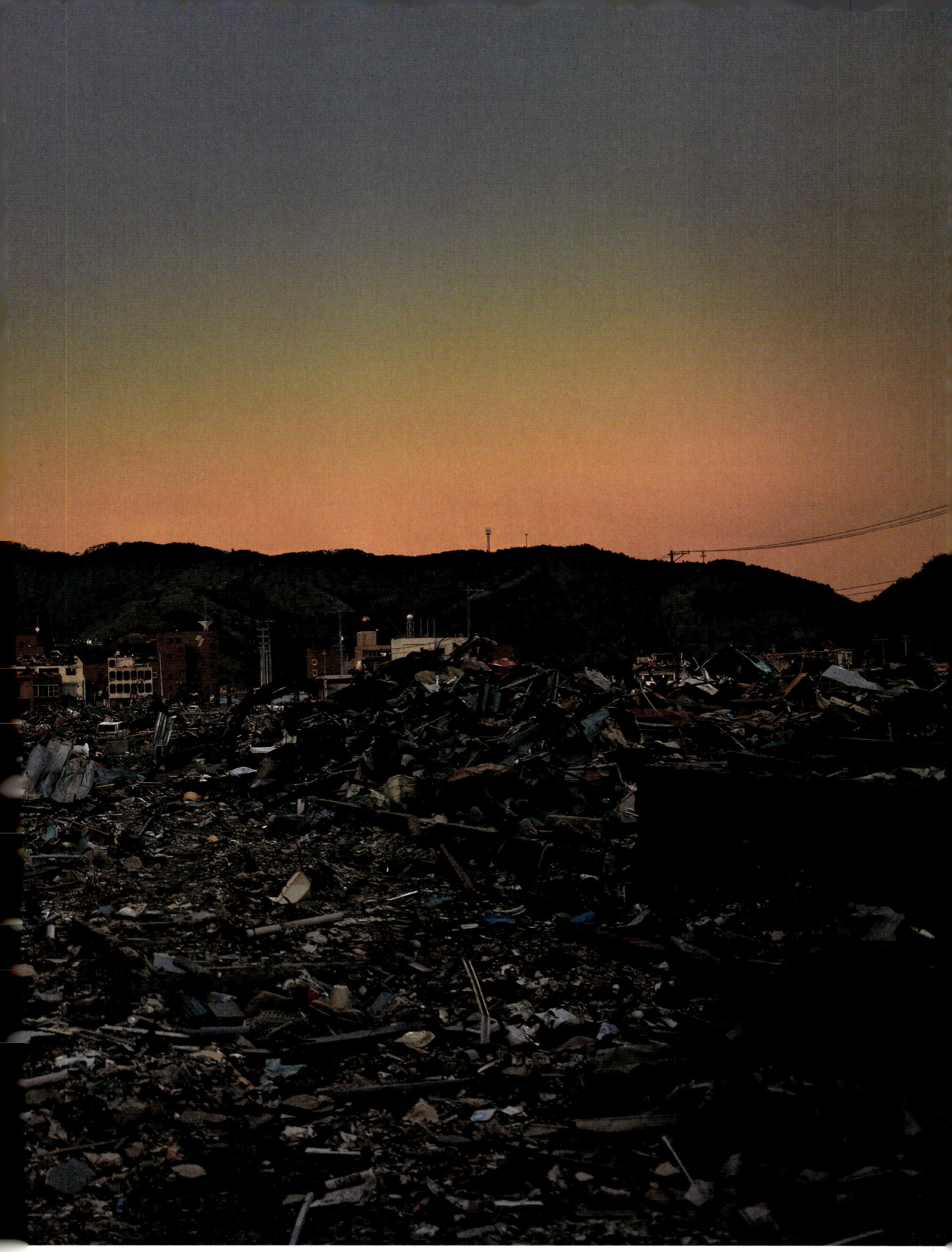

After the earthquake, Japan's coastline became lower.
City of Ishinomaki, Miyagi prefecture

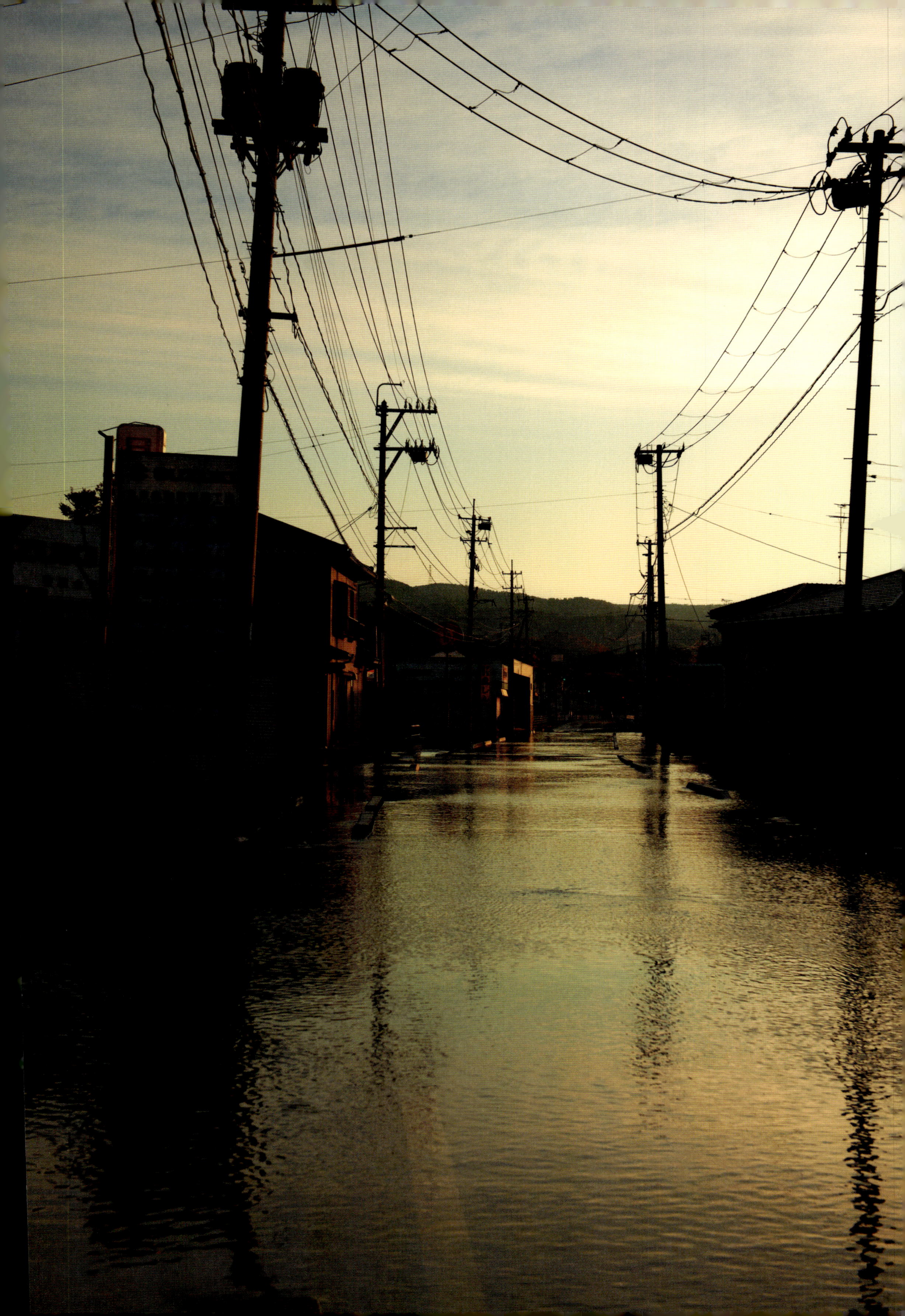

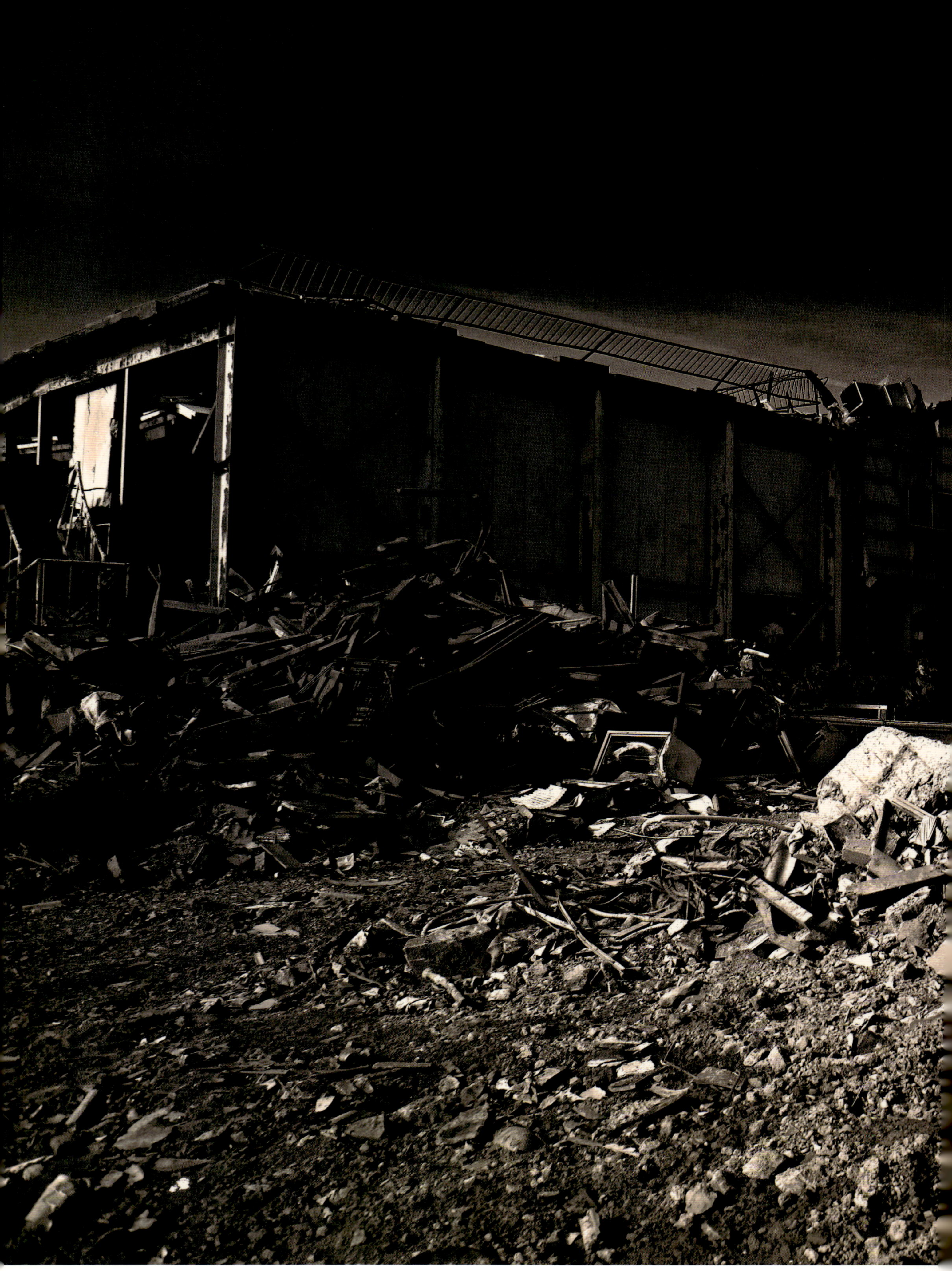

Onagawa Cho, Oj ka County, Miyagi prefecture

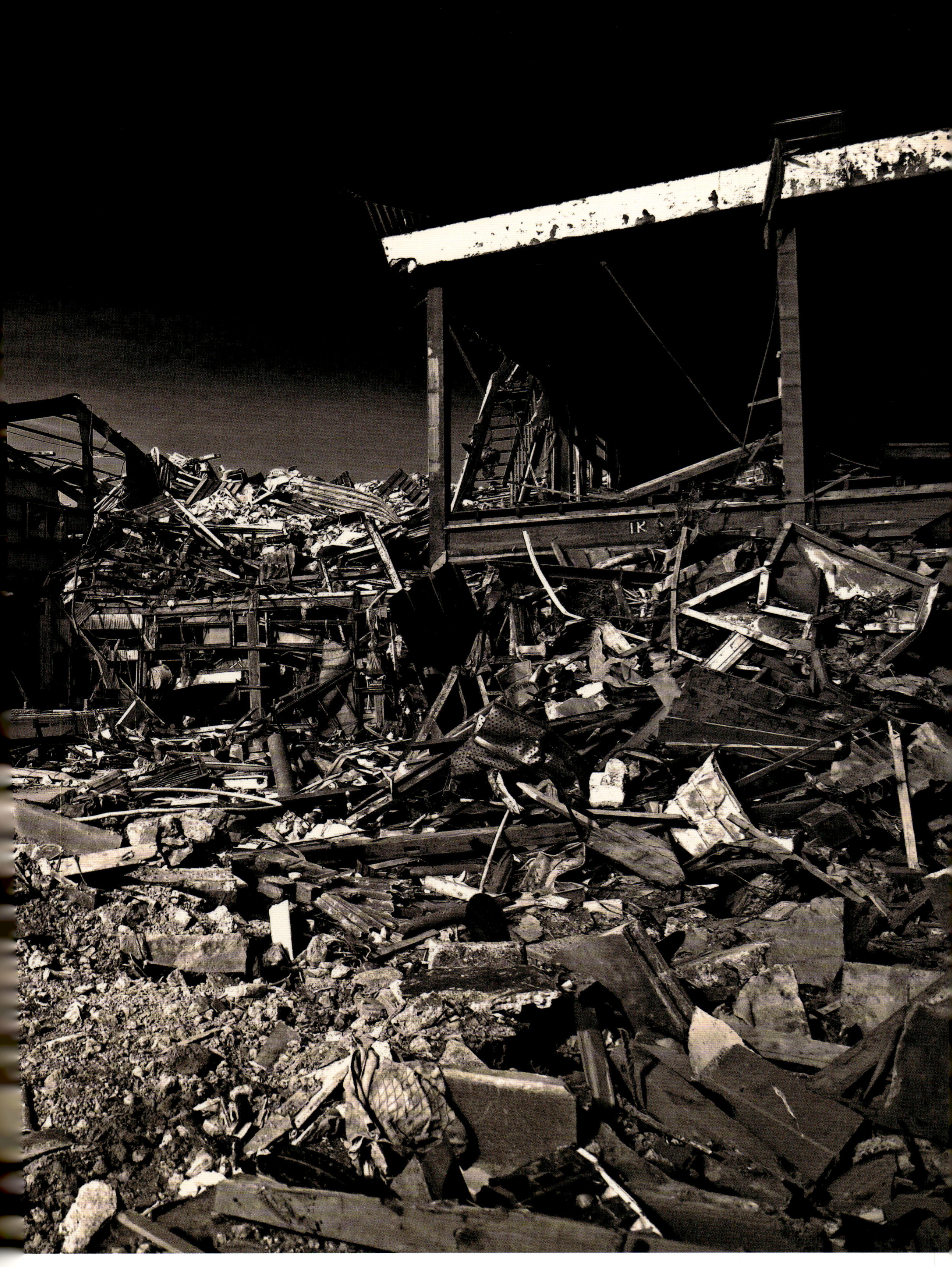

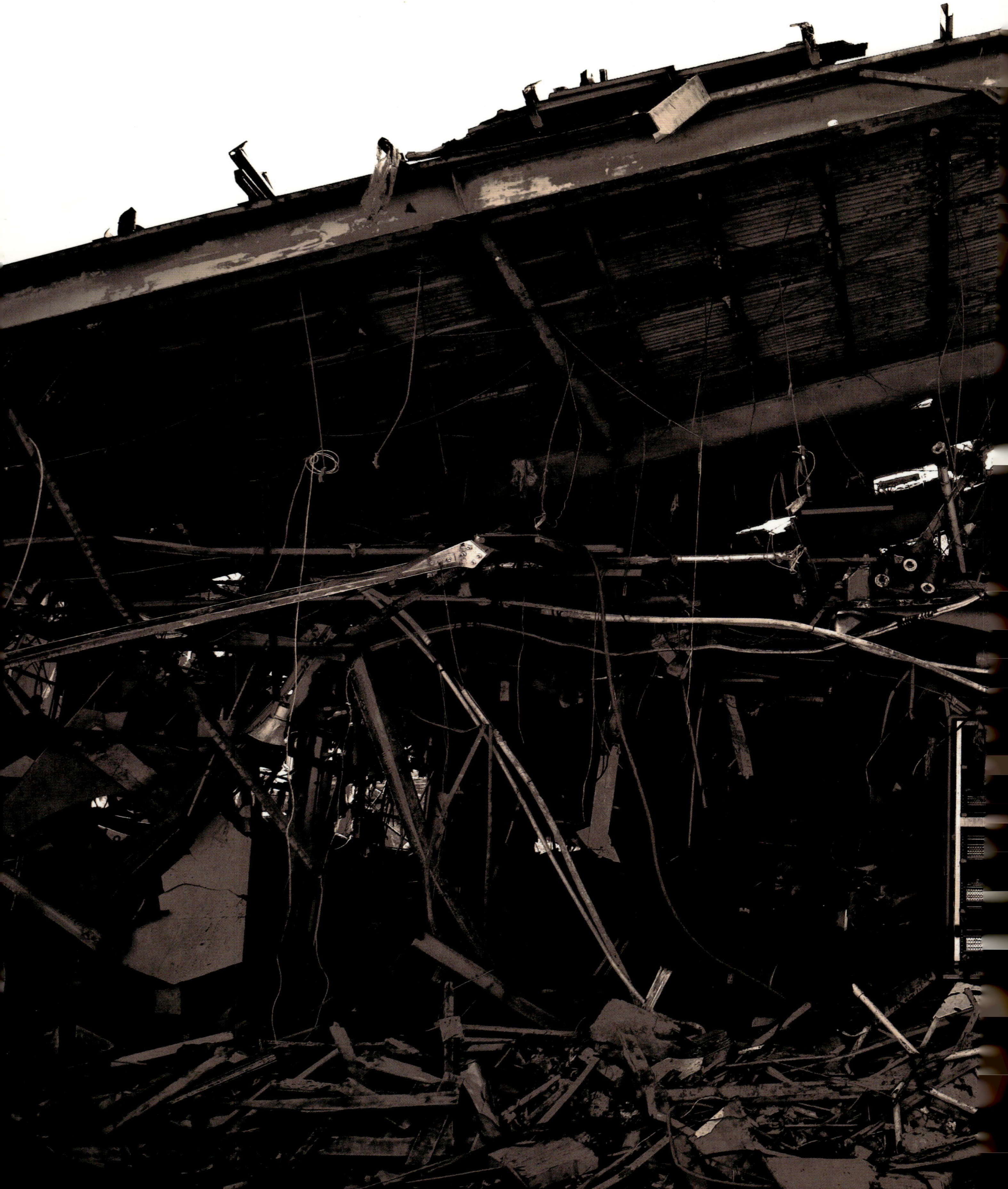

Onagawa Cho, Ojika County, Miyagi prefecture

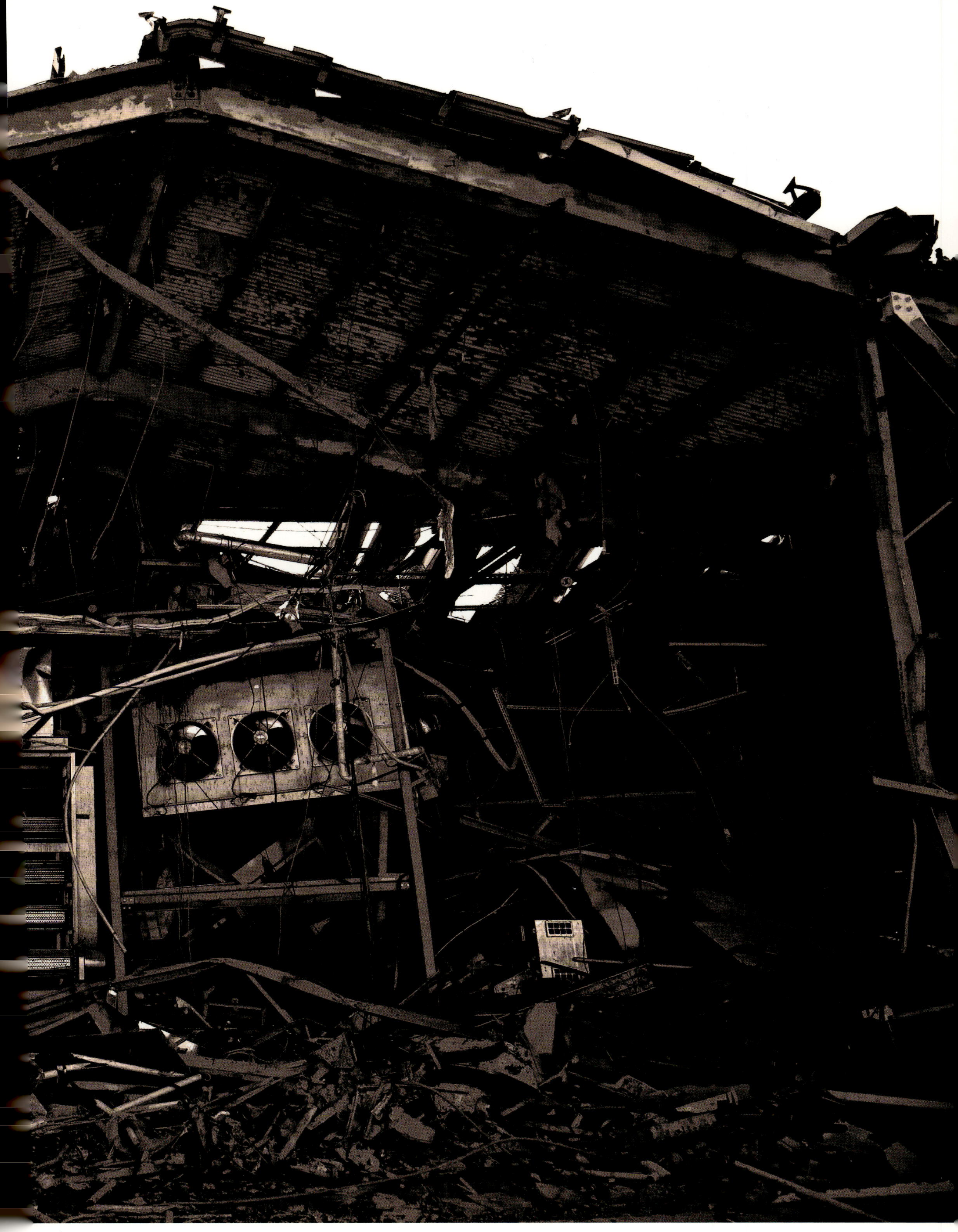

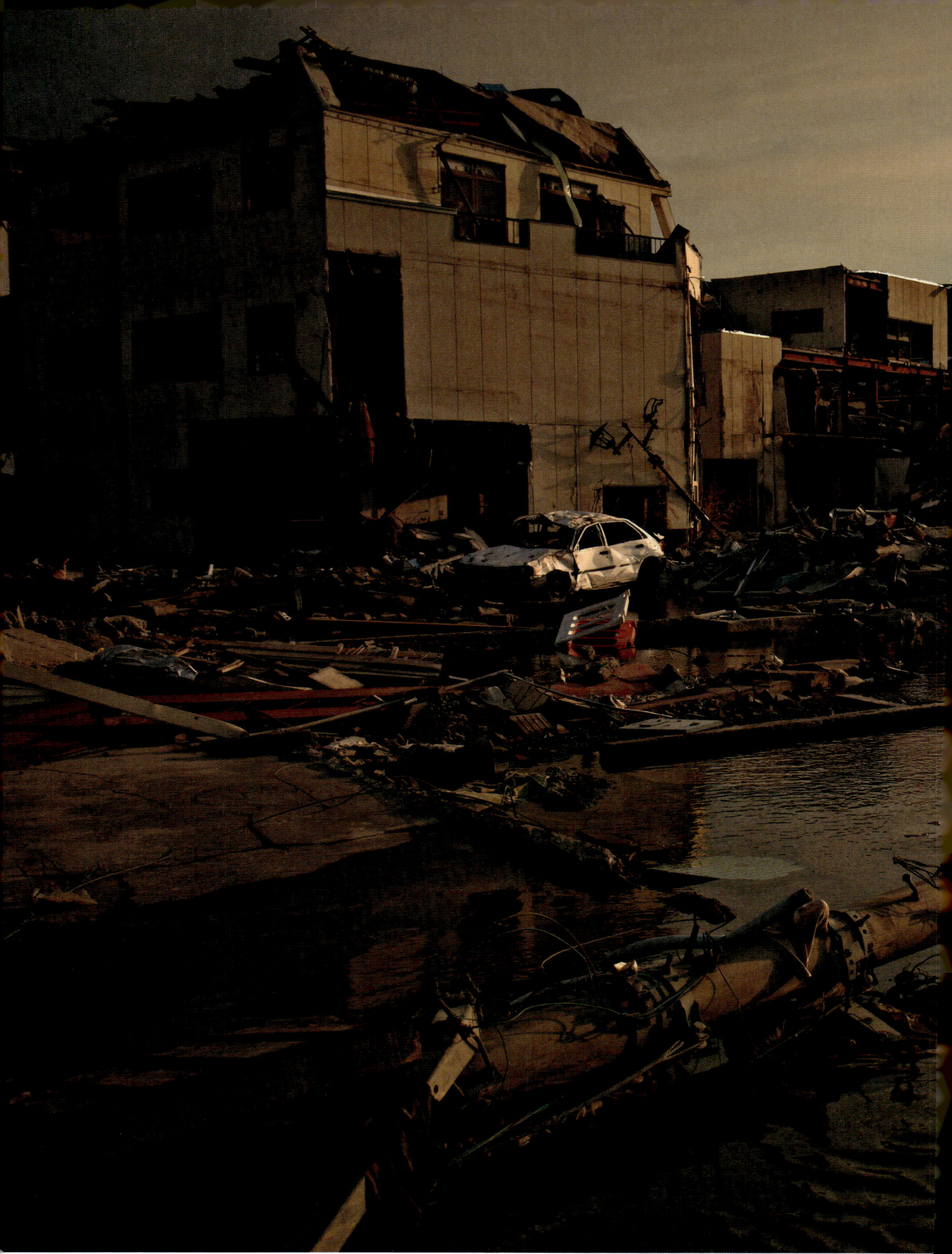

The flooded central town at high tide.
Onagawa Cho, Ojika County, Miyagi prefecture

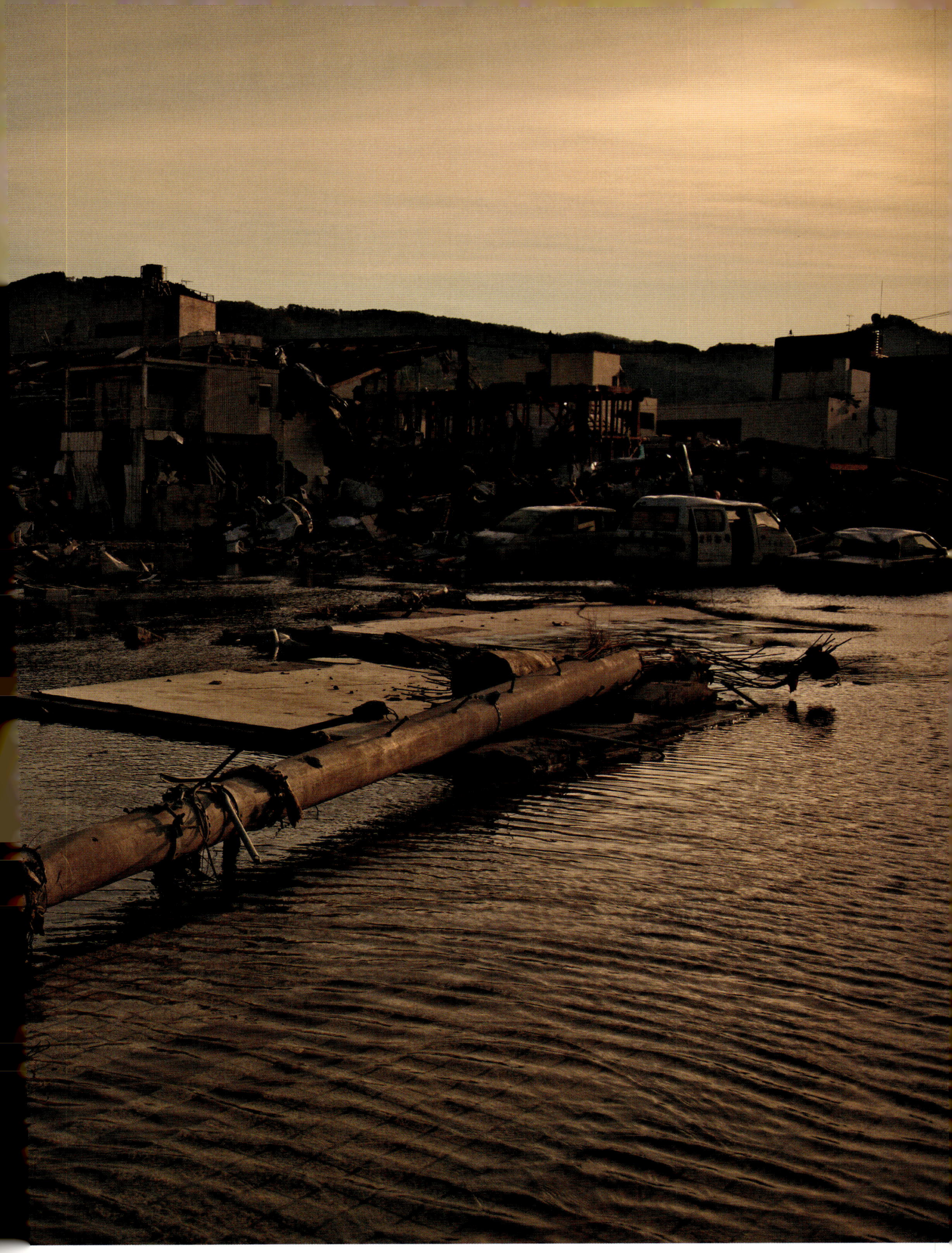

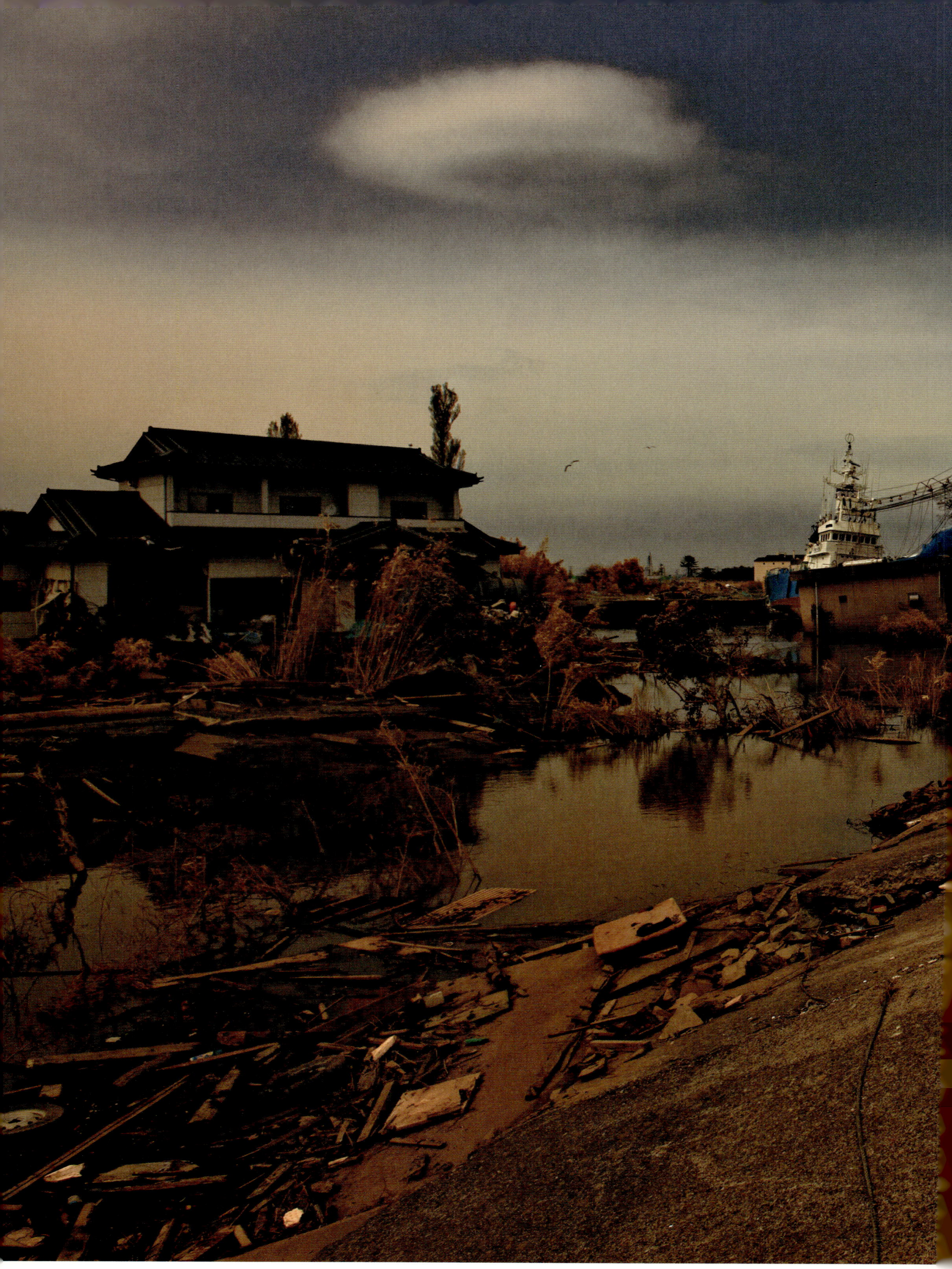

A large freighter in the center of a residential area.
City of Higashi Matsushima, Miyagi prefecture

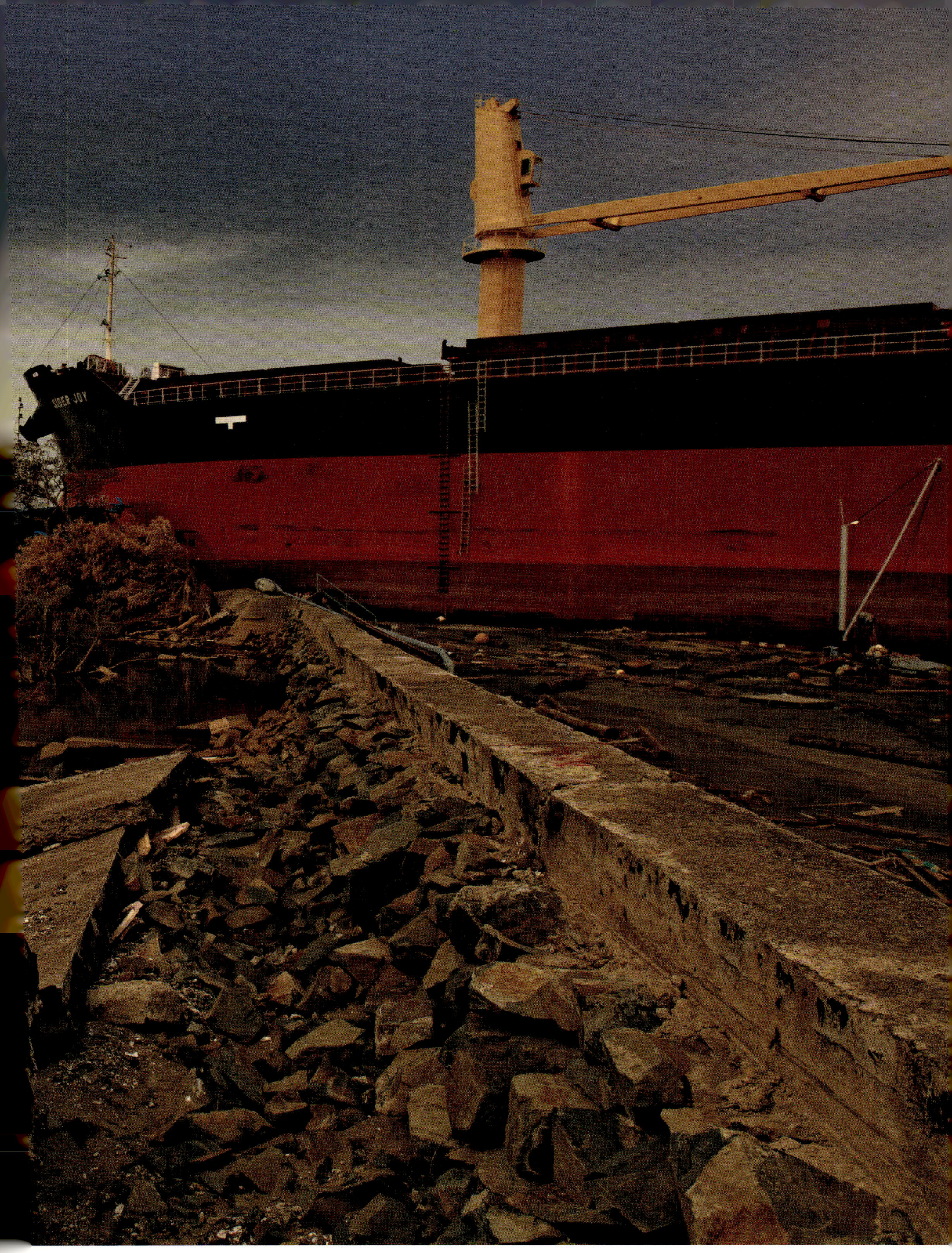
SIDER JOY

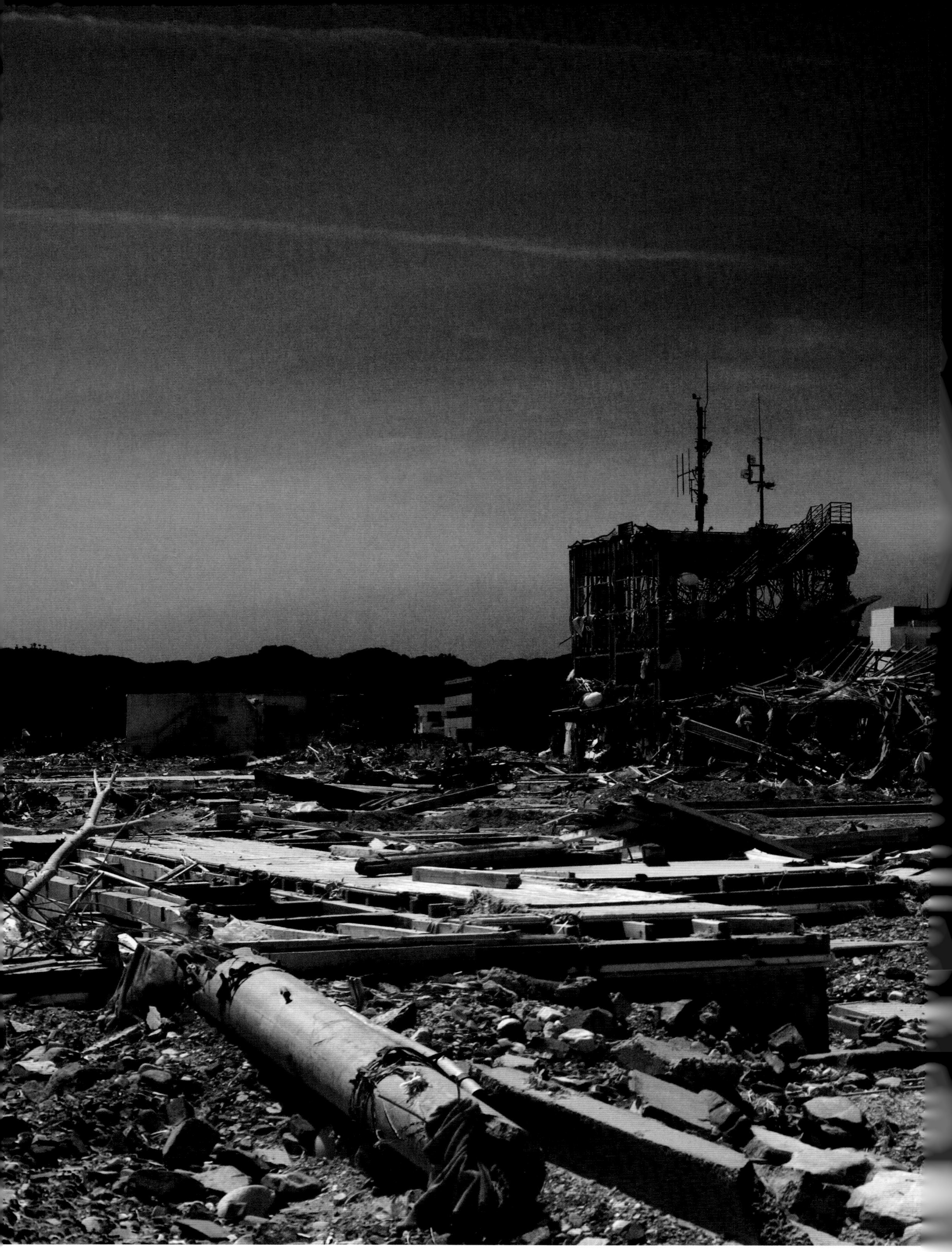

The Government Office of Disaster Measures.
Minami Sanriku Cho, Motoyoshi County, Miyagi prefecture

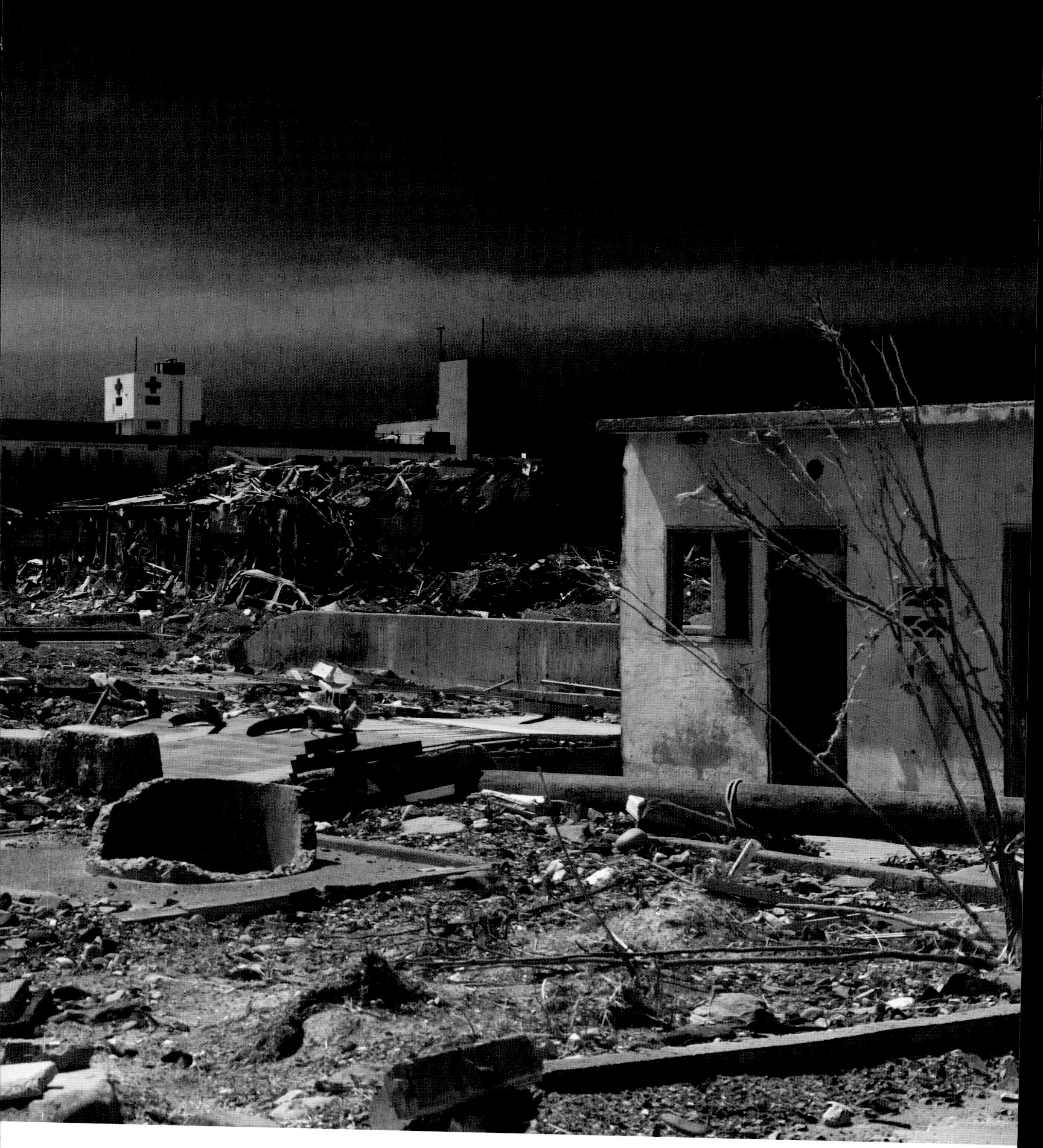

Onagawa Cho, Oji<a County, Miyagi prefecture

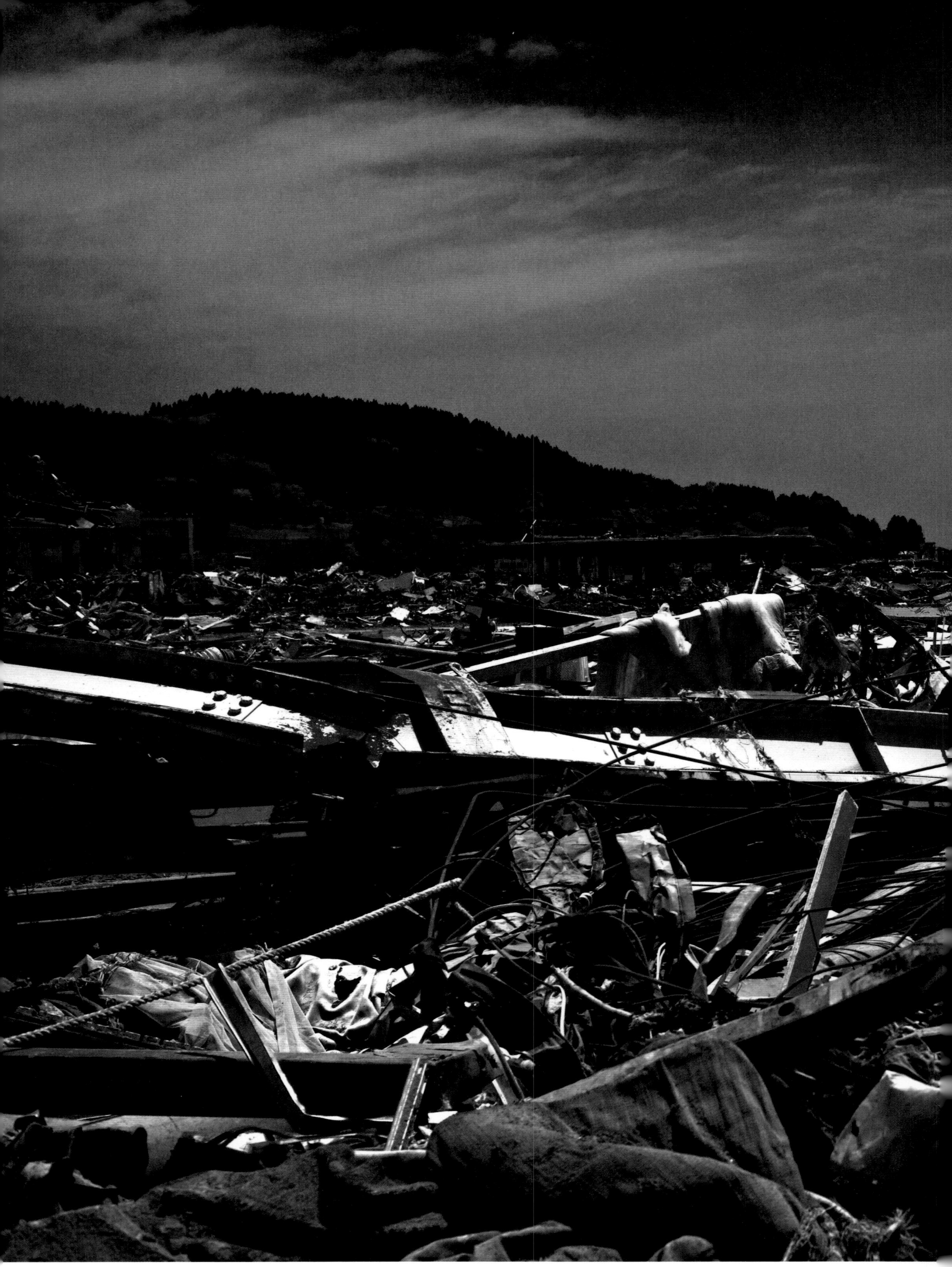

Minami Sanriku Cho, Motoyoshi County, Miyagi prefecture

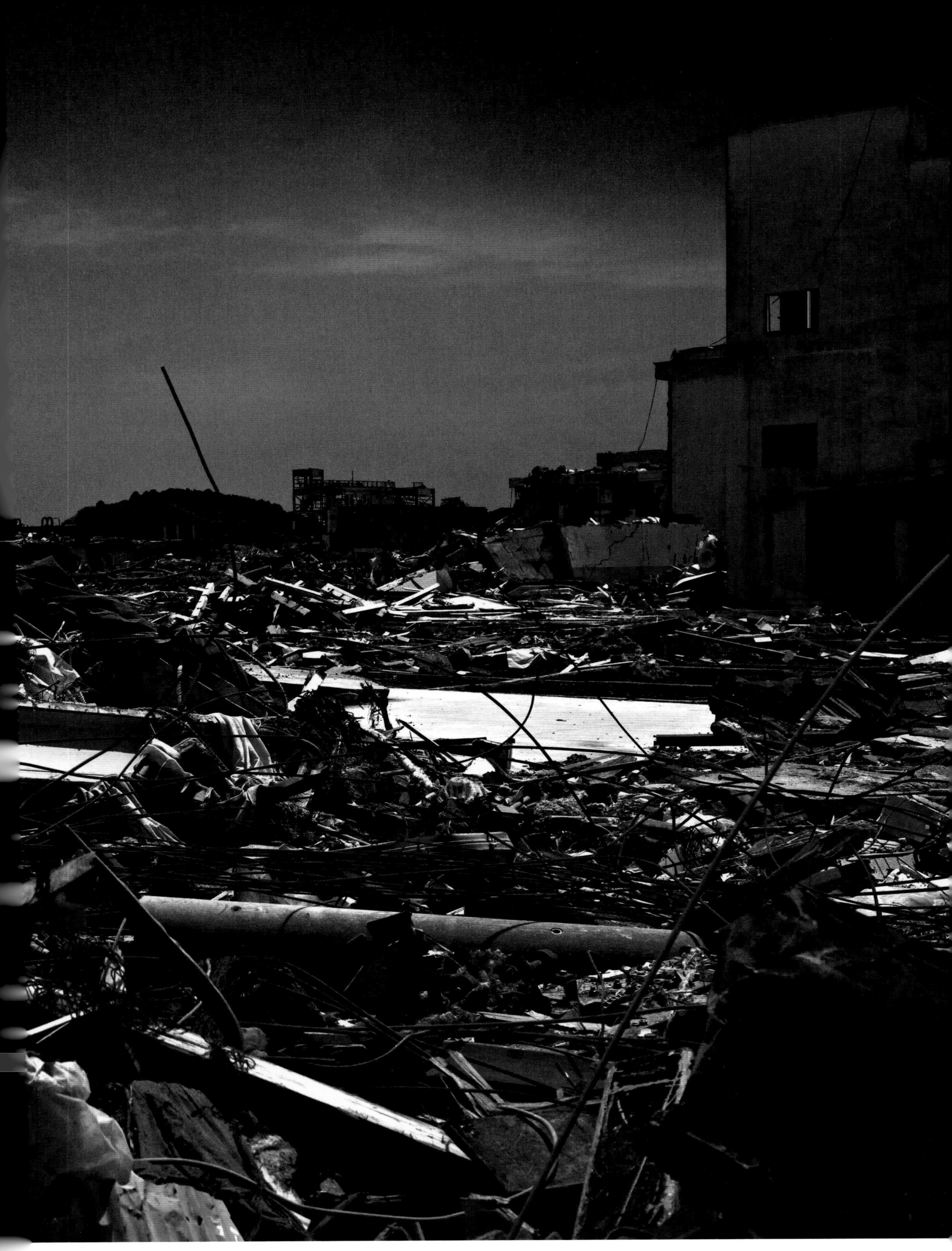

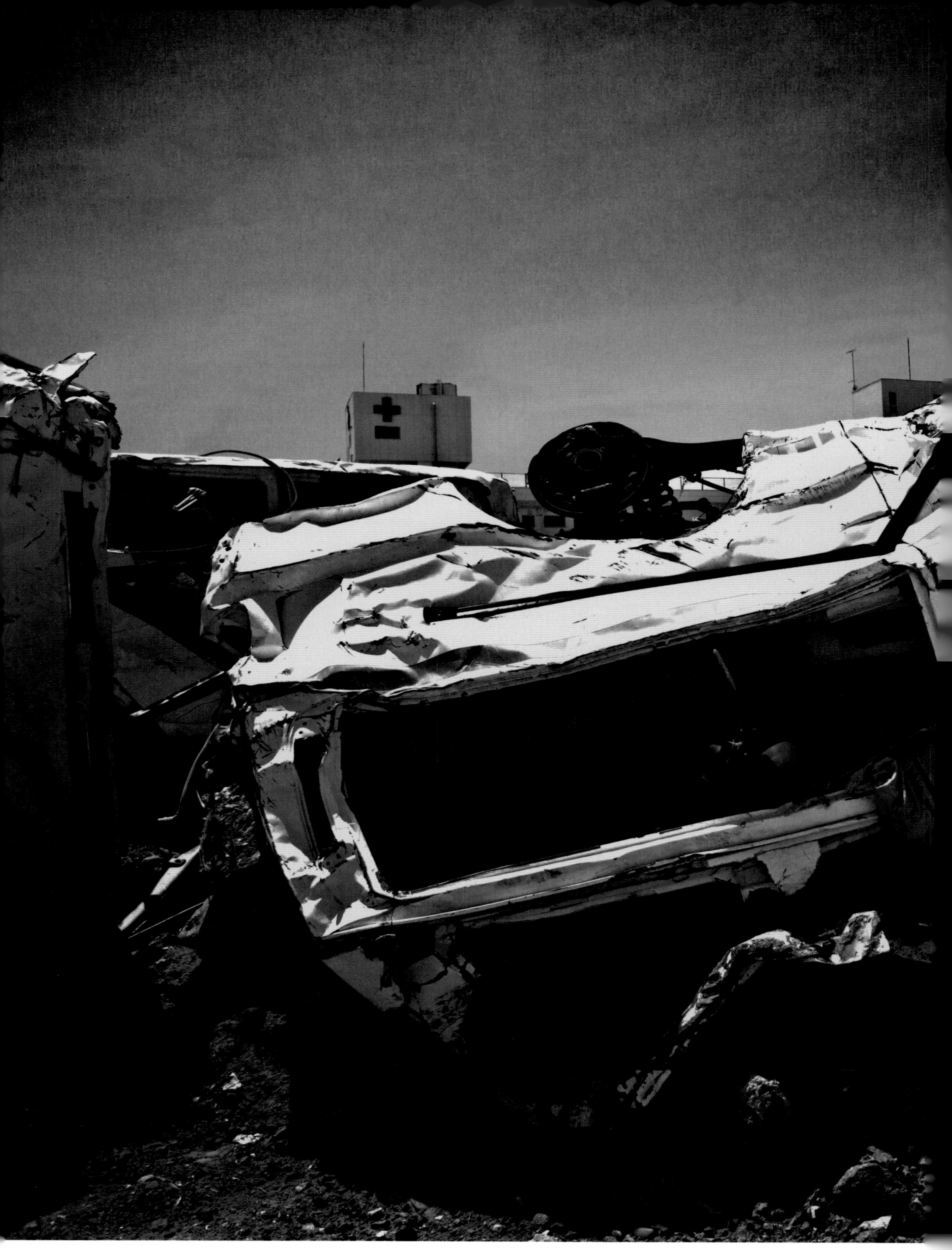

An ambulance.
Minami Sanriku Cho, Motoyoshi County, Miyagi prefecture

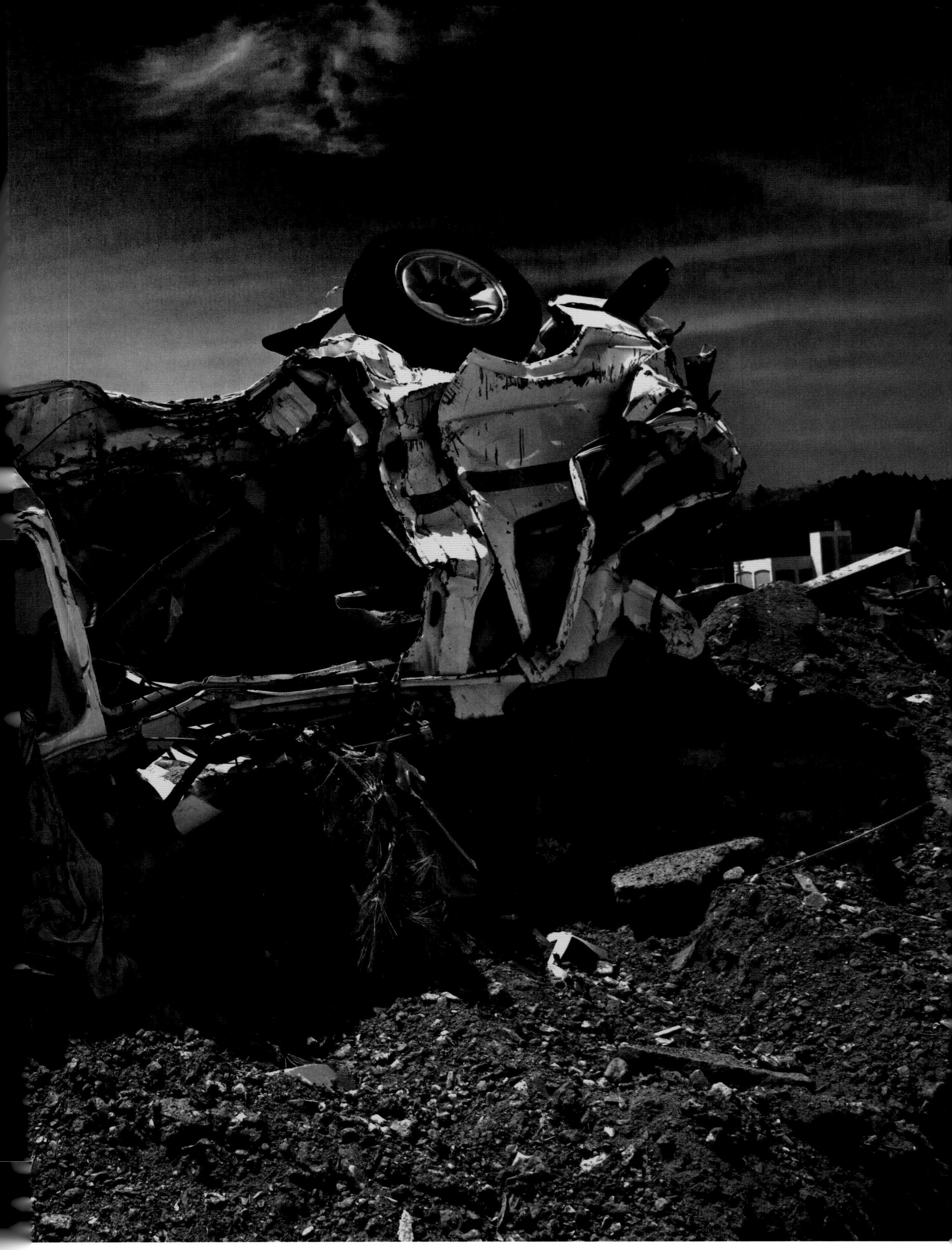

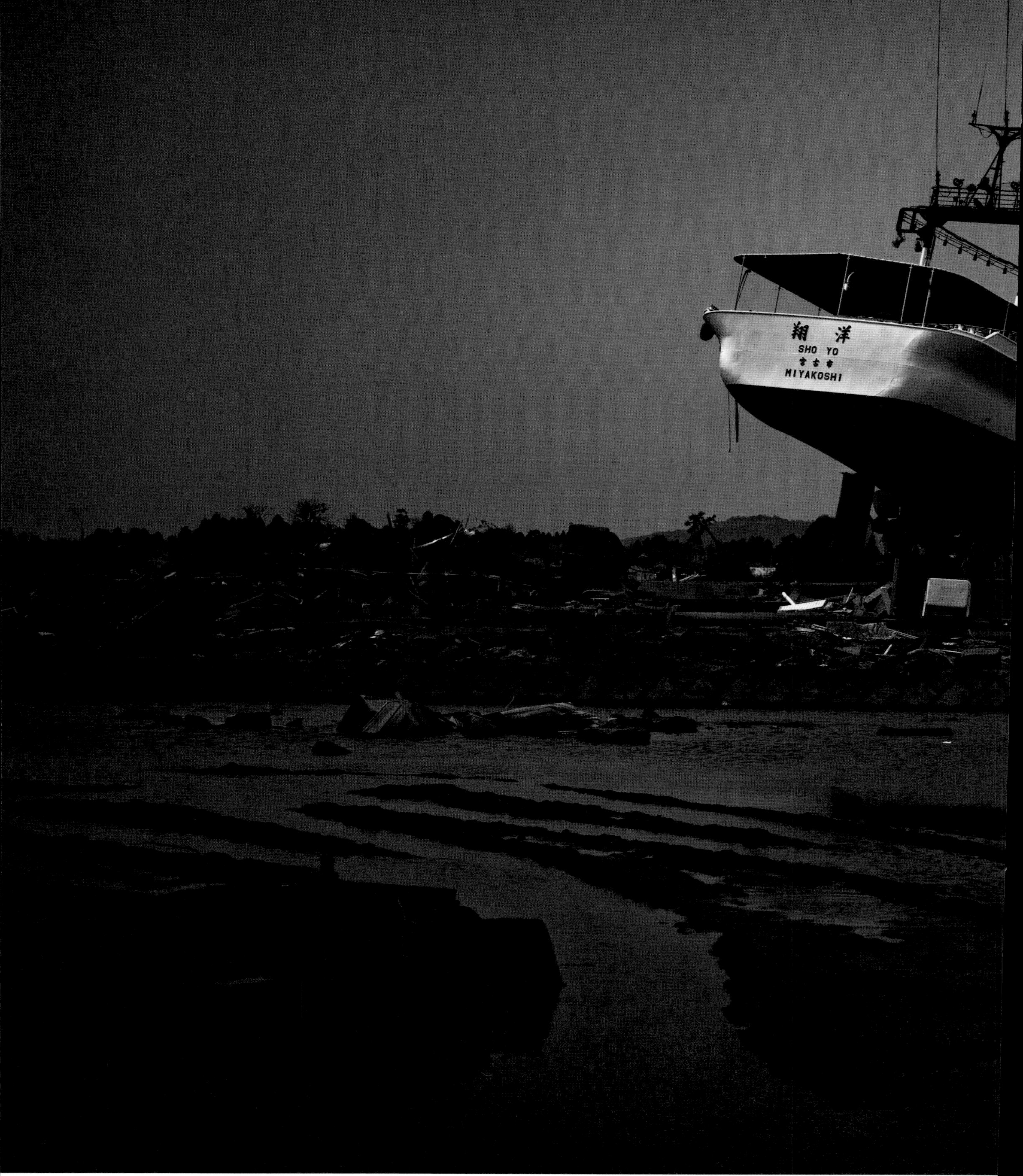

City of Higashi Matsushima, Miyagi prefecture

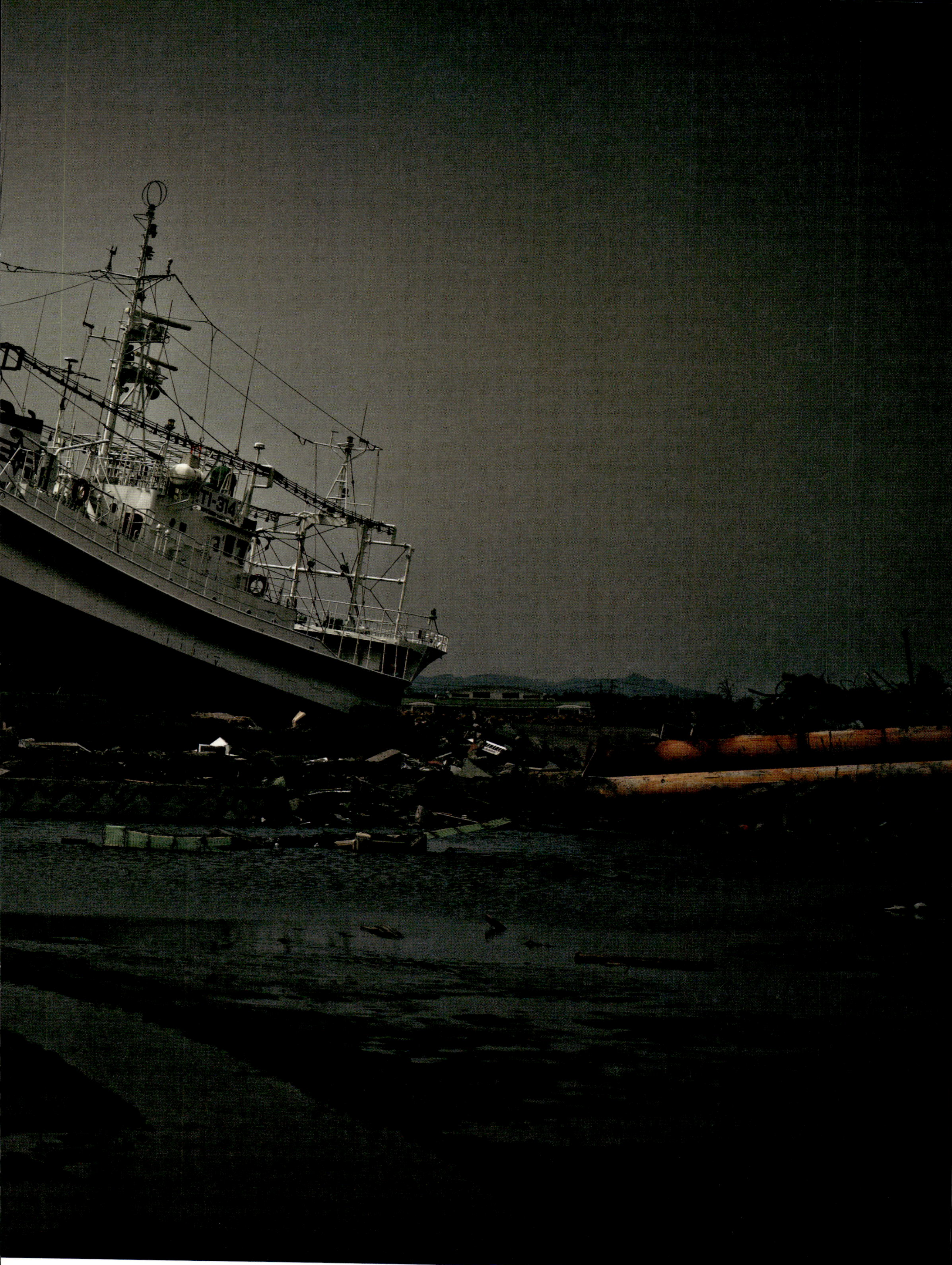
TI-314

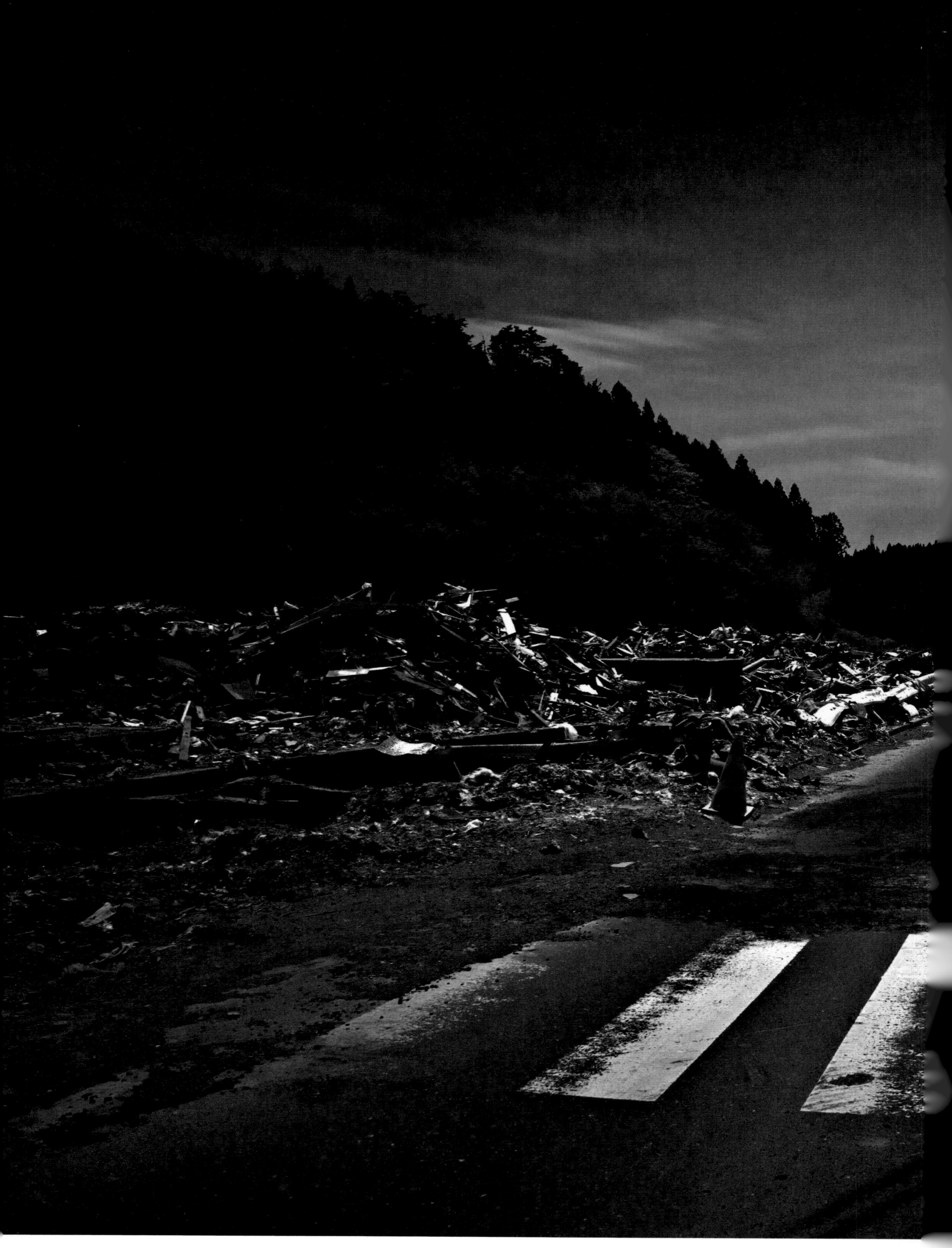

Unused utility poles installed after the tsunami.
Minami Sanriku Cho, Motoyoshi County, Miyagi prefecture

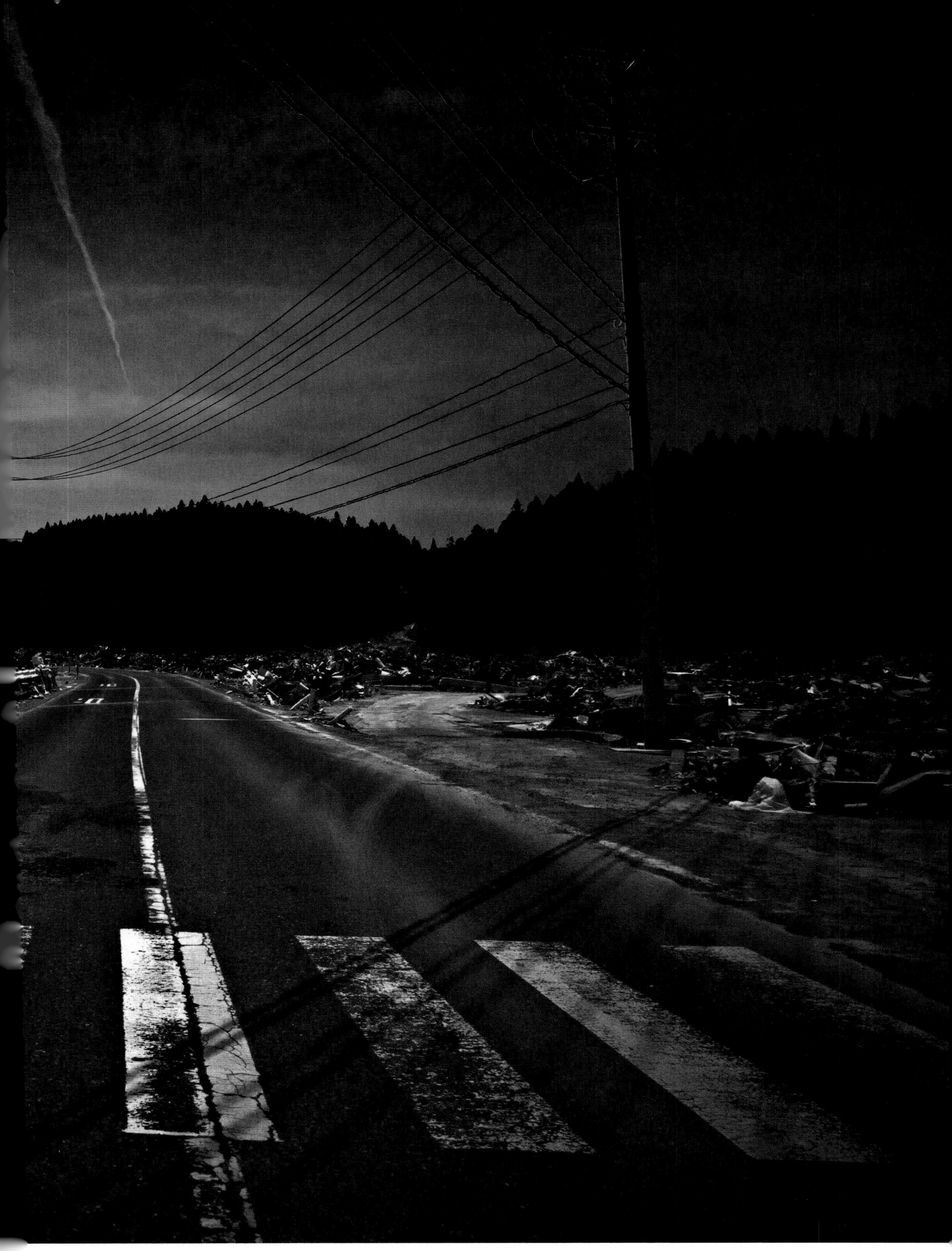

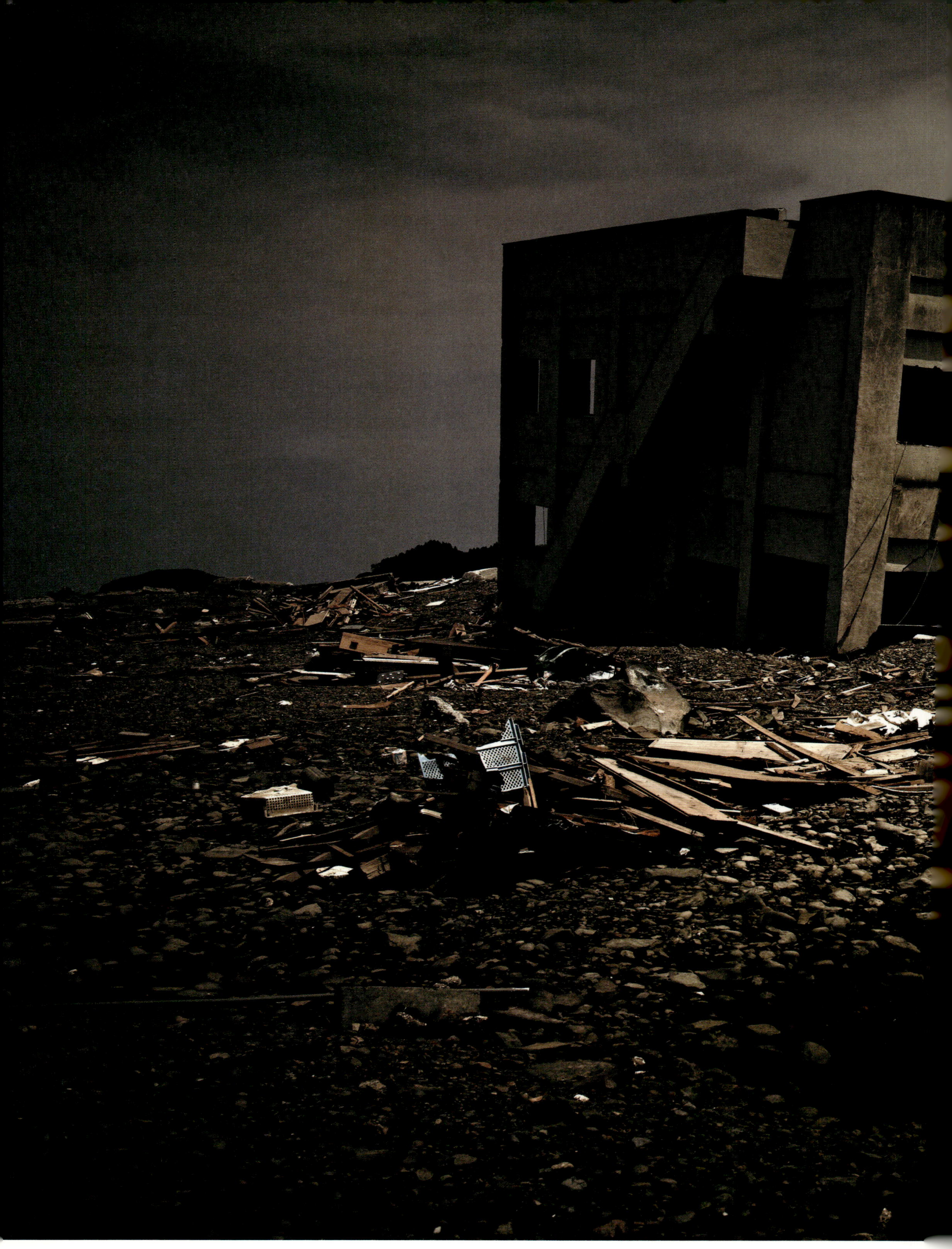

Before the tsunami, there were no buildings here.
Tokura, Jurisdiction of Minami Sanriku Cho, Motoyoshi County, Miyagi prefecture

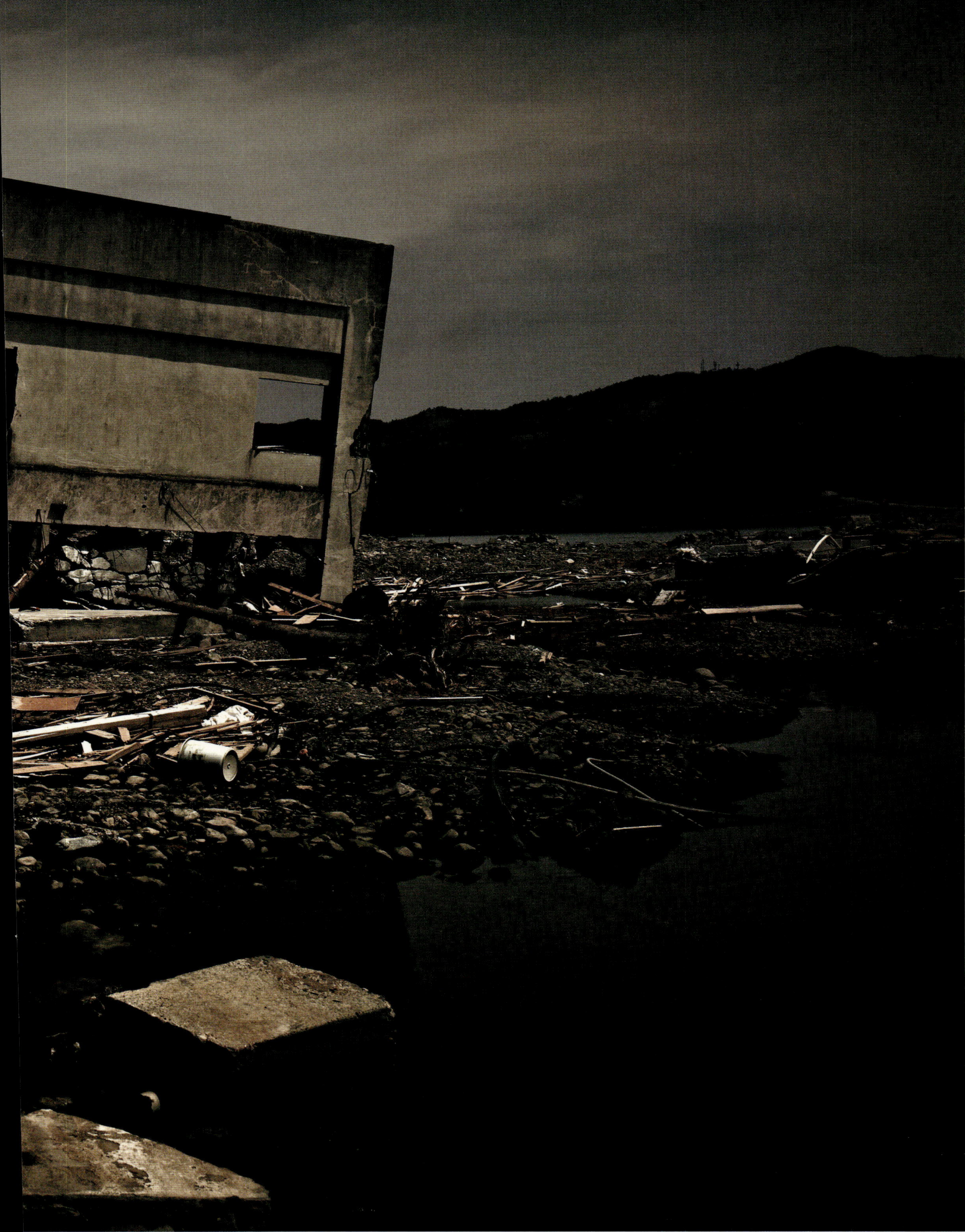

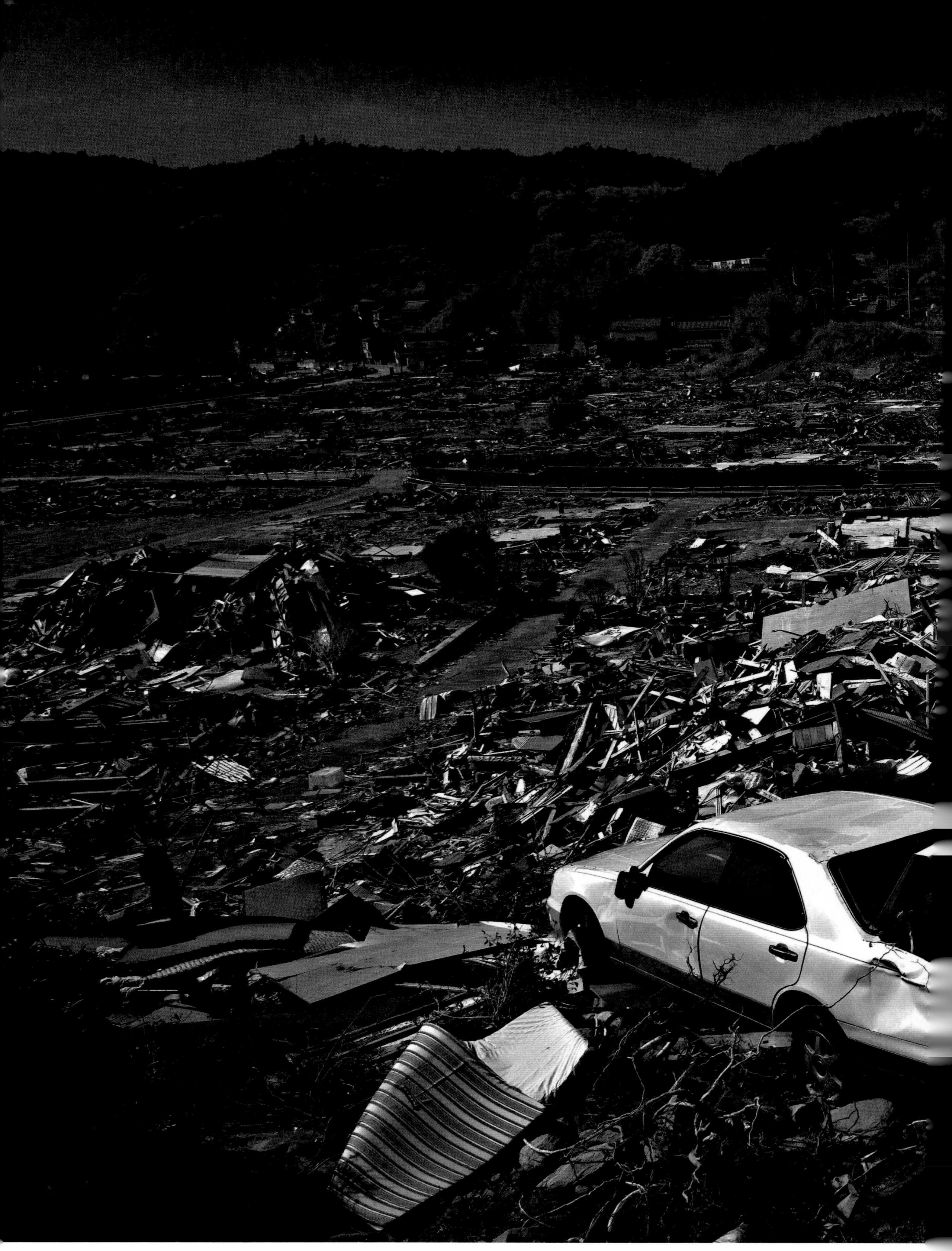

There was a town here.
Ogatsu-cho, City of Ishinomaki, Miyagi prefecture

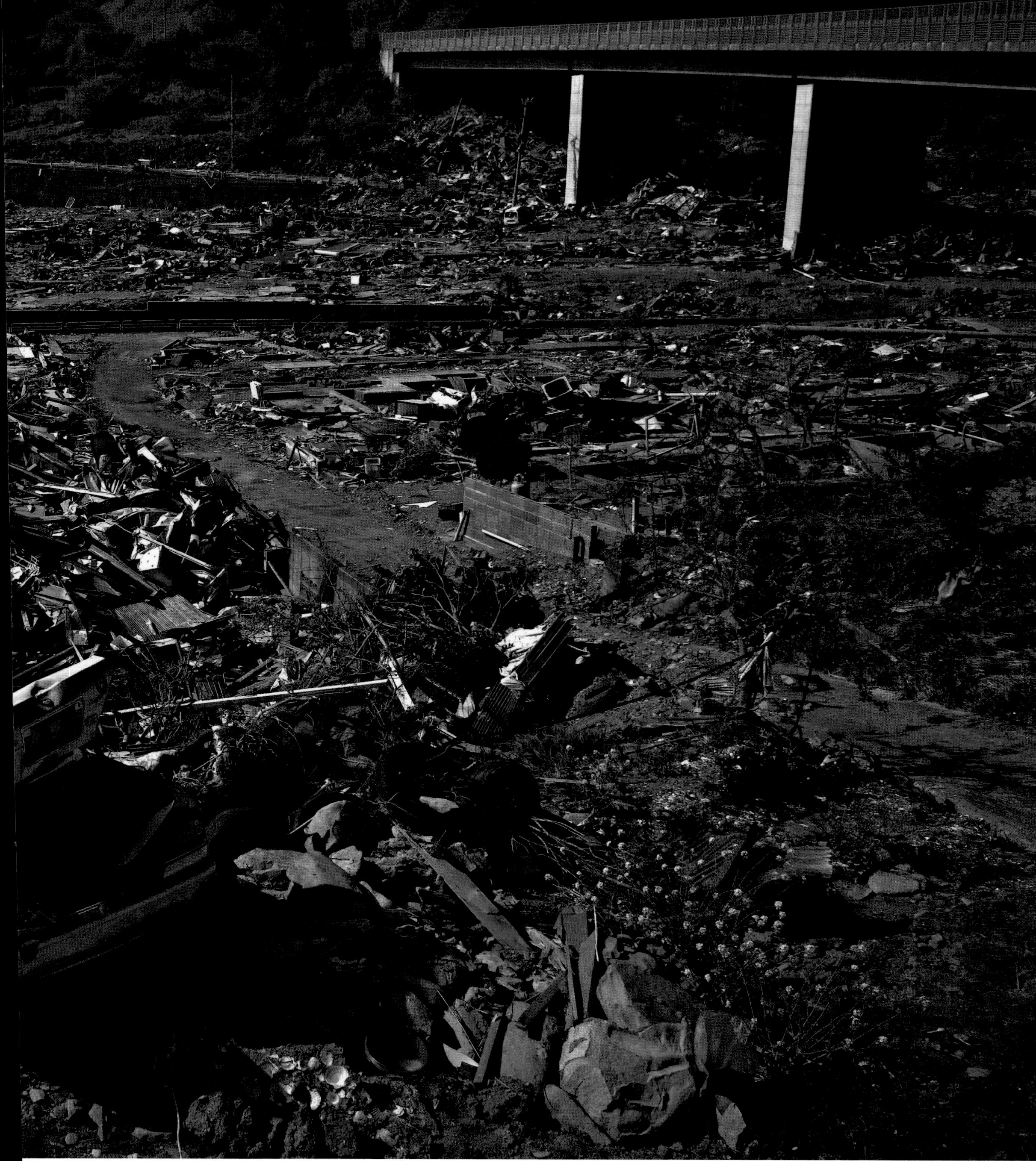

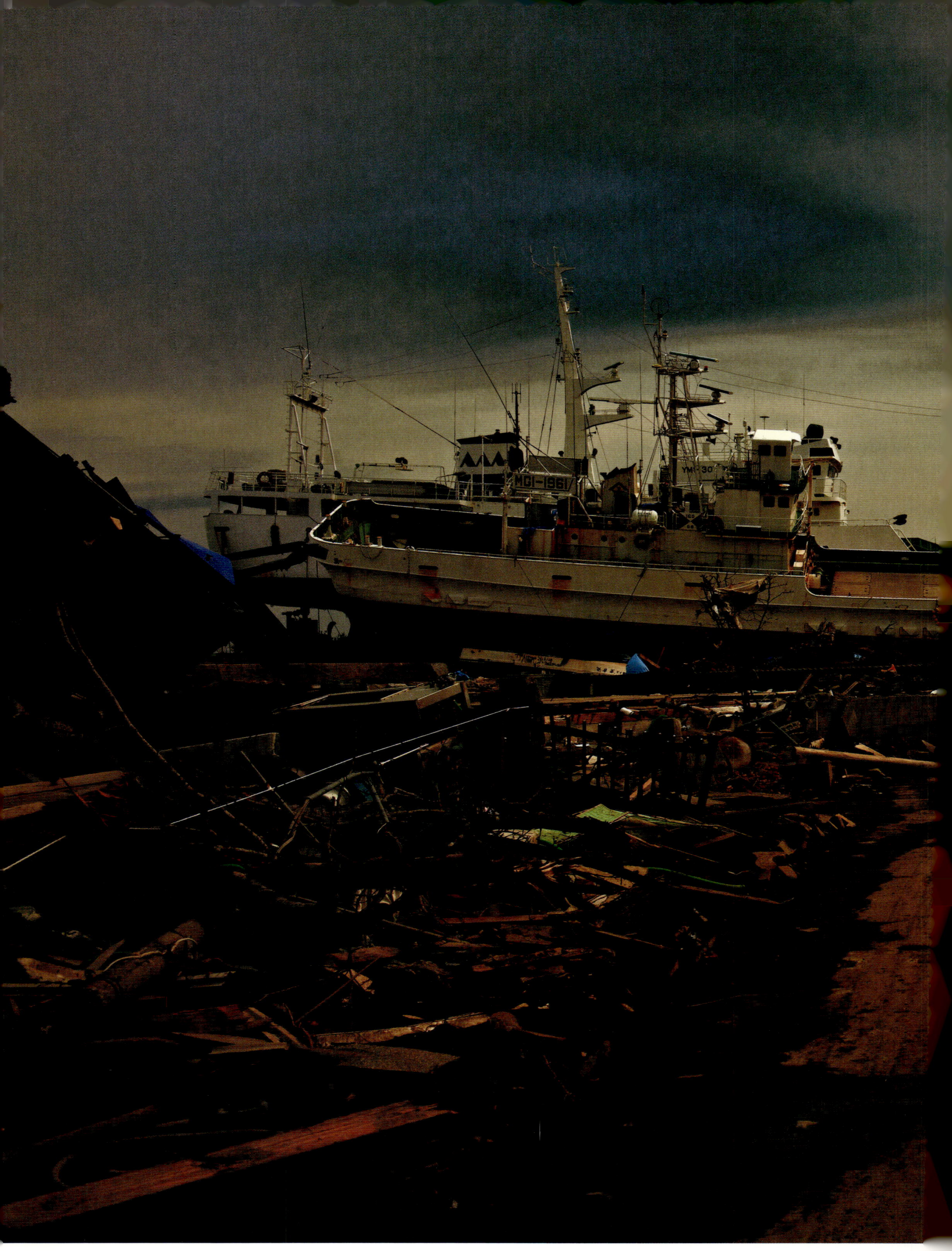

The residential area.
City of Higashi Matsushima, Miyagi prefecture

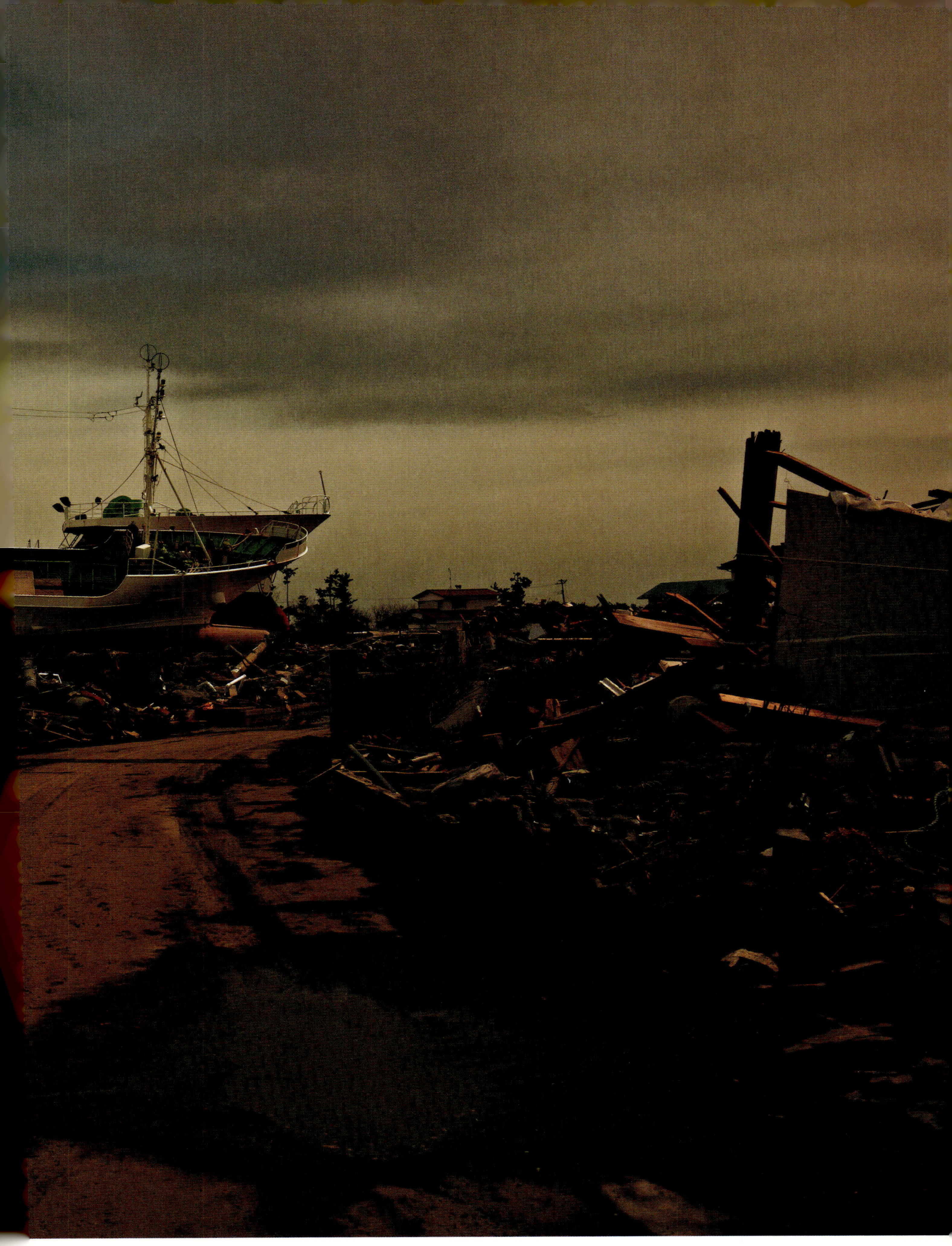

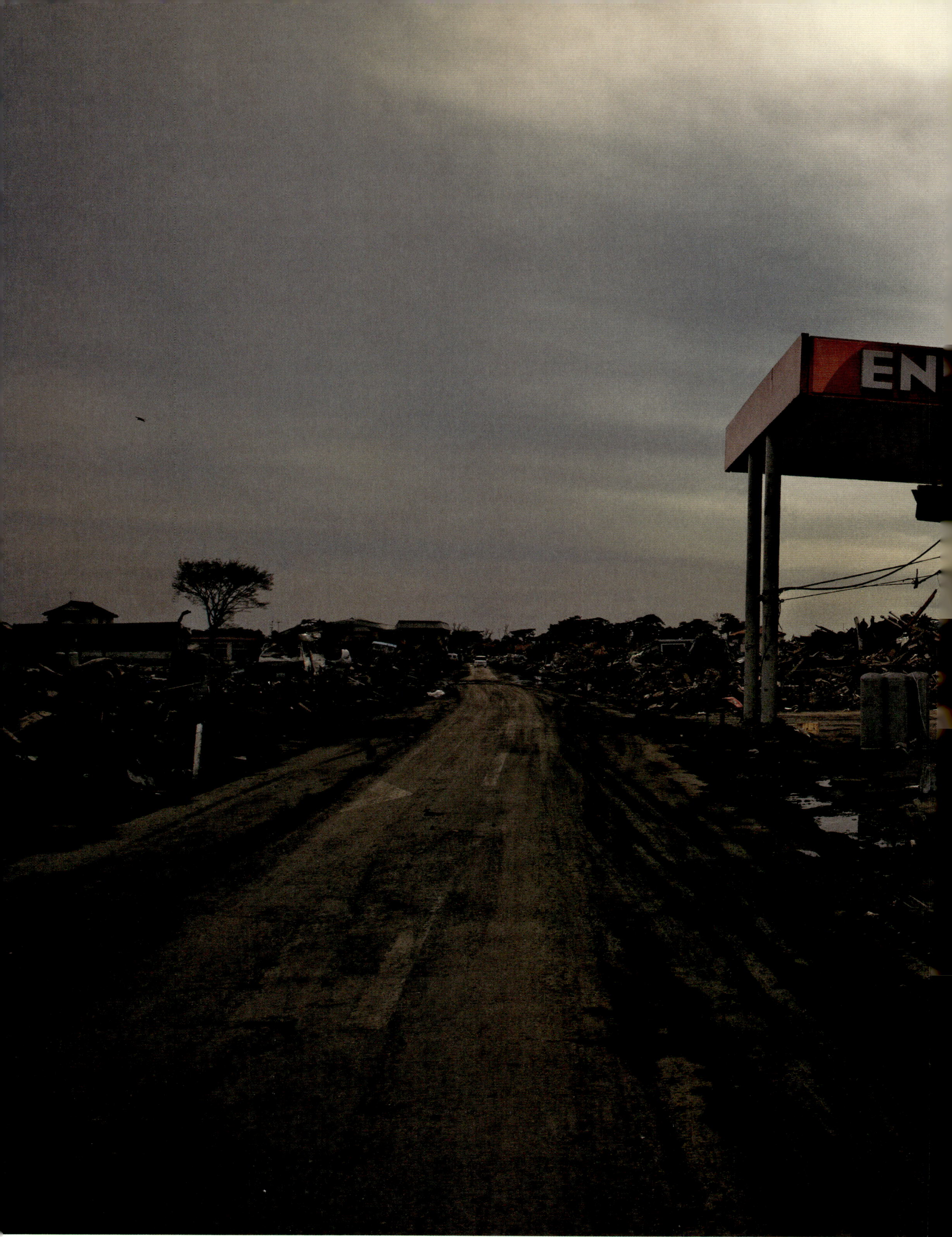

A gas station.
City of Higashi Matsushima, Miyagi prefecture

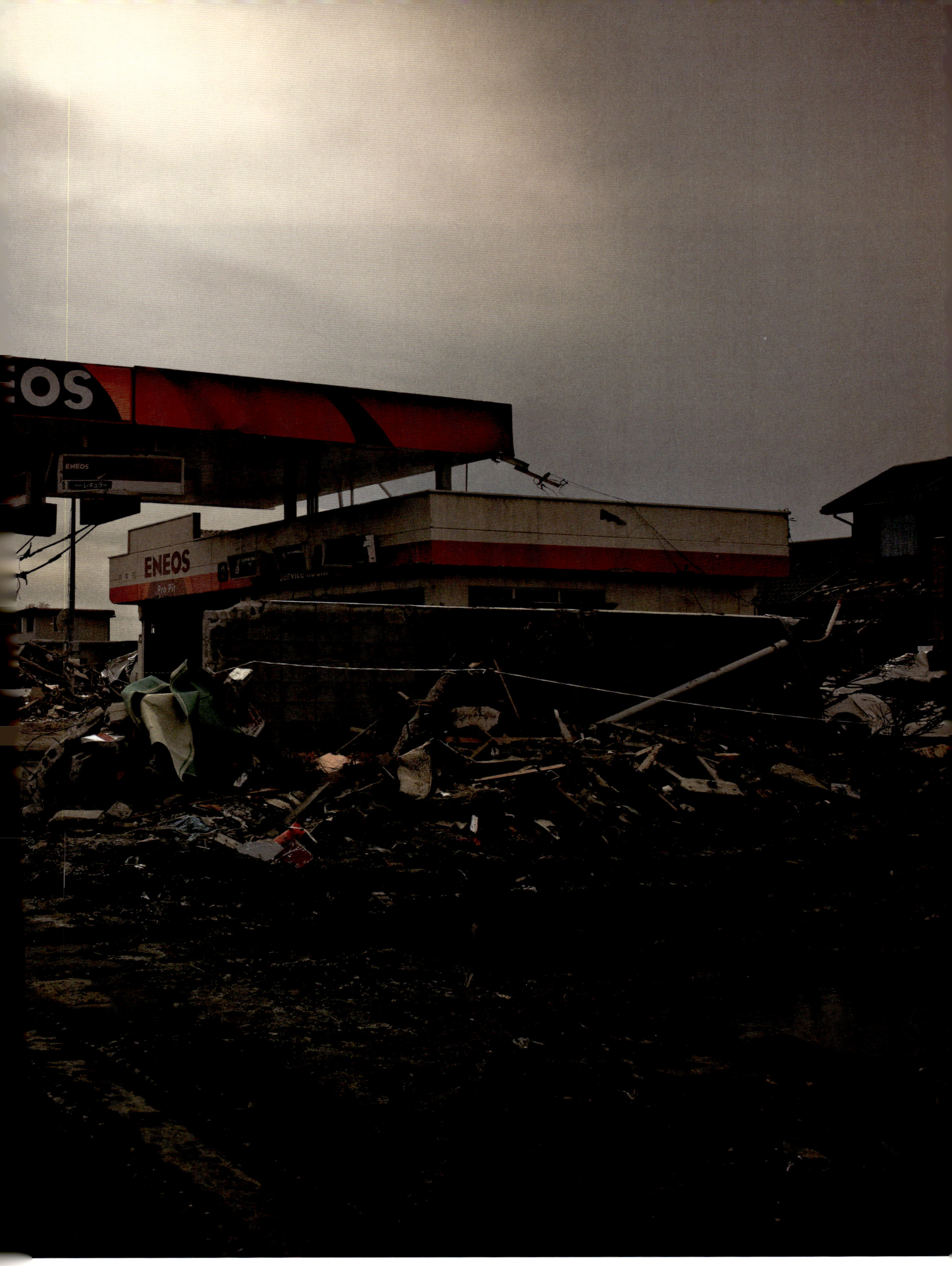
ENEOS
ENEOS
Pro Pit

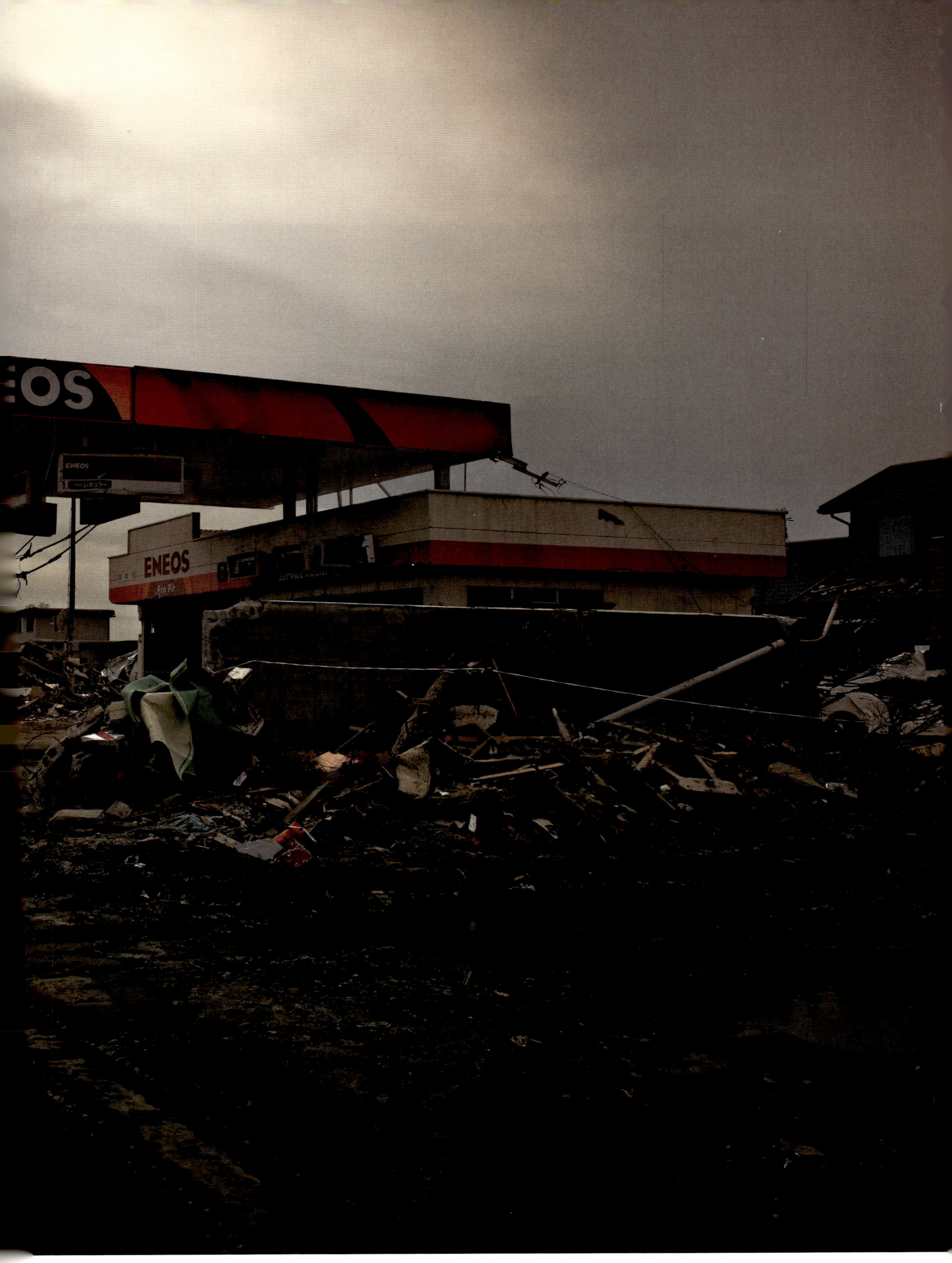
ENEOS
Pro Pit

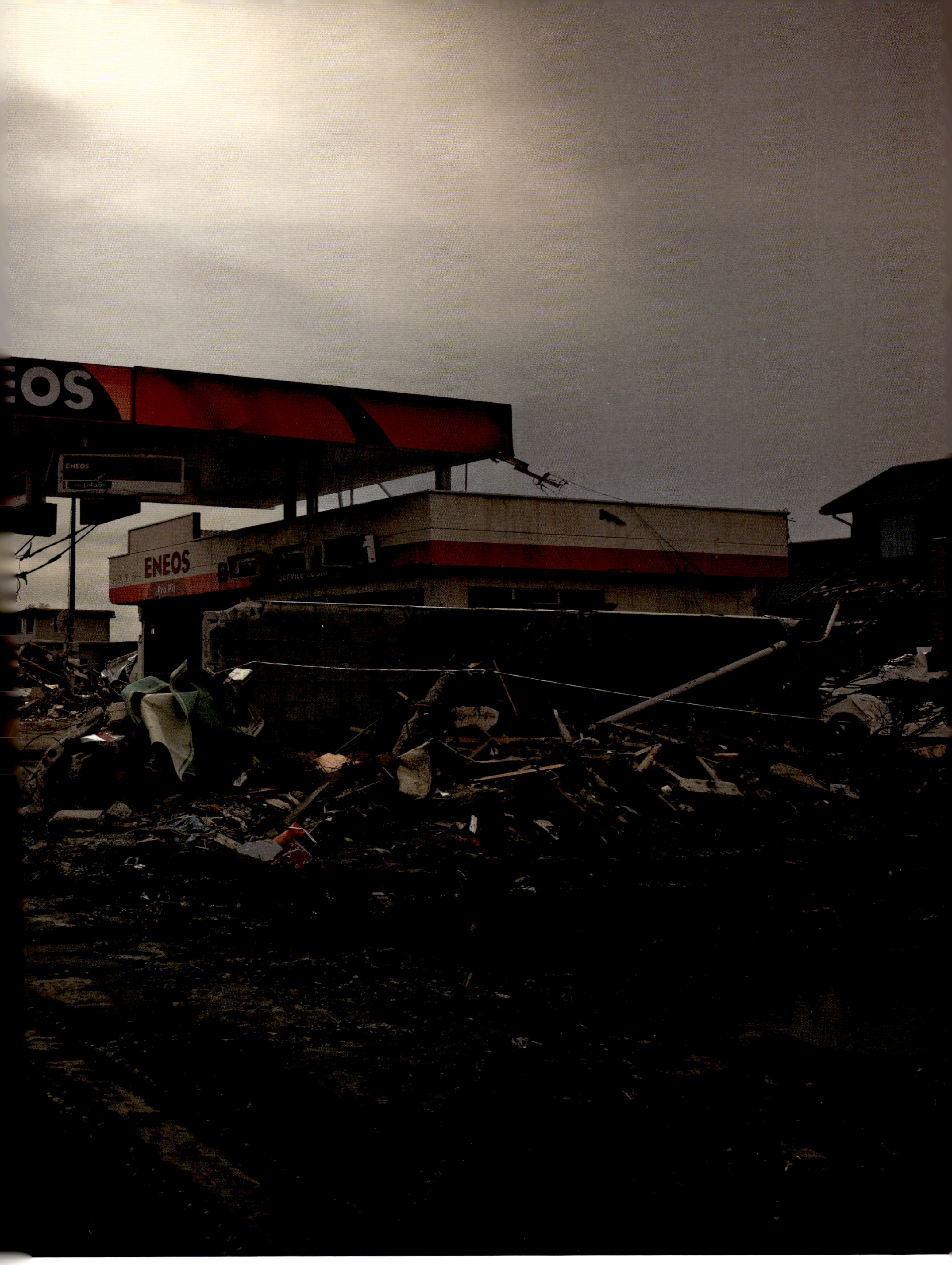
EOS
ENEOS
ENEOS

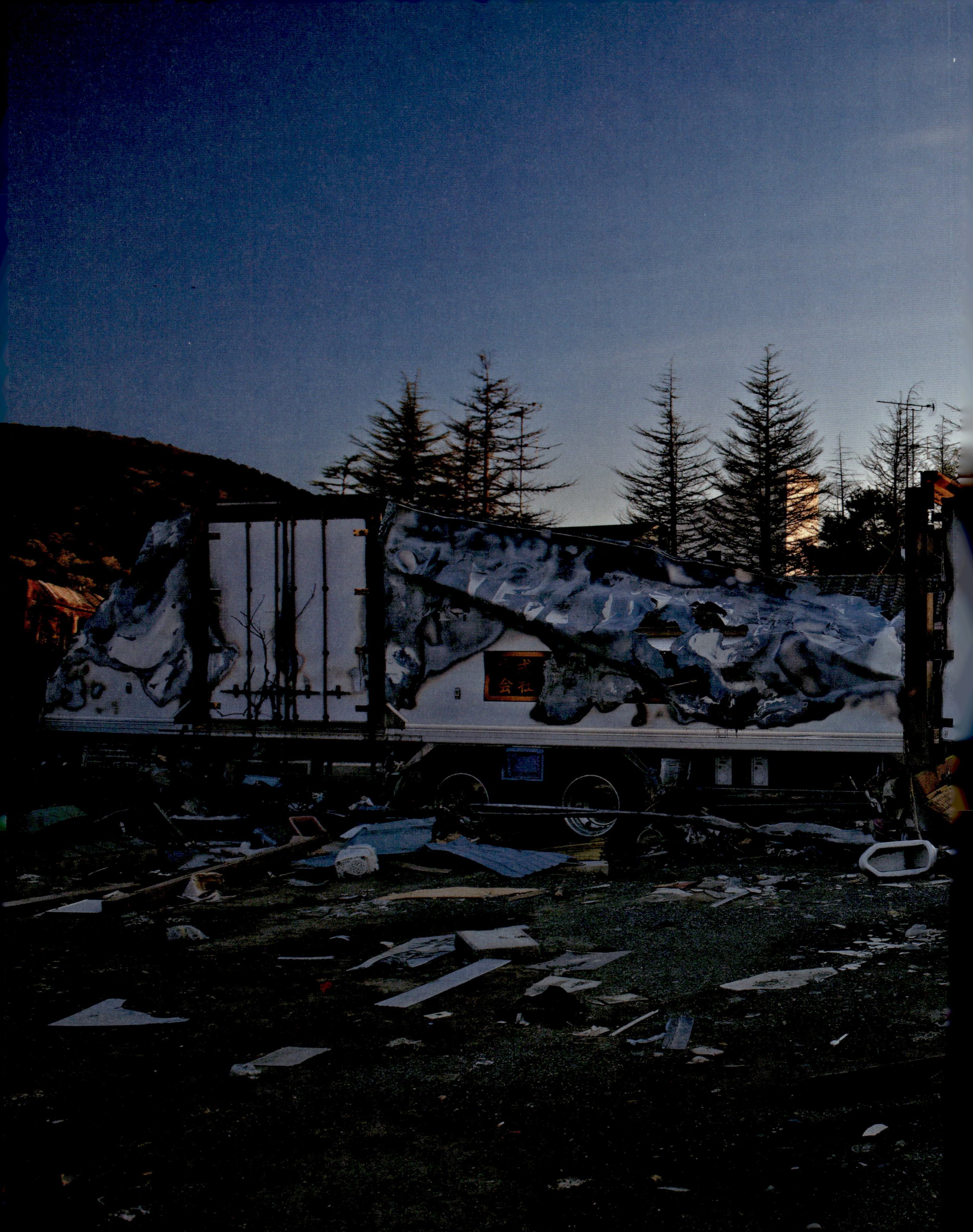

City of Ishinomaki, Miyagi prefecture

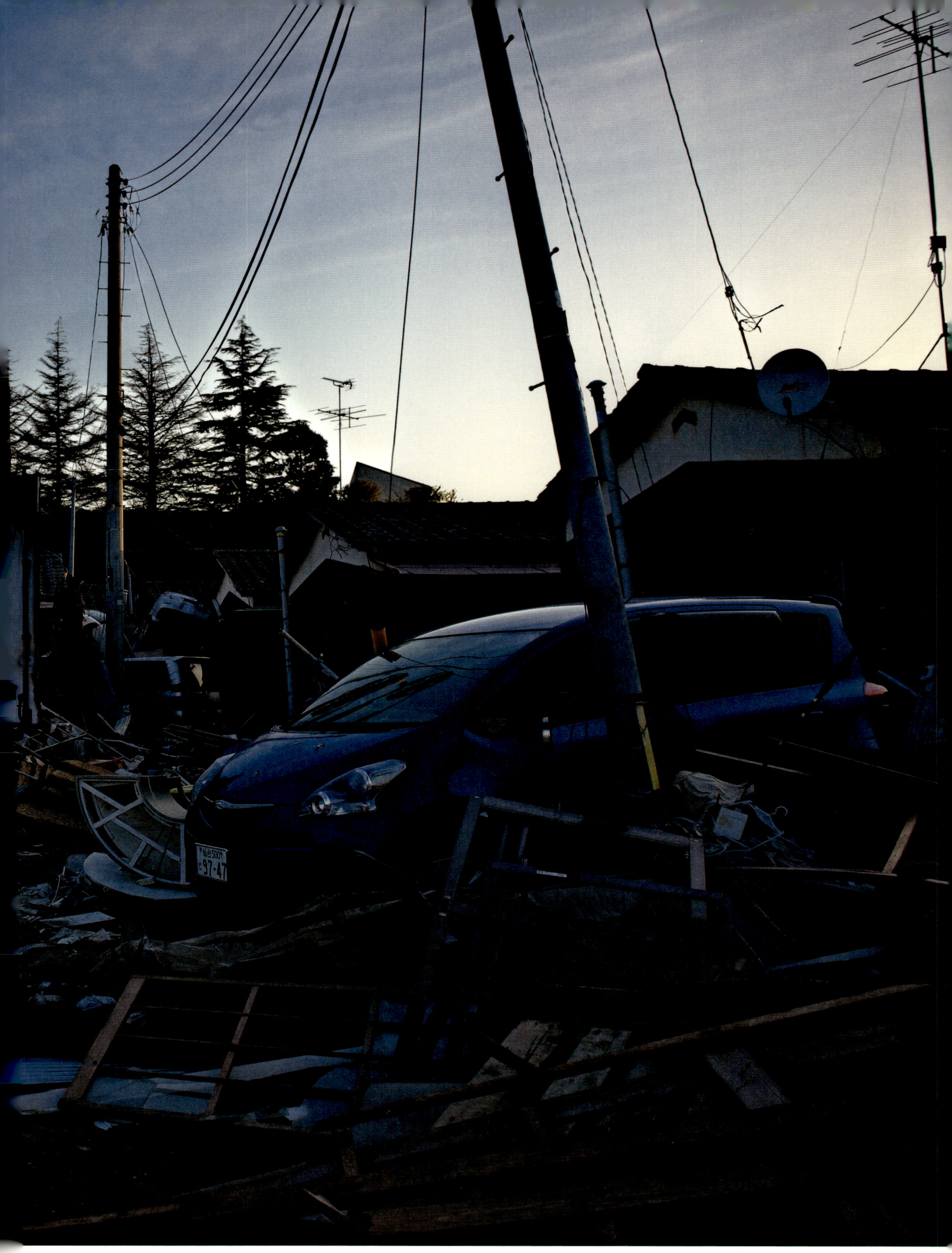
仙台500
97-47

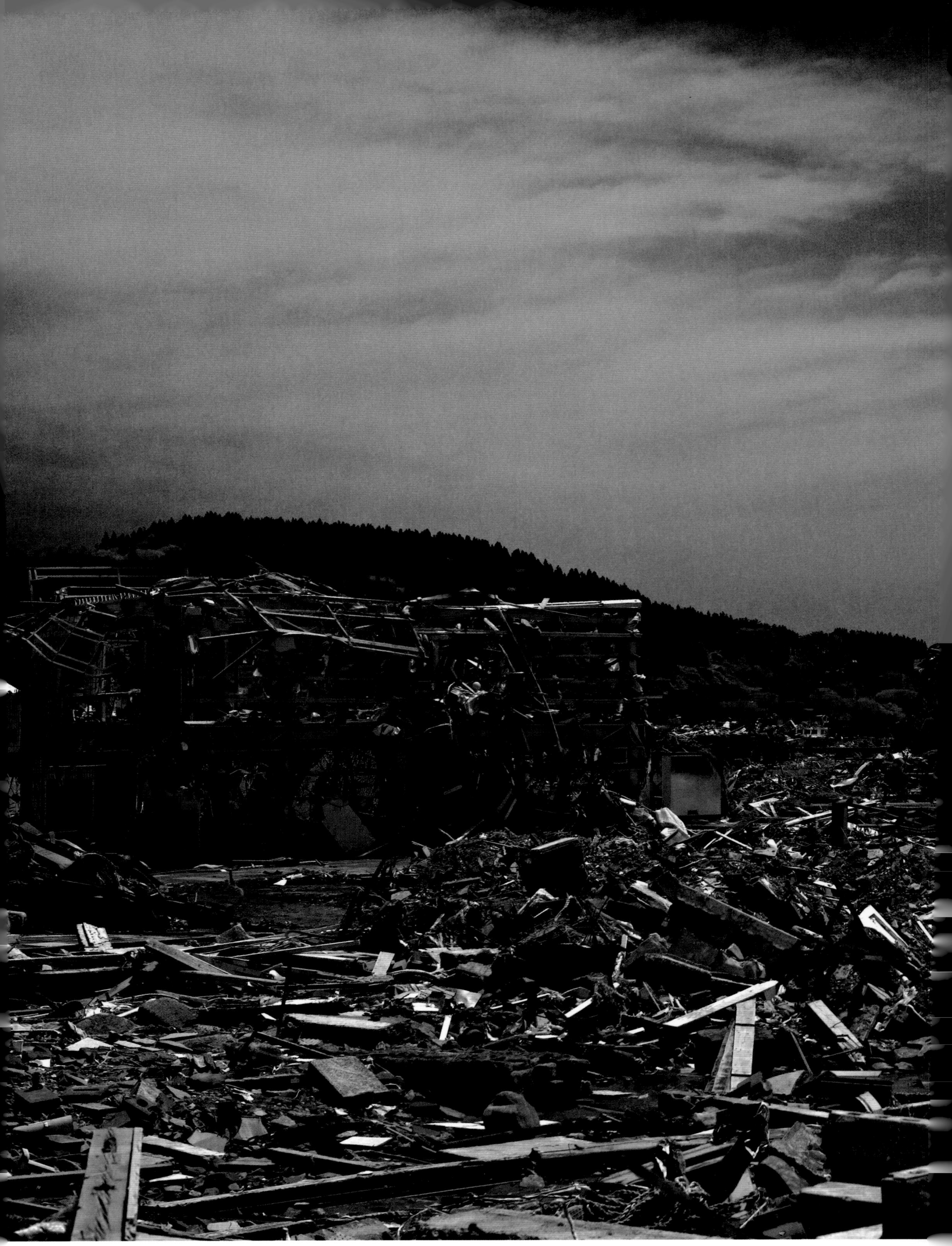

Minami Sanriku Cho, Motoyoshi County, Miyagi prefecture

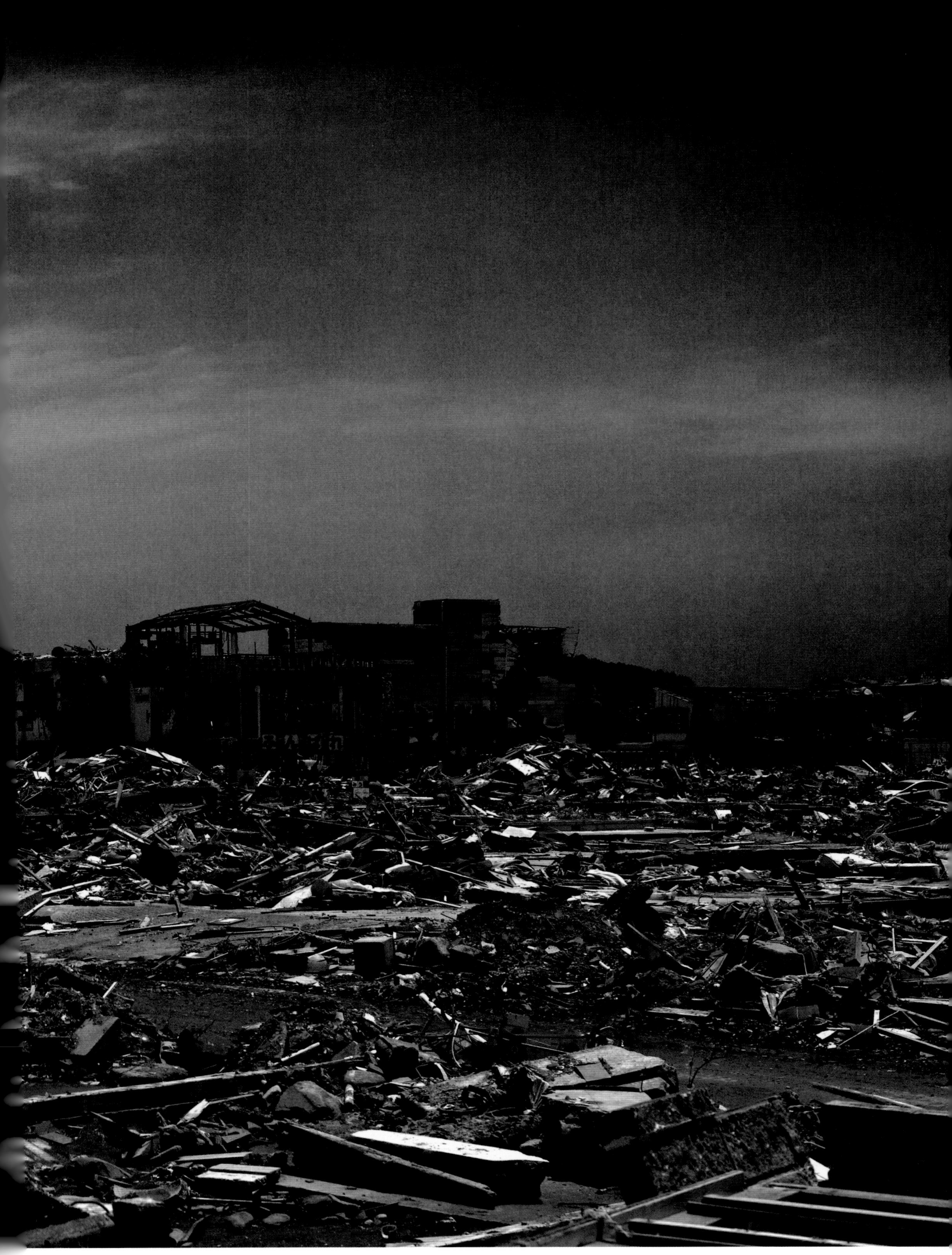

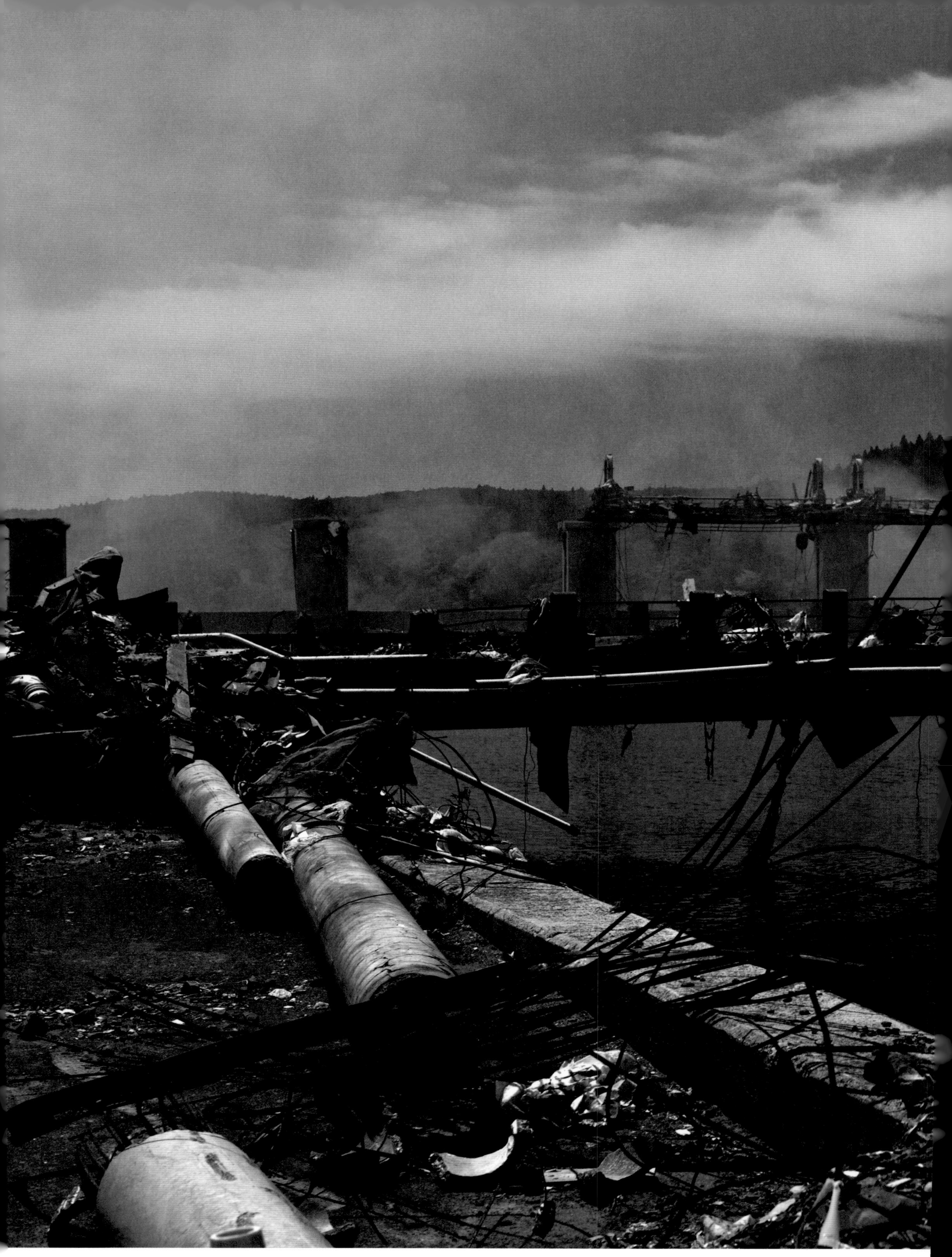

Two sluiceways for protection against tsunami.
Minami Sanriku Cho, Motoyoshi County, Miyagi prefecture

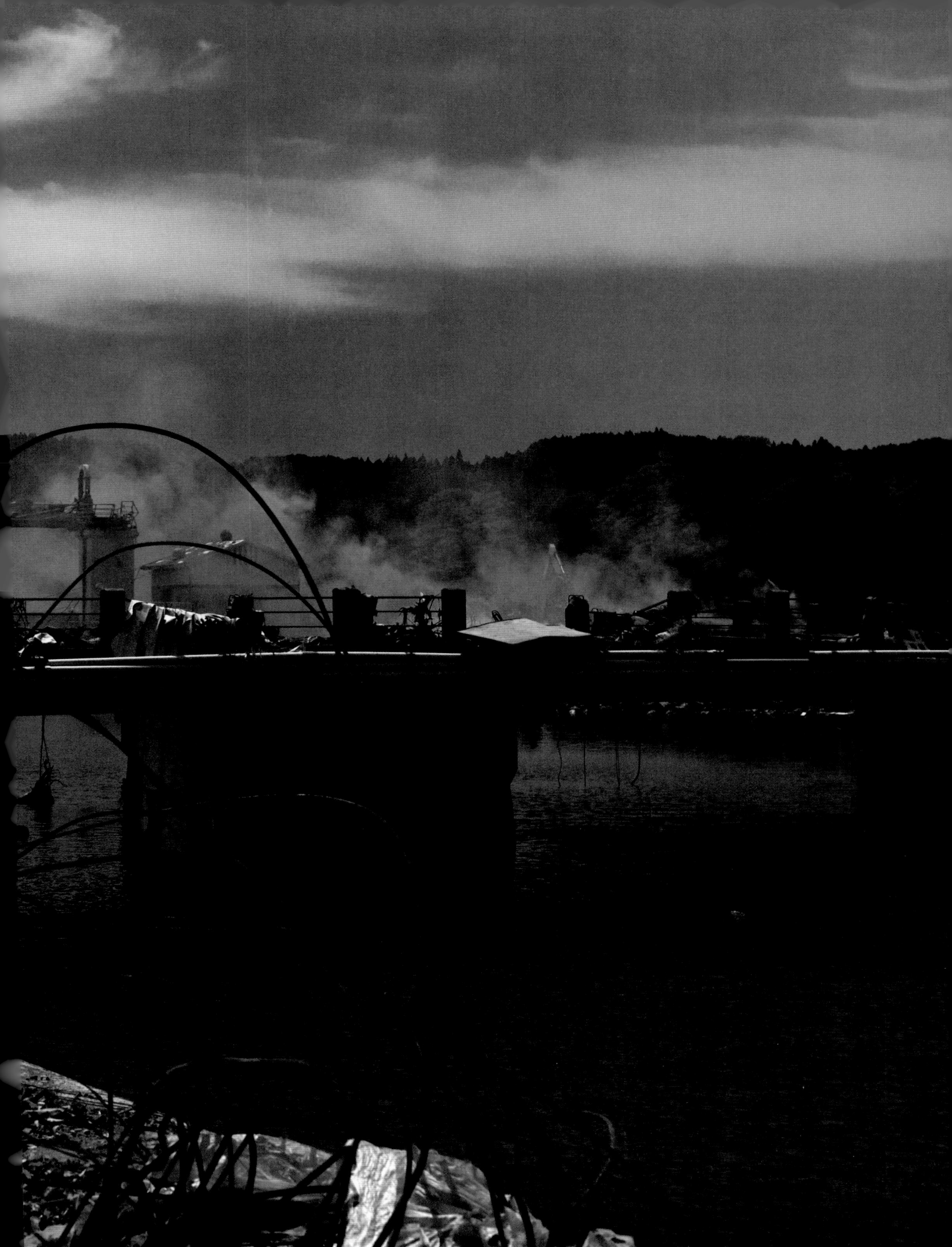

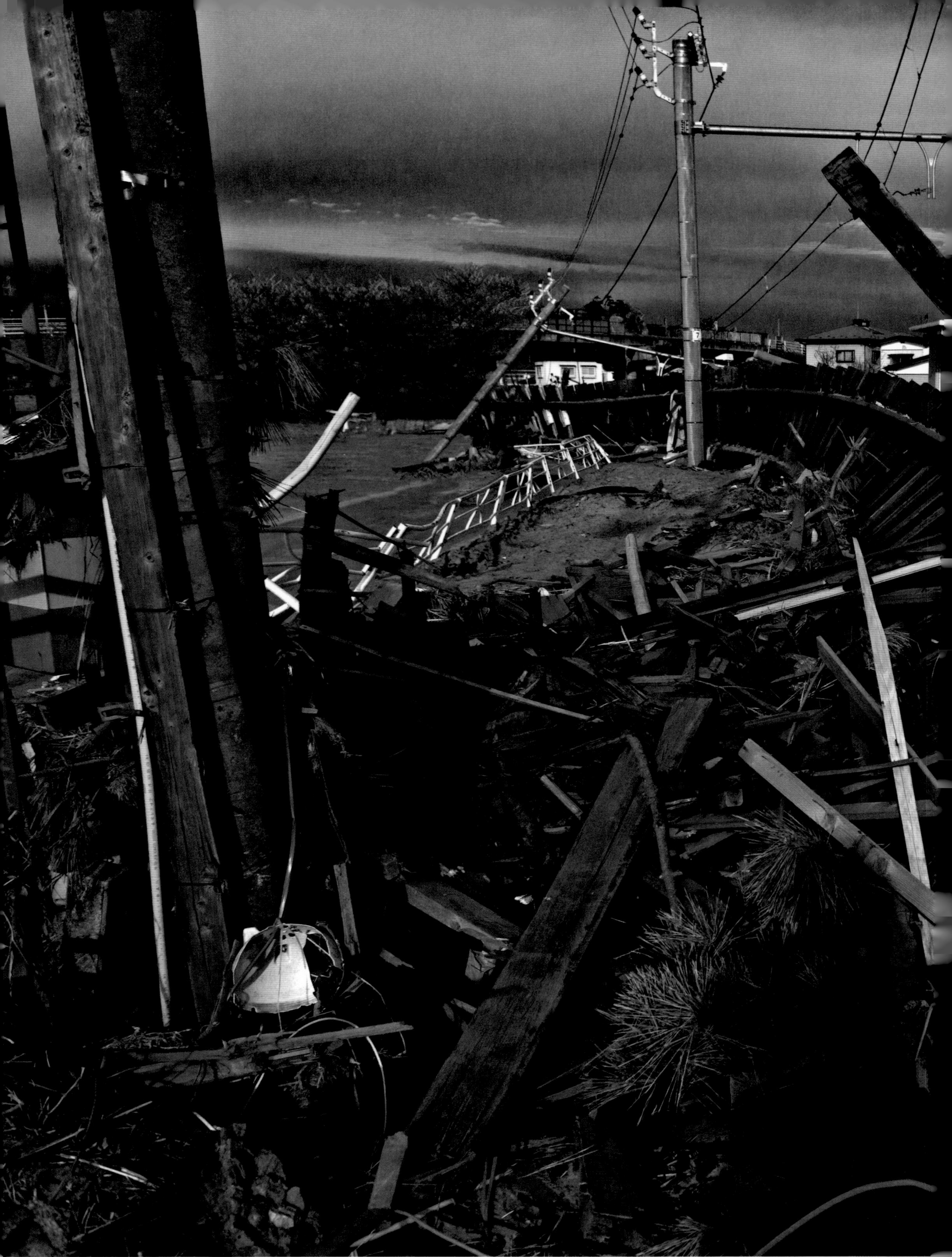

A railway.
City of Higashi Matsushima, Miyagi prefecture

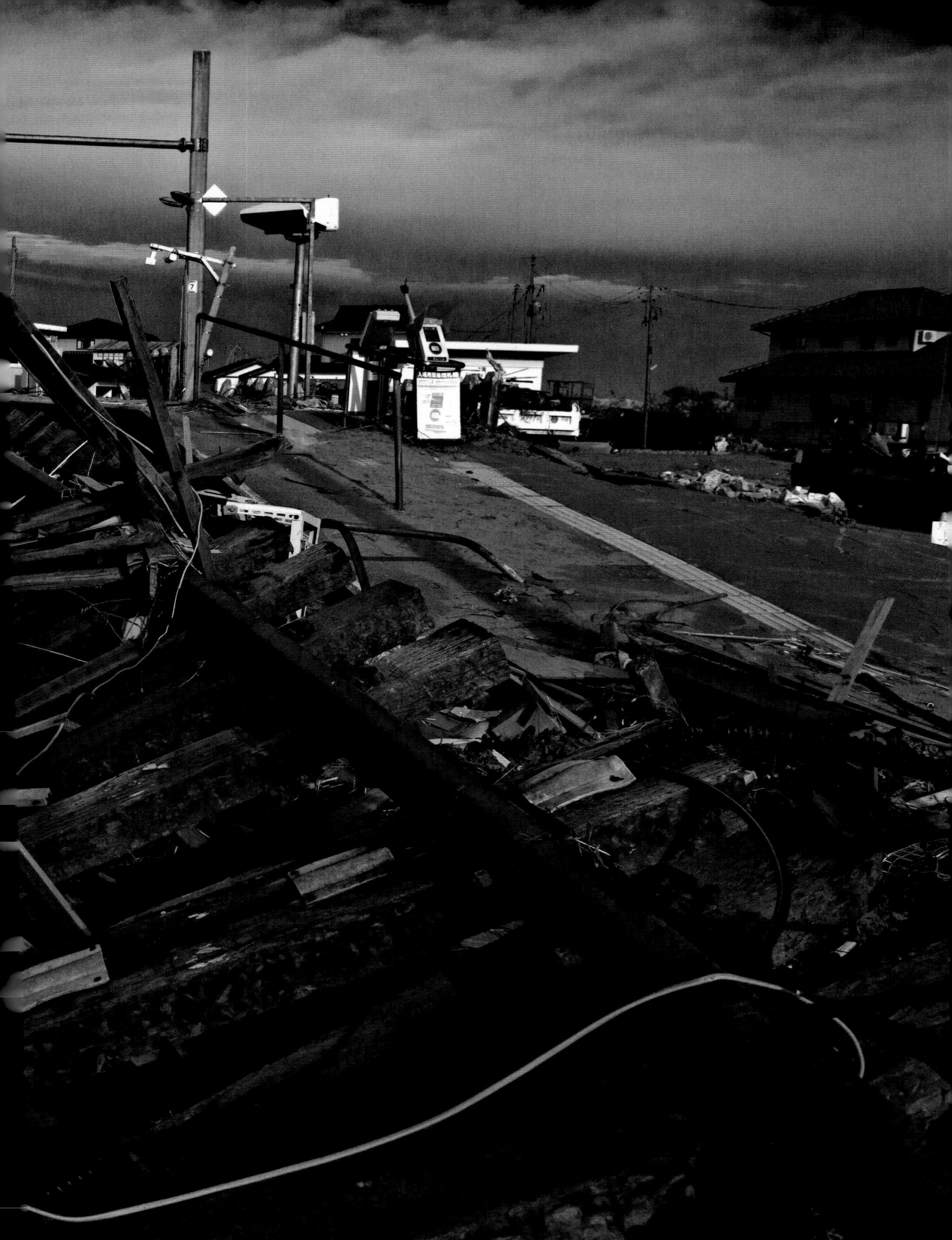

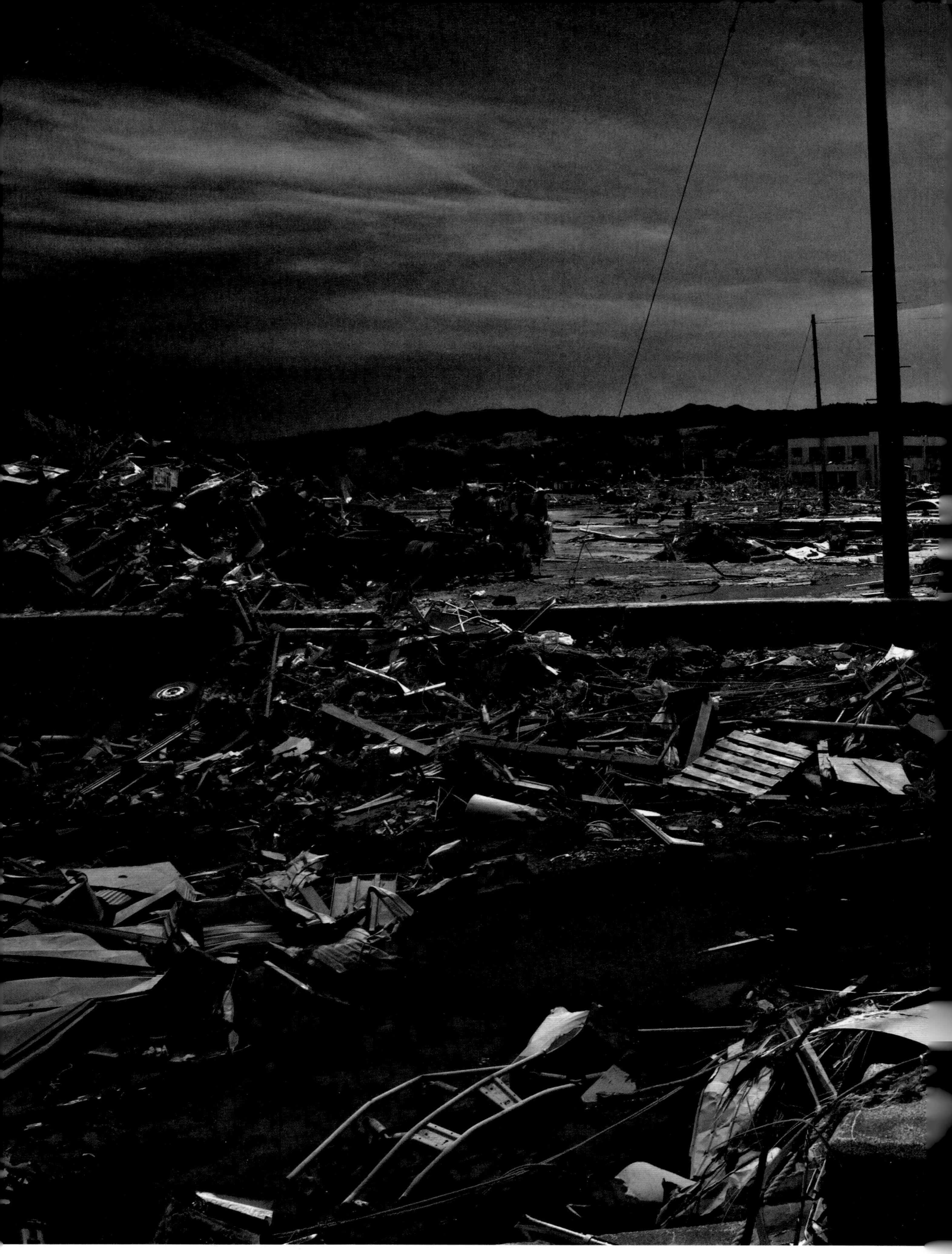

Minami Sanriku Cho, Motoyoshi County, Miyagi prefecture

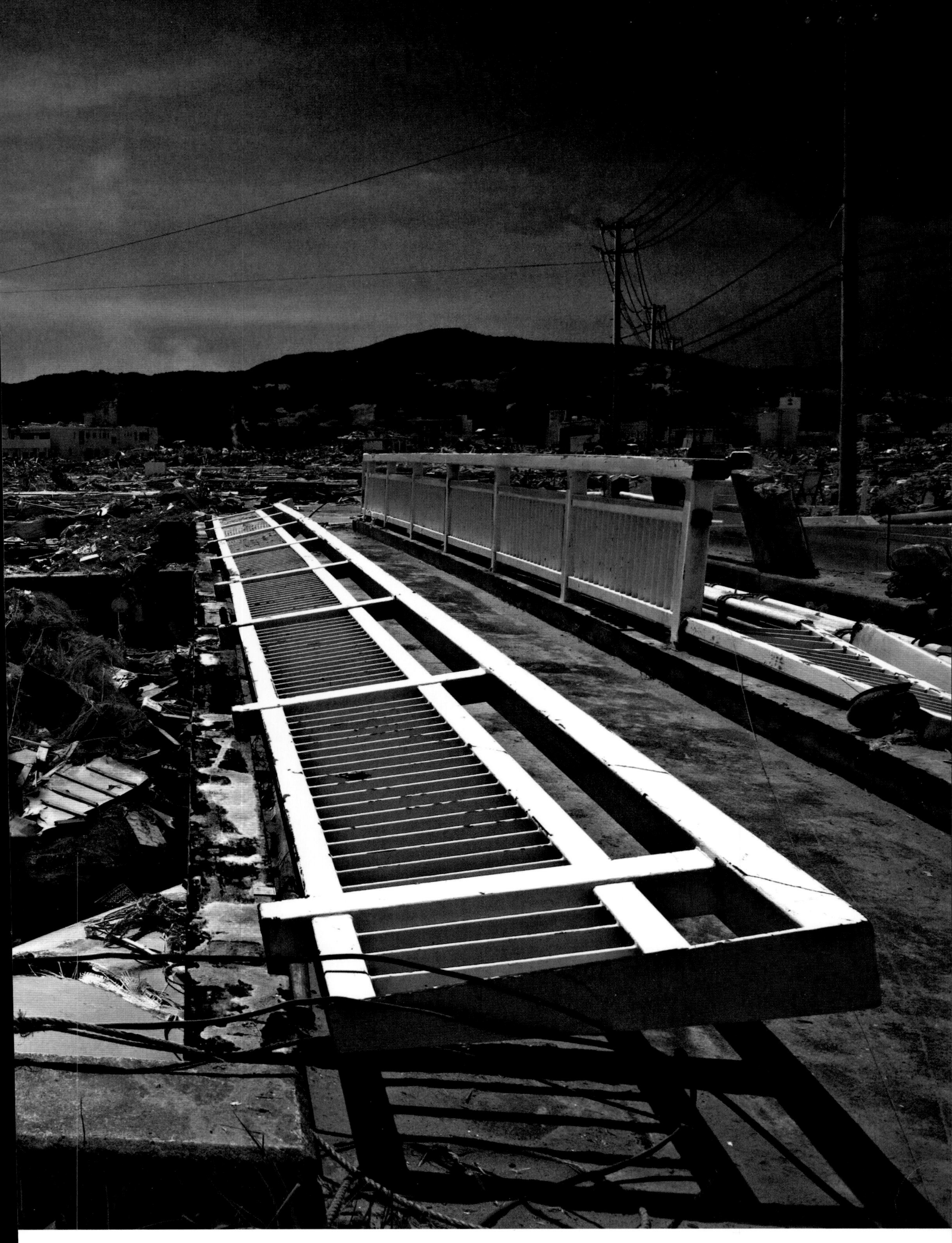

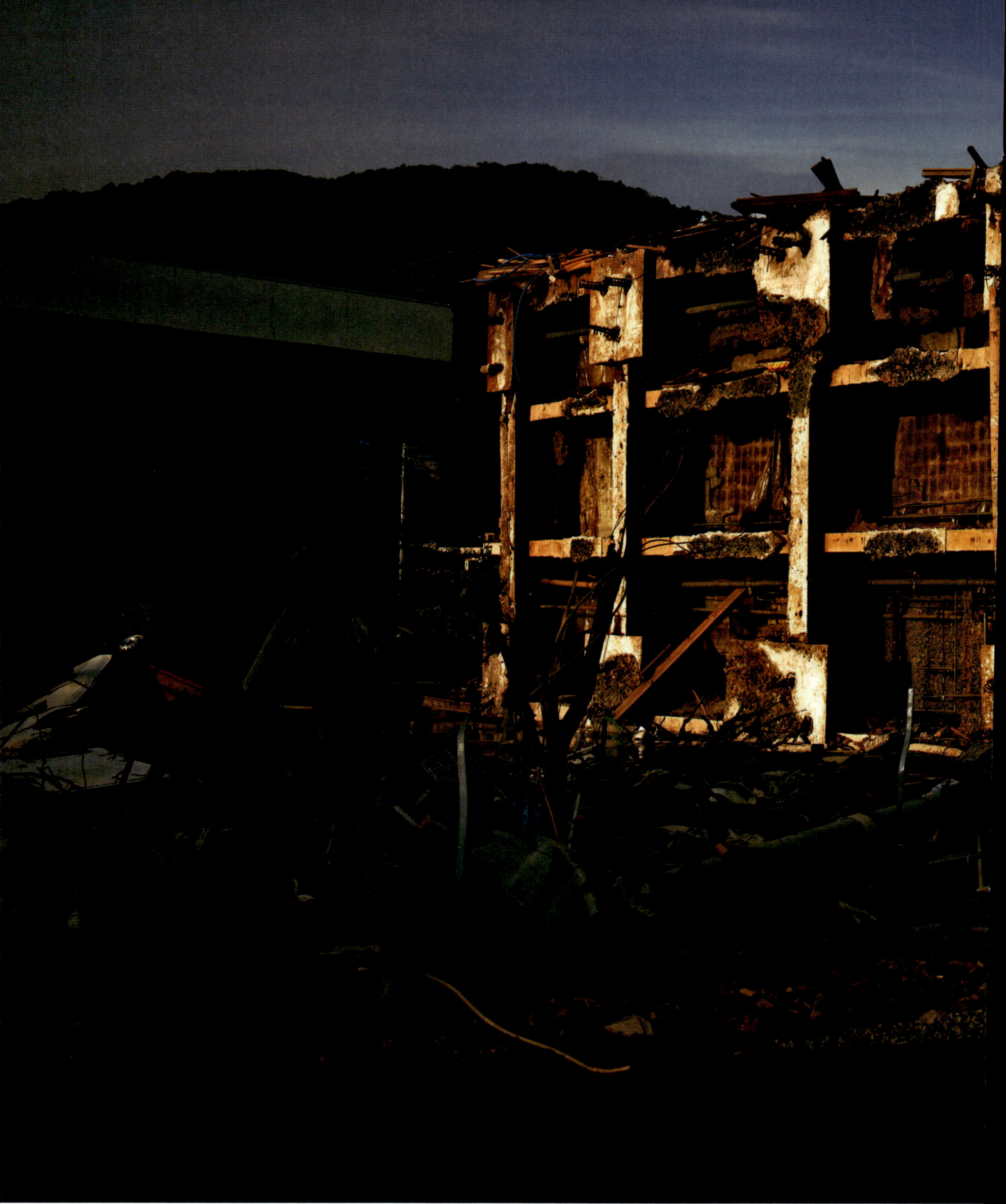

The exposed foundation of a fallen building.
Onagawa Cho, Ojika County, Miyagi prefecture

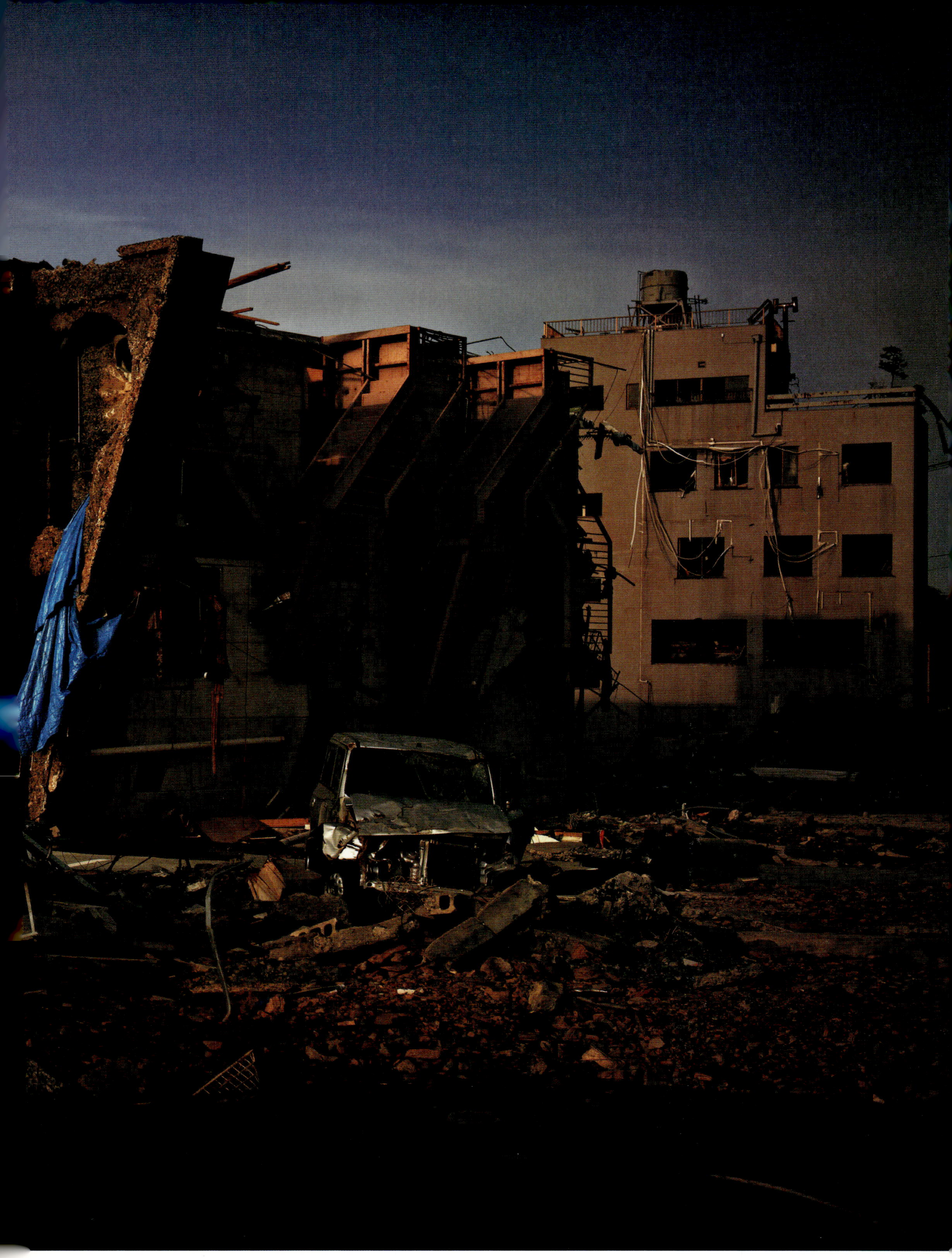

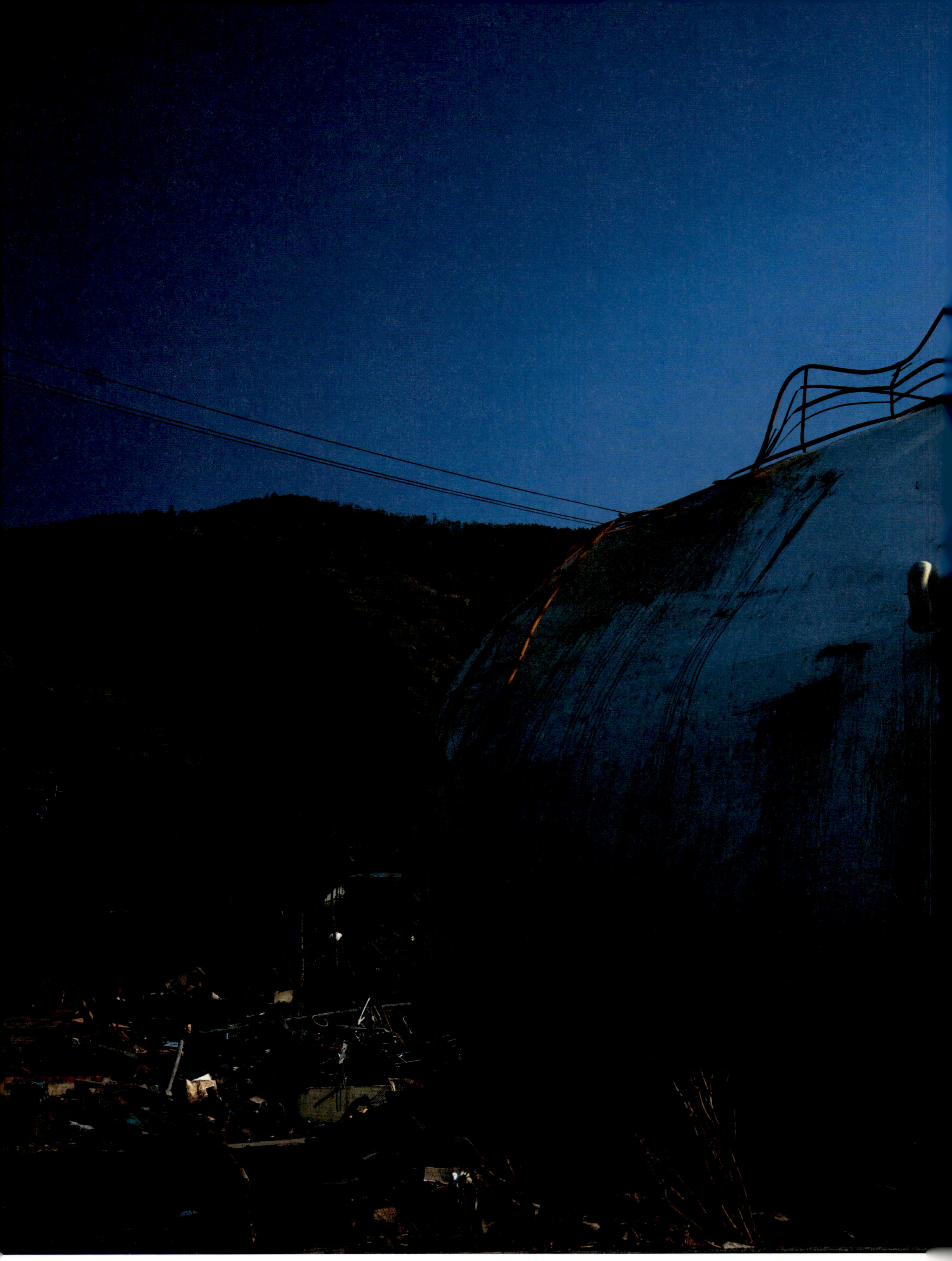

A fish oil tank dropped into the residential district.
Onagawa Cho, Ojika County, Miyagi prefecture

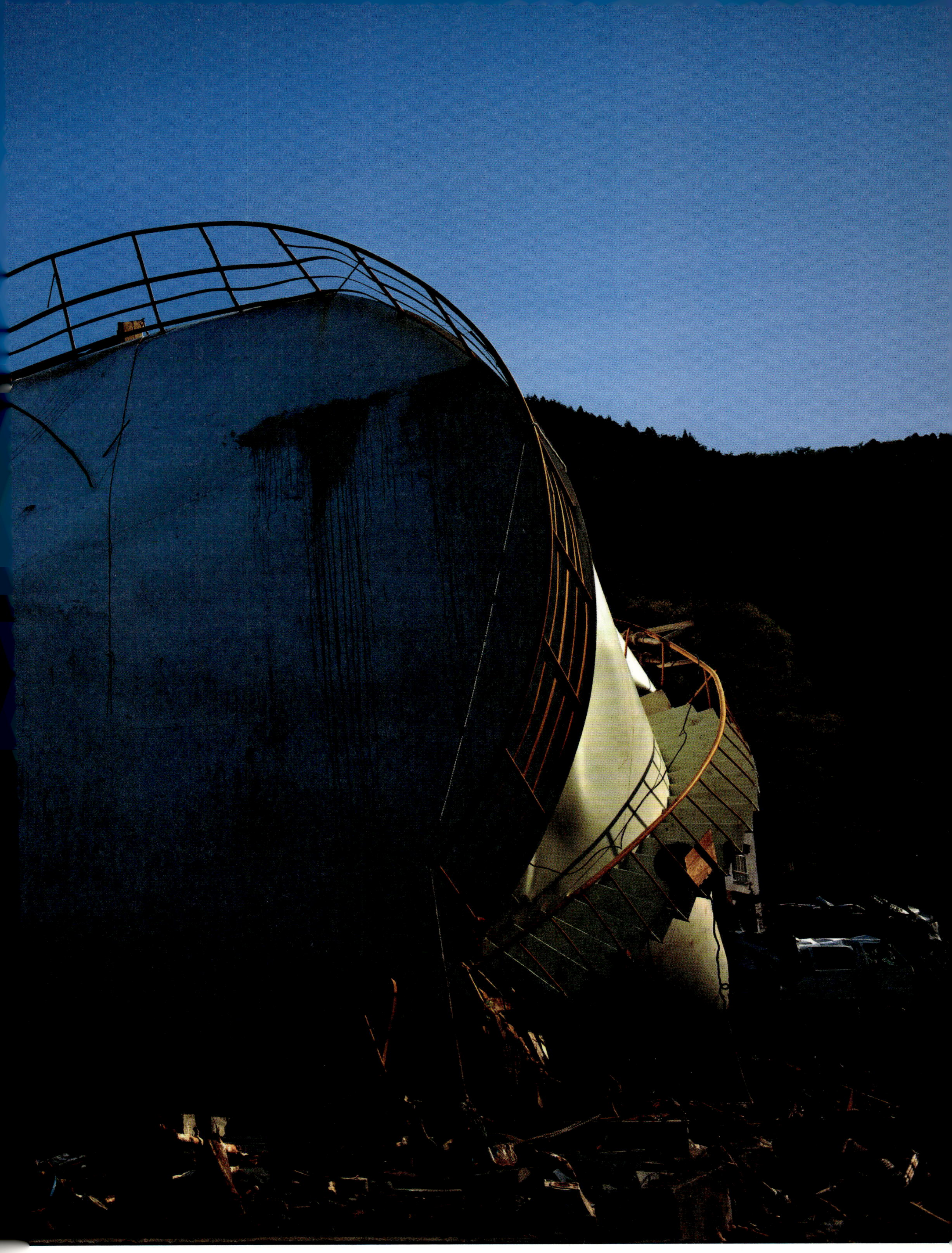

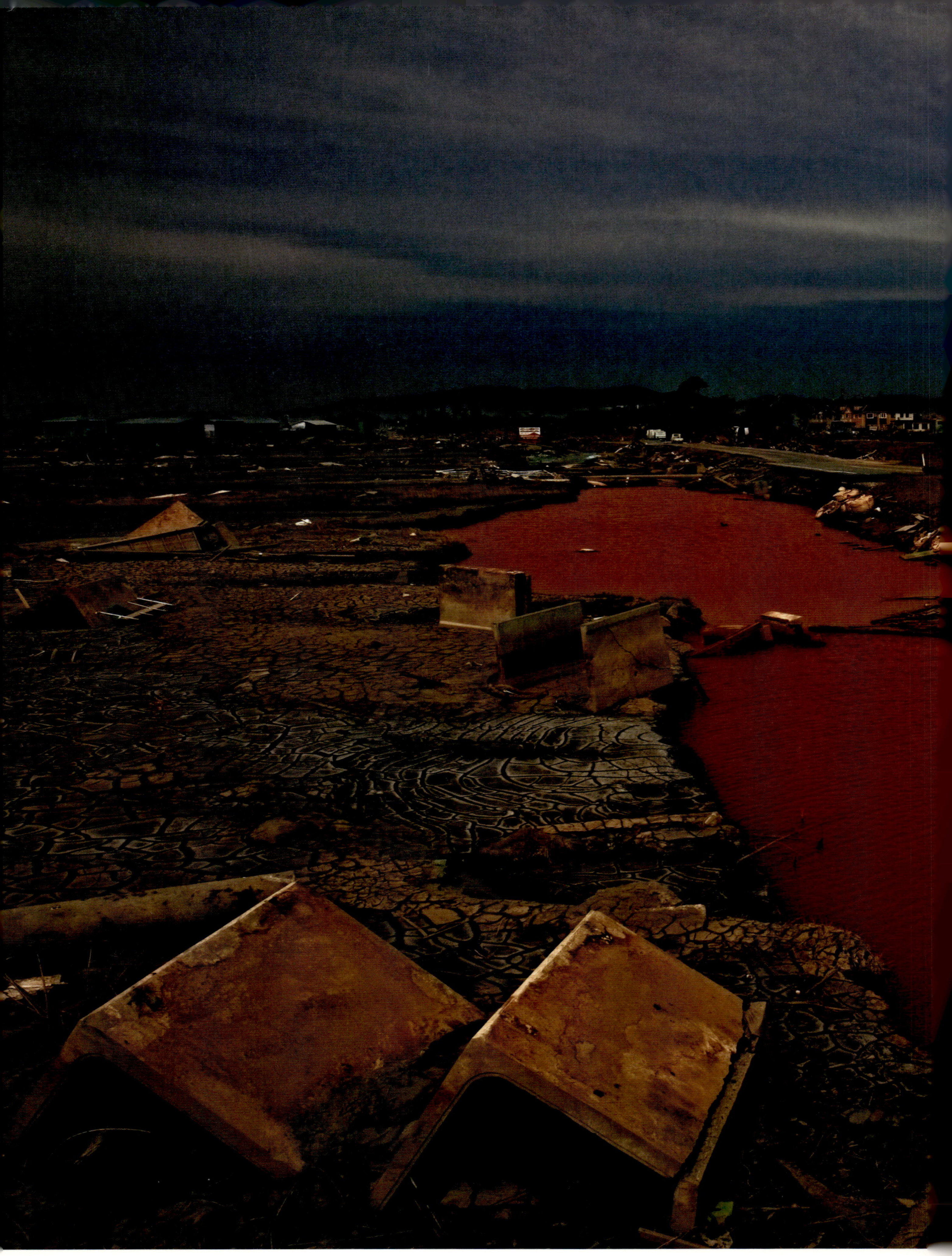

A newly created red river of rust, sulfuric acid and melted clay.
City of Higashi Matsushima, Miyagi prefecture

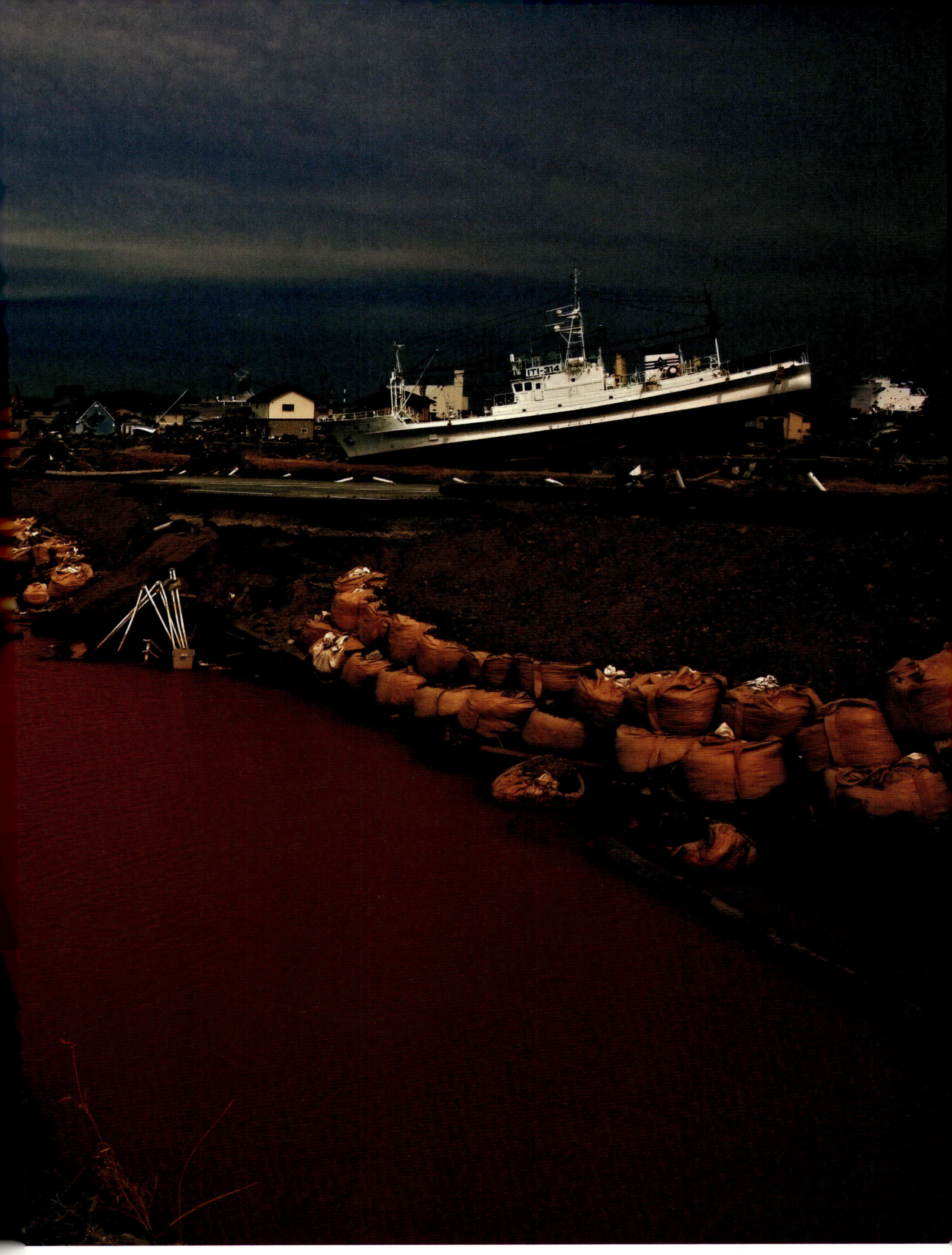
ITI-314

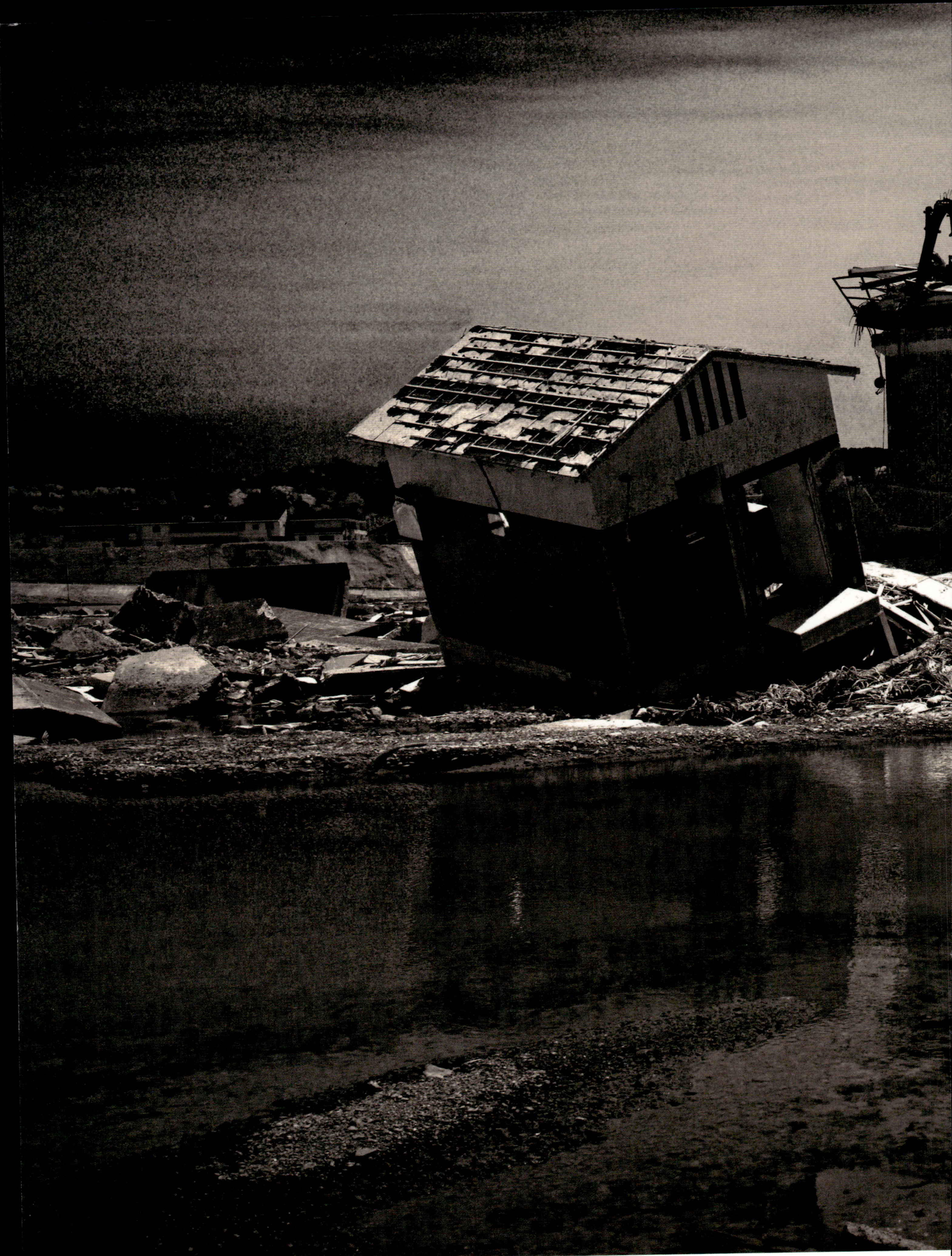

An anti-tsunami sluiceway with newly flooded land in the foreground.
Tokura, Jurisdiction of Minami Sanriku Cho, Motoyoshi County, Miyagi prefecture

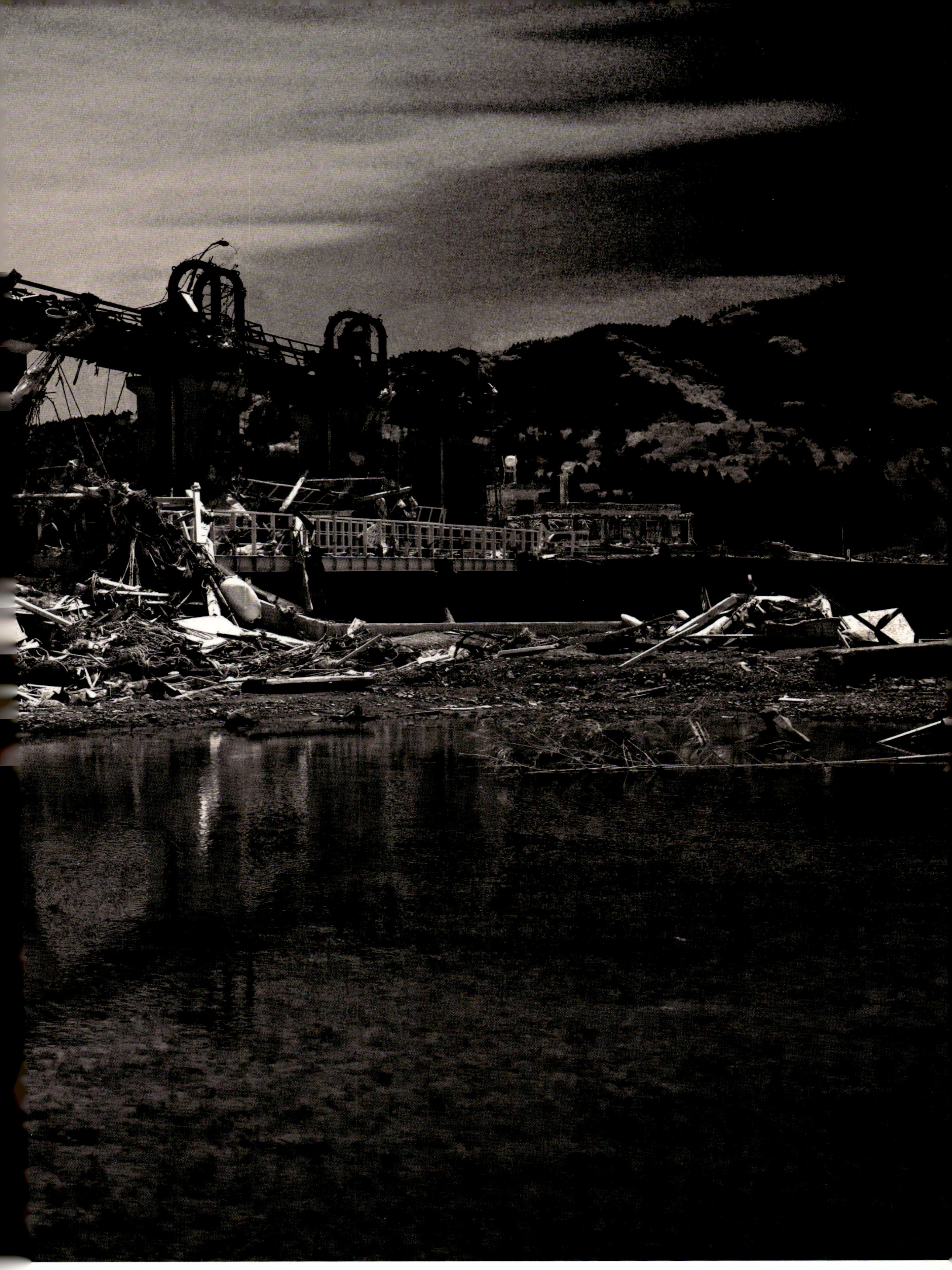

Pages 210-211. The view from the Sanriku Railway. City of Ofunato, Iwate prefecture

Pages 212-213. The town center. City of Ofunato, Iwate prefecture

Pages 214-215. A gasoline truck on the wall of a ship building factory. Kamaishi port, City of Kamaishi, Iwate prefecture

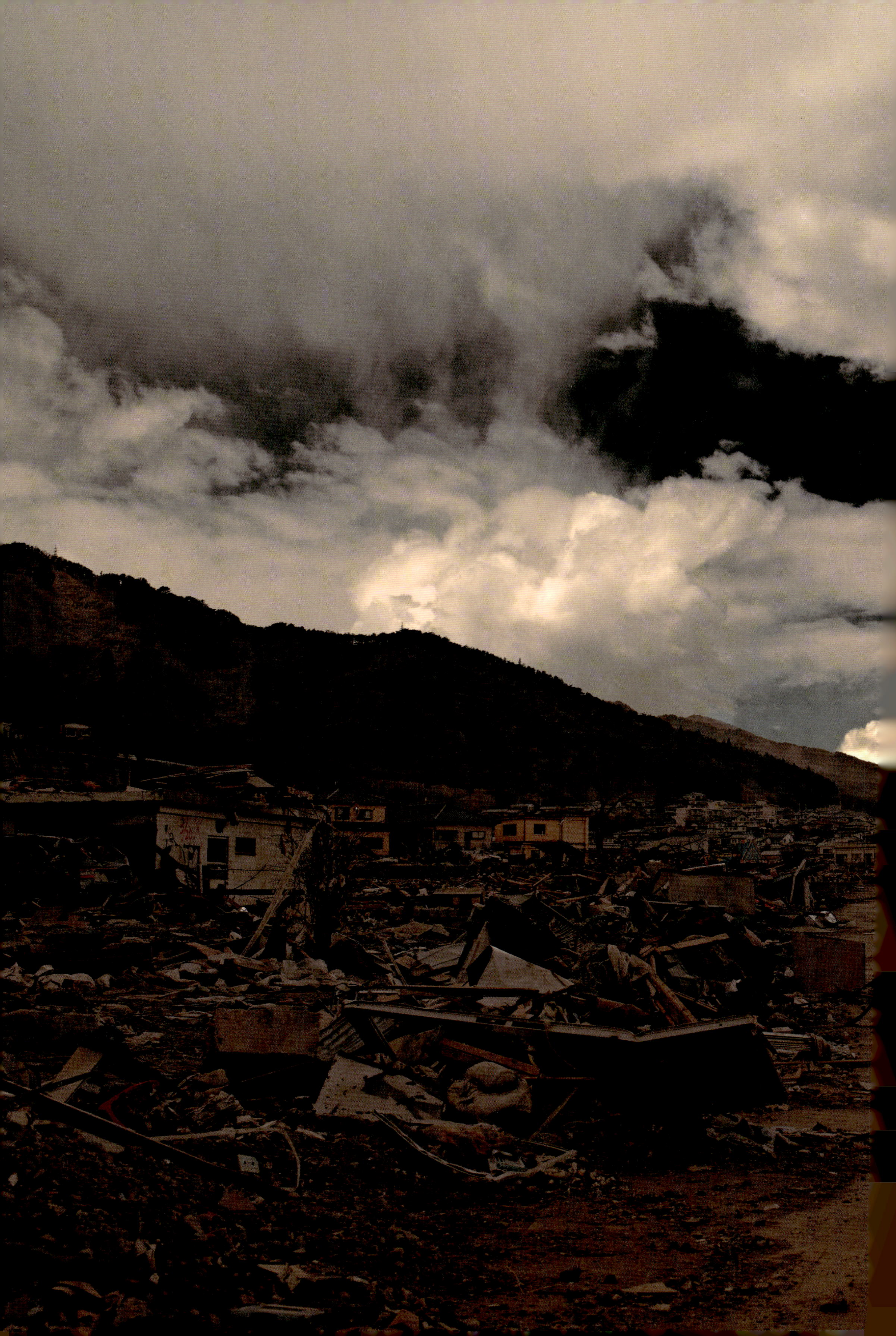

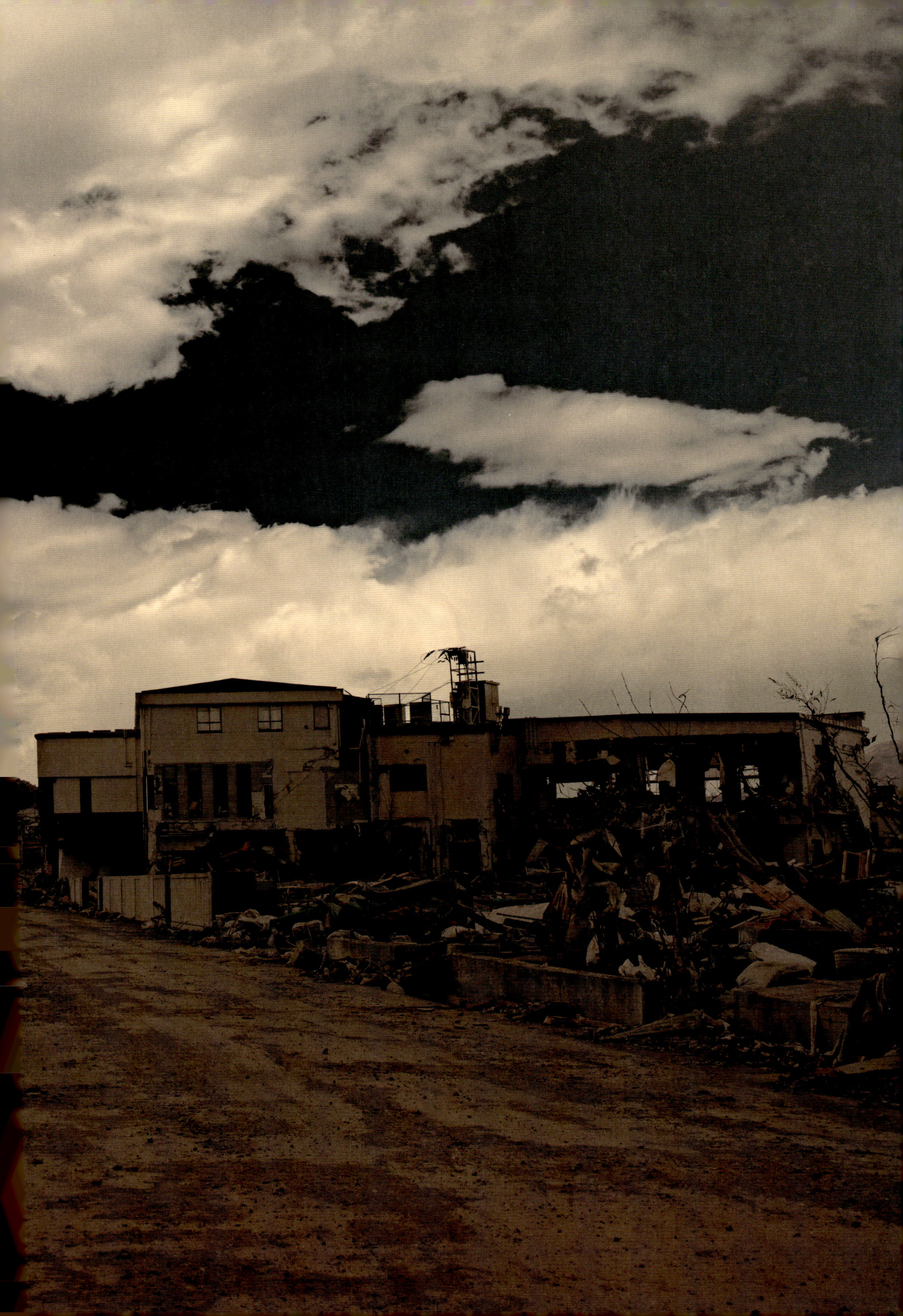

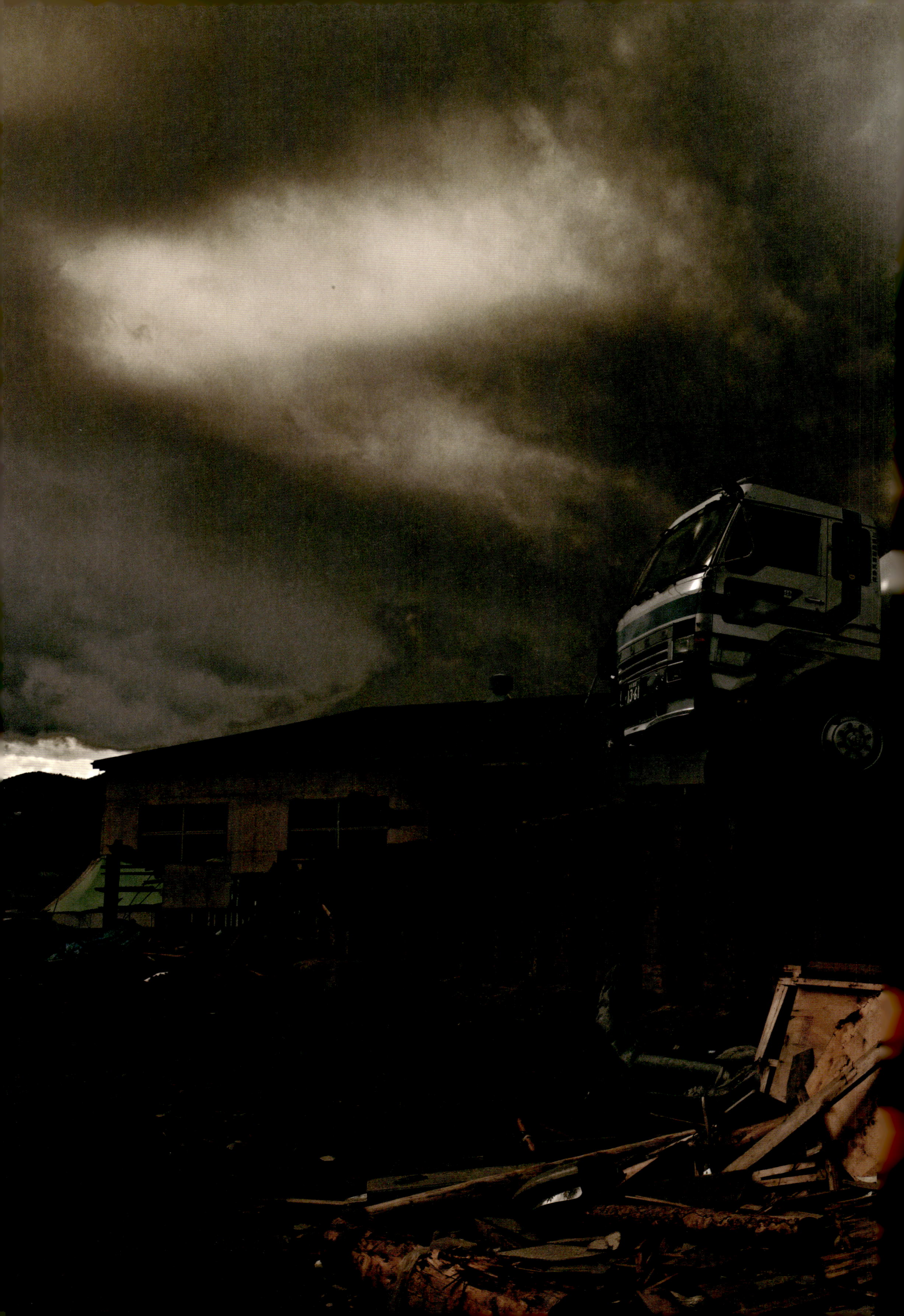

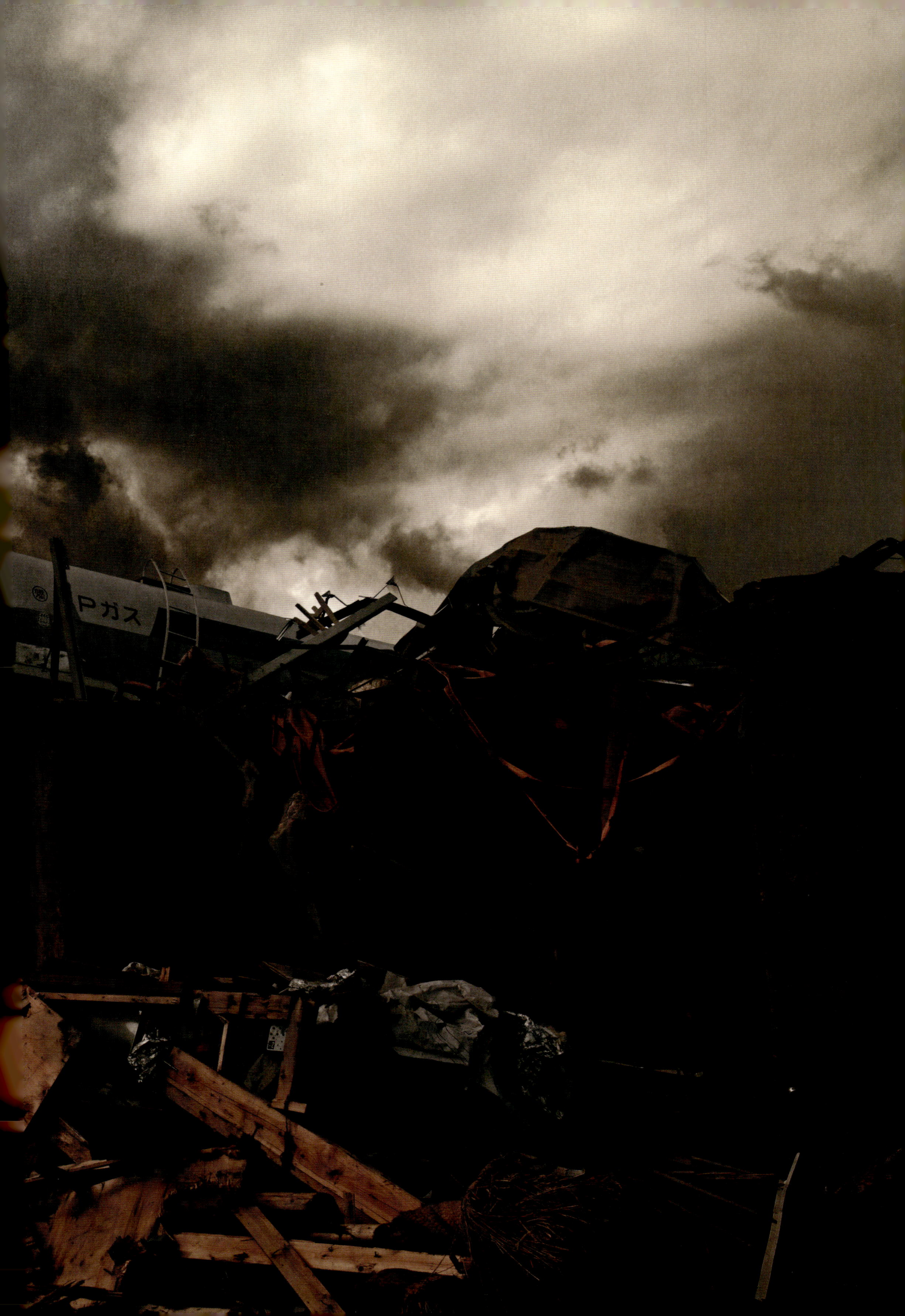
Pガス

FUKUSHIMA: 18

MONTHS AFTER

Fukushima: 18 months after

Yasushi Handa

Eighteen months had passed since the earthquake and a massive tsunami caused an unimaginable nuclear crisis at the power plants in Fukushima Prefecture. Due to the danger of radiation, a 20-kilometer perimeter around the plant was declared off limits; but, on August 10, 2012, Narahamachi was slated as a town to be removed from that category. That step meant certain areas would now be open to adults during the day, under certain conditions. One day later, early in the morning, I crossed that threshold.

It was the beginning of the Obon holiday, a time when many Japanese return to their hometowns for family reunions to mark the Buddhist tradition of praying for one's dead ancestors and cleaning gravesites. As such, even though it was early, the roads on the Joban Expressway were packed. That heightened the eerie feeling of finding myself alone as I drove over the Iwaki junction, and exited along the Hirono interchange, the last exit before the blockade. Through the haze, I could see the towering smokestacks of the Hirono thermal power plant in the distance. I was now on a road that had been blocked and guarded by policemen the night before. To the right, I saw J Village, which had been the training center for Japan's national soccer team, before it became the emergency base camp for the nuclear power plant workers. I could feel my body stiffening from the tension.

At the last rest area in Nakago, I picked up a long-sleeve shirt and mask, which I placed beside my Tyvek suit. I didn't want to suit up before entering Narahamachi out of concern that it might offend someone. This was a hazardous area, but still a time for families to focus on their roots and family heritage. My assumption, however, was wrong because the only traffic on the road was associated with work at the power plants. With the exception of the occasional police car, there were no regular passenger cars besides mine in either lane.

Within half an hour, I arrived at the Narahamachi town office. On a hill, I could see what used to be a splendid three-story wooden building that was now on the verge of collapsing. I parked my car along the disfigured slope near the town office. Here, I put on my nuclear radiation protective clothing, my heavy boots with iron-plated soles, and my gas mask and goggles. Between the heat and stress, I was immediately drenched with sweat. I started the car and headed towards Yamadahama, an area near the ocean that had been devastated by the tsunami eighteen months prior. I drove through a railroad crossing covered with shattered glass. Driving downhill, I mentally prepared myself to see a ravaged landscape, as I had seen the year before in Tohoku. Yet, what I saw was a lovely green hillock, like a beautiful plateau. It calmed me. But that sense of calm quickly turned to dismay as I realized the sloping hillside was in fact the ruins of rice fields strewn with the remains of what had been a civilized and picturesque life along the coastline. Tall weeds had taken over, which now served as a plush green blanket over a vast landscape of destruction, including battered cars and the remains of homes.

I felt as though I had entered an alternate reality. I got out of my car, took out my camera, and looked through the viewfinder. In an instant, everything blurred as the heat and sweat from my body caused my goggles fog up. It was 32 degrees Celsius, just a hair under 90 degrees Fahrenheit, and my radiation dosimeter read 0.7~1.0 μSv per hour at eye level. (Back in Tokyo, it had read 0.05 μSv per hour.) From where I stood, I could see patches of barren land, which had probably been stripped clean for radioactive decontamination. When I entered the weeds, huge numbers of grasshoppers and frogs leapt with my every footstep. I could vaguely see their path of movement through my clouded goggles. Without people to tend the land, wild and hearty nature had taken over. My goggles were too fogged over to shoot pictures, so I removed them. I felt so unencumbered to have a clear view, but within a few minutes I was having trouble breathing. The protective suit, while very light, didn't breathe and the heat was unbearable. I was concerned about heatstroke, so I toyed with the idea of removing the mask, which would expose me to radioactive pollution.

Close to 2000 workers, wearing these same kinds of suits, face the same predicament as they daily toil away at the nuclear power plant. It struck me as too much to ask.

I was overcome with sorrow, thinking of how my mother had passed away from heatstroke the summer before when the government asked citizens to refrain from using air conditioning to conserve energy. She was an elderly woman who had previously stayed close to her air conditioner at the height of summer. But, like many other elderly Japanese, she blindly heeded calls to endure the heat, and died for her obedience. She was found curled up on her futon in a sweltering room. Yes, a natural calamity triggered a man-made disaster, which was then aggravated by the incompetence of the TEPCO power company and government officials. More innocent people lost their lives because officials failed to think through the consequences of their policies. My mother was one of them. The image of her shriveled body lingers in my mind.

I drove to the top of a hill along a residential area, but I couldn't get a sense of what the town was like. When I had entered the devastated coastal areas along Sanriku in Tohoku, I was overcome by shock. All I could do was cry and join my hands in prayer for the loss of so much and so many. It was different here. Located on a hill, it had been spared the destructive power of waves. Homes and buildings were instead damaged by the earthquake and the hundreds of aftershocks that rocked the region for weeks afterwards. So at first glance, the town looked fine; yet it was completely silent since everyone had evacuated long ago. You could feel that the sense of life, like time, had come to a standstill. The backdrop reminded me of a painting by Giorgio de Chirico, emanating a strange forlorn atmosphere steeped in fear.

Laundry blew on a clothesline. Children's toys littered the ground. Some yards had been overtaken by weeds, while others remained clear. The streets were pristine, which indicated they had most likely been decontaminated. In short, it was far different from what I had imagined a ghost town would be like. I couldn't help but feel an overwhelming wave of sadness, as I contemplated the heartrending pleas and resolution of most former residents to return to their homes, their land, and their lives. Every detail of the town seemed to echo this heartfelt determination to resume what was once a normal life. Despite such calls, which all of us can understand and sympathize with, the government plans to designate the area as a temporary dumping ground for radioactive waste. It's beyond cruel.

The sound of silence was broken by the approach of a car, which jolted me back to reality. It was a police car, driving very slowly. The officers glared at me as though I were a criminal. It didn't bother me because they were doing their job. On the way here, I had stopped near Tatsuta Station on the JR Joban Line, and saw storefronts and vending machines that had been wrenched open with crowbars. The town is no longer considered a hazard zone, but no one is allowed to enter at night. Yes, thieves in the night, preying on opportunity. It made my blood boil.

I returned to my car and began driving toward Odaka-ku, Minamisoma City, which is on the other side of the nuclear power plant. If I headed straight, it was only 20 kilometers away; but the road was blocked. If I returned to the Tohoku Expressway, I'd get stuck in the holiday traffic jam so I took a road crossing a ridge, which took me down a meandering mountain road. I almost immediately regretted my decision because when I glanced at my radiation dosimeter, it read an outrageously high number: 3.0 μSv per hour. I knew it was extraordinarily difficult to remove residual radiation from mountainous areas, but I hadn't anticipated such a high level. Nonetheless, I kept driving, passing through Kawauchimura toward Iitatemura. Eventually, I came to a road block. The officers in the police car watched me, and I had no choice but to turn around and retrace my path. As expected, traffic was heavy on the Joban and Banetsu expressways, leading to the Tohoku Expressway. Glancing at other drivers, I imagined they were heading to see family or sightseeing. Everyone was dressed lightly, which made me even more aware of my protective gear and how it intensified the heat. I felt awkward, but I only had a few protective suits so I couldn't change for the sake of appearances. I glanced again at my radiation dosimeter, which read 0.3 μSv per hour. It was six times higher than in Tokyo, but it seemed low after coming from an area registering a monstrous 3.0 μSv per hour. I put my windows down and took in a deep breath. Humans adapt quickly to their circumstances; scary though they may be in this instance.

After exiting the Tohoku Expressway, the heavy traffic continued which meant I arrived at Odaka-ku around sunset. Clouds were heavy and hanging low. I turned right at the Ooi crossing of Route 6 to enter Odaka. I stopped the car on the bridge that leads to what used to be the center of town. A huge murder of crows watched me at a close distance. I got out of my car to peer down at the city. There was no one to be seen, as the rain began to fall. It was getting dark so I decided to use a tripod to shoot pictures. I took the polarizing filter off the lens, but my protective suit didn't have a pocket so I set it on the rail. In a flash, a crow snatched it and flew off. I screamed at the birds, in a fit of anger. When I looked down, I noticed that places on the rail, along the sidewalk, and anywhere else water pooled, had been stained black. It suddenly hit me that it must be the traces of "black rain," like the rain that fell on Hiroshima after the atomic bombing. Chills ran down my spine.

Once off the bridge, I turned left, entering what used to be considered the heart of the city. The asphalt streets were nothing but rubble. Some stores and buildings were completely crushed, some disfigured, and many seemingly on the verge of collapse at any moment. Lights from a traffic signal were dazzling and changing their colors for no car, for no one.

The rain tapered off, and the glow of the evening sun was mesmerizing. Yet, it couldn't conceal the ruins, which cast a long shadow of sadness.

I retraced my route, and checked into a hotel in a different part of the city. I finally disrobed and put on normal clothes before heading out to dinner. By that time, the rain had returned, pounding the pavement. I clutched my umbrella, remembering the hideous black rain. I saw a group of young people talking joyfully as they walked through the rain with no umbrellas. Surely they knew the danger of being exposed to such rain. I couldn't help but think of their futures and feel my heart sink.

Later in my hotel room, everything suddenly began to shake. I turned on the TV, and soon heard that an earthquake, with a seismic intensity of 5, was centered off the coast of Fukushima Prefecture. It was a strong quake, but it somehow didn't seem that powerful. I went to bed, thinking that I had grown too accustomed to the rumbling of the earth. A few days later, a correction was issued, saying that the quake had indeed been less powerful.

I woke up to the sound of heavy rain. I drove the same route I had the night before to return to the downtown area of Odaka. It was early, so traffic was light. Like the day before, where I turned right at Ooi crossing, no one followed me. The rain had stopped, and the crows scoured the streets, as though they were patrolling their territory. I drove without pause, forcing them to scatter. I slowed down as I approached the station. Under the cover of darkness, the town had looked different. In the daylight, I could see the horrific state of the dilapidated buildings, each further humbled by the continuous aftershocks. Dangerous buildings had bright yellow tape running in a cross-like pattern across doorways; it was visually striking.

A cat sat in the middle of the road. As I drove closer, it didn't budge. I stared at it and noticed it had extraordinarily long whiskers on only one side of its face. I wondered if radiation had caused the deformity. Its eyes were sunken and slimy with thick puss. Crows leered and seemed poised to attack. I got out of my car and threw the cat a piece of bread. Ignoring the bread, it suddenly hissed, exposing its sharp teeth and bristling its fur in a fit of anger. Left behind by owners, pets turned feral, fending for food and life against other wild creatures, like the crows. Prolonged exposure to radiation would surely cut this cat's life short. As it weakens, it will eventually fall prey to the crows. These street creatures are also victims of this man-made disaster.

I left the town, and drove up a mountain road leading to a pasture used for grazing cows. Cowsheds were concealed behind huge swathes of weeds, which prevented me from getting a clear view. Trying to peer through an opening, I noted an enormous web spanning between beams that had been spun by an equally impressive poisonous spider, with a body measuring 5 centimeters. The ground beneath the cracks in the eaves was black, where rain had fallen.

I moved on, and came upon a beautiful meadow, surrounded by an electric fence. It was a ranch, where cows poisoned by radiation were slated for slaughter. There were placards and signs protesting the government's decision to kill the animals, but what other options were there? I felt sorry for all concerned.

I passed the hill and headed to the coastline. The cracked road had been overtaken by weeds, which made the path hard to follow. I saw a group of what appeared to be volunteers removing radioactive materials. All of them wore short sleeves, and some of them wore shorts and flip flops. I struck up a conversation with one of the men, who showed me his Geiger counter, which he wore on a string around his neck. "I've already been exposed to more than180 μSv today," he said, laughing.

I wanted to criticize him for wearing such useless clothes, but I exhaled, feeling somehow lightened by his cheerful mood. Without a word I accelerated, leaving the group to continue its work.

The coastal area, which used to be lined with luxurious rice fields, was nothing more than a swamp. Water birds, similar to cranes, were gracefully feeding on fish. A lone house stood near the beach, somehow defying the odds that had destroyed so many homes. For a moment, the scenery evoked the majestic tranquility one feels upon entering a famous national park. But a more detailed assessment, tallying the fallen utility poles and the submerged ruins of what used to be homes, calls one back to the stark reality of loss.

I stood there, physically and emotionally exhausted. I longed to go home; but first I had to go to Iitatemura. I drove along another winding road. When I reached the village, dark clouds filled the sky again. Just like Narahamachi and Odaka, I saw no one. Houses and a school courtyard were covered in weeds. The village, located in a mountainous region, had only been partially decontaminated so radiation levels were staggering. Along the way, I saw a number of massive piles covered with blue fabric; it was radioactive waste. Unsurprisingly, the level of radiation grew stronger near the blue masses.

I wanted to go farther, but I had reached a hazard zone where only those with special permits were allowed to enter.

Huge raindrops fell on my front windshield. I decided to go home, and left Iitatemura. Along the way, I shed my protective gear, placing it in a plastic bag. I almost immediately felt more at ease, but also more fatigued. The clouds began to part, revealing rays of sunlight. The forecast had called for heavy rain all day; but, the skies to the west were clear. I pointed my car in the direction of Tokyo, as I entered the Jobando Express.

I was suddenly overwhelmed by an almost desperate desire to see Narahamachi again. I made a U-turn at the Iwaki junction. I no longer had protective clothing.

Postscript

Fear of things we can't see, like radiation, is tricky. First, we tend to be driven by irrational fear, like characters in the science-fiction film *Alien*, waiting for something terrible to burst out of nowhere at any moment. But once that fear subsides, we start to let our guard down and get lazy about protecting ourselves. At some point, symptoms appear, bringing us back to the dreadful reality, which includes our own carelessness. Recently, a subcontractor made news when it sent employees into the nuclear power plants with lead shields over their Geiger counters so they could continue working beyond the acceptable level of radiation exposure. It was scandalous, but they apparently did so because they needed the work. There were no other jobs, and this one paid well. That was their excuse. Were they unaware of the risk to their lives just to make a living? The government has guidelines on acceptable limits of radiation exposure for workers at the Fukushima power plants. When a worker reaches the limit, they can no longer enter the plant. But people don't feel the immediate impact of radiation, so they throw caution to the wind. It's like a frog in warm water. If you drop it in a pot of hot water, it will immediately escape; but, if you drop it in a pot of warm water, it will linger, unaware that the temperature is rising. It's dead before it knows it. So it is with humans, who understand the theory of radiation poisoning but nonetheless take the risk for short-term benefits. Once you ignore the danger, you discount the risk. Such is the folly of humans.

The same thing might be said about the dead who occupied the towns swept away by the tsunami. Within a millennium, spanning the Meiji, Showa, and Heisei eras, the coastal region of Tohoku has been battered repeatedly by the forces of nature. Why did people defy logic, and cling stubbornly to their desire to rebuild towns despite their vulnerability? Kunio Yanagida, known as the father of Japanese folklorists, visited the areas devastated by a tsunami following the Meiji Sanriku Great Earthquake in 1896. Yanagida understood that locals worshiped their ancestors, and were deeply attached to the region that their ancestors had toiled to transform from a desolate wasteland into the land of glorious rice fields. Yet, in his book "Yukiguni no Haru (Spring in Snow Country)," he explained what happened after the tsunami disaster: "In short, the rich lost their property. The poor went to the coastline every day, saying they were searching for missing people, but in reality they were scavenging for valuables to bring home. Rarely was anything returned to its rightful owner. It was difficult to launch a recovery plan because people with knowhow had become cowards. People of means secured land on higher ground, but felt guilty for abandoning their homes and neighbors on lower land. On the other side of the spectrum, were those who brushed the disaster aside and focused on making a living; they moved to the beaches, where it was easy to run a fishery and a trading company. Then there were those who came from other regions, settling in areas without permission as they sought out opportunities in a time of loss. Therefore, the village looked basically the same. In fact, there were far more people living in the area than prior to the tsunami."

We are at the starting block of reconstruction, with the entire world watching our efforts. In the future, we expect a divergence in the world's energy policies. What differs between our time and that of Yanagida's is that we can share information in an instant. We can access the world's best and brightest minds in our quest to rebuild. We should strive to avoid the obvious mistakes that this man-made disaster has revealed, and leave the next generation with a safer and better plan for its precious towns.

Map of Affected Area

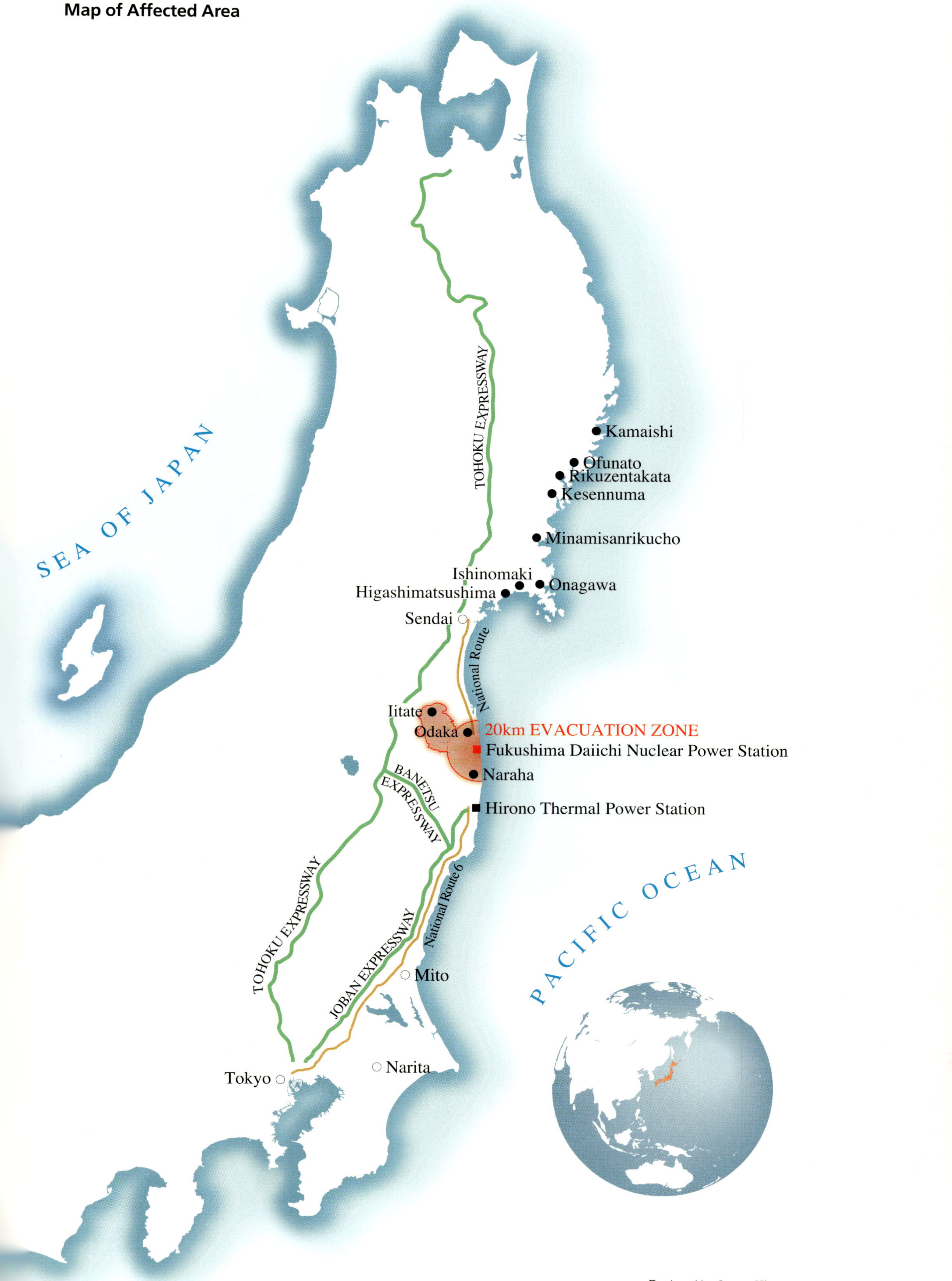

Designed by Osamu Hirota

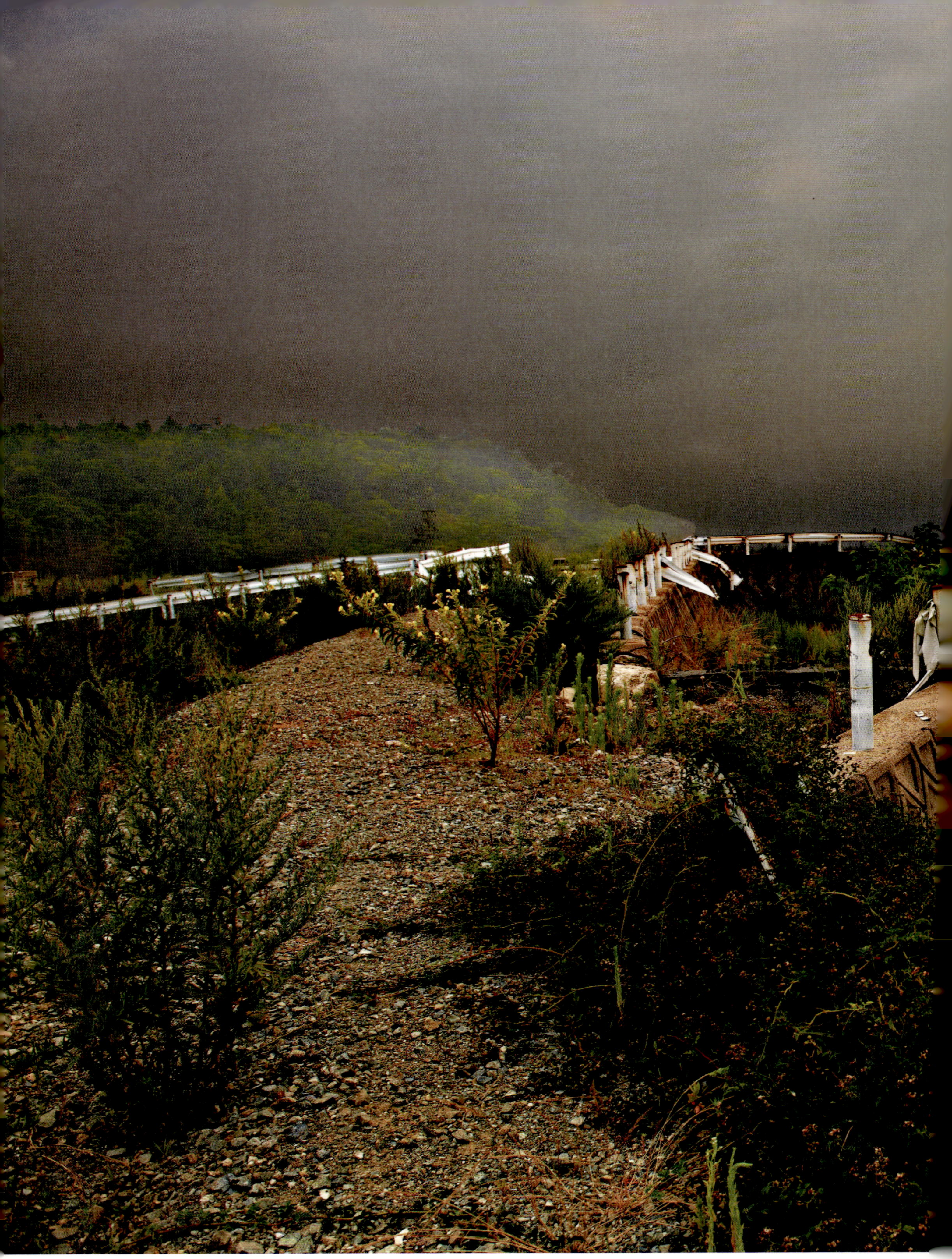

A devastated road and lone building.
Naraha-machi, Futaba County, Fukushima prefecture

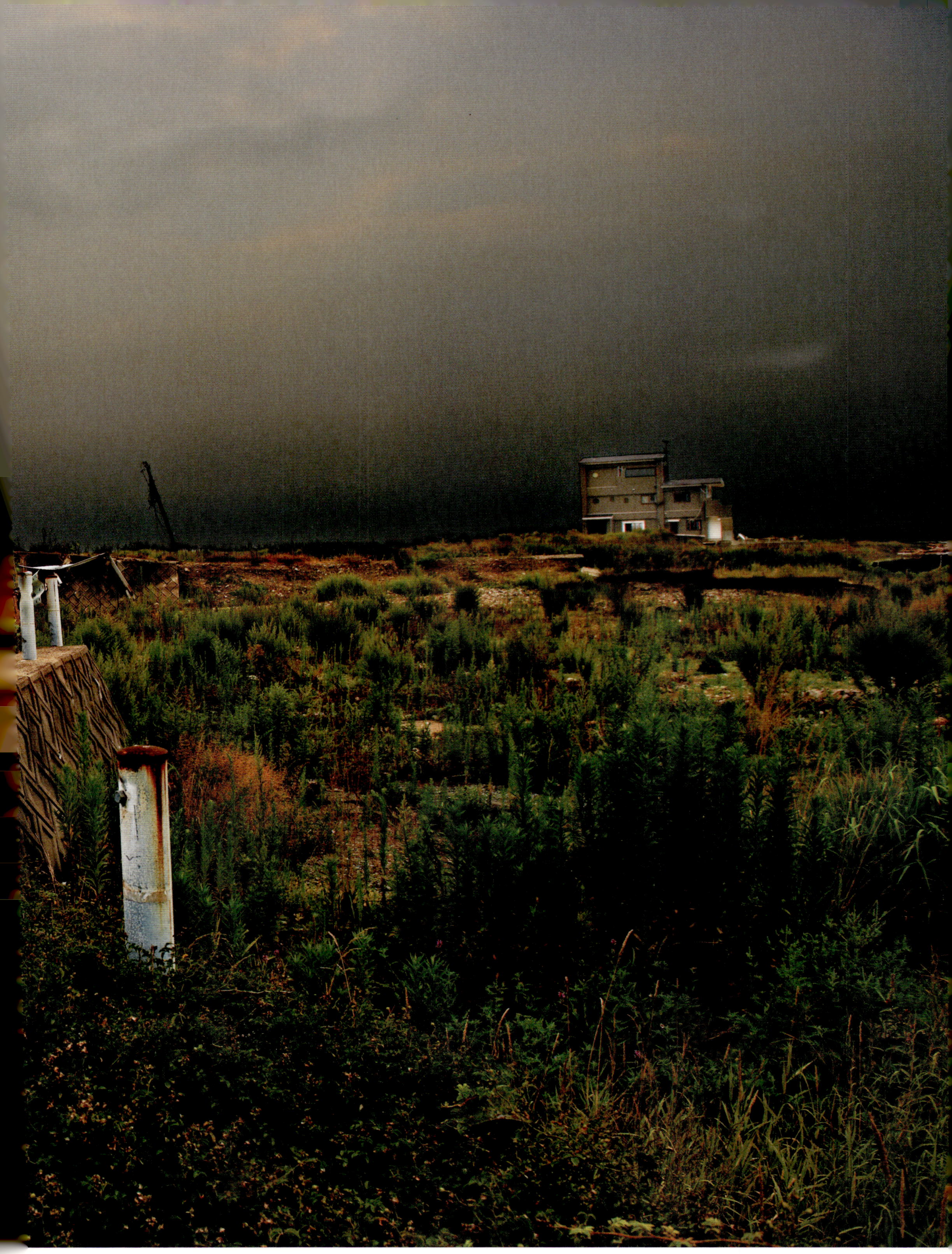

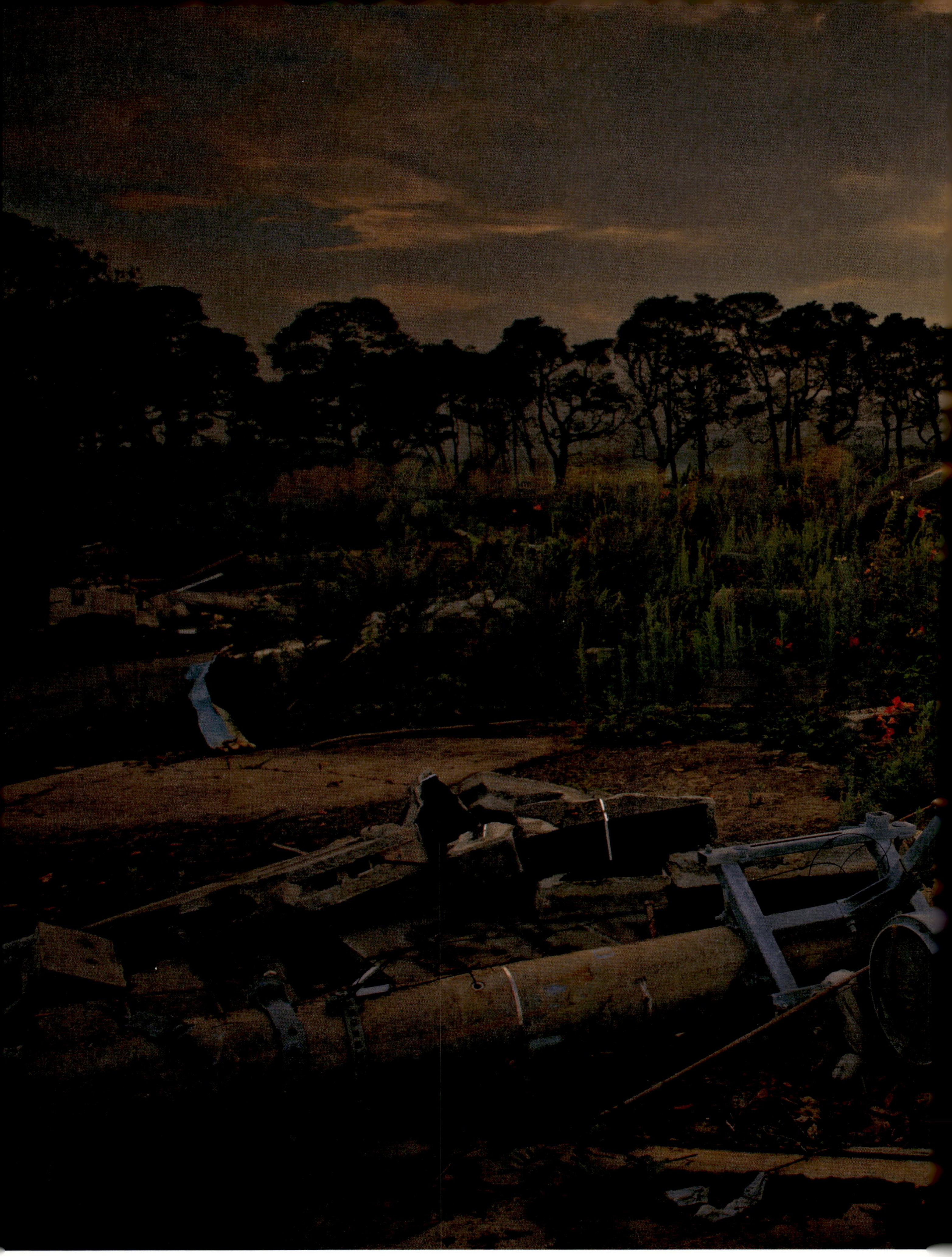

A former residential area.
Naraha-machi, Futaba County, Fukushima prefecture

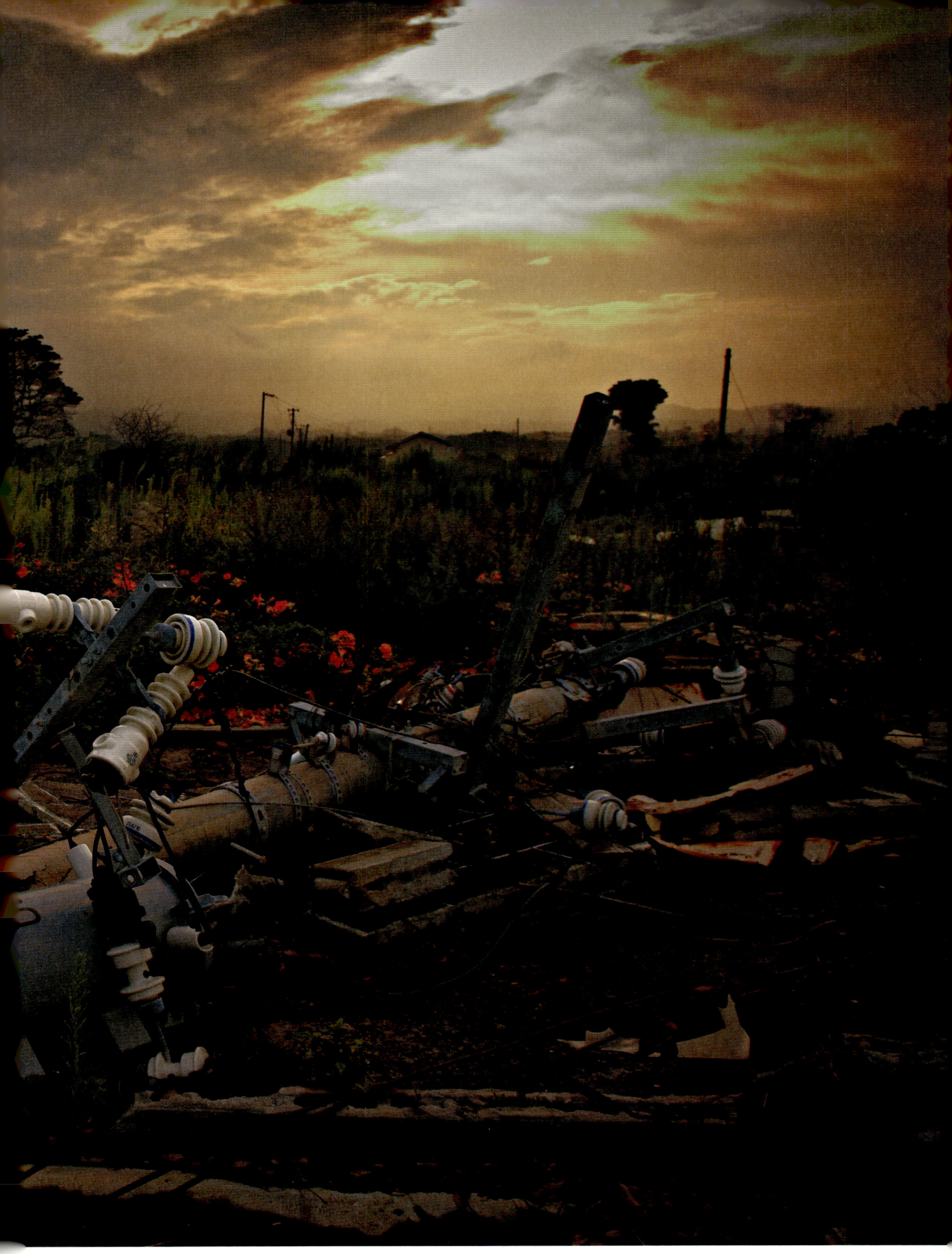

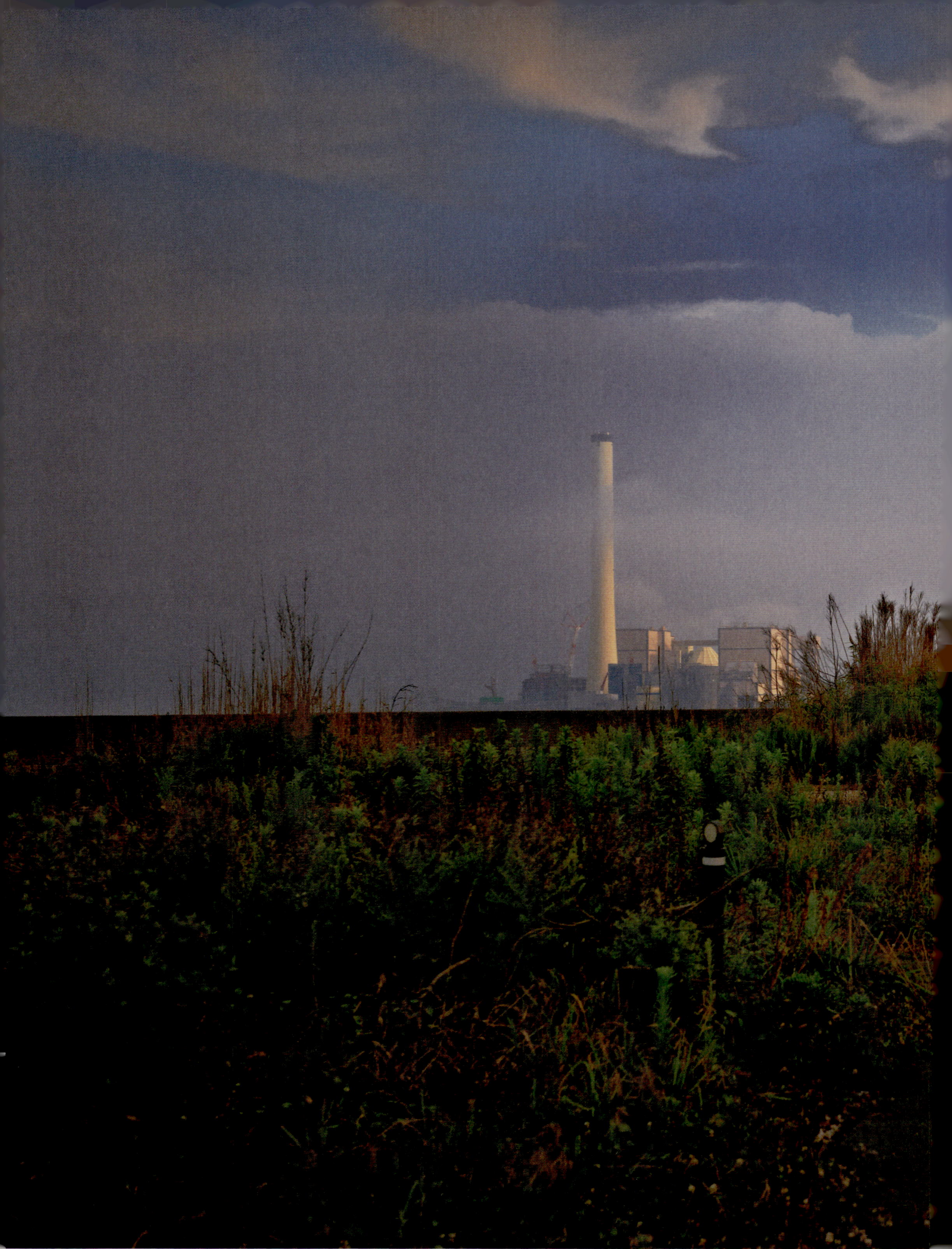

A view of Hirono Thermal Power Plant from Naraha-machi.
Naraha-machi, Futaba County, Fukushima prefecture

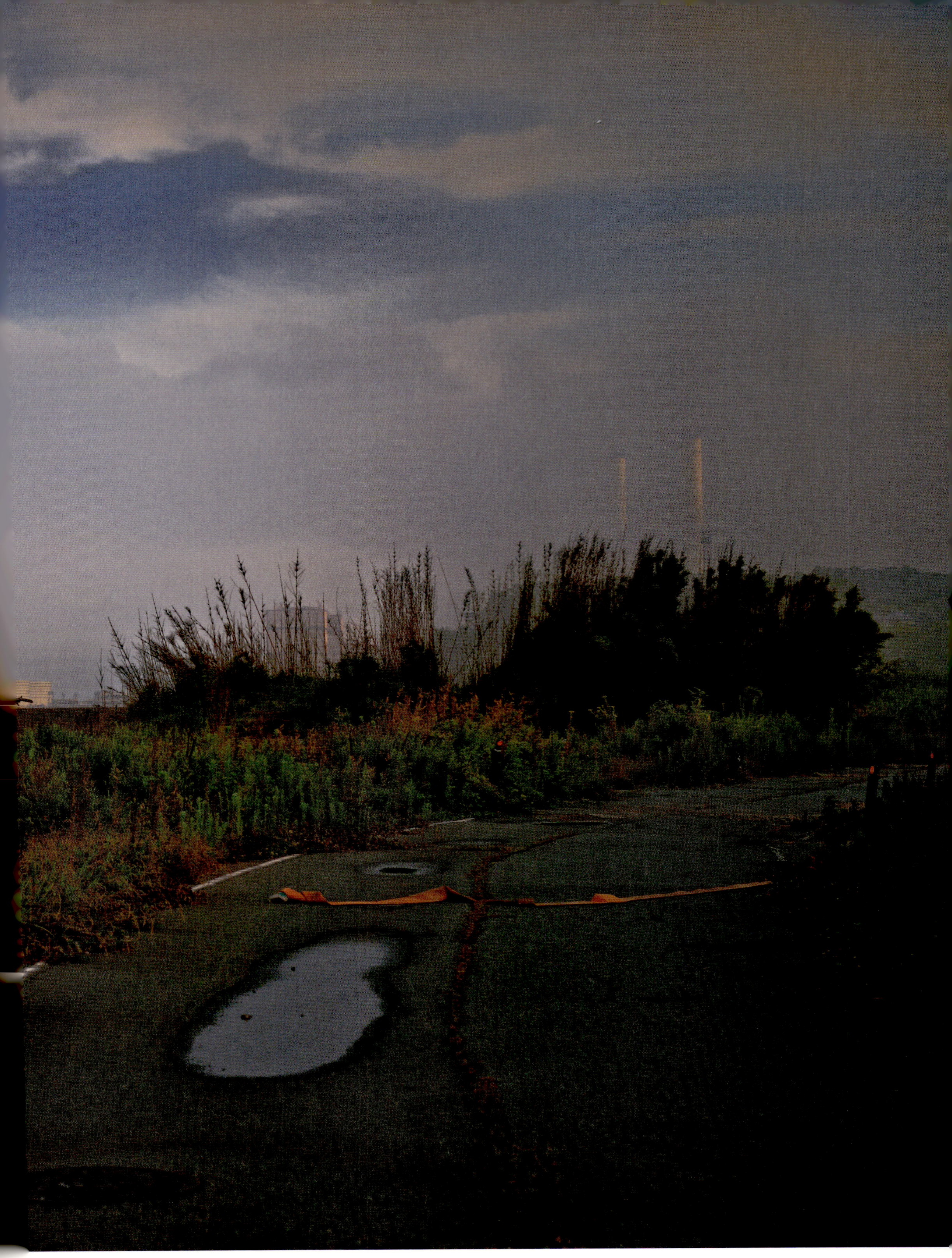

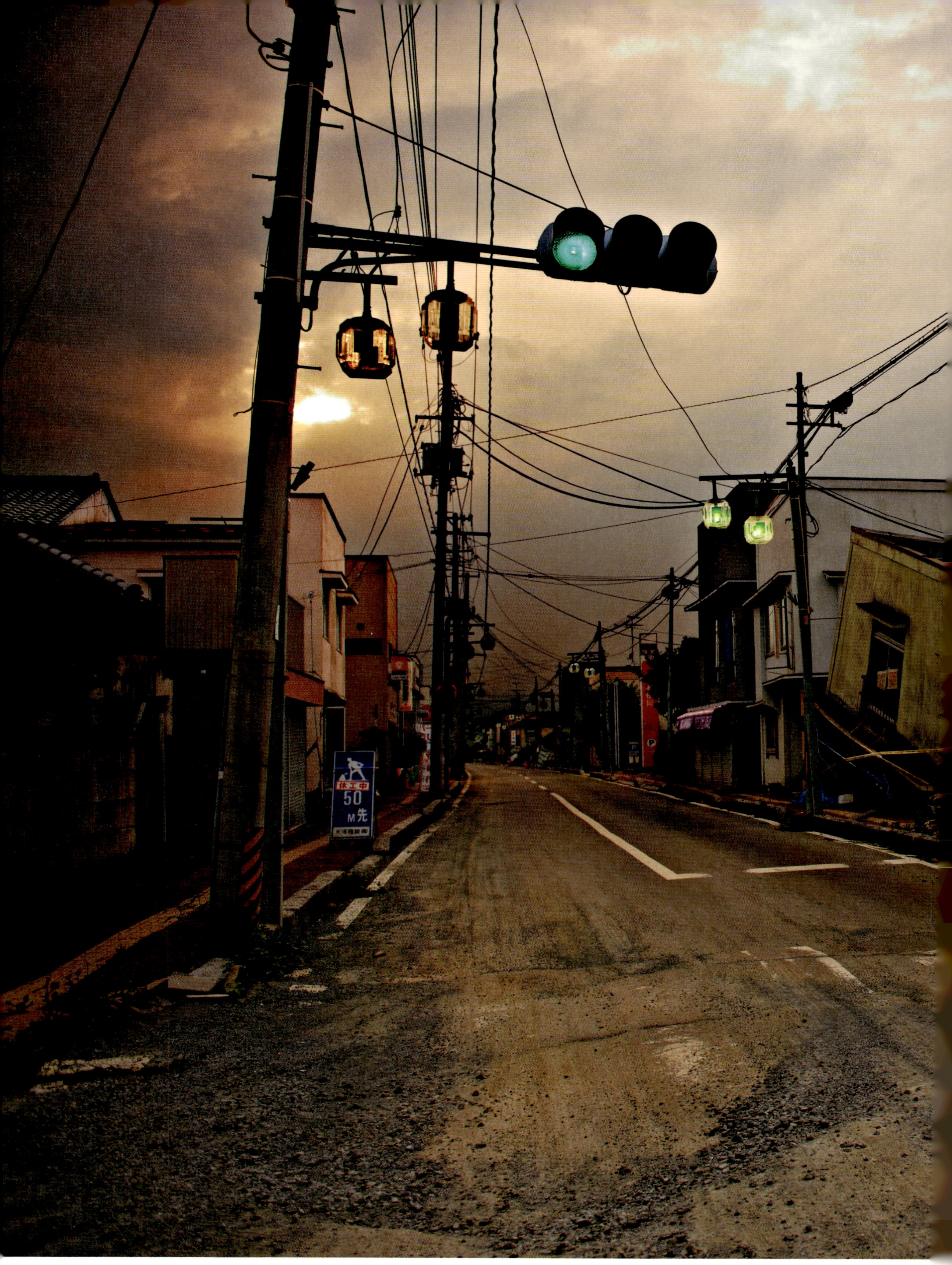

The town center.
Odaka Ward, Soma County, Fukushima prefecture

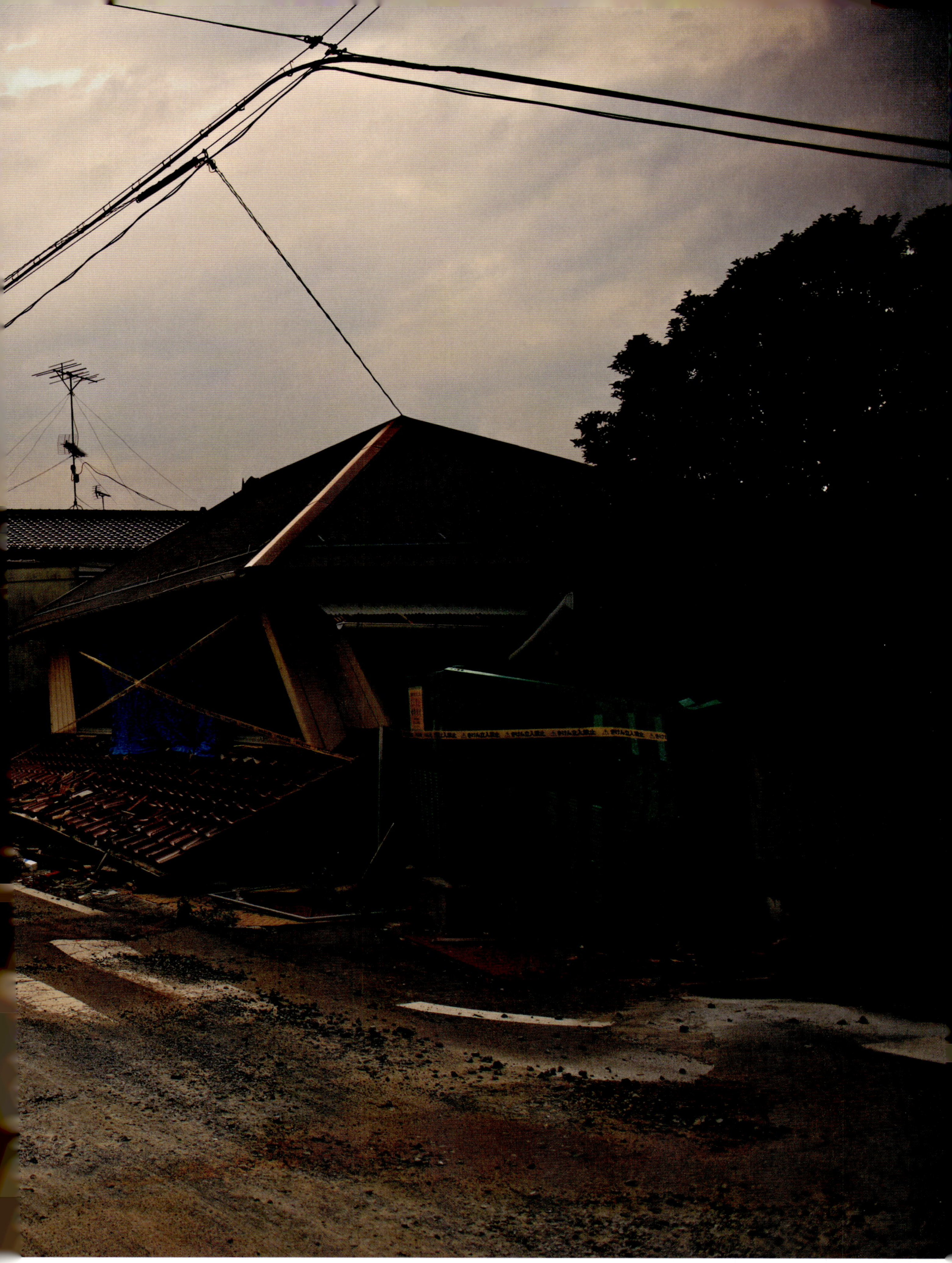

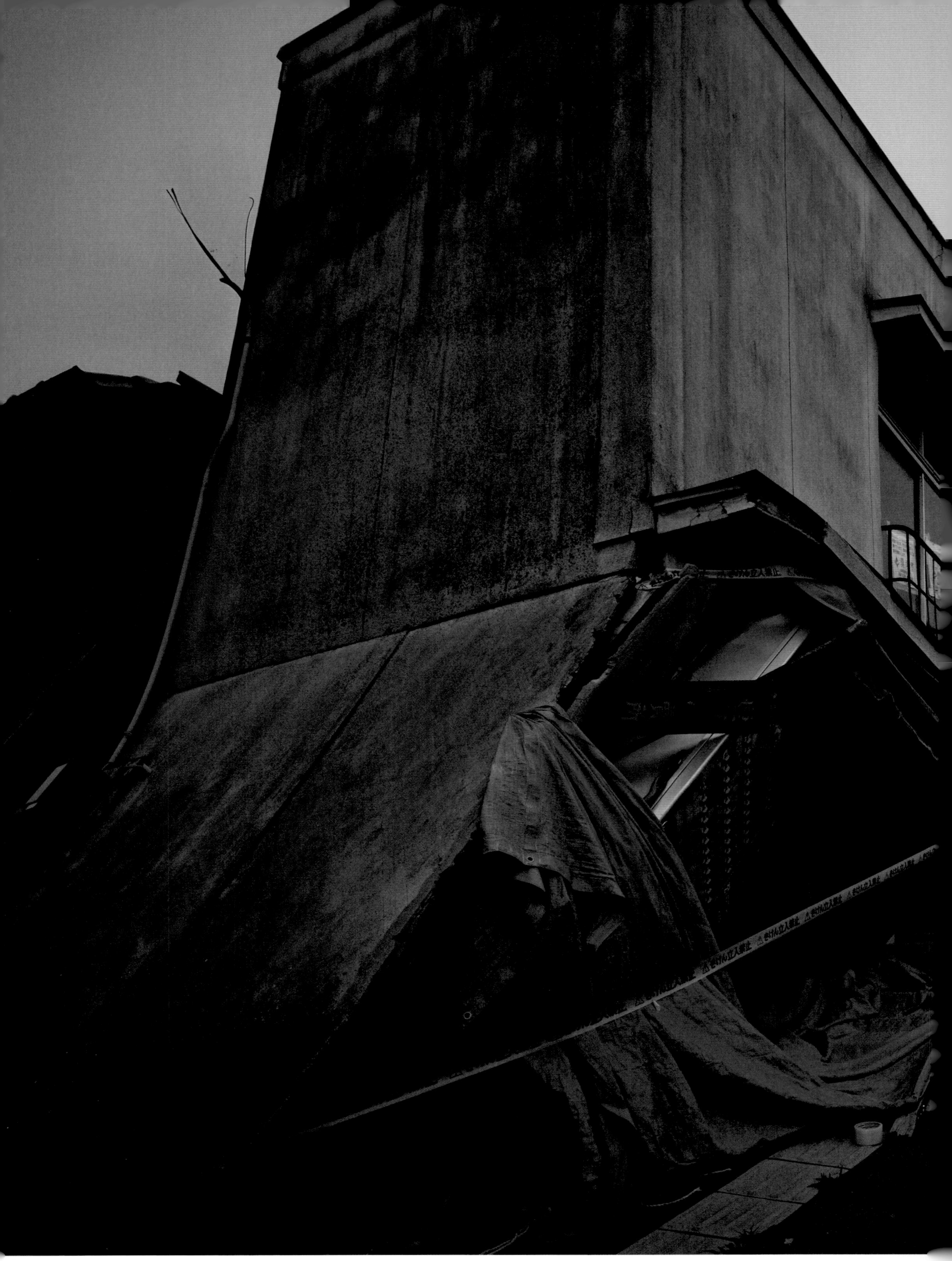

The result of 200 aftershocks.
Odaka Ward, Soma County, Fukushima prefecture

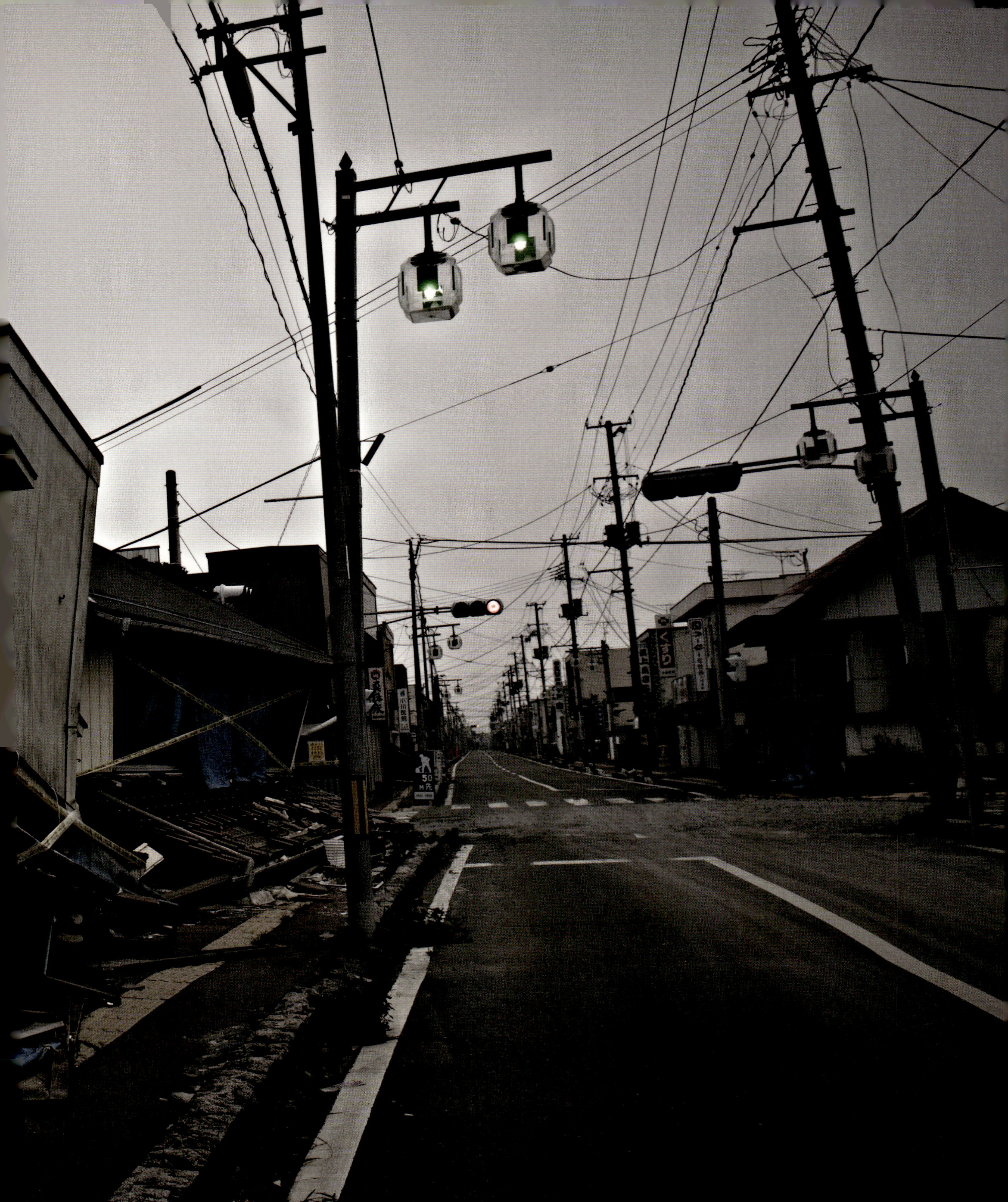

くすり
50
M先

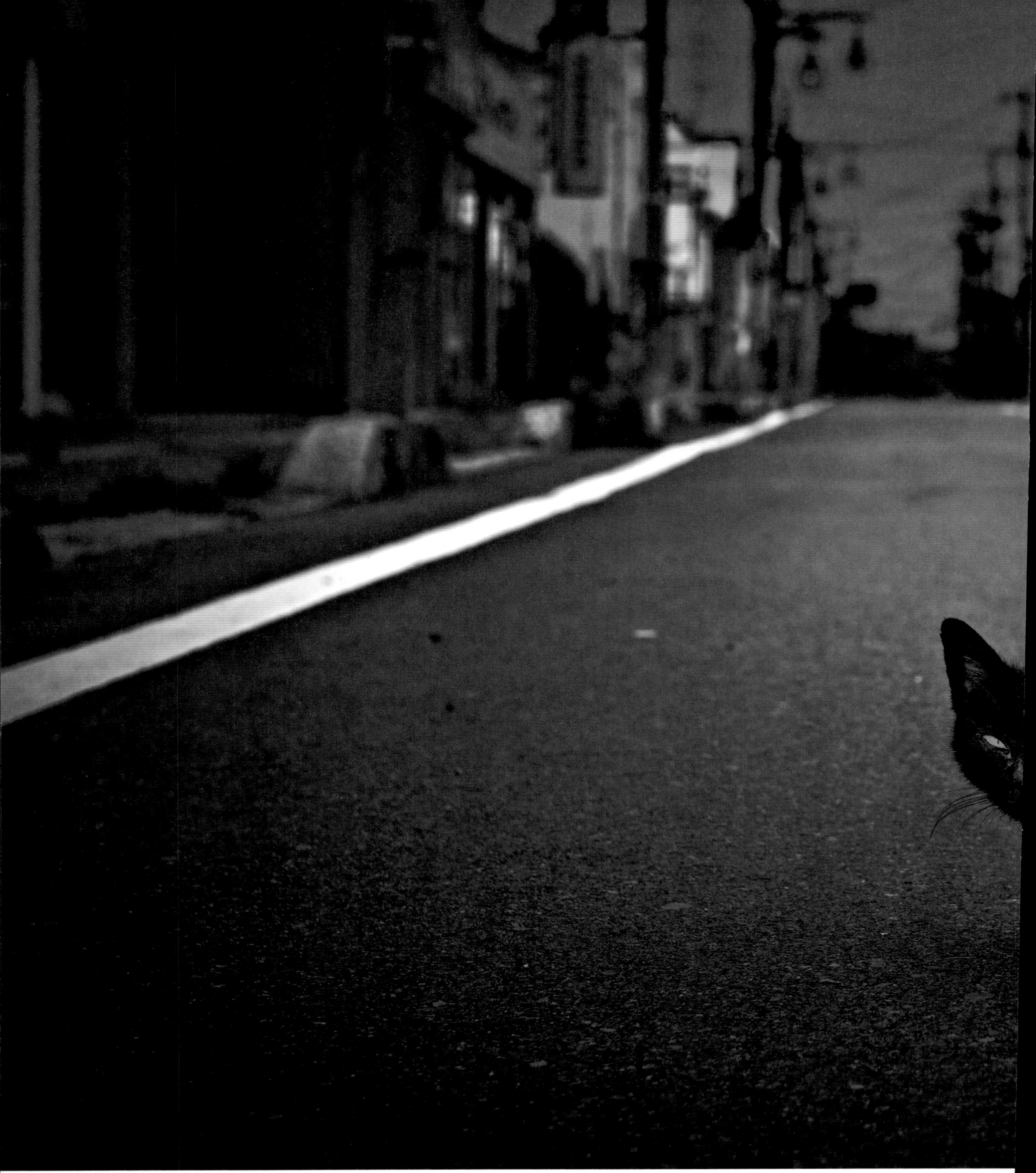

A cat with deformed whiskers.
Odaka Ward, Soma County, Fukushima prefecture

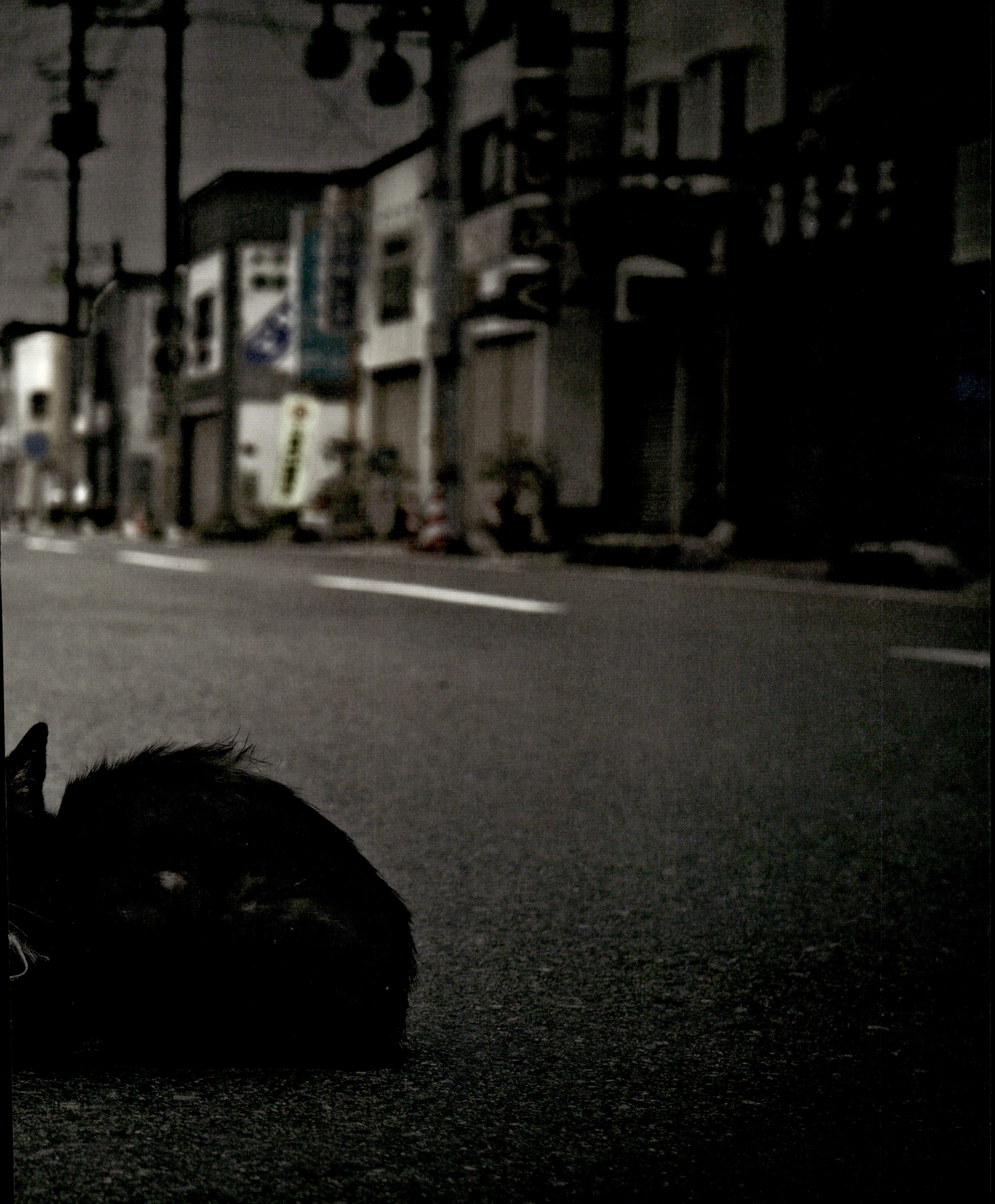

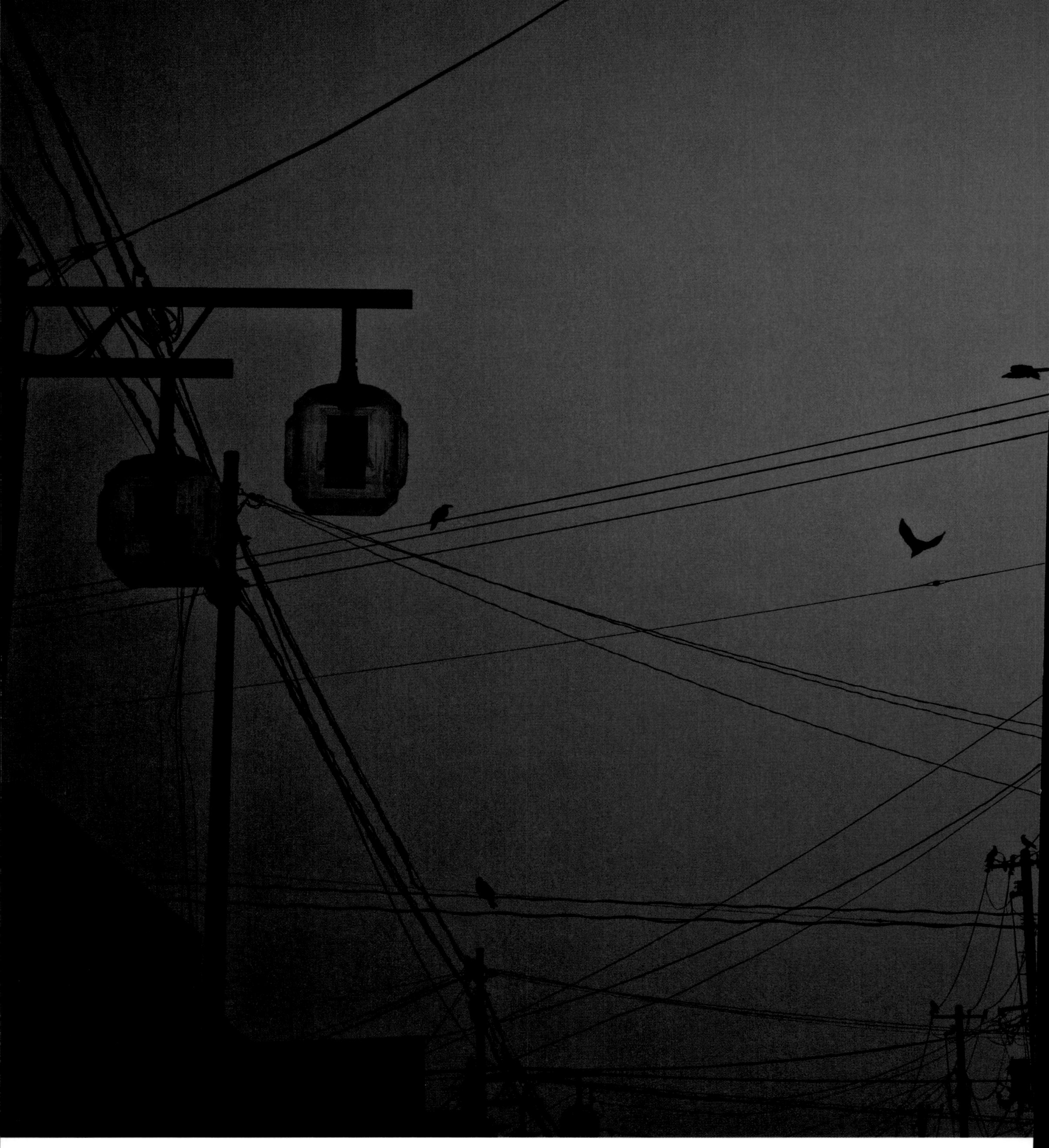

With no humans left, the crows inherited the town.
Odaka Ward, Soma County, Fukushima prefecture

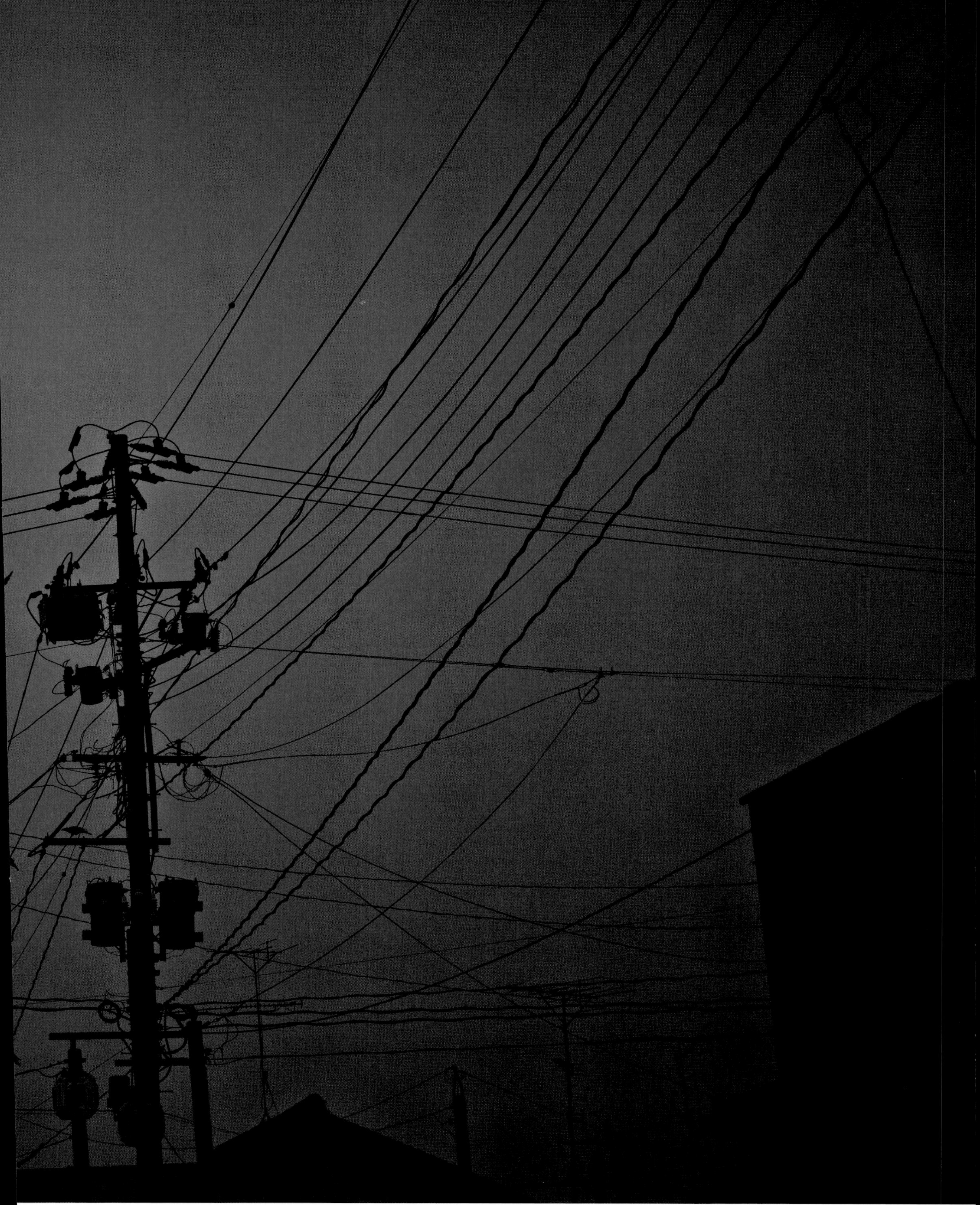

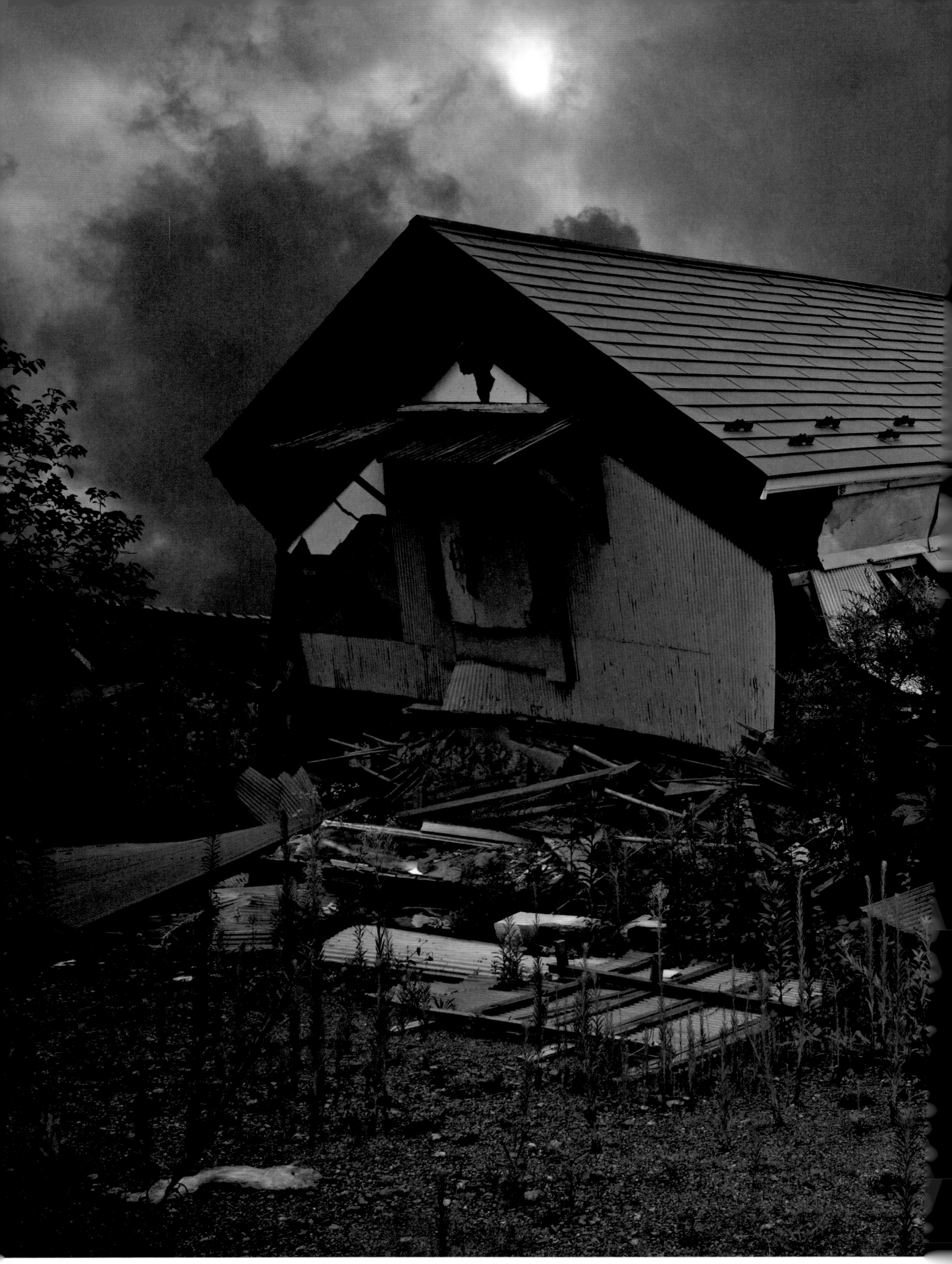

A house surrounded by unnaturally tall weeds in the ghost town.
Odaka Ward, Soma County, Fukushima prefecture

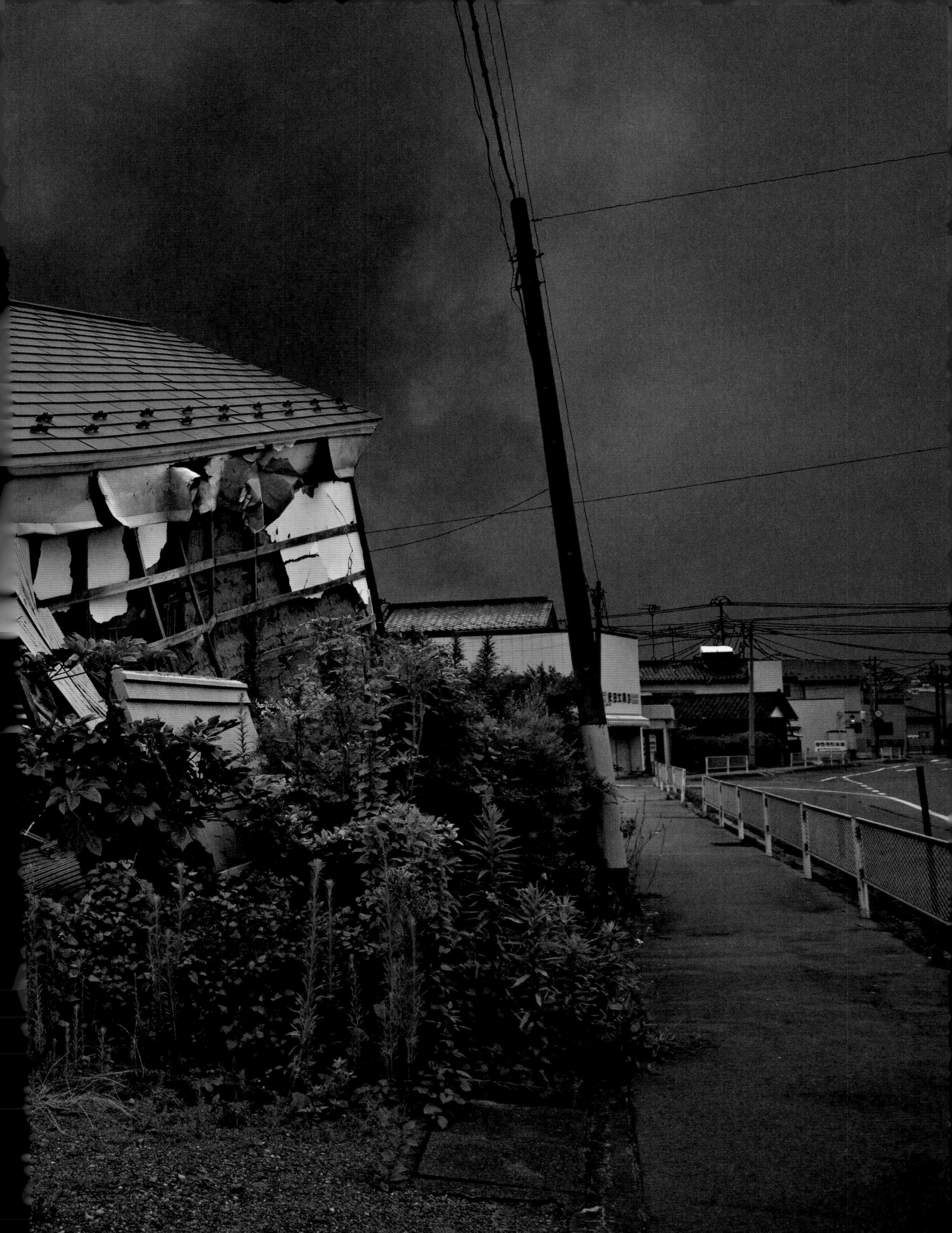

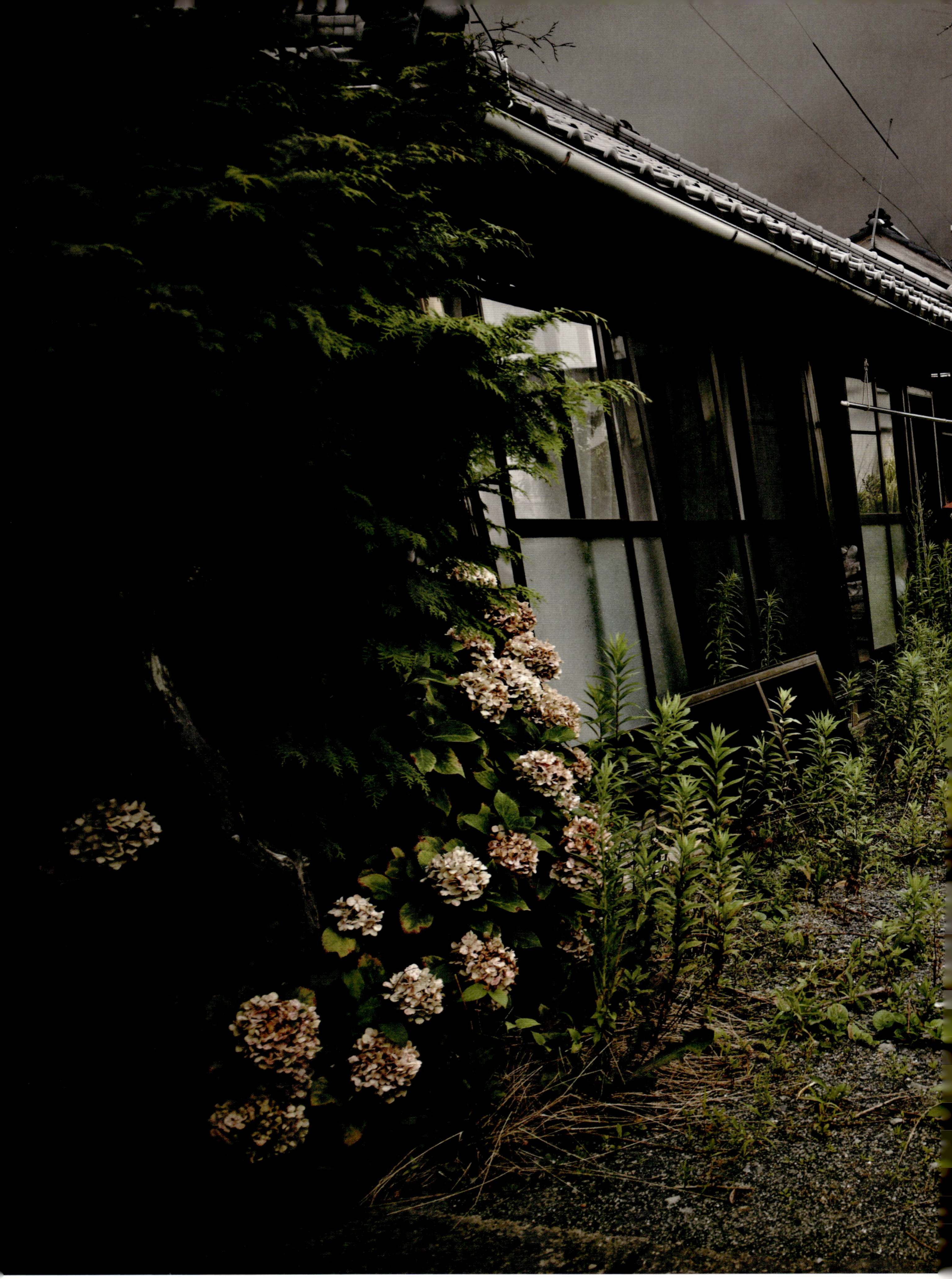

A child's tricycle engulfed by overgrown weeds.
Odaka Ward, Soma County, Fukushima prefecture

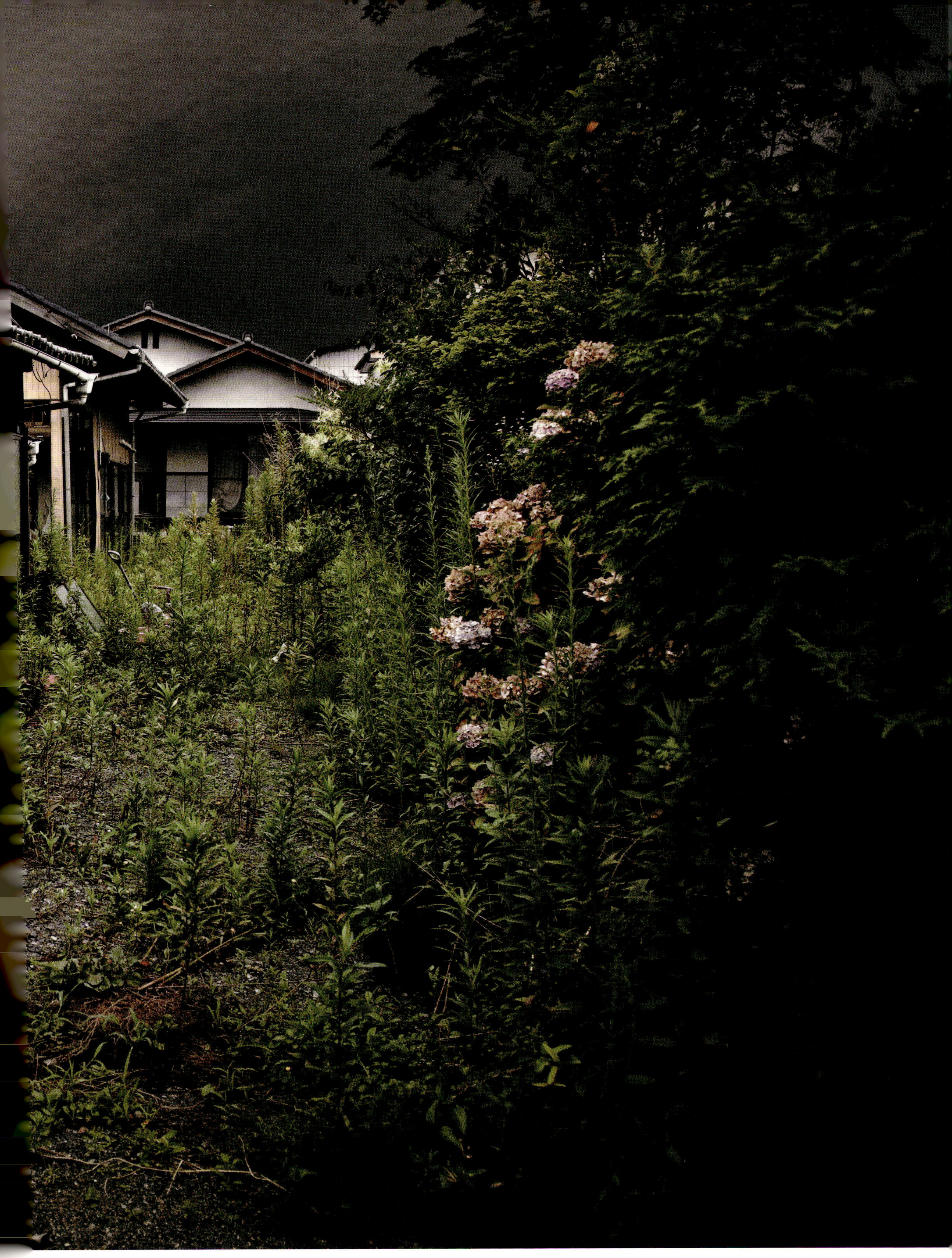

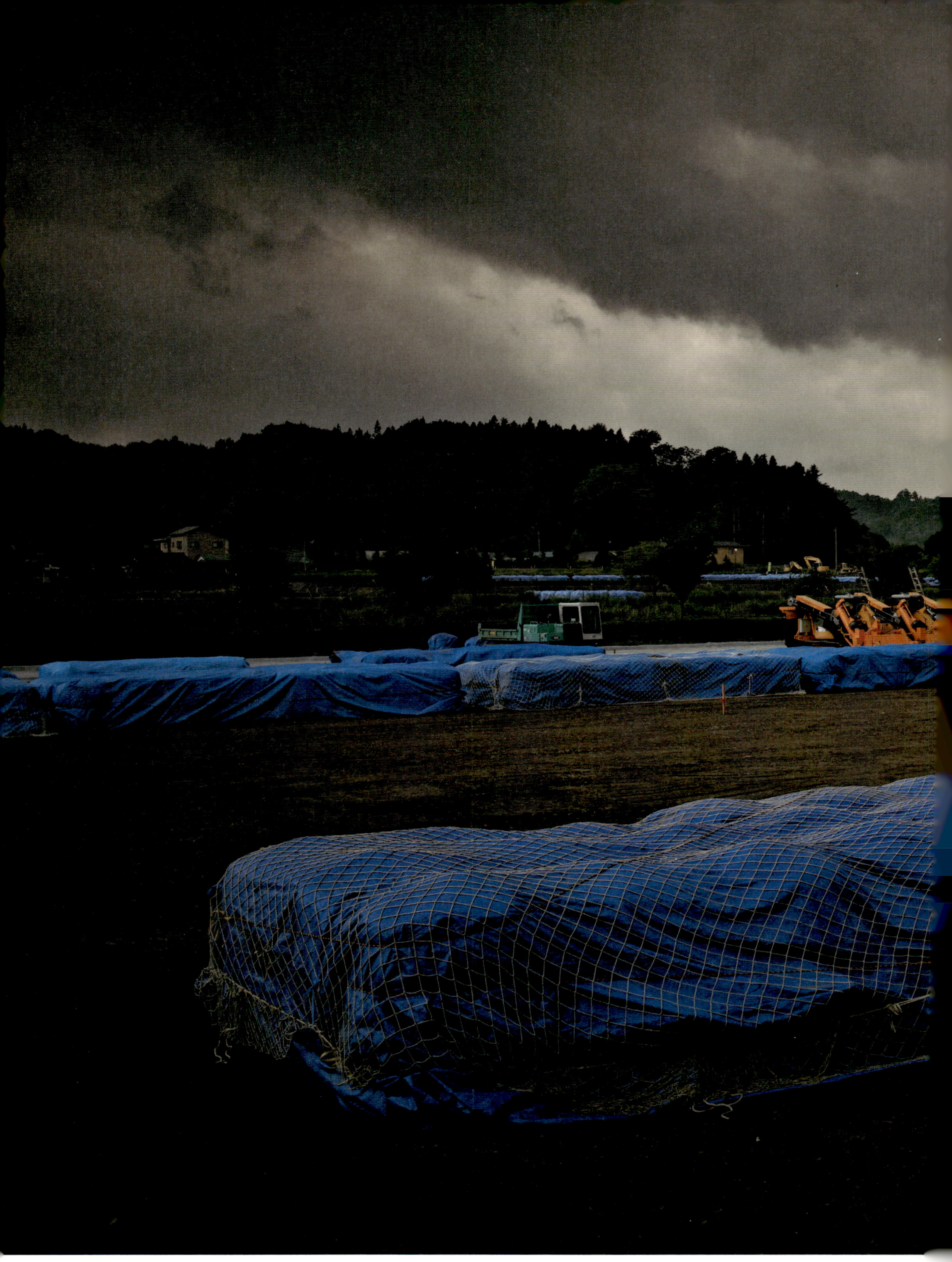

Radioactive waste wrapped in blue tarps.
Iitate Village, Soma County, Fukushima prefecture

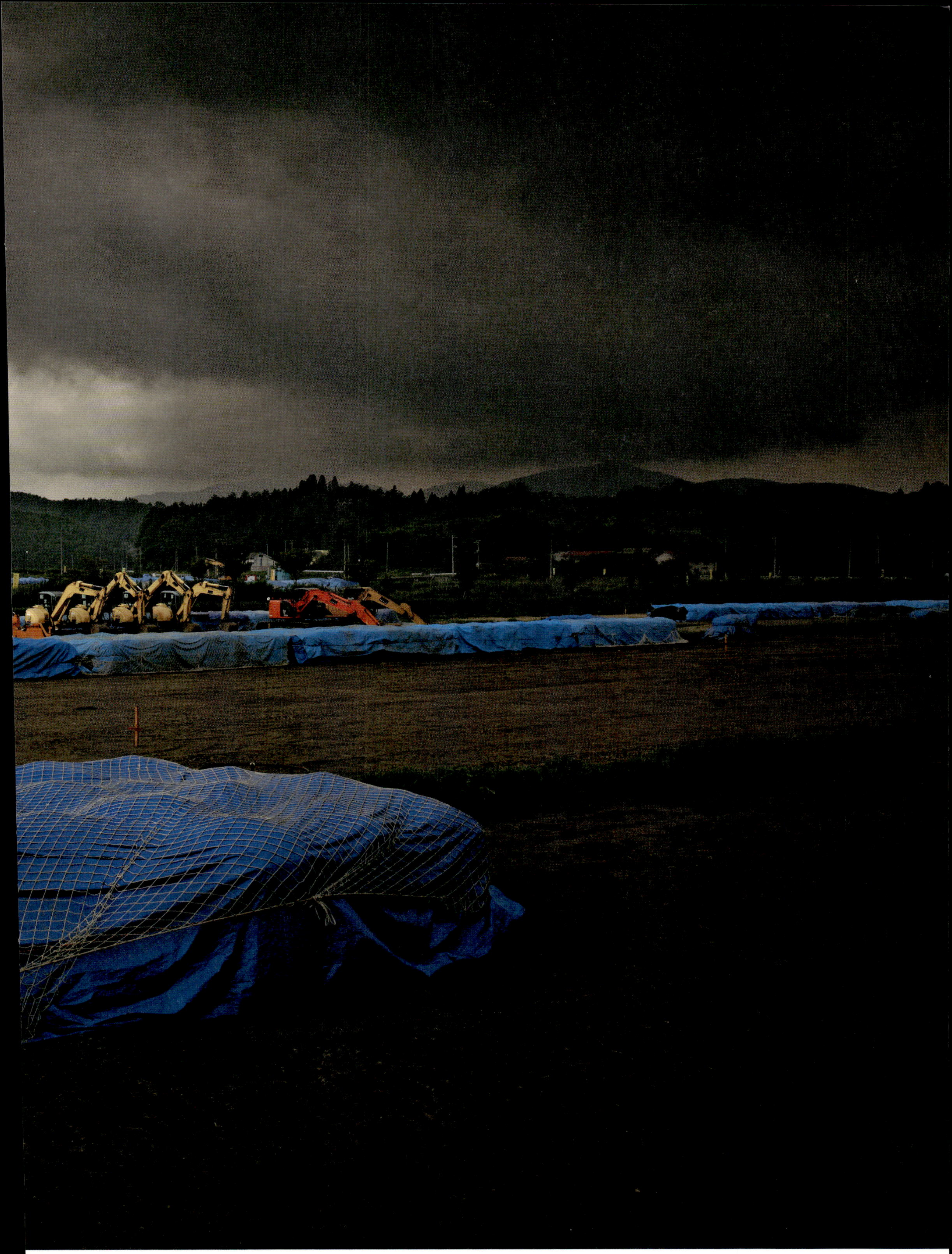

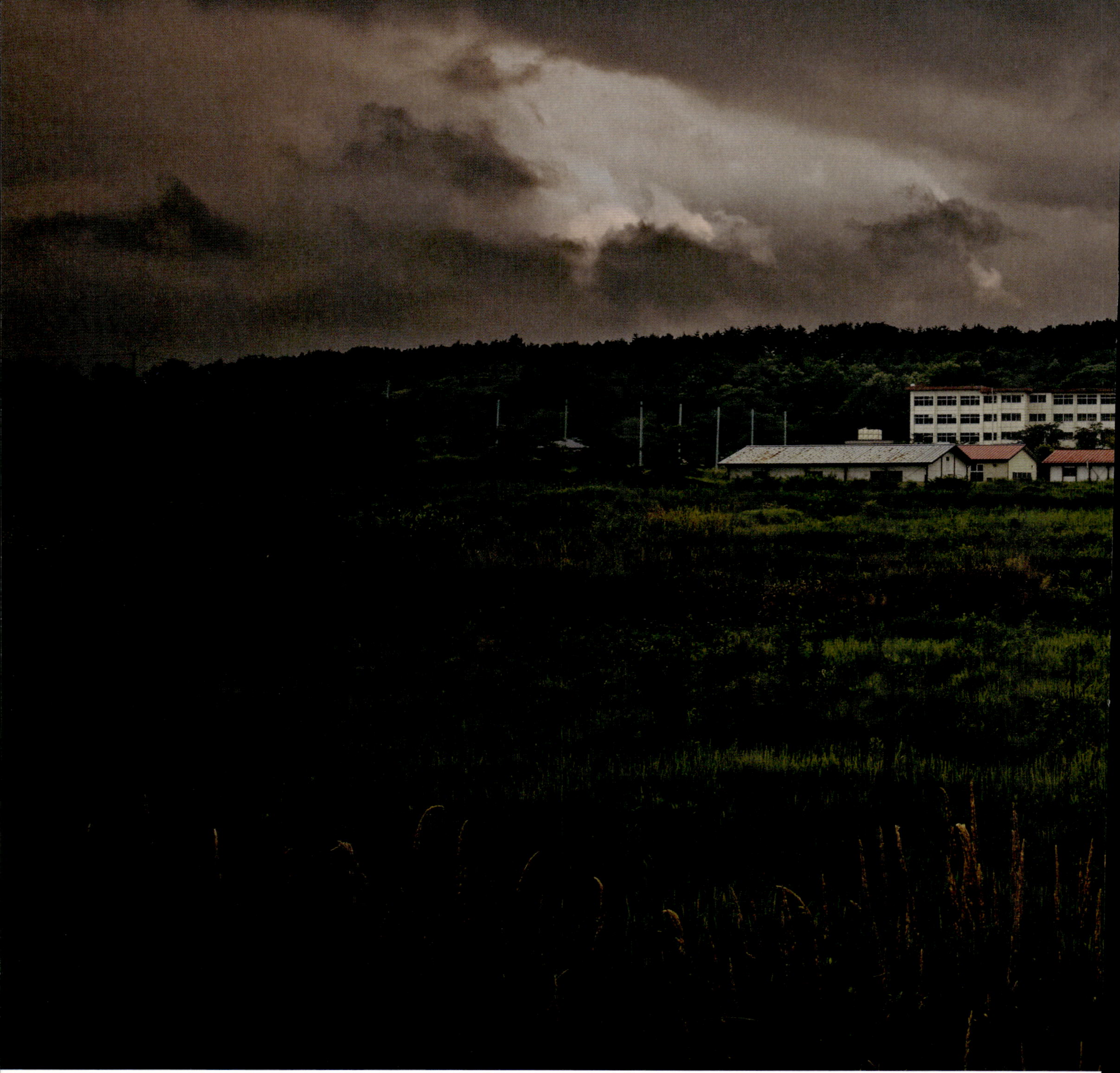

The Minami Soma Agricultural High School surrounded by a sea of weeds.
Iitate Village, Soma County, Fukushima prefecture

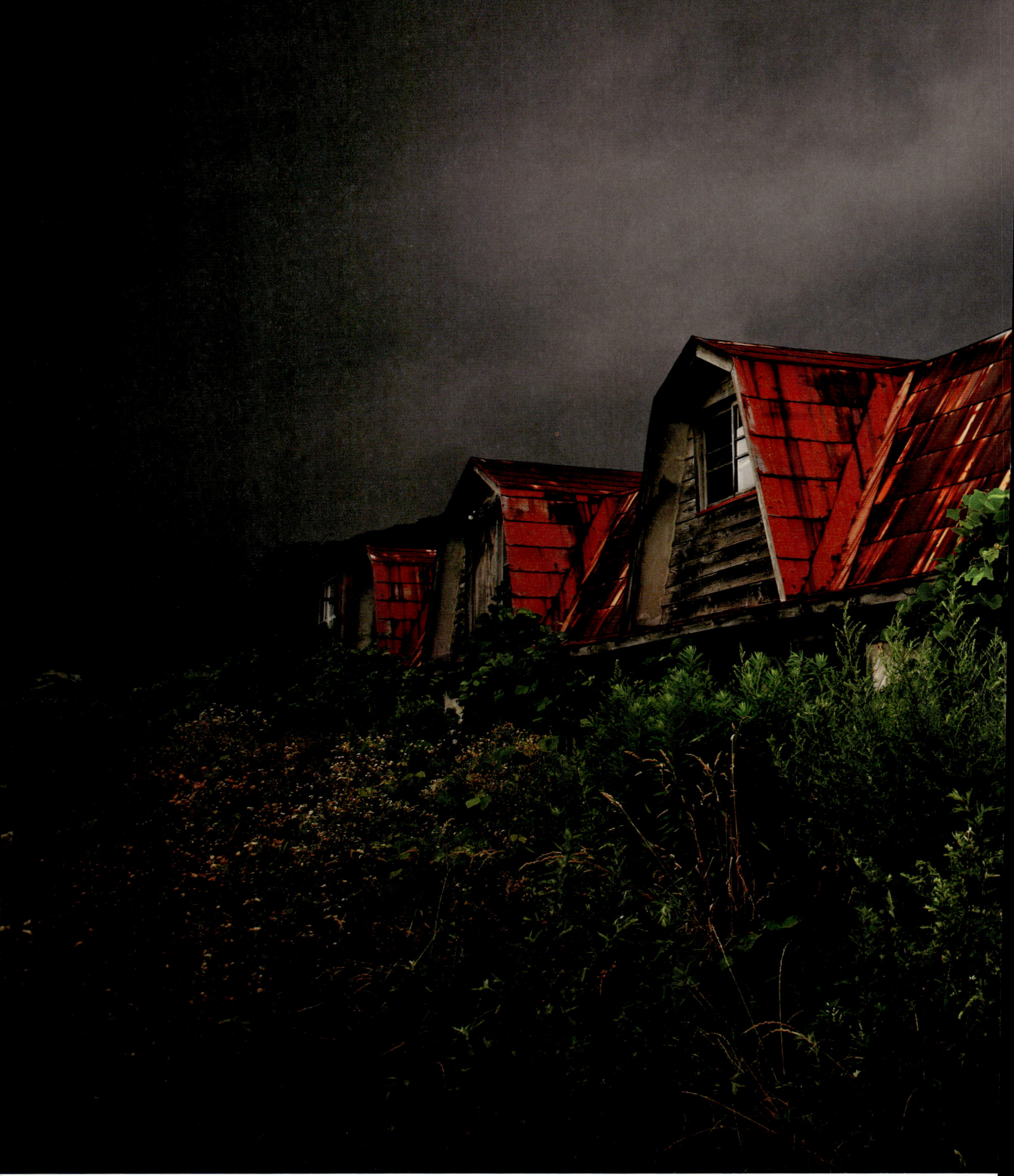

A dairy barn covered in recent overgrowth.
Odaka Ward, Soma County, Fukushima prefecture

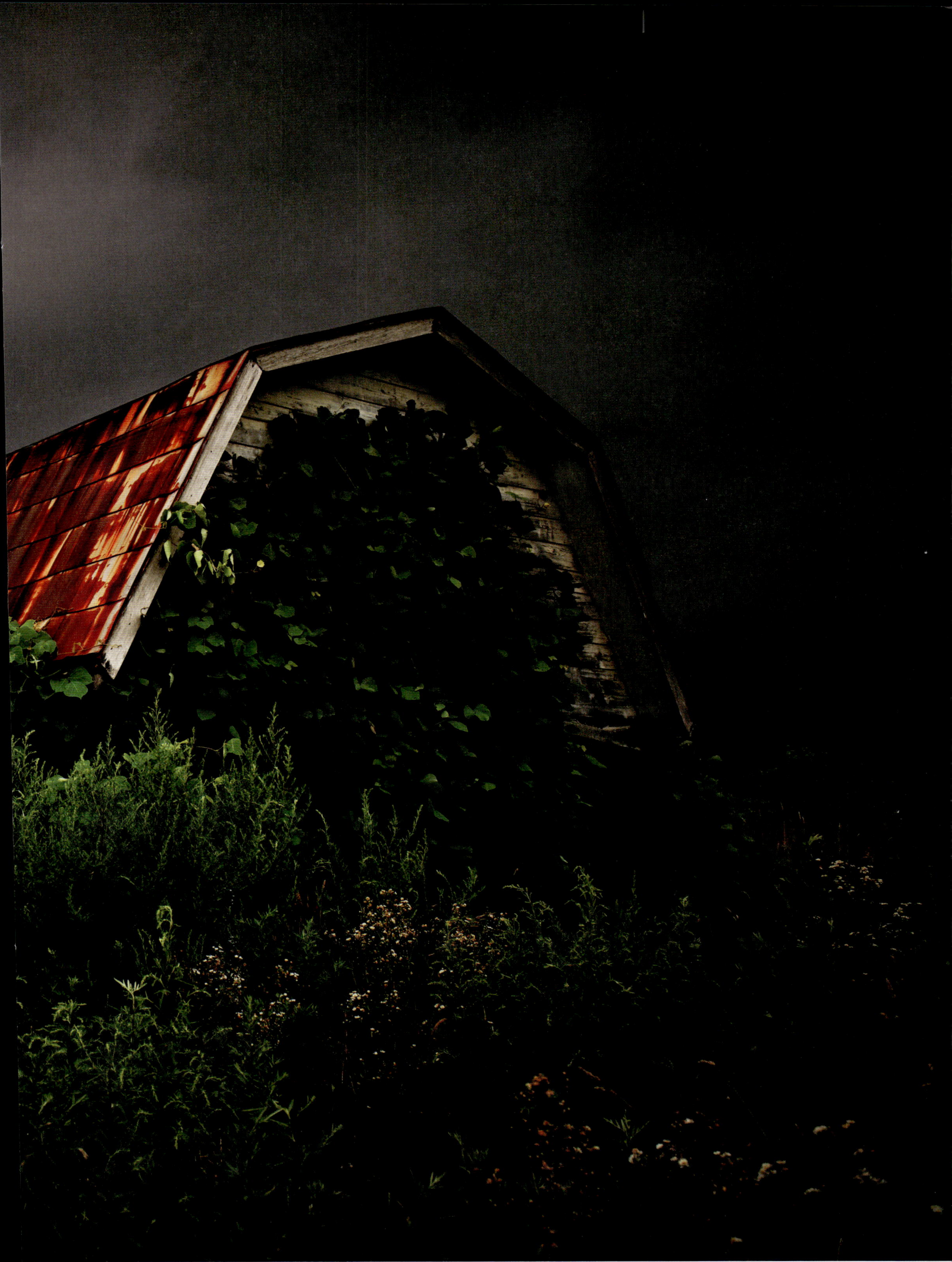

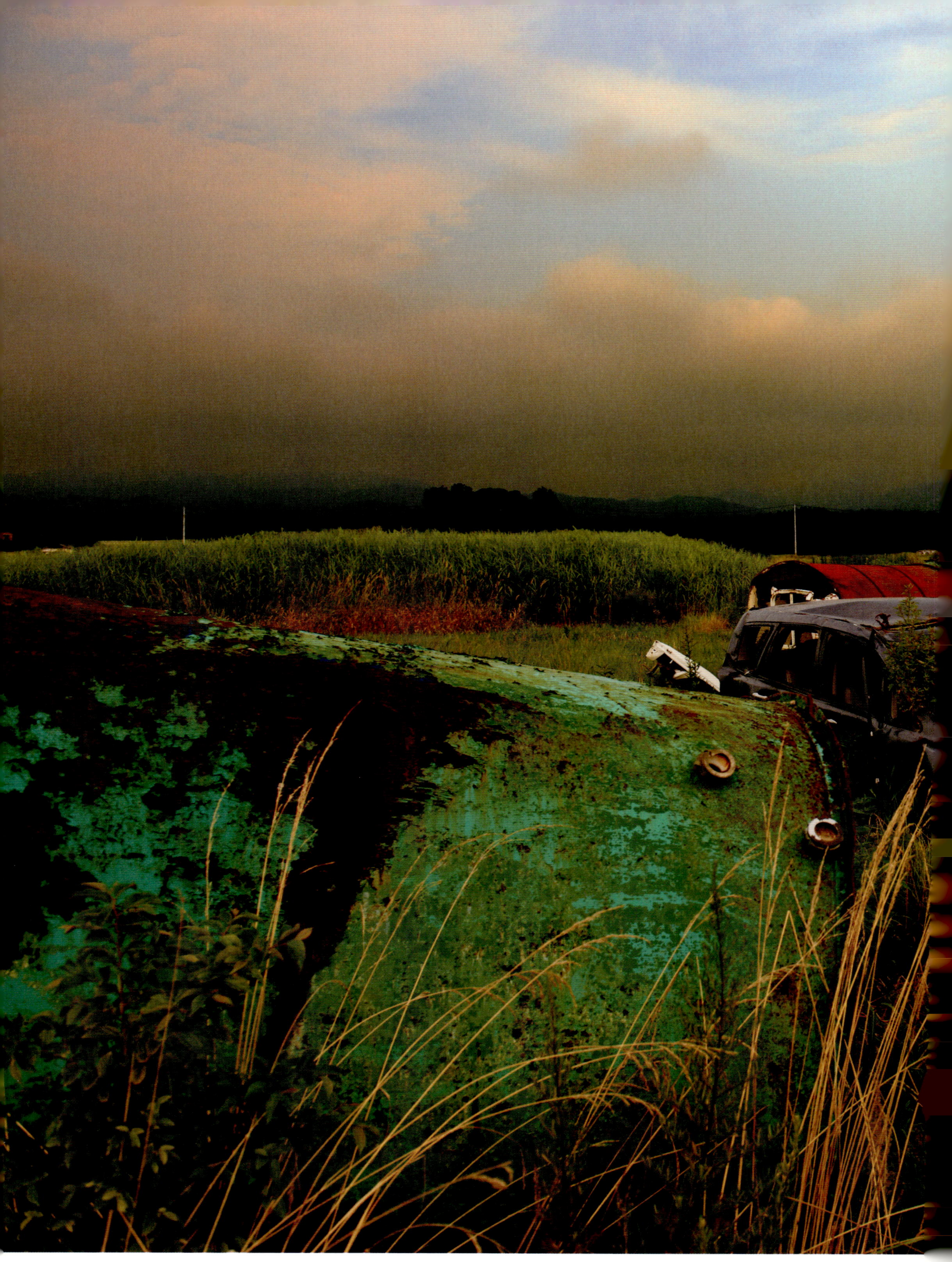

Naraha-machi, Futaba County, Fukushima prefecture

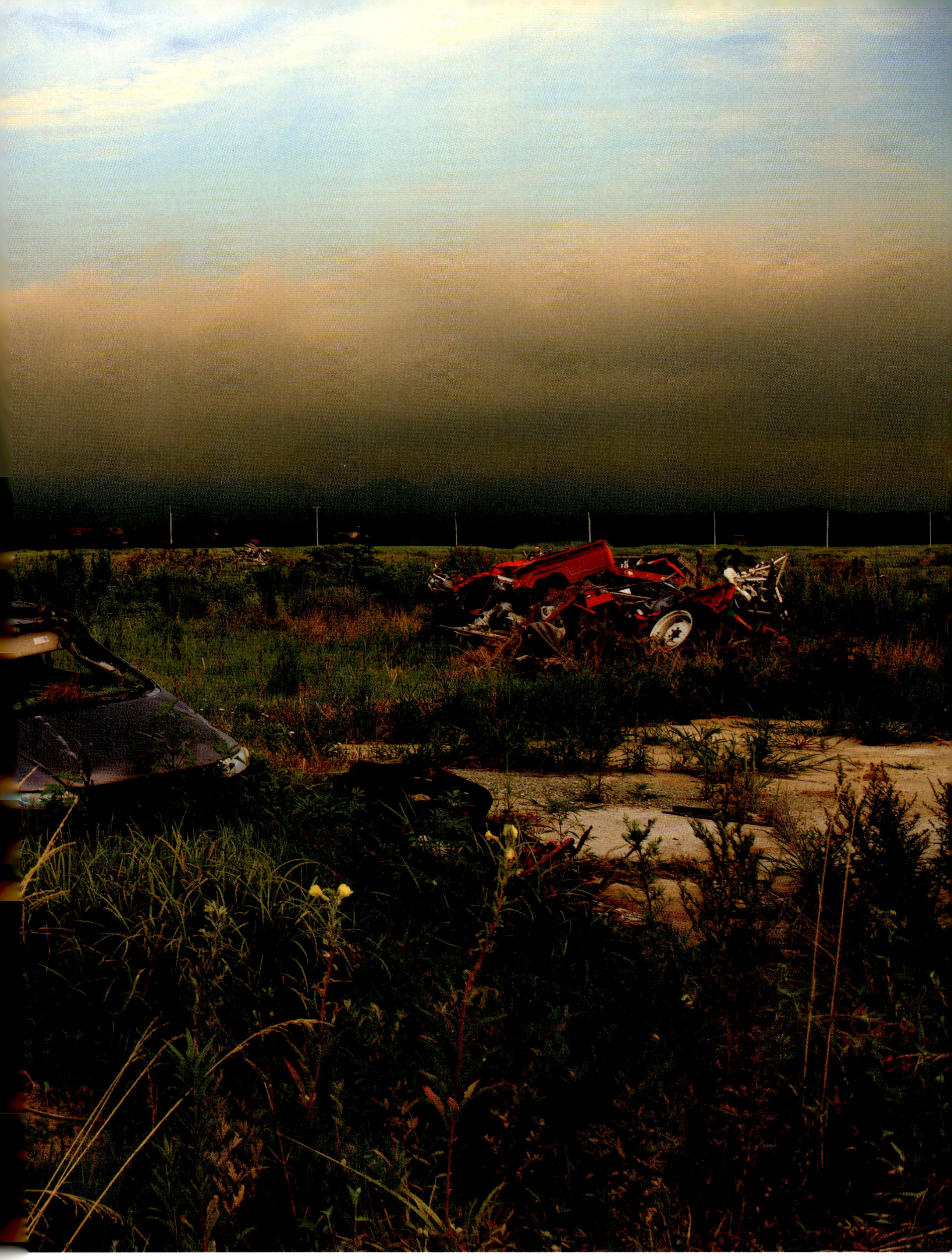

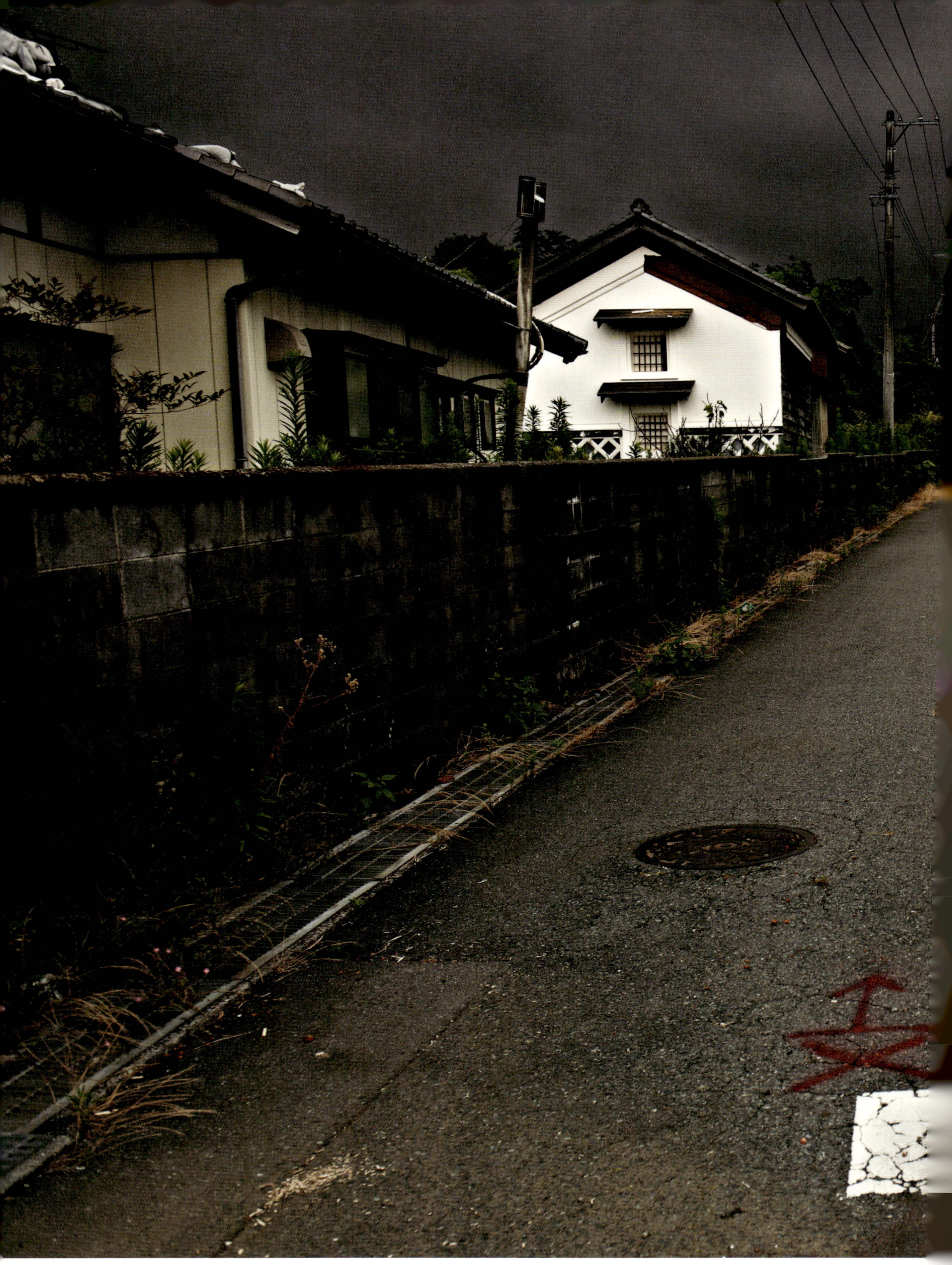

Fallen roof tiles from repeated aftershocks cleared during radioactive waste removal.
Odaka Ward, Soma County, Fukushima prefecture

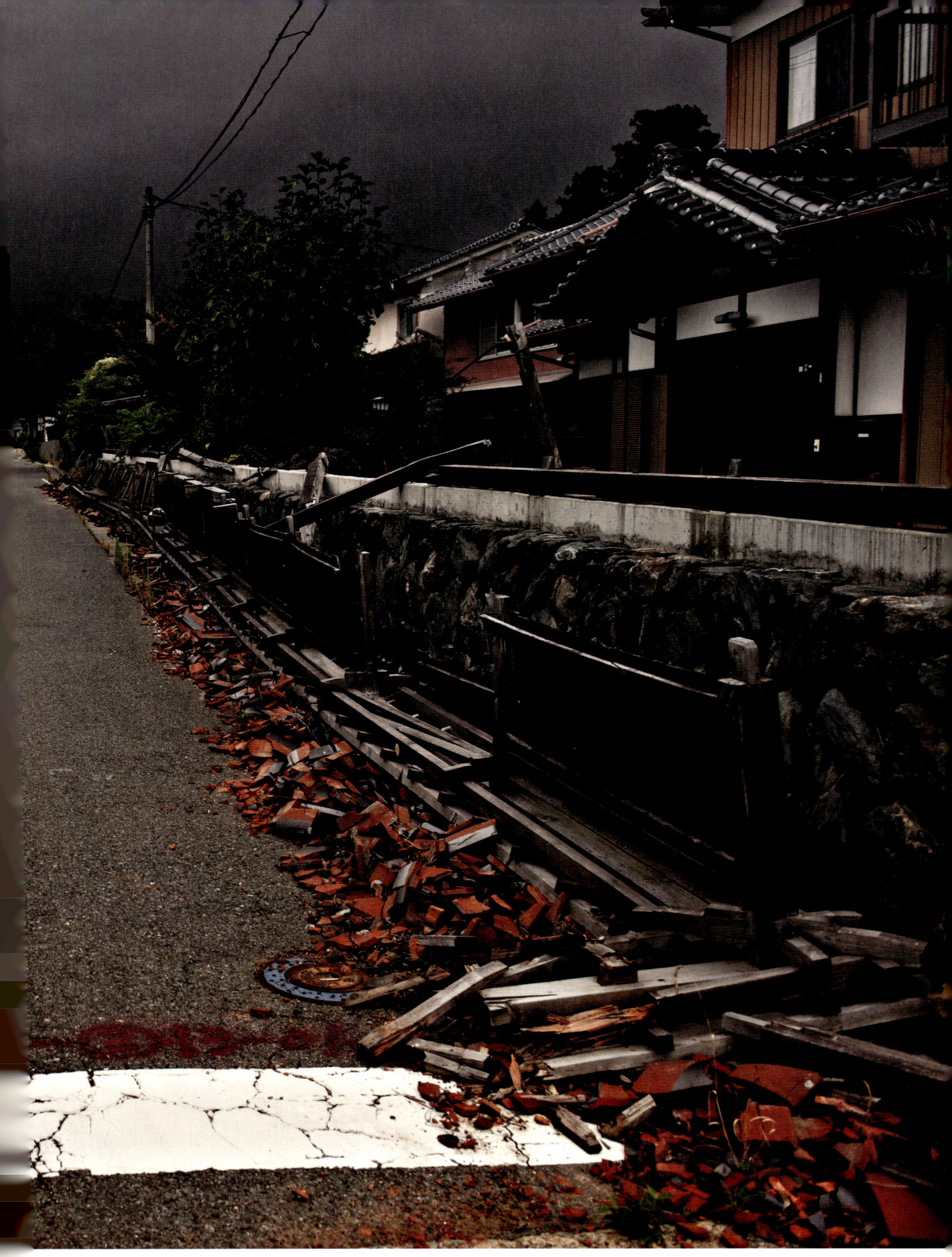

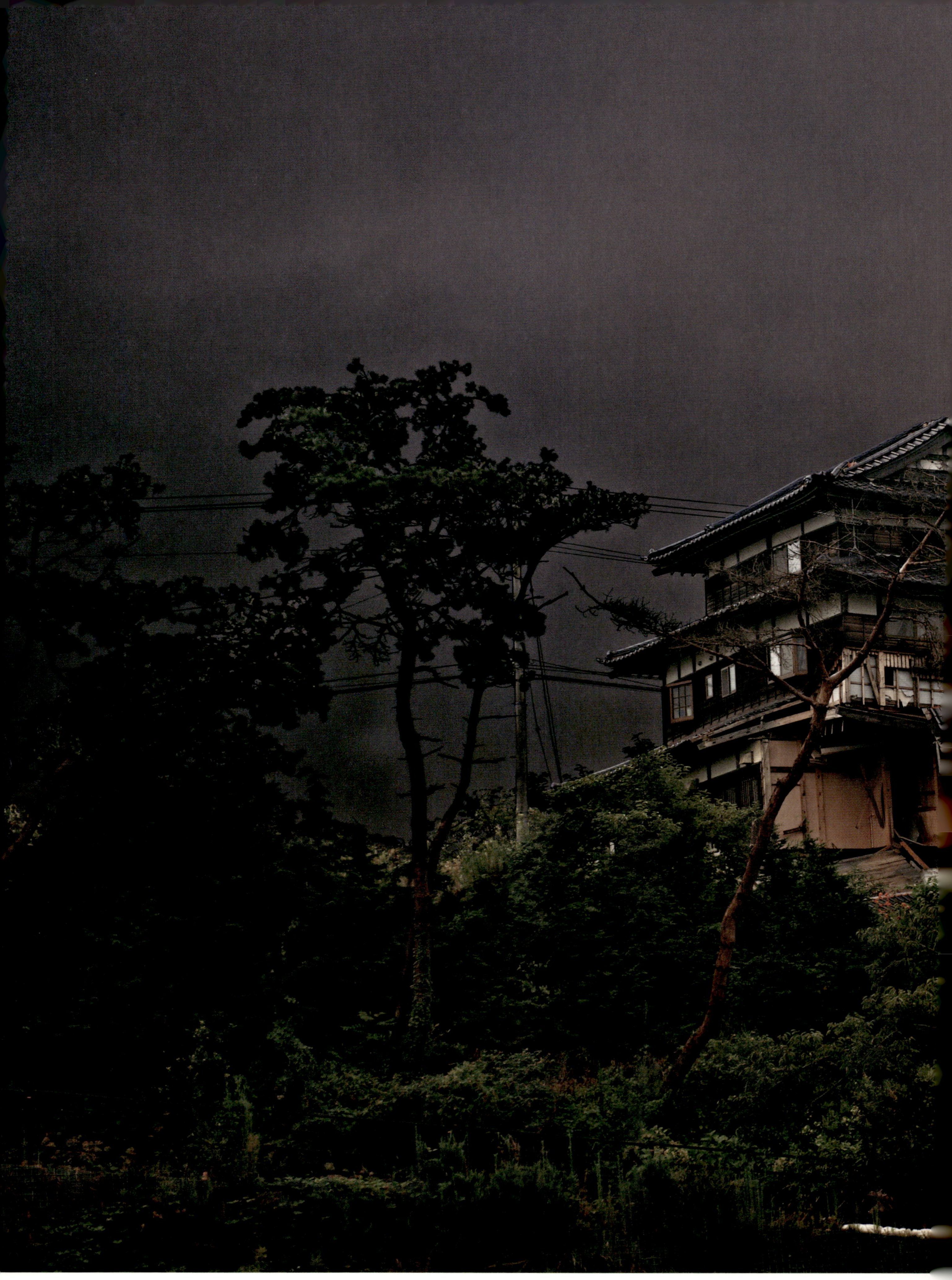

An earthquake damaged three-story wooden building on the top of a hill.
Odaka Ward, Soma County, Fukushima prefecture

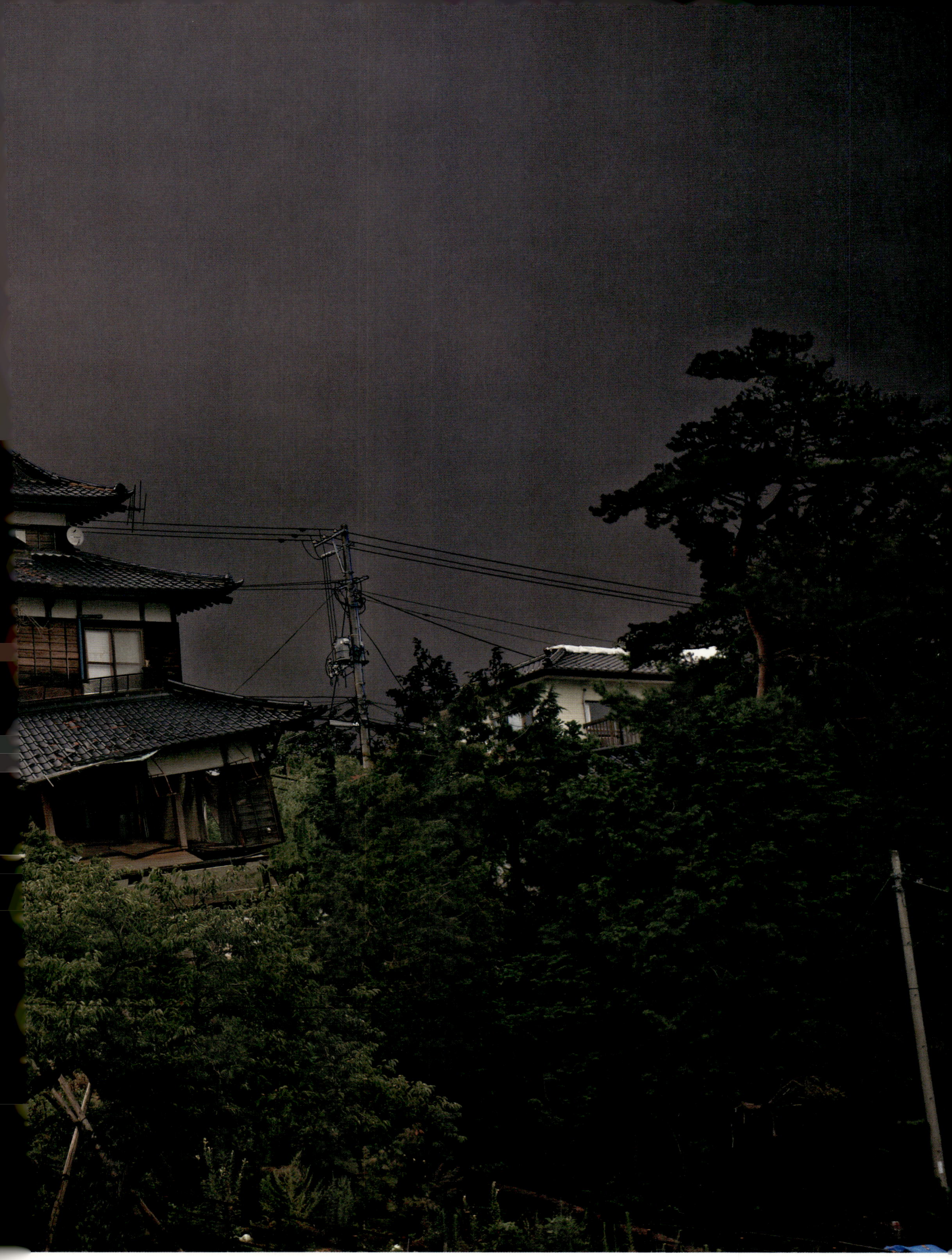

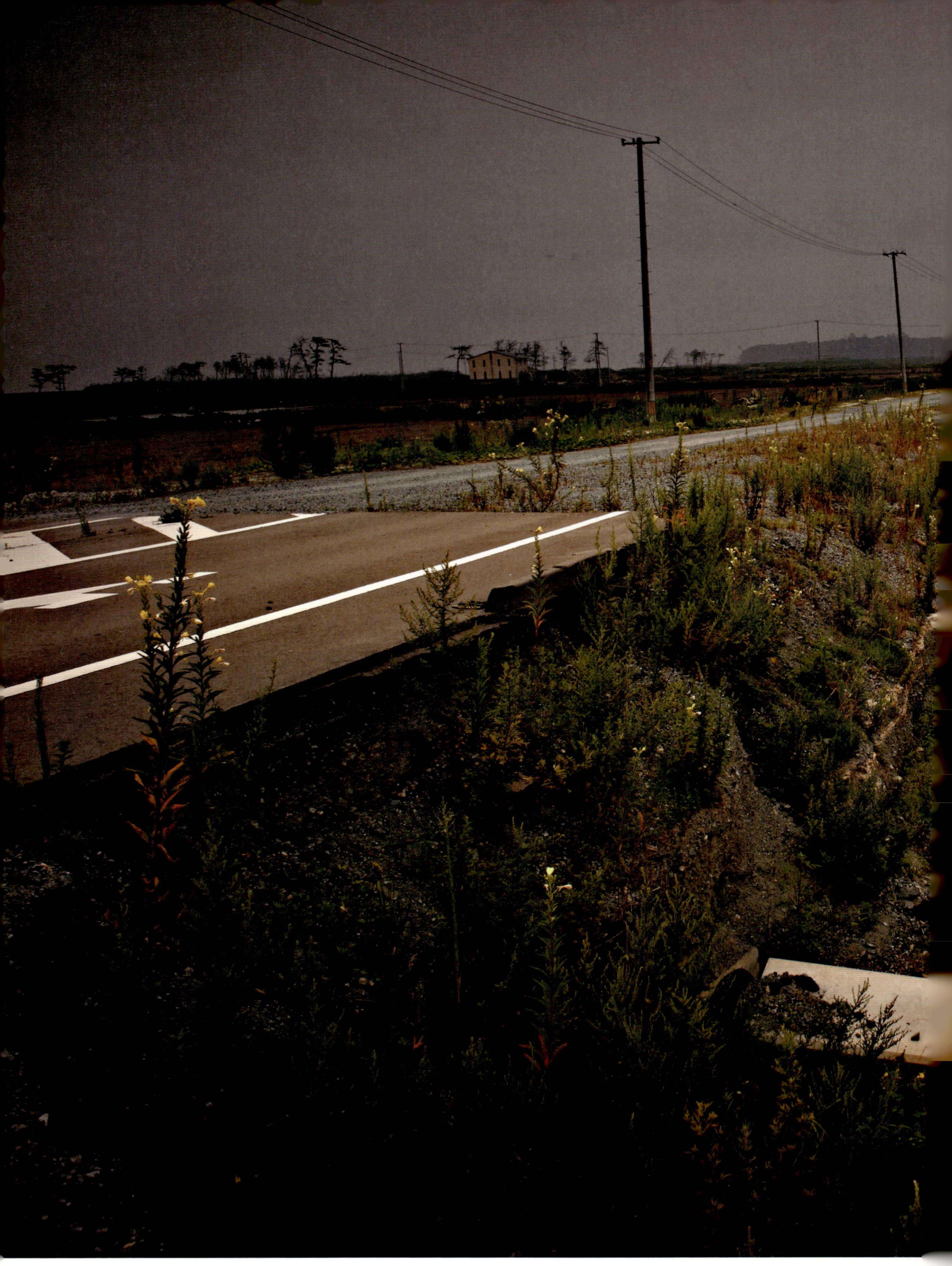

A former field became wetlands.
Odaka Ward, Soma County, Fukushima prefecture

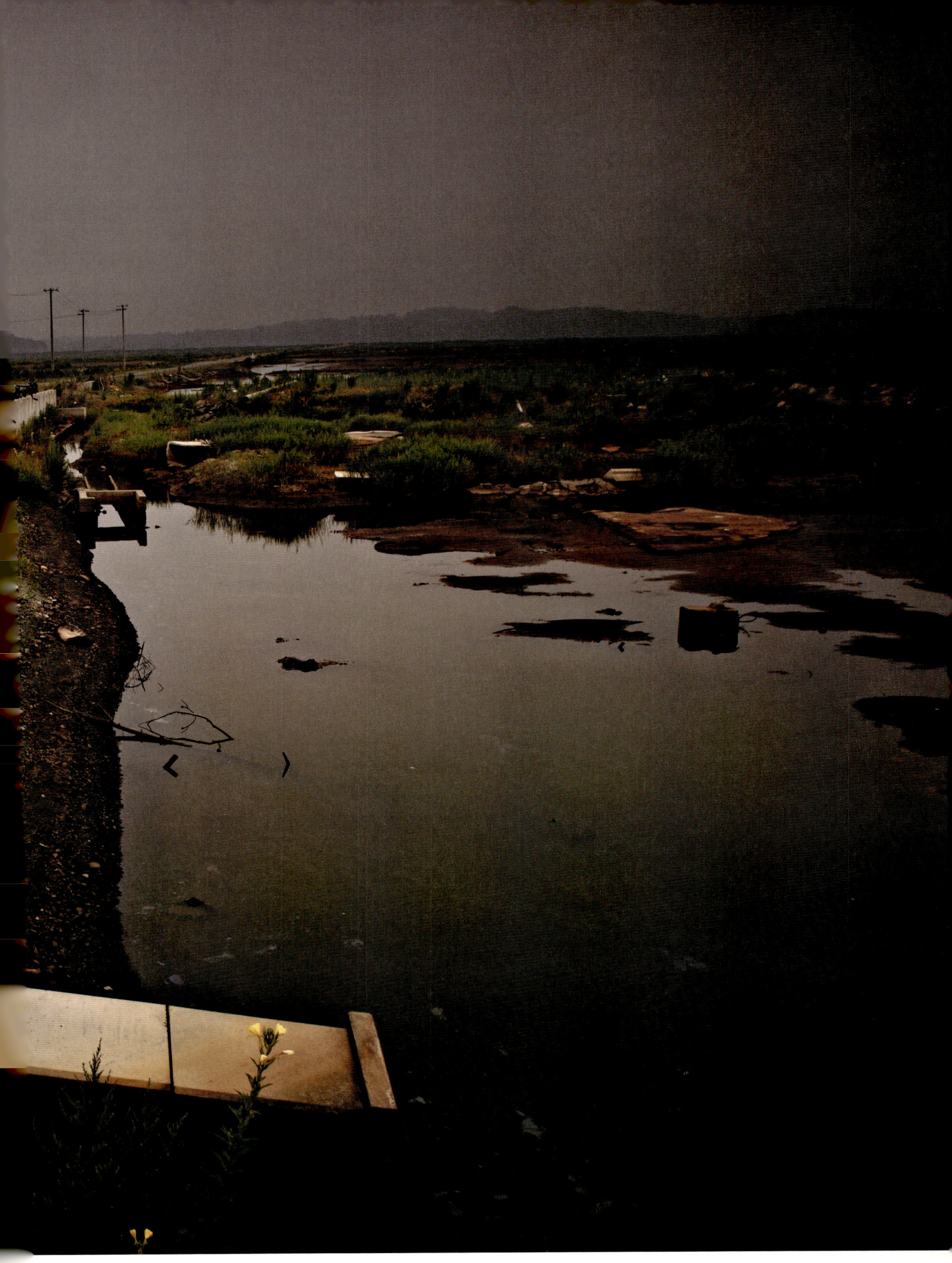

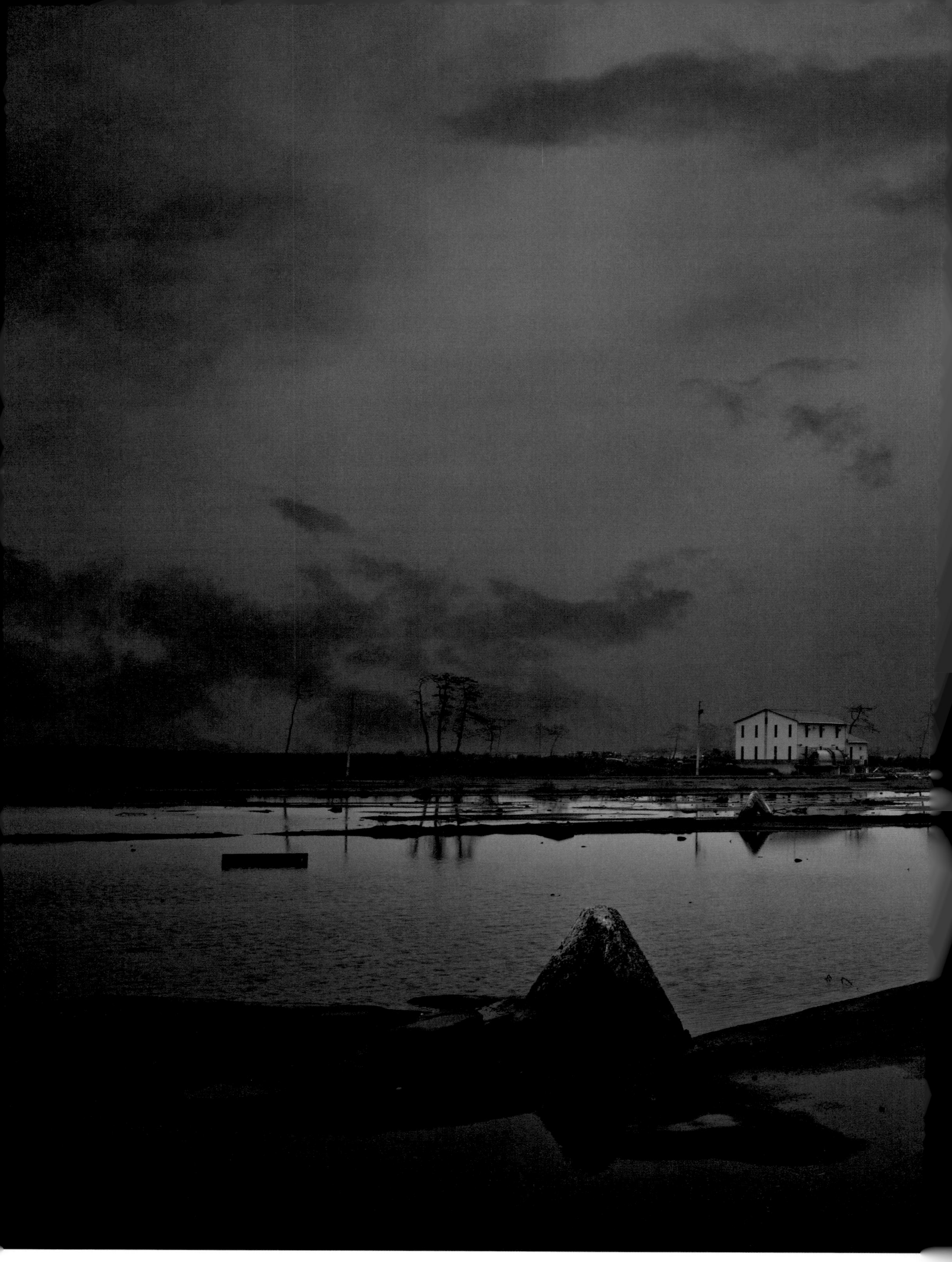

Another view of former rice fields.
Odaka Ward, Soma County, Fukushima prefecture

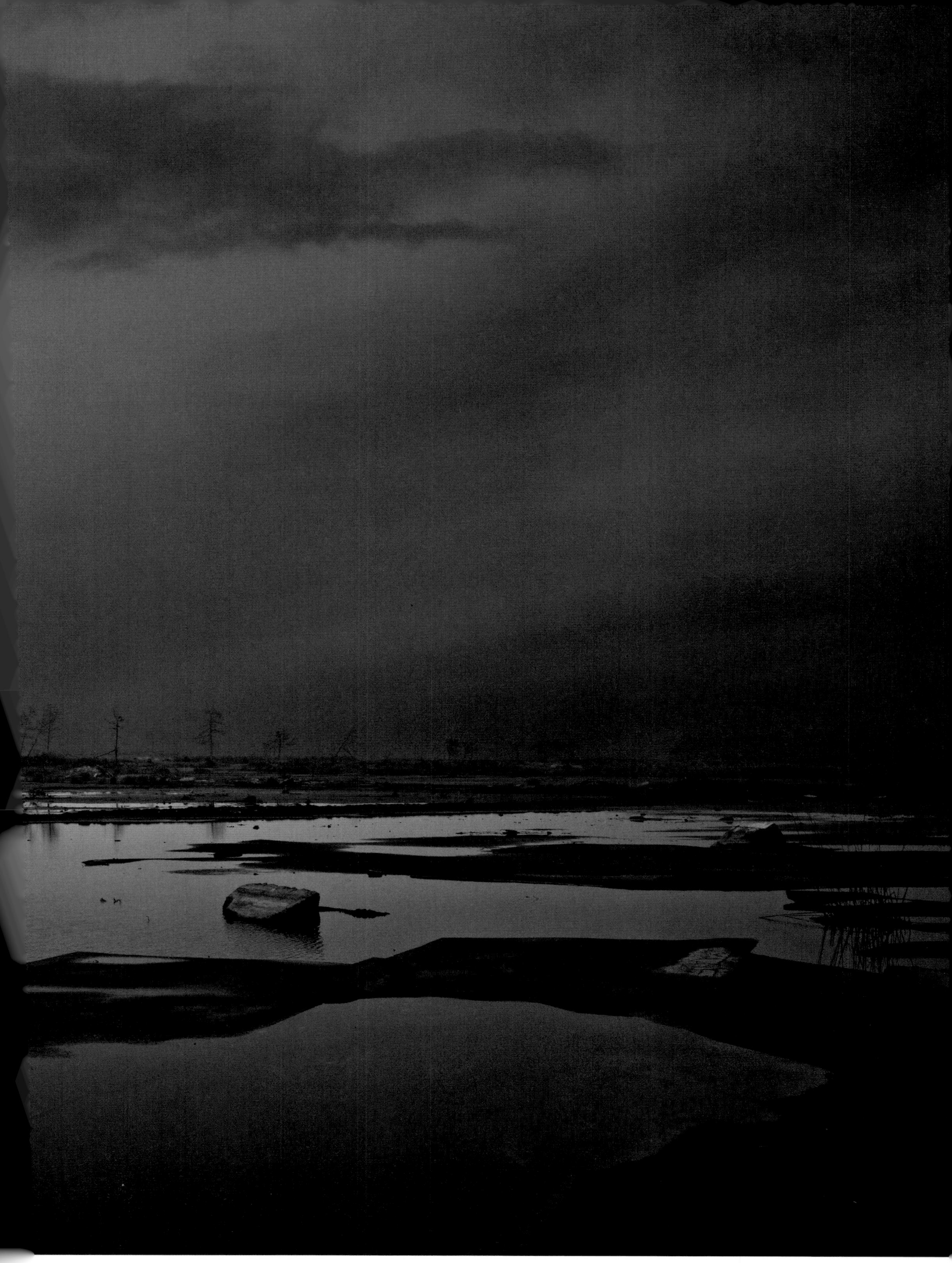

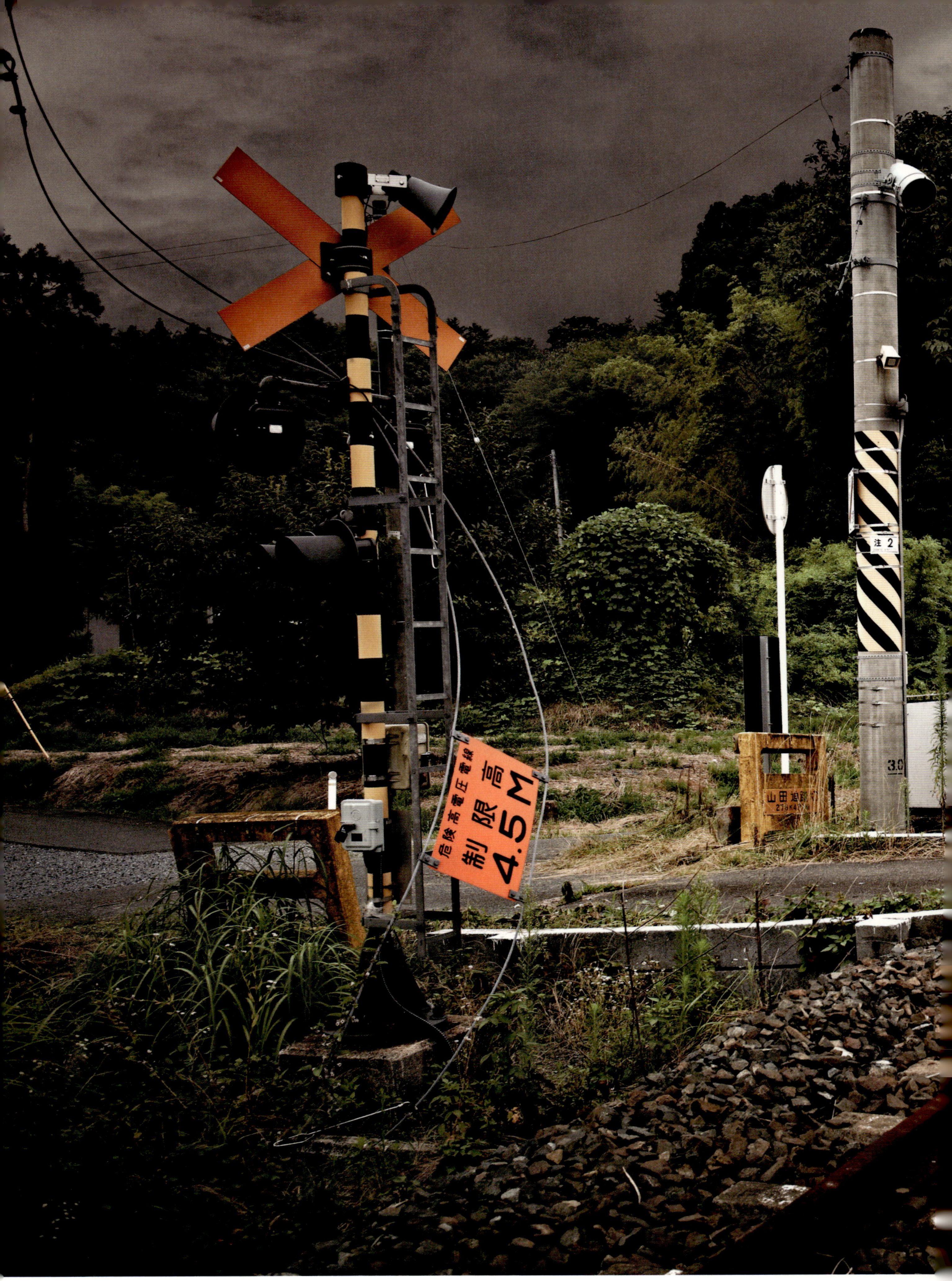

A railway crossing covered in weeds.
Odaka Ward, Soma County, Fukushima prefecture

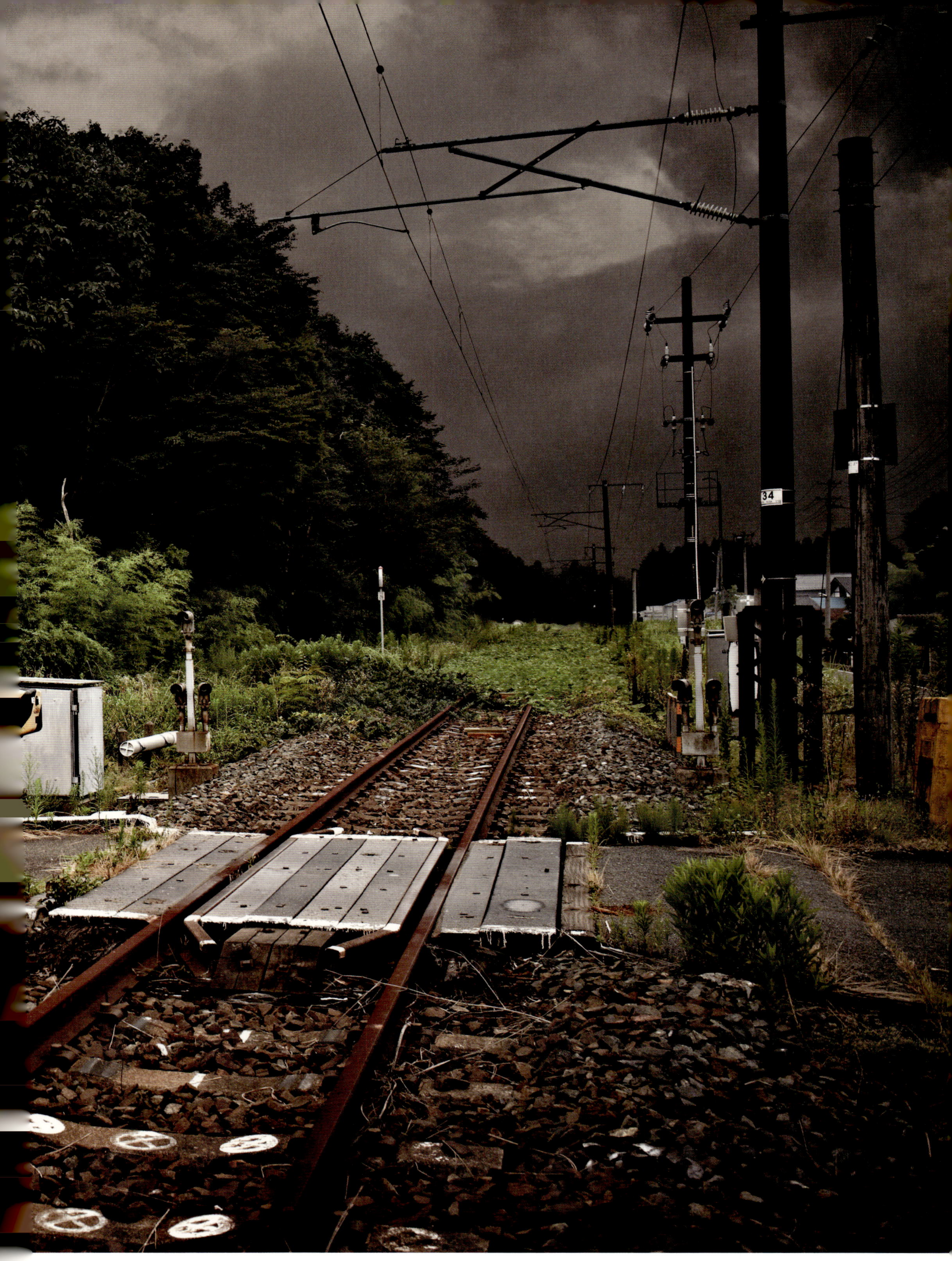
34